# TRANSMETROPOLITAN
## lust for life

**WARREN ELLIS**
WRITER

**DARICK ROBERTSON**
PENCILLER

**KIM DEMULDER**
**RODNEY RAMOS**
INKERS

**NATHAN EYRING**
COLORIST

**CLEM ROBINS**
LETTERER

TRANSMETROPOLITAN
created by
warren ellis
and
darick robertson

Dedicated to Tibor Sardy, with appreciation.

Special thanks to

Janice Corfield-Ricciardi, Andre Ricciardi,

Mike O'Brien, Larry Young

and Meredith Miller.

—DARICK ROBERTSON

For Niki, for Lilith, and for my father.

—WARREN ELLIS


KAREN BERGER
VP-EXECUTIVE EDITOR
STUART MOORE
EDITOR-ORIGINAL SERIES
JULIE ROTTENBERG
ASSOCIATE EDITOR-ORIGINAL SERIES
CLIFF CHIANG
ASSISTANT EDITOR-ORIGINAL SERIES
RICK TAYLOR
EDITOR-COLLECTED EDITION
JIM SPIVEY
ASSOCIATE EDITOR-COLLECTED EDITION
ROBBIN BROSTERMAN
SENIOR ART DIRECTOR
PAUL LEVITZ
PRESIDENT & PUBLISHER
GEORG BREWER
VP-DESIGN & RETAIL PRODUCT DEVELOPMENT
RICHARD BRUNING
SENIOR VP-CREATIVE DIRECTOR
PATRICK CALDON
SENIOR VP-FINANCE & OPERATIONS
CHRIS CARAMALIS
VP-FINANCE
TERRI CUNNINGHAM
VP-MANAGING EDITOR
ALISON GILL
VP-MANUFACTURING
RICH JOHNSON
VP-BOOK TRADE SALES
HANK KANALZ
VP-GENERAL MANAGER, WILDSTORM
LILLIAN LASERSON
SENIOR VP & GENERAL COUNSEL
JIM LEE
EDITORIAL DIRECTOR-WILDSTORM
DAVID MCKILLIPS
VP-ADVERTISING & CUSTOM PUBLISHING
JOHN NEE
VP-BUSINESS DEVELOPMENT
GREGORY NOVECK
SENIOR VP-CREATIVE AFFAIRS
CHERYL RUBIN
SENIOR VP-BRAND MANAGEMENT
BOB WAYNE
VP-SALES & MARKETING



TRANSMETROPOLITAN:
LUST FOR LIFE
Published by DC Comics.



DC Comics, 1700 Broadway, New York, NY 10019
A Warner Bros. Entertainment Company
Printed in Canada. Fourth Printing.

ISBN: 1-56389-481-5

Cover illustration by DARICK ROBERTSON.
Cover color by NATHAN EYRING.
Publication design by MURPHY FOGELNEST.

**EXCLUSIVE TO THE WORD**

by **Spider Jerusalem** [author of "waving and drowning"]

# I HATE IT HERE

—Yesterday, here in the middle of the City, I saw a wolf turn into a Russian ex-gymnast and hand over a business card that read YOUR OWN PERSONAL TRANSHUMAN SECURITY WHORE! STERILIZED INNARDS! ACCEPTS ALL CREDIT CARDS to a large man who wore trained attack cancers on his face and possessed seventy-five indentured Komodo Dragons instead of legs. And they had sex. Right in front of me. And six of the Komodo Dragons spat napalm on my new shoes.

Now listen. I'm told I'm a FAMOUS JOURNALIST these days. I'm told the five years I spent away from the City have vanished like the name of the guy you picked up last night, and that it's like I never left. (I was driven away, let me remind you, by things like Sickness, Hate and The Death of Truth.)

So why do I have to put up with this shabby crap on my front doorstep? Now my beautiful new apartment stinks of wet fur and burning dragon spit, and I think one of the cancers mated with the doormat. It keeps cursing at me in a thick Mexican accent. I may have to have it shot.

If you loved me, you'd all kill yourselves today.

— SPIDER JERUSALEM

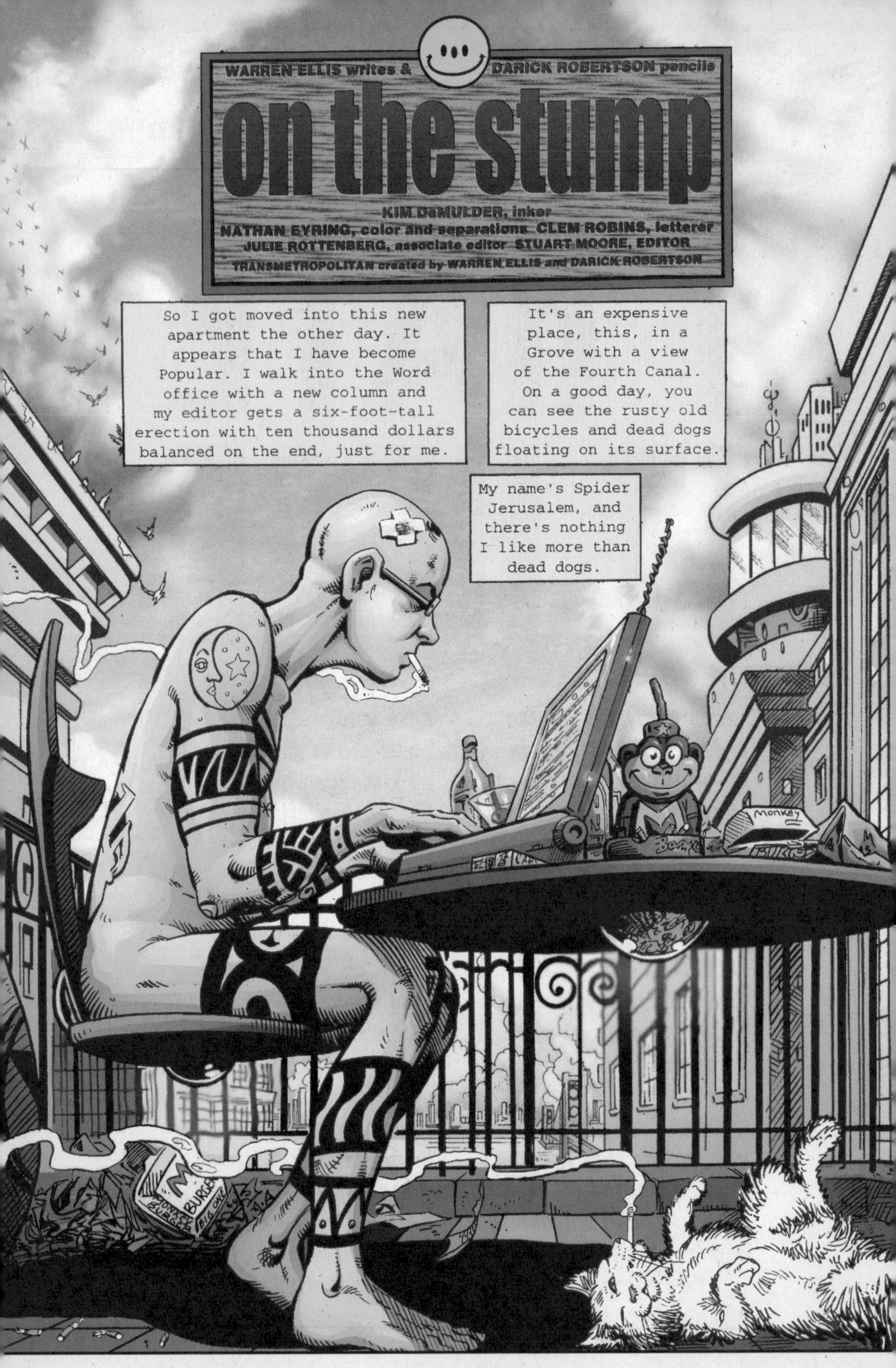
WARREN ELLIS writes & DARICK ROBERTSON pencils
on the stump
KIM DeMULDER, inker
NATHAN EYRING, color and separations CLEM ROBINS, letterer
JULIE ROTTENBERG, associate editor STUART MOORE, EDITOR
TRANSMETROPOLITAN created by WARREN ELLIS and DARICK ROBERTSON
So I got moved into this new apartment the other day. It appears that I have become Popular. I walk into the Word office with a new column and my editor gets a six-foot-tall erection with ten thousand dollars balanced on the end, just for me.
It's an expensive place, this, in a Grove with a view of the Fourth Canal. On a good day, you can see the rusty old bicycles and dead dogs floating on its surface.
My name's Spider Jerusalem, and there's nothing I like more than dead dogs.
Monkey
MONKEY BURGER
BURGER
BIG ONE

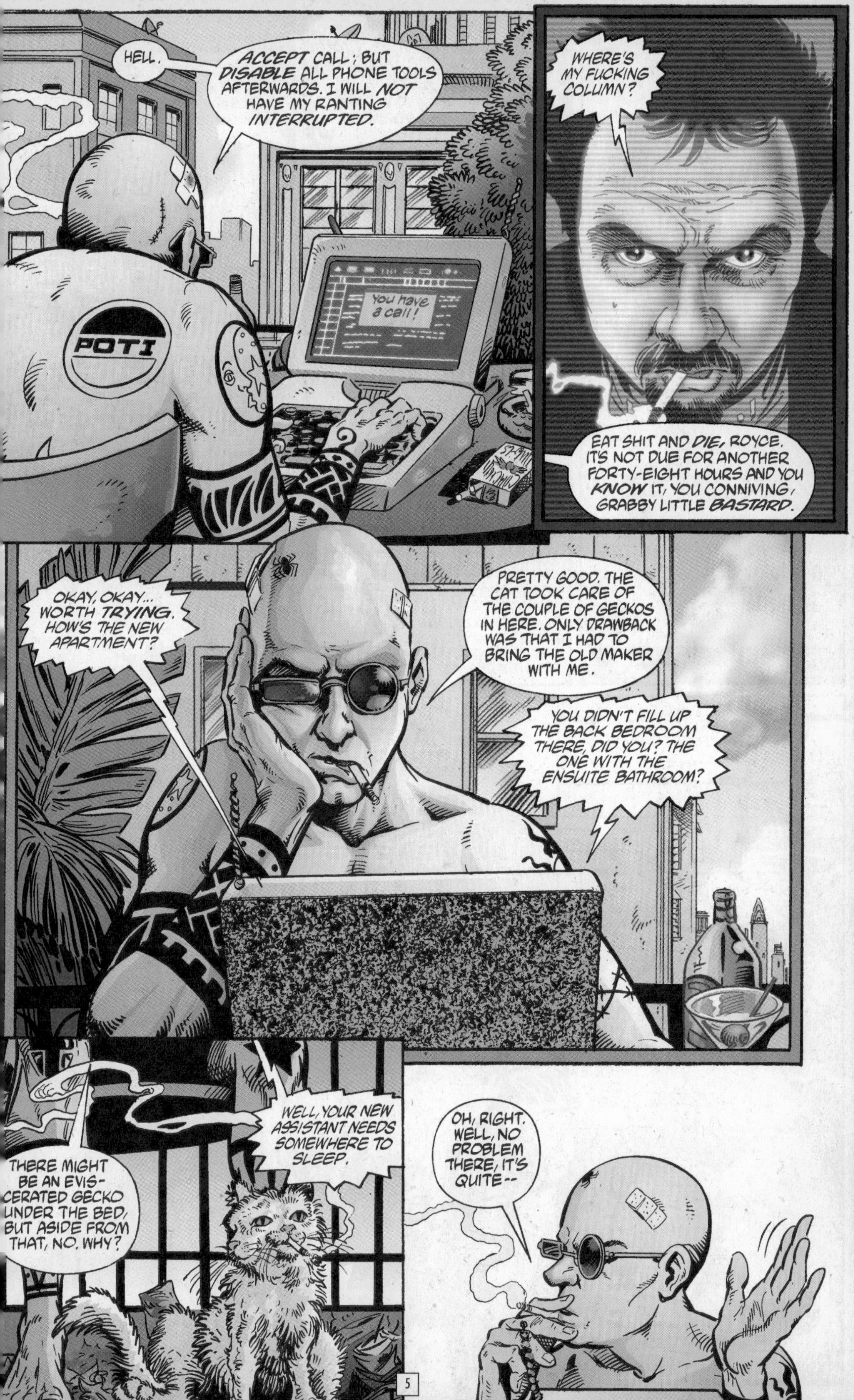

HELL.
ACCEPT CALL; BUT DISABLE ALL PHONE TOOLS AFTERWARDS. I WILL NOT HAVE MY RANTING INTERRUPTED.
You have a call!
POTI
WHERE'S MY FUCKING COLUMN?
EAT SHIT AND DIE, ROYCE. IT'S NOT DUE FOR ANOTHER FORTY-EIGHT HOURS AND YOU KNOW IT, YOU CONNIVING, GRABBY LITTLE BASTARD.
OKAY, OKAY... WORTH TRYING. HOW'S THE NEW APARTMENT?
PRETTY GOOD. THE CAT TOOK CARE OF THE COUPLE OF GECKOS IN HERE. ONLY DRAWBACK WAS THAT I HAD TO BRING THE OLD MAKER WITH ME.
YOU DIDN'T FILL UP THE BACK BEDROOM THERE, DID YOU? THE ONE WITH THE ENSUITE BATHROOM?
THERE MIGHT BE AN EVIS-CERATED GECKO UNDER THE BED, BUT ASIDE FROM THAT, NO. WHY?
WELL, YOUR NEW ASSISTANT NEEDS SOMEWHERE TO SLEEP.
OH, RIGHT. WELL, NO PROBLEM THERE, IT'S QUITE--

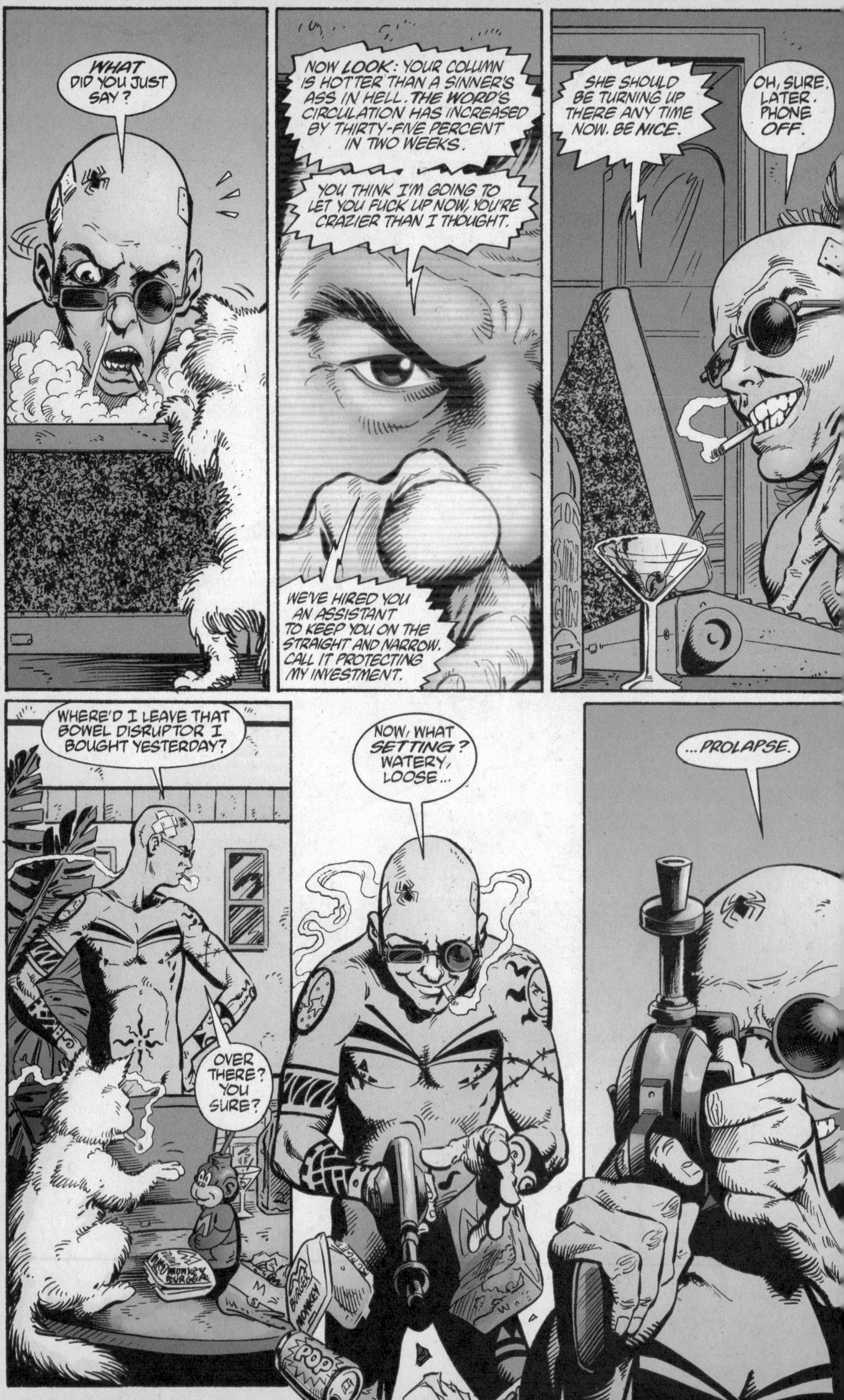
WHAT DID YOU JUST SAY?
NOW LOOK: YOUR COLUMN IS HOTTER THAN A SINNER'S ASS IN HELL. THE WORD'S CIRCULATION HAS INCREASED BY THIRTY-FIVE PERCENT IN TWO WEEKS.
YOU THINK I'M GOING TO LET YOU FUCK UP NOW, YOU'RE CRAZIER THAN I THOUGHT.
WE'VE HIRED YOU AN ASSISTANT TO KEEP YOU ON THE STRAIGHT AND NARROW. CALL IT PROTECTING MY INVESTMENT.
SHE SHOULD BE TURNING UP THERE ANY TIME NOW. BE NICE.
OH, SURE. LATER. PHONE OFF.
WHERE'D I LEAVE THAT BOWEL DISRUPTOR I BOUGHT YESTERDAY?
OVER THERE? YOU SURE?
MONKEY BURGER
NOW, WHAT SETTING? WATERY, LOOSE...
POP
...PROLAPSE.

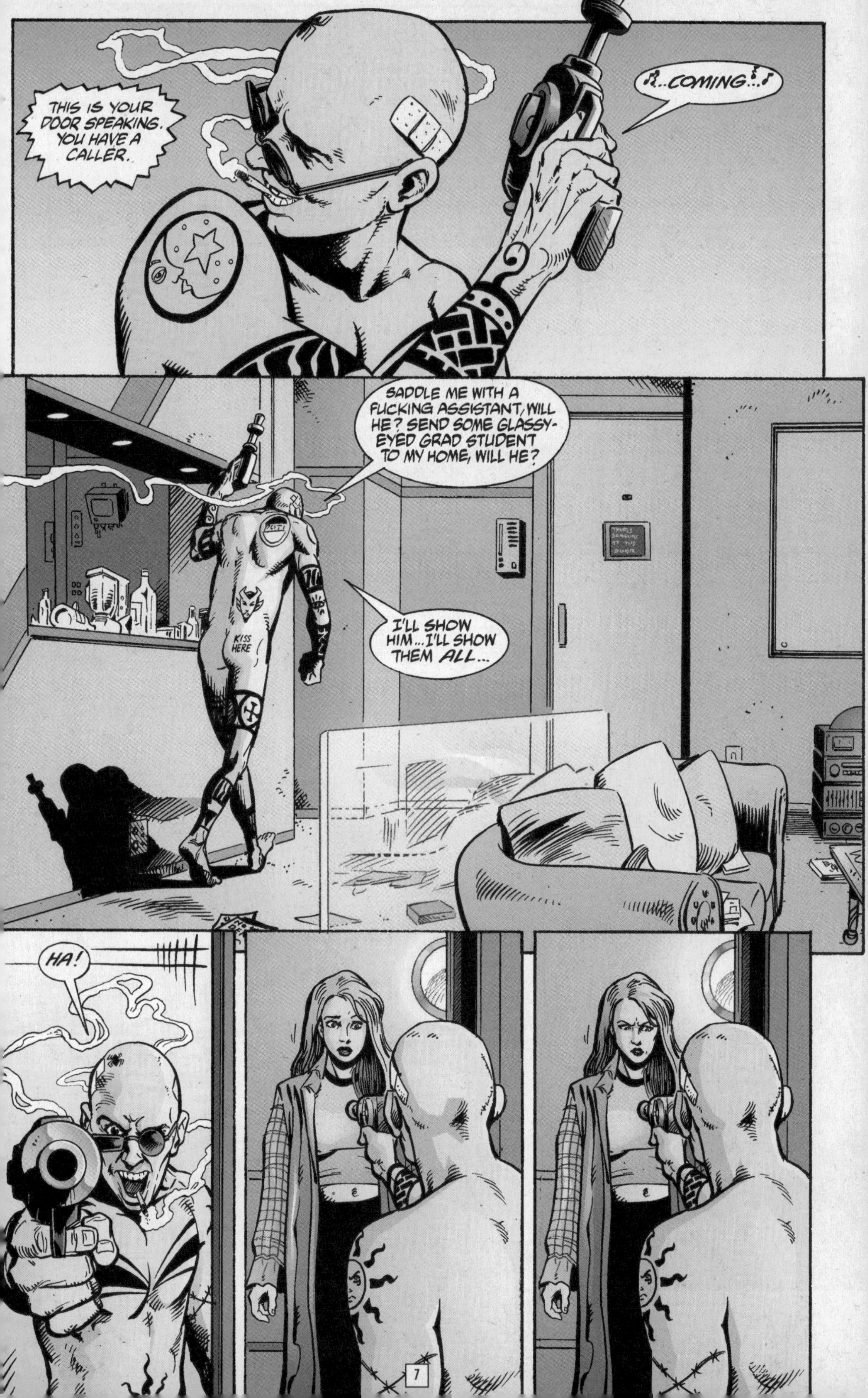
THIS IS YOUR DOOR SPEAKING. YOU HAVE A CALLER.
♫...COMING...♪
SADDLE ME WITH A FUCKING ASSISTANT, WILL HE? SEND SOME GLASSY-EYED GRAD STUDENT TO MY HOME, WILL HE?
KISS HERE
I'LL SHOW HIM...I'LL SHOW THEM ALL...
HA!

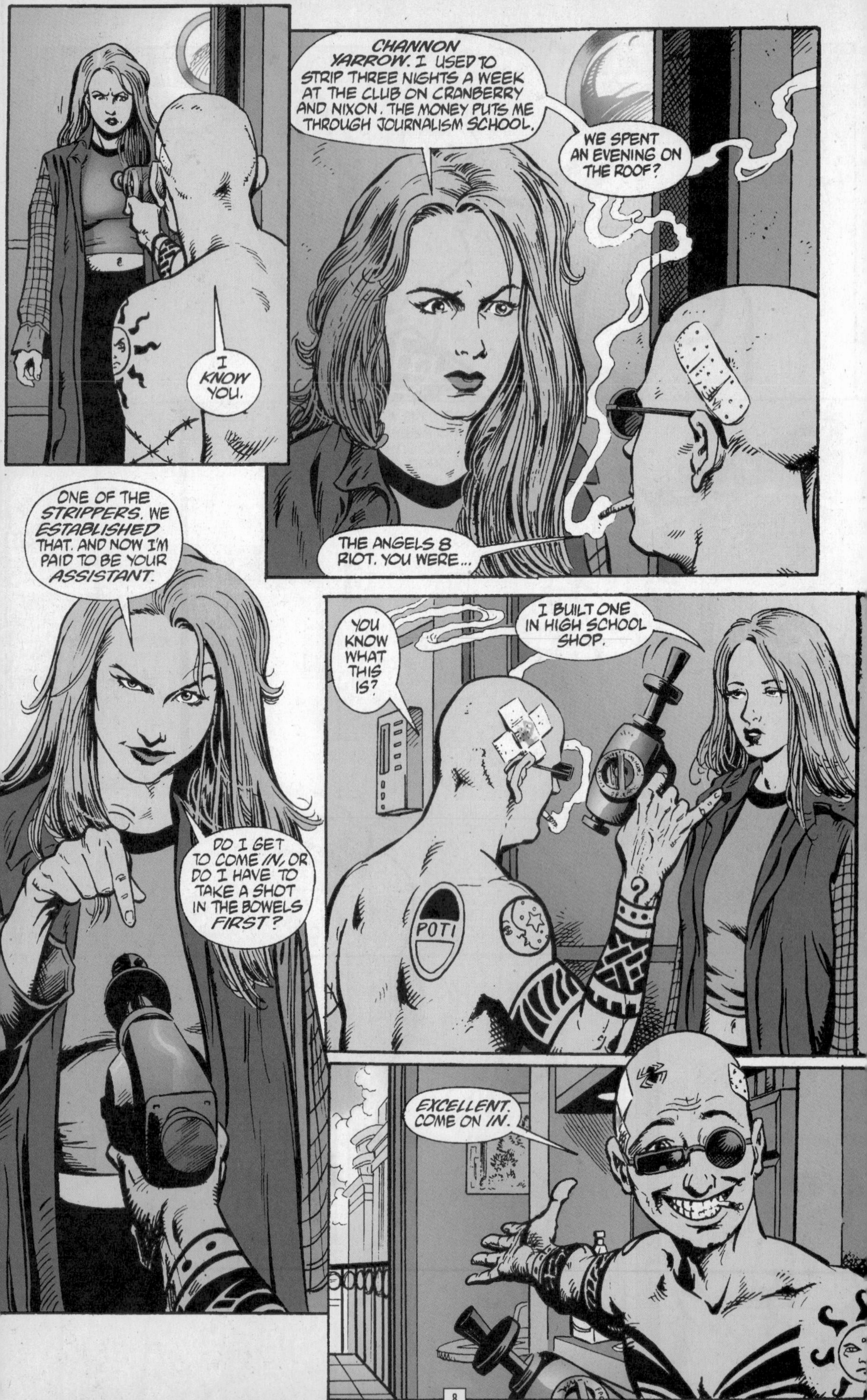
I KNOW YOU.
CHANNON YARROW. I USED TO STRIP THREE NIGHTS A WEEK AT THE CLUB ON CRANBERRY AND NIXON. THE MONEY PUTS ME THROUGH JOURNALISM SCHOOL.
WE SPENT AN EVENING ON THE ROOF?
THE ANGELS 8 RIOT. YOU WERE...
ONE OF THE STRIPPERS. WE ESTABLISHED THAT. AND NOW I'M PAID TO BE YOUR ASSISTANT.
DO I GET TO COME IN, OR DO I HAVE TO TAKE A SHOT IN THE BOWELS FIRST?
YOU KNOW WHAT THIS IS?
I BUILT ONE IN HIGH SCHOOL SHOP.
POTI
EXCELLENT. COME ON IN.

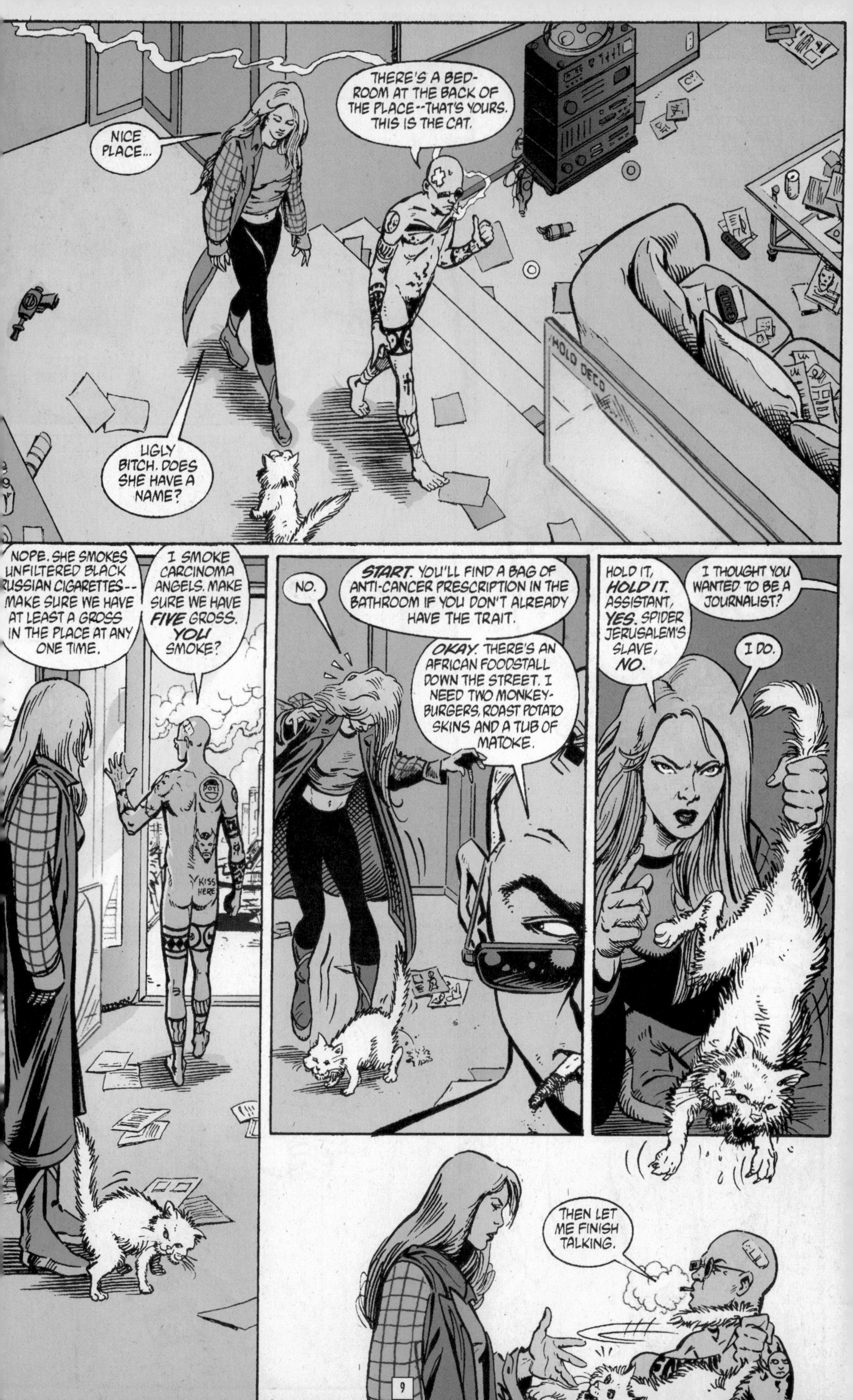

NICE PLACE...
THERE'S A BED-ROOM AT THE BACK OF THE PLACE--THAT'S YOURS. THIS IS THE CAT.
UGLY BITCH. DOES SHE HAVE A NAME?
HOLO DECO
NOPE. SHE SMOKES UNFILTERED BLACK RUSSIAN CIGARETTES--MAKE SURE WE HAVE AT LEAST A GROSS IN THE PLACE AT ANY ONE TIME.
I SMOKE CARCINOMA ANGELS. MAKE SURE WE HAVE FIVE GROSS. YOU SMOKE?
KISS HERE
NO.
START. YOU'LL FIND A BAG OF ANTI-CANCER PRESCRIPTION IN THE BATHROOM IF YOU DON'T ALREADY HAVE THE TRAIT.
OKAY. THERE'S AN AFRICAN FOODSTALL DOWN THE STREET. I NEED TWO MONKEY-BURGERS, ROAST POTATO SKINS AND A TUB OF MATOKE.
HOLD IT, HOLD IT. ASSISTANT, YES. SPIDER JERUSALEM'S SLAVE, NO.
I THOUGHT YOU WANTED TO BE A JOURNALIST?
I DO.
THEN LET ME FINISH TALKING.

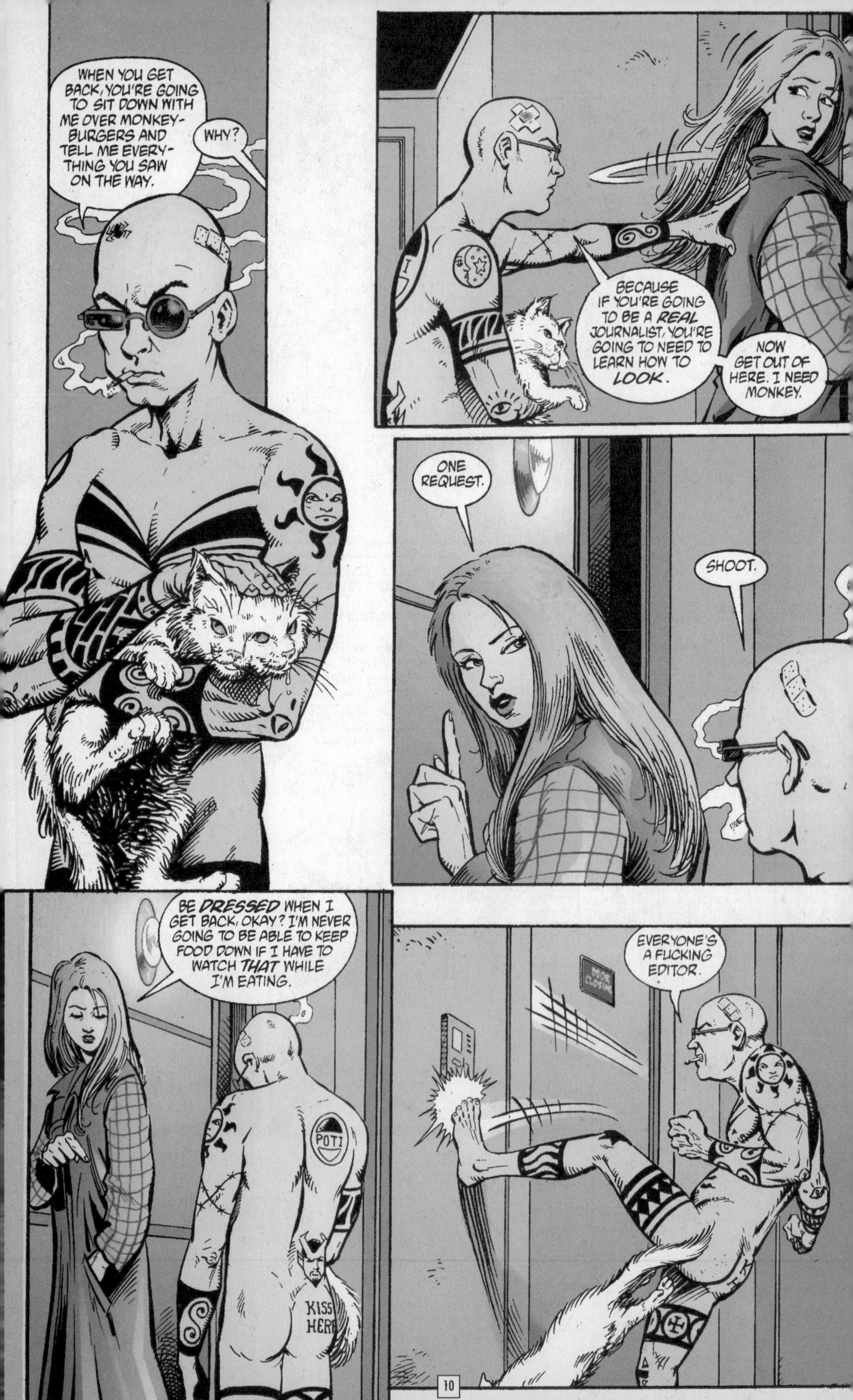
WHEN YOU GET BACK, YOU'RE GOING TO SIT DOWN WITH ME OVER MONKEY-BURGERS AND TELL ME EVERYTHING YOU SAW ON THE WAY.
WHY?
BECAUSE IF YOU'RE GOING TO BE A REAL JOURNALIST, YOU'RE GOING TO NEED TO LEARN HOW TO LOOK.
NOW GET OUT OF HERE. I NEED MONKEY.
ONE REQUEST.
SHOOT.
BE DRESSED WHEN I GET BACK, OKAY? I'M NEVER GOING TO BE ABLE TO KEEP FOOD DOWN IF I HAVE TO WATCH THAT WHILE I'M EATING.
POTI
KISS HERE
EVERYONE'S A FUCKING EDITOR.

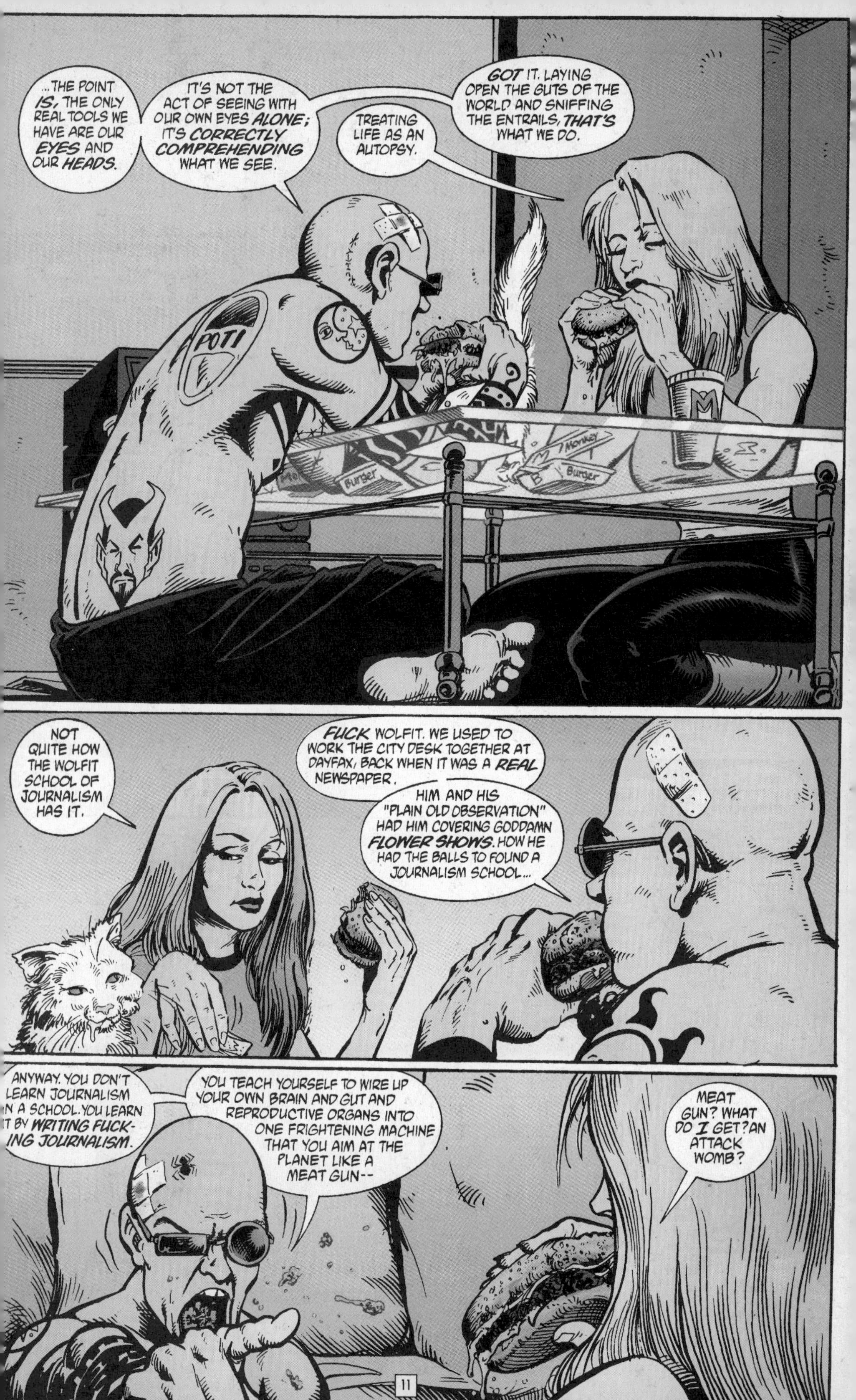
...THE POINT IS, THE ONLY REAL TOOLS WE HAVE ARE OUR EYES AND OUR HEADS.
IT'S NOT THE ACT OF SEEING WITH OUR OWN EYES ALONE; IT'S CORRECTLY COMPREHENDING WHAT WE SEE.
TREATING LIFE AS AN AUTOPSY.
GOT IT. LAYING OPEN THE GUTS OF THE WORLD AND SNIFFING THE ENTRAILS, THAT'S WHAT WE DO.
POTI
Burger
Monkey
Burger
NOT QUITE HOW THE WOLFIT SCHOOL OF JOURNALISM HAS IT.
FUCK WOLFIT. WE USED TO WORK THE CITY DESK TOGETHER AT DAYFAX, BACK WHEN IT WAS A REAL NEWSPAPER.
HIM AND HIS "PLAIN OLD OBSERVATION" HAD HIM COVERING GODDAMN FLOWER SHOWS. HOW HE HAD THE BALLS TO FOUND A JOURNALISM SCHOOL...
ANYWAY. YOU DON'T LEARN JOURNALISM IN A SCHOOL. YOU LEARN IT BY WRITING FUCKING JOURNALISM.
YOU TEACH YOURSELF TO WIRE UP YOUR OWN BRAIN AND GUT AND REPRODUCTIVE ORGANS INTO ONE FRIGHTENING MACHINE THAT YOU AIM AT THE PLANET LIKE A MEAT GUN--
MEAT GUN? WHAT DO I GET? AN ATTACK WOMB?

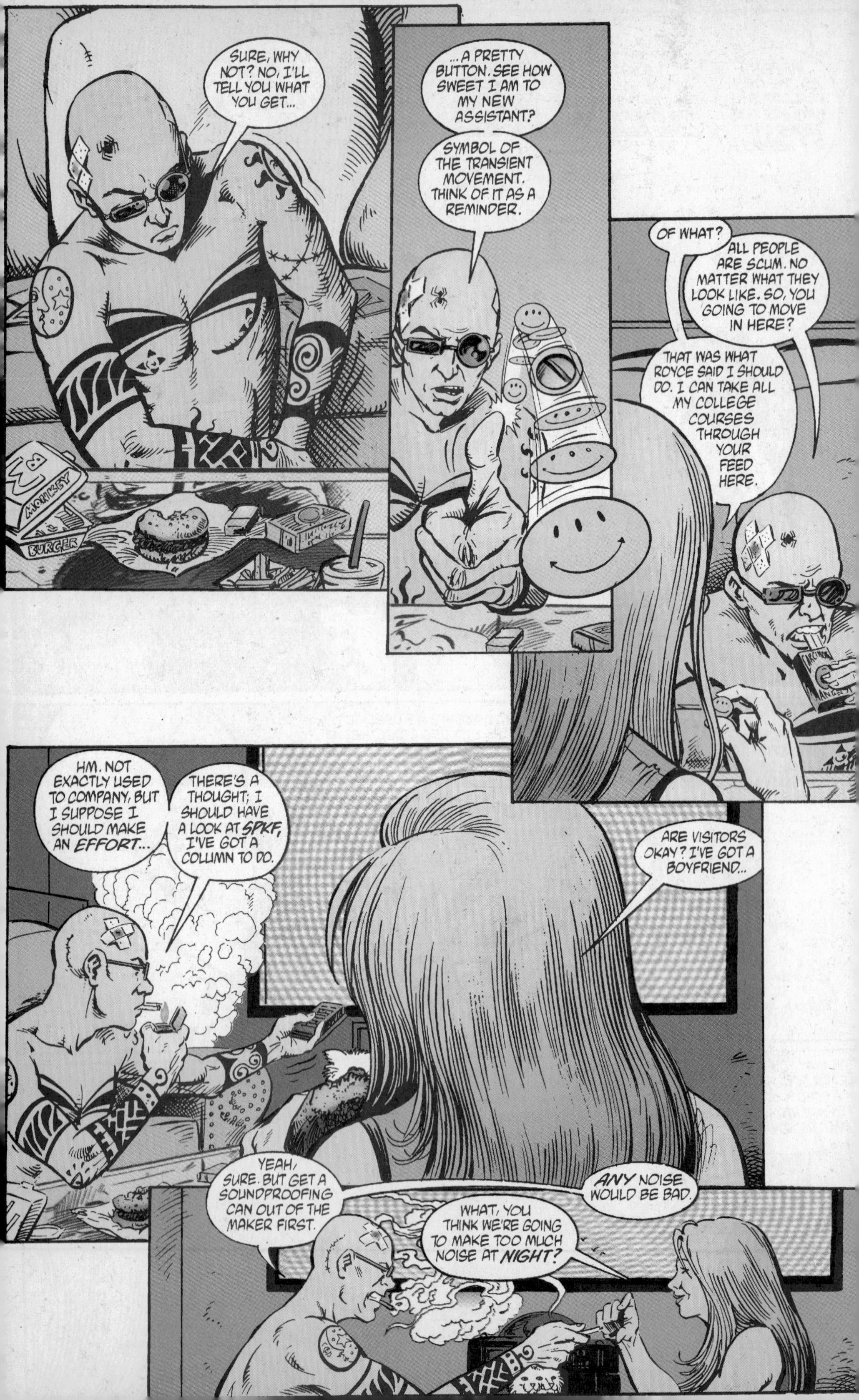
SURE, WHY NOT? NO, I'LL TELL YOU WHAT YOU GET...
...A PRETTY BUTTON. SEE HOW SWEET I AM TO MY NEW ASSISTANT?
SYMBOL OF THE TRANSIENT MOVEMENT. THINK OF IT AS A REMINDER.
OF WHAT?
ALL PEOPLE ARE SCUM. NO MATTER WHAT THEY LOOK LIKE. SO, YOU GOING TO MOVE IN HERE?
THAT WAS WHAT ROYCE SAID I SHOULD DO. I CAN TAKE ALL MY COLLEGE COURSES THROUGH YOUR FEED HERE.
HM. NOT EXACTLY USED TO COMPANY, BUT I SUPPOSE I SHOULD MAKE AN EFFORT...
THERE'S A THOUGHT; I SHOULD HAVE A LOOK AT SPKF, I'VE GOT A COLUMN TO DO.
ARE VISITORS OKAY? I'VE GOT A BOYFRIEND...
YEAH, SURE. BUT GET A SOUNDPROOFING CAN OUT OF THE MAKER FIRST.
ANY NOISE WOULD BE BAD.
WHAT, YOU THINK WE'RE GOING TO MAKE TOO MUCH NOISE AT NIGHT?
MONKEY
BURGER

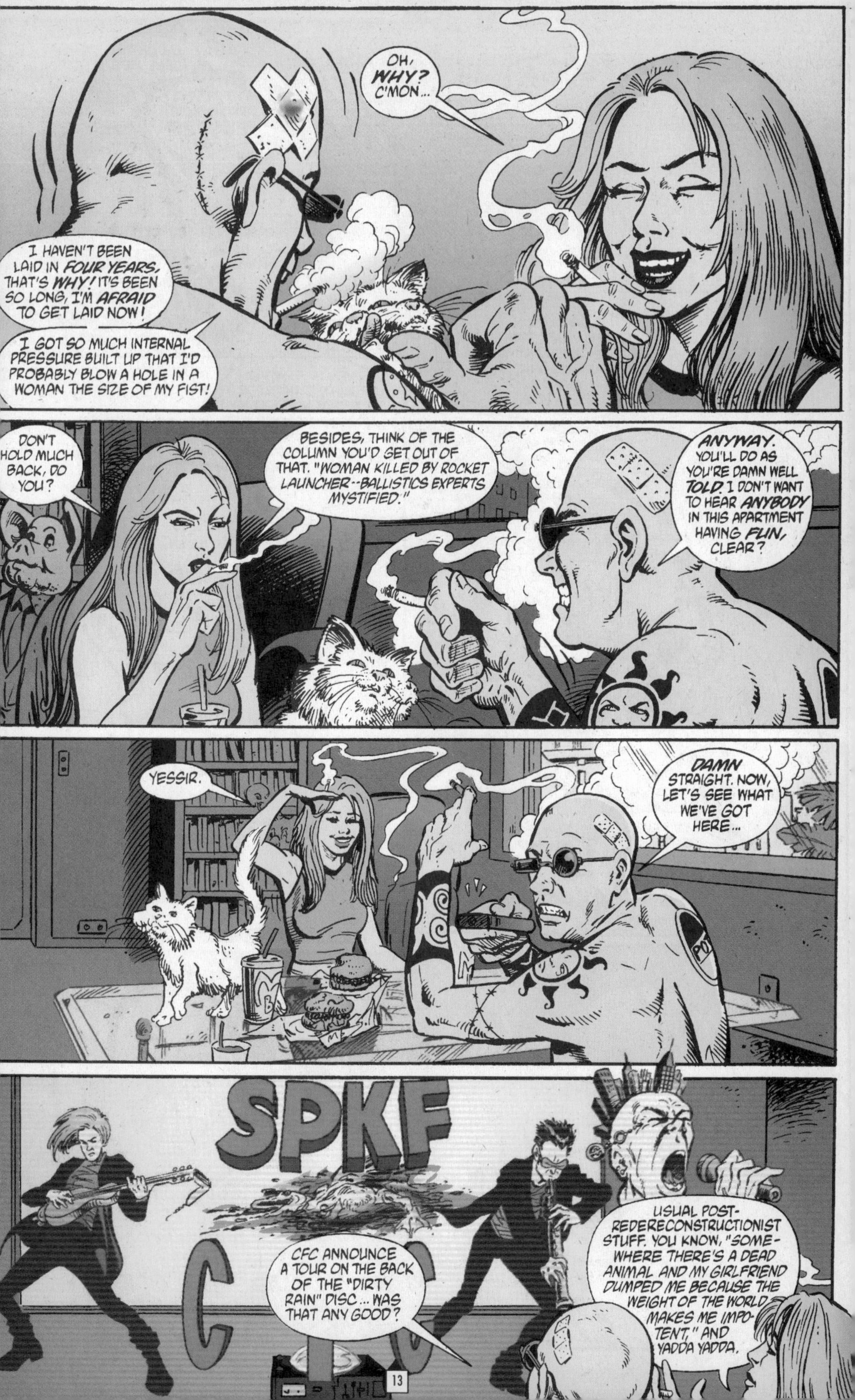

OH, WHY? C'MON...
I HAVEN'T BEEN LAID IN FOUR YEARS, THAT'S WHY! IT'S BEEN SO LONG, I'M AFRAID TO GET LAID NOW!
I GOT SO MUCH INTERNAL PRESSURE BUILT UP THAT I'D PROBABLY BLOW A HOLE IN A WOMAN THE SIZE OF MY FIST!
DON'T HOLD MUCH BACK, DO YOU?
BESIDES, THINK OF THE COLUMN YOU'D GET OUT OF THAT. "WOMAN KILLED BY ROCKET LAUNCHER--BALLISTICS EXPERTS MYSTIFIED."
ANYWAY. YOU'LL DO AS YOU'RE DAMN WELL TOLD. I DON'T WANT TO HEAR ANYBODY IN THIS APARTMENT HAVING FUN, CLEAR?
YESSIR.
DAMN STRAIGHT. NOW, LET'S SEE WHAT WE'VE GOT HERE...
SPKF
CFC ANNOUNCE A TOUR ON THE BACK OF THE "DIRTY RAIN" DISC... WAS THAT ANY GOOD?
USUAL POST-REDERECONSTRUCTIONIST STUFF. YOU KNOW, "SOMEWHERE THERE'S A DEAD ANIMAL AND MY GIRLFRIEND DUMPED ME BECAUSE THE WEIGHT OF THE WORLD MAKES ME IMPOTENT," AND YADDA YADDA.

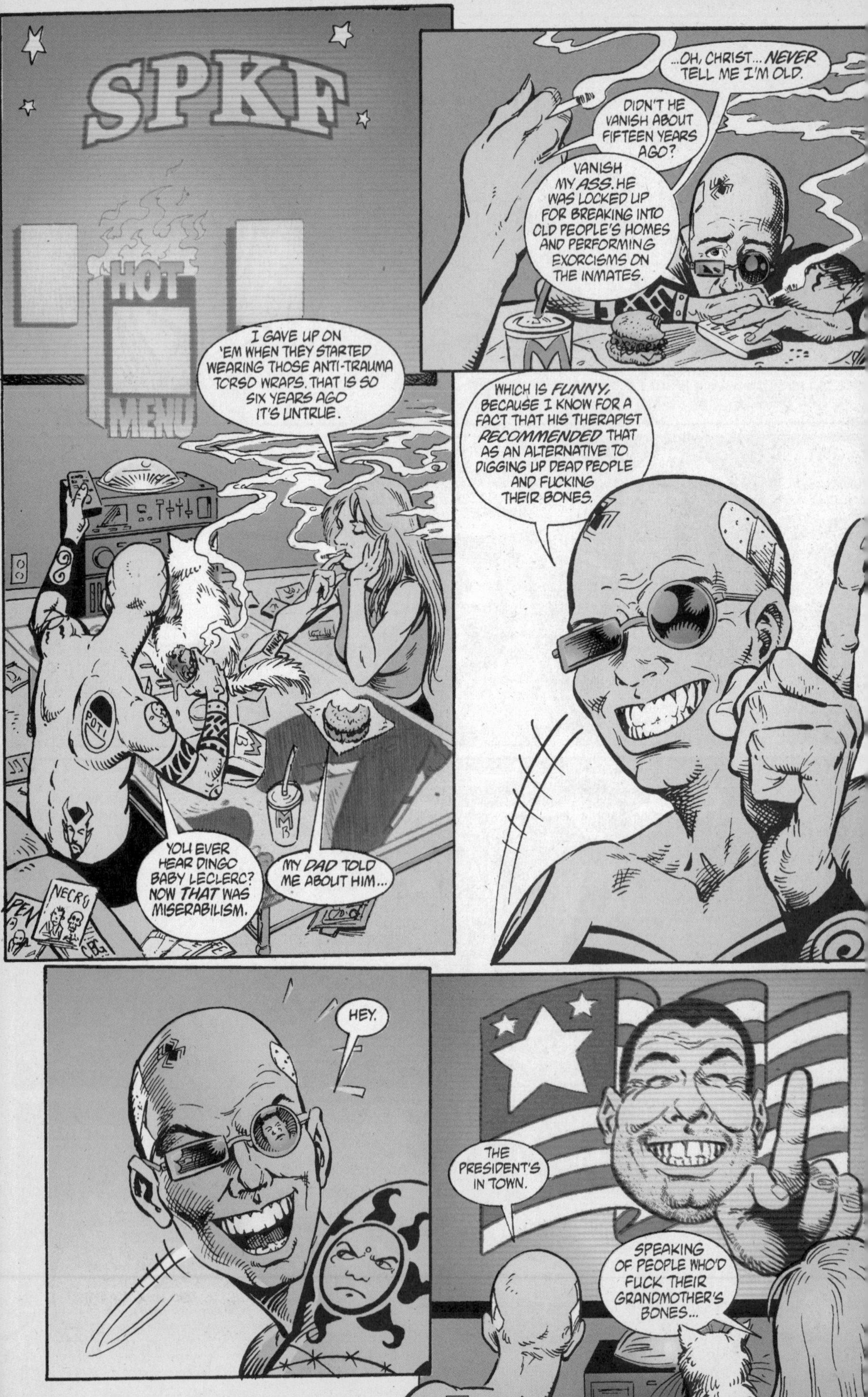
SPKF
HOT
MENU
I GAVE UP ON 'EM WHEN THEY STARTED WEARING THOSE ANTI-TRAUMA TORSO WRAPS. THAT IS SO SIX YEARS AGO IT'S UNTRUE.
YOU EVER HEAR DINGO BABY LECLERC? NOW THAT WAS MISERABILISM.
MY DAD TOLD ME ABOUT HIM...
DIDN'T HE VANISH ABOUT FIFTEEN YEARS AGO?
...OH, CHRIST... NEVER TELL ME I'M OLD.
VANISH MY ASS. HE WAS LOCKED UP FOR BREAKING INTO OLD PEOPLE'S HOMES AND PERFORMING EXORCISMS ON THE INMATES.
WHICH IS FUNNY, BECAUSE I KNOW FOR A FACT THAT HIS THERAPIST RECOMMENDED THAT AS AN ALTERNATIVE TO DIGGING UP DEAD PEOPLE AND FUCKING THEIR BONES.
HEY.
THE PRESIDENT'S IN TOWN.
SPEAKING OF PEOPLE WHO'D FUCK THEIR GRANDMOTHER'S BONES...
NECRO

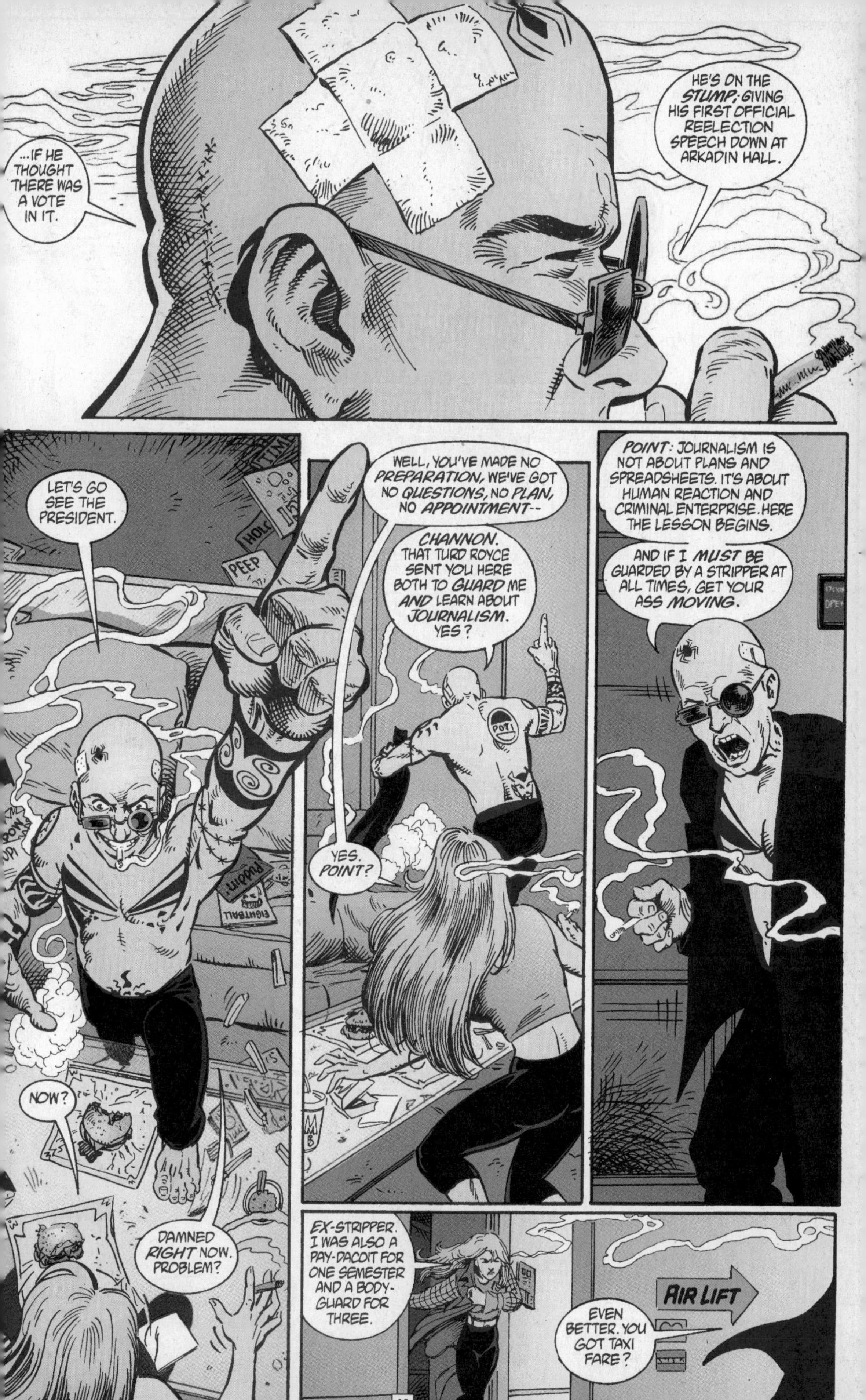
...IF HE THOUGHT THERE WAS A VOTE IN IT.
HE'S ON THE STUMP; GIVING HIS FIRST OFFICIAL REELECTION SPEECH DOWN AT ARKADIN HALL.
LET'S GO SEE THE PRESIDENT.
NOW?
DAMNED RIGHT NOW. PROBLEM?
WELL, YOU'VE MADE NO PREPARATION, WE'VE GOT NO QUESTIONS, NO PLAN, NO APPOINTMENT--
CHANNON. THAT TURD ROYCE SENT YOU HERE BOTH TO GUARD ME AND LEARN ABOUT JOURNALISM. YES?
YES. POINT?
POINT: JOURNALISM IS NOT ABOUT PLANS AND SPREADSHEETS. IT'S ABOUT HUMAN REACTION AND CRIMINAL ENTERPRISE. HERE THE LESSON BEGINS.
AND IF I MUST BE GUARDED BY A STRIPPER AT ALL TIMES, GET YOUR ASS MOVING.
EX-STRIPPER. I WAS ALSO A PAY-DACOIT FOR ONE SEMESTER AND A BODY-GUARD FOR THREE.
AIR LIFT
EVEN BETTER. YOU GOT TAXI FARE?

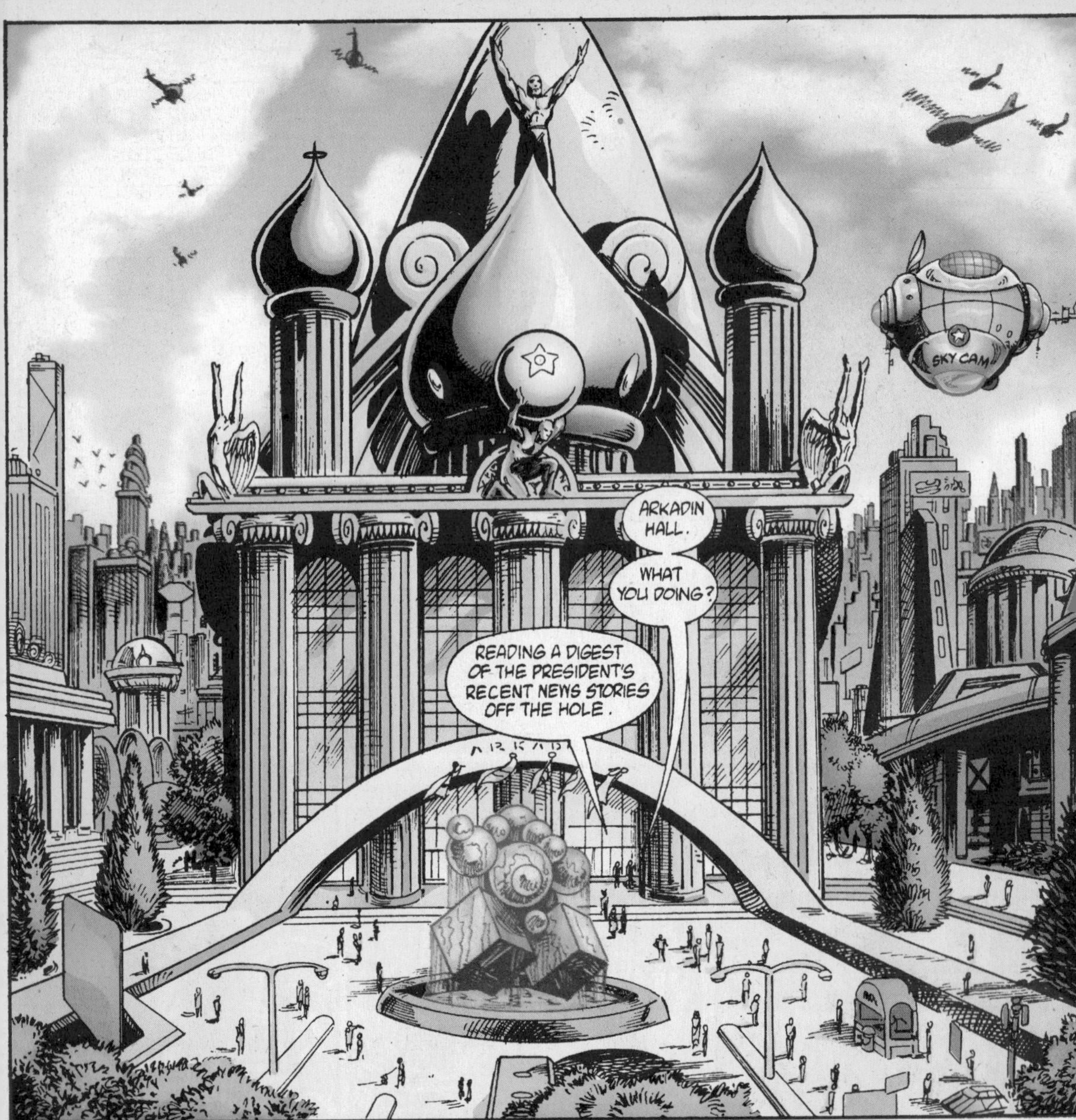
SKY CAM
ARKADIN HALL.
WHAT YOU DOING?
READING A DIGEST OF THE PRESIDENT'S RECENT NEWS STORIES OFF THE HOLE.

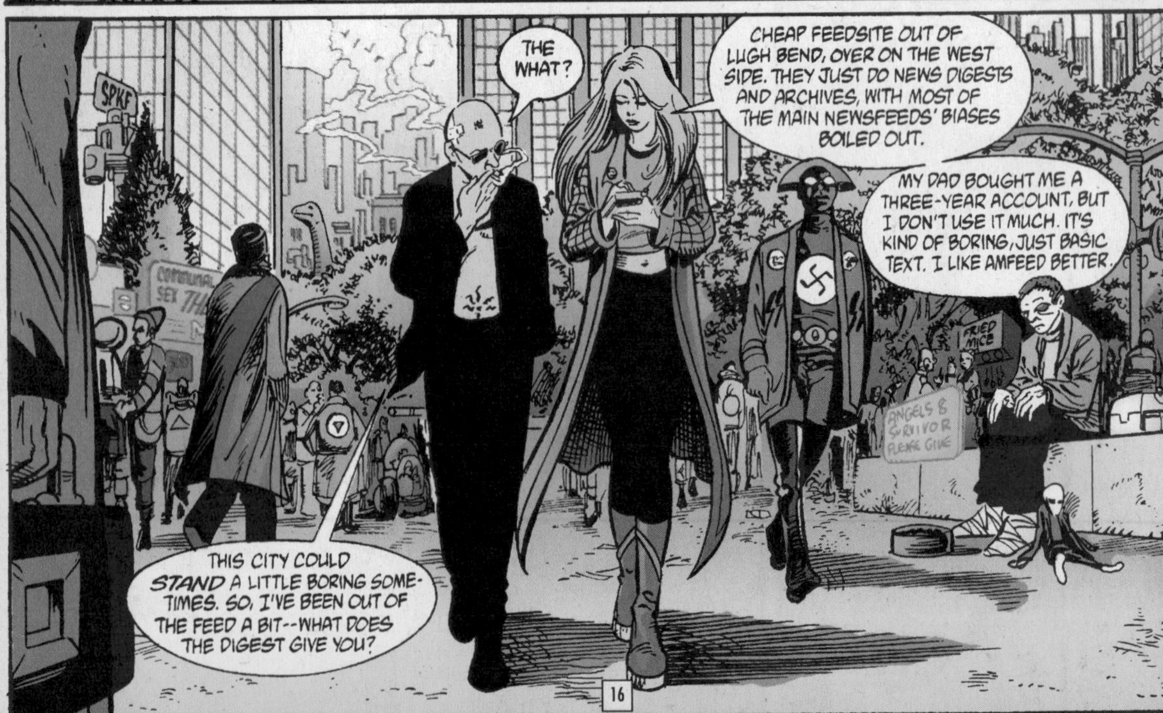
THE WHAT?
CHEAP FEEDSITE OUT OF LUGH BEND, OVER ON THE WEST SIDE. THEY JUST DO NEWS DIGESTS AND ARCHIVES, WITH MOST OF THE MAIN NEWSFEEDS' BIASES BOILED OUT.
MY DAD BOUGHT ME A THREE-YEAR ACCOUNT, BUT I DON'T USE IT MUCH. IT'S KIND OF BORING, JUST BASIC TEXT. I LIKE AMFEED BETTER.
THIS CITY COULD STAND A LITTLE BORING SOMETIMES. SO, I'VE BEEN OUT OF THE FEED A BIT--WHAT DOES THE DIGEST GIVE YOU?
SPKF
FRIED MICE
ANGELS & SURVIVOR PLEASE GIVE

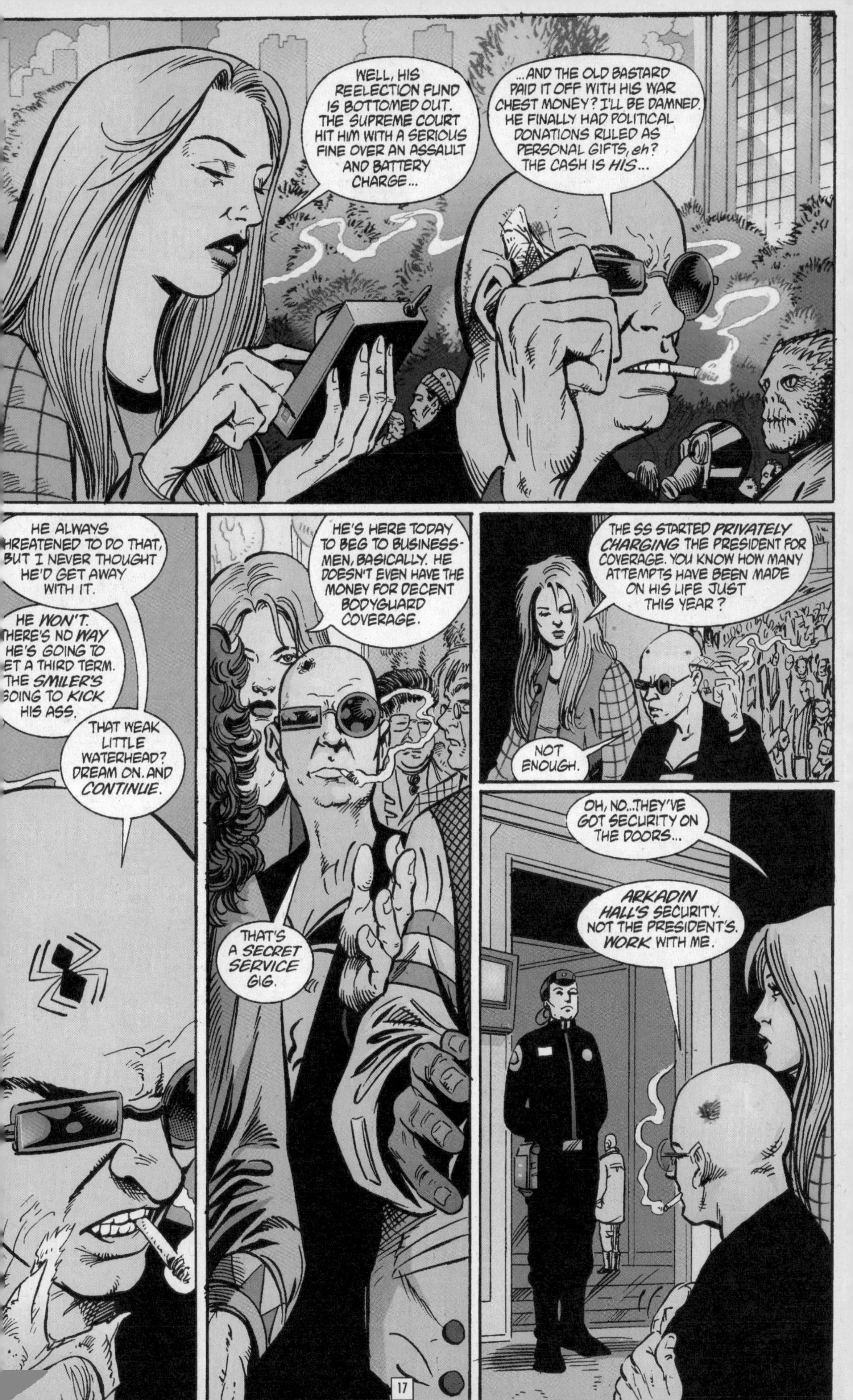
WELL, HIS REELECTION FUND IS BOTTOMED OUT. THE SUPREME COURT HIT HIM WITH A SERIOUS FINE OVER AN ASSAULT AND BATTERY CHARGE...
...AND THE OLD BASTARD PAID IT OFF WITH HIS WAR CHEST MONEY? I'LL BE DAMNED. HE FINALLY HAD POLITICAL DONATIONS RULED AS PERSONAL GIFTS, eh? THE CASH IS HIS...
HE ALWAYS THREATENED TO DO THAT, BUT I NEVER THOUGHT HE'D GET AWAY WITH IT.
HE WON'T. THERE'S NO WAY HE'S GOING TO GET A THIRD TERM. THE SMILER'S GOING TO KICK HIS ASS.
THAT WEAK LITTLE WATERHEAD? DREAM ON. AND CONTINUE.
HE'S HERE TODAY TO BEG TO BUSINESSMEN, BASICALLY. HE DOESN'T EVEN HAVE THE MONEY FOR DECENT BODYGUARD COVERAGE.
THAT'S A SECRET SERVICE GIG.
THE SS STARTED PRIVATELY CHARGING THE PRESIDENT FOR COVERAGE. YOU KNOW HOW MANY ATTEMPTS HAVE BEEN MADE ON HIS LIFE JUST THIS YEAR?
NOT ENOUGH.
OH, NO...THEY'VE GOT SECURITY ON THE DOORS...
ARKADIN HALL'S SECURITY. NOT THE PRESIDENT'S. WORK WITH ME.

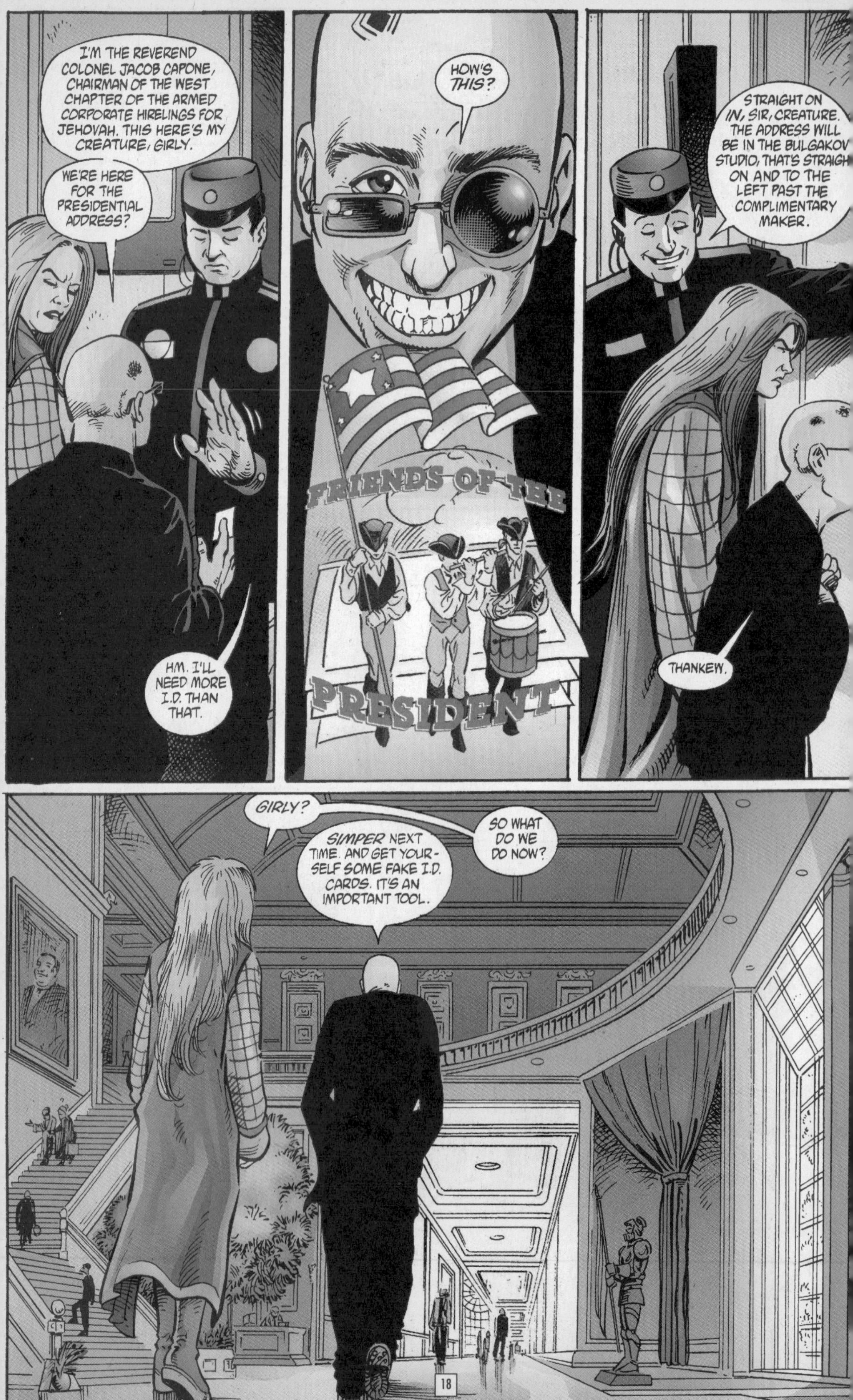
I'M THE REVEREND COLONEL JACOB CAPONE, CHAIRMAN OF THE WEST CHAPTER OF THE ARMED CORPORATE HIRELINGS FOR JEHOVAH. THIS HERE'S MY CREATURE, GIRLY.
WE'RE HERE FOR THE PRESIDENTIAL ADDRESS?
H.M. I'LL NEED MORE I.D. THAN THAT.
HOW'S THIS?
FRIENDS OF THE PRESIDENT
STRAIGHT ON IN, SIR, CREATURE. THE ADDRESS WILL BE IN THE BULGAKOV STUDIO, THAT'S STRAIGH ON AND TO THE LEFT PAST THE COMPLIMENTARY MAKER.
THANKEW.
GIRLY?
SIMPER NEXT TIME. AND GET YOURSELF SOME FAKE I.D. CARDS. IT'S AN IMPORTANT TOOL.
SO WHAT DO WE DO NOW?

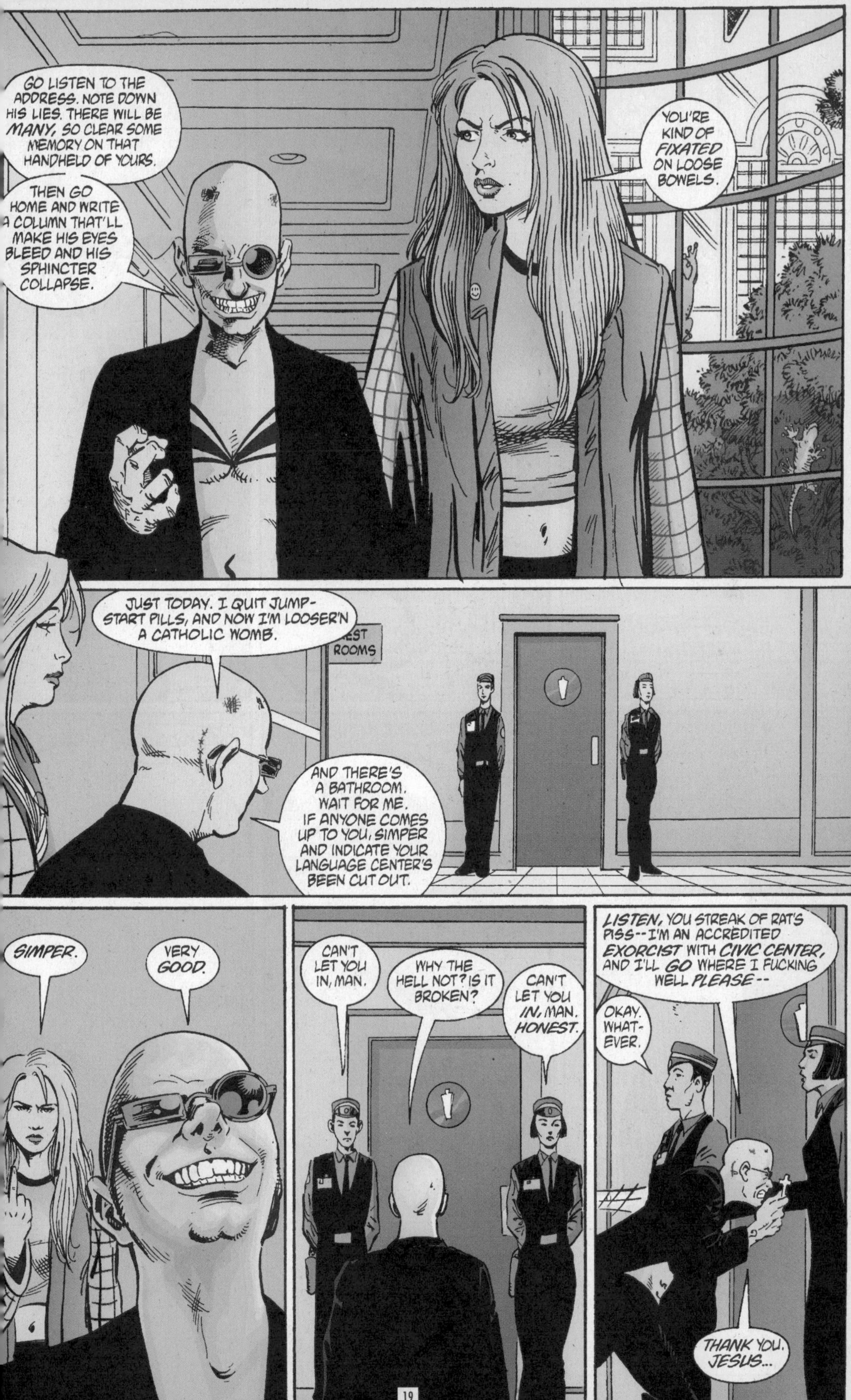
GO LISTEN TO THE ADDRESS. NOTE DOWN HIS LIES. THERE WILL BE MANY, SO CLEAR SOME MEMORY ON THAT HANDHELD OF YOURS.
THEN GO HOME AND WRITE A COLUMN THAT'LL MAKE HIS EYES BLEED AND HIS SPHINCTER COLLAPSE.
YOU'RE KIND OF FIXATED ON LOOSE BOWELS.
JUST TODAY. I QUIT JUMP-START PILLS, AND NOW I'M LOOSER'N A CATHOLIC WOMB.
REST ROOMS
AND THERE'S A BATHROOM. WAIT FOR ME. IF ANYONE COMES UP TO YOU, SIMPER AND INDICATE YOUR LANGUAGE CENTER'S BEEN CUT OUT.
SIMPER.
VERY GOOD.
CAN'T LET YOU IN, MAN.
WHY THE HELL NOT? IS IT BROKEN?
CAN'T LET YOU IN, MAN. HONEST.
LISTEN, YOU STREAK OF RAT'S PISS--I'M AN ACCREDITED EXORCIST WITH CIVIC CENTER, AND I'LL GO WHERE I FUCKING WELL PLEASE--
OKAY. WHAT-EVER.
THANK YOU. JESUS...

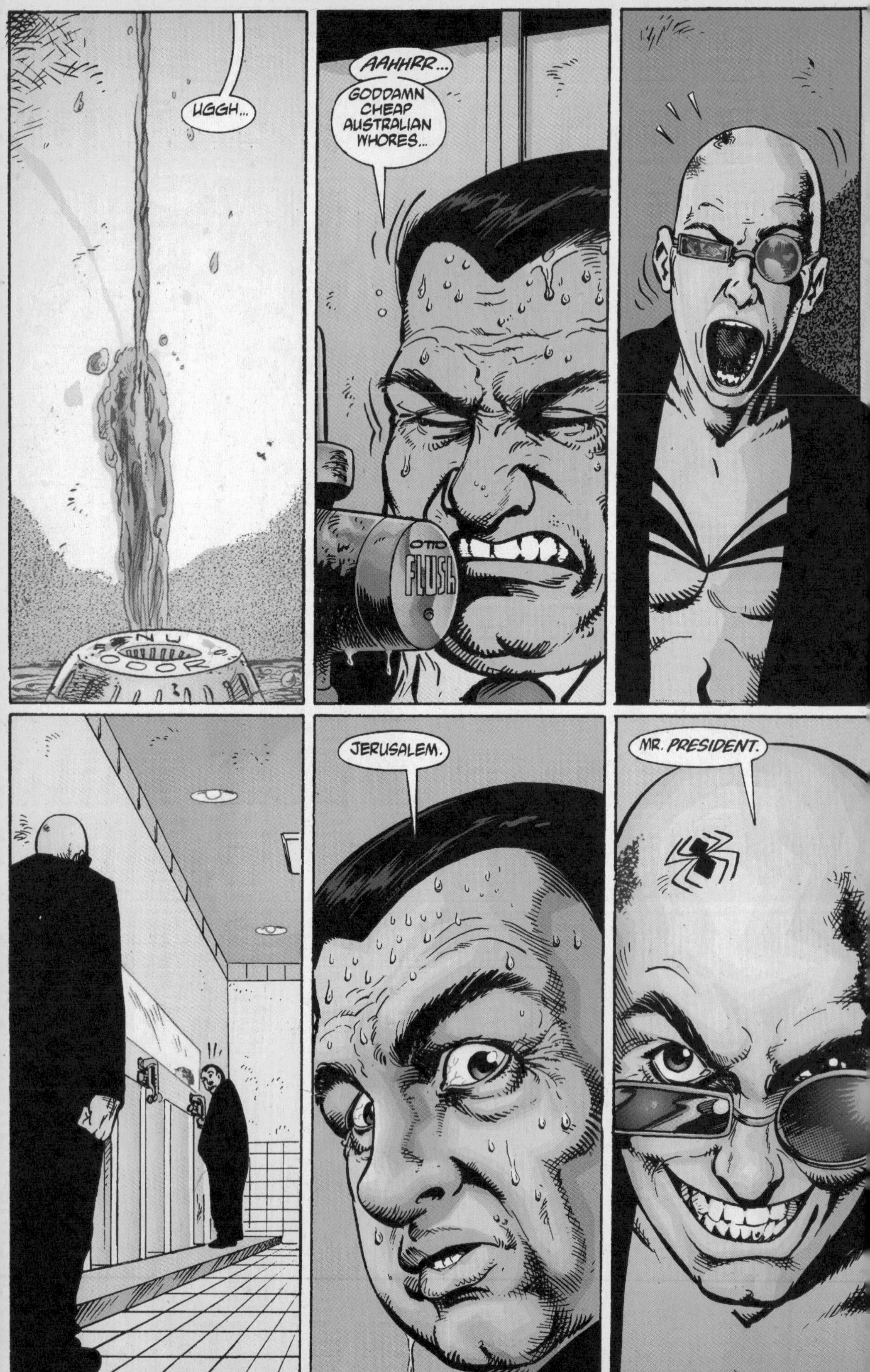
UGGH...
AAHHRR...
GODDAMN CHEAP AUSTRALIAN WHORES...
FLUSH
JERUSALEM.
MR. PRESIDENT.

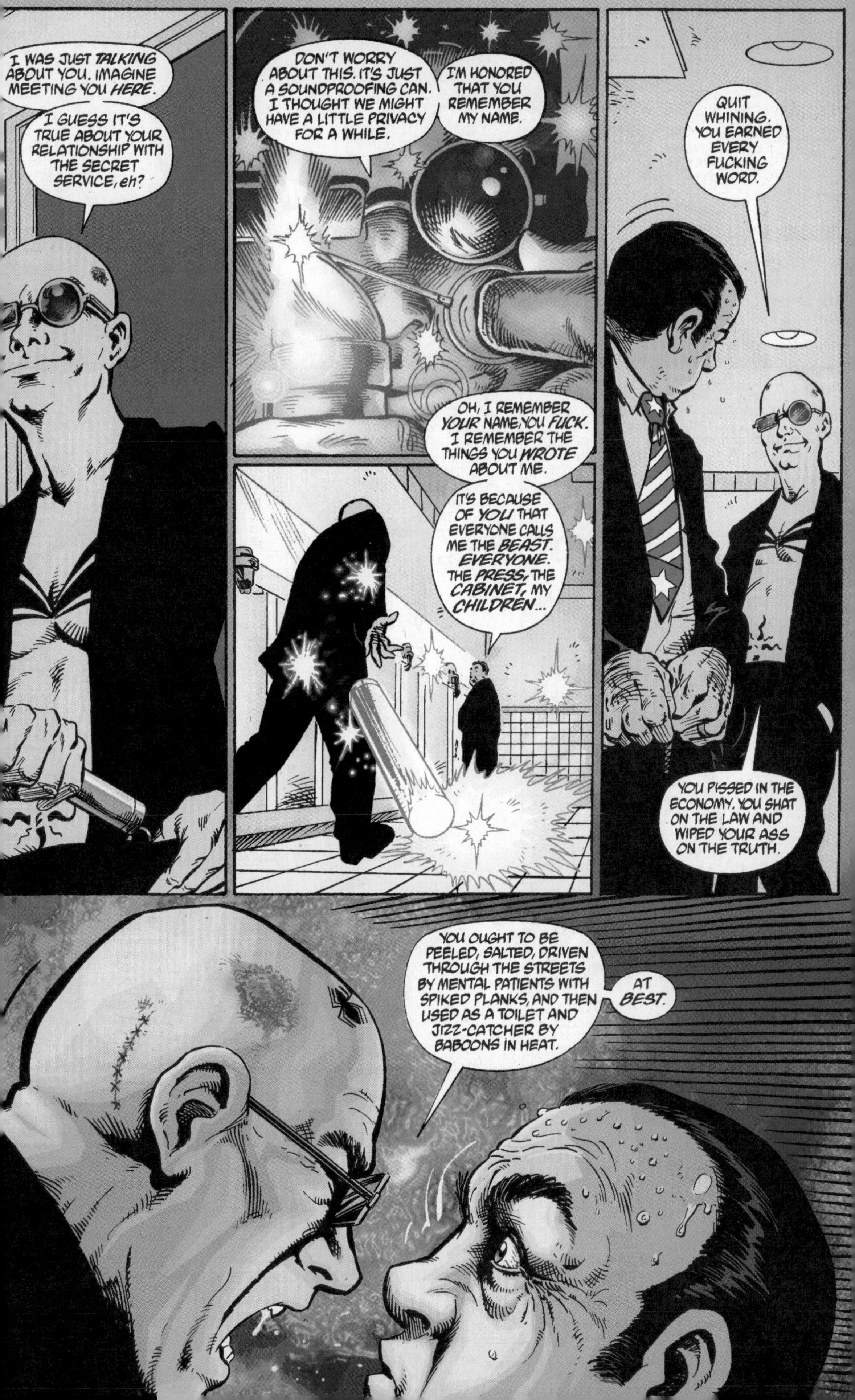
I WAS JUST TALKING ABOUT YOU. IMAGINE MEETING YOU HERE.
I GUESS IT'S TRUE ABOUT YOUR RELATIONSHIP WITH THE SECRET SERVICE, eh?
DON'T WORRY ABOUT THIS. IT'S JUST A SOUNDPROOFING CAN. I THOUGHT WE MIGHT HAVE A LITTLE PRIVACY FOR A WHILE.
I'M HONORED THAT YOU REMEMBER MY NAME.
OH, I REMEMBER YOUR NAME, YOU FUCK. I REMEMBER THE THINGS YOU WROTE ABOUT ME.
IT'S BECAUSE OF YOU THAT EVERYONE CALLS ME THE BEAST. EVERYONE. THE PRESS, THE CABINET, MY CHILDREN...
QUIT WHINING. YOU EARNED EVERY FUCKING WORD.
YOU PISSED IN THE ECONOMY. YOU SHAT ON THE LAW AND WIPED YOUR ASS ON THE TRUTH.
YOU OUGHT TO BE PEELED, SALTED, DRIVEN THROUGH THE STREETS BY MENTAL PATIENTS WITH SPIKED PLANKS, AND THEN USED AS A TOILET AND JIZZ-CATCHER BY BABOONS IN HEAT.
AT BEST.

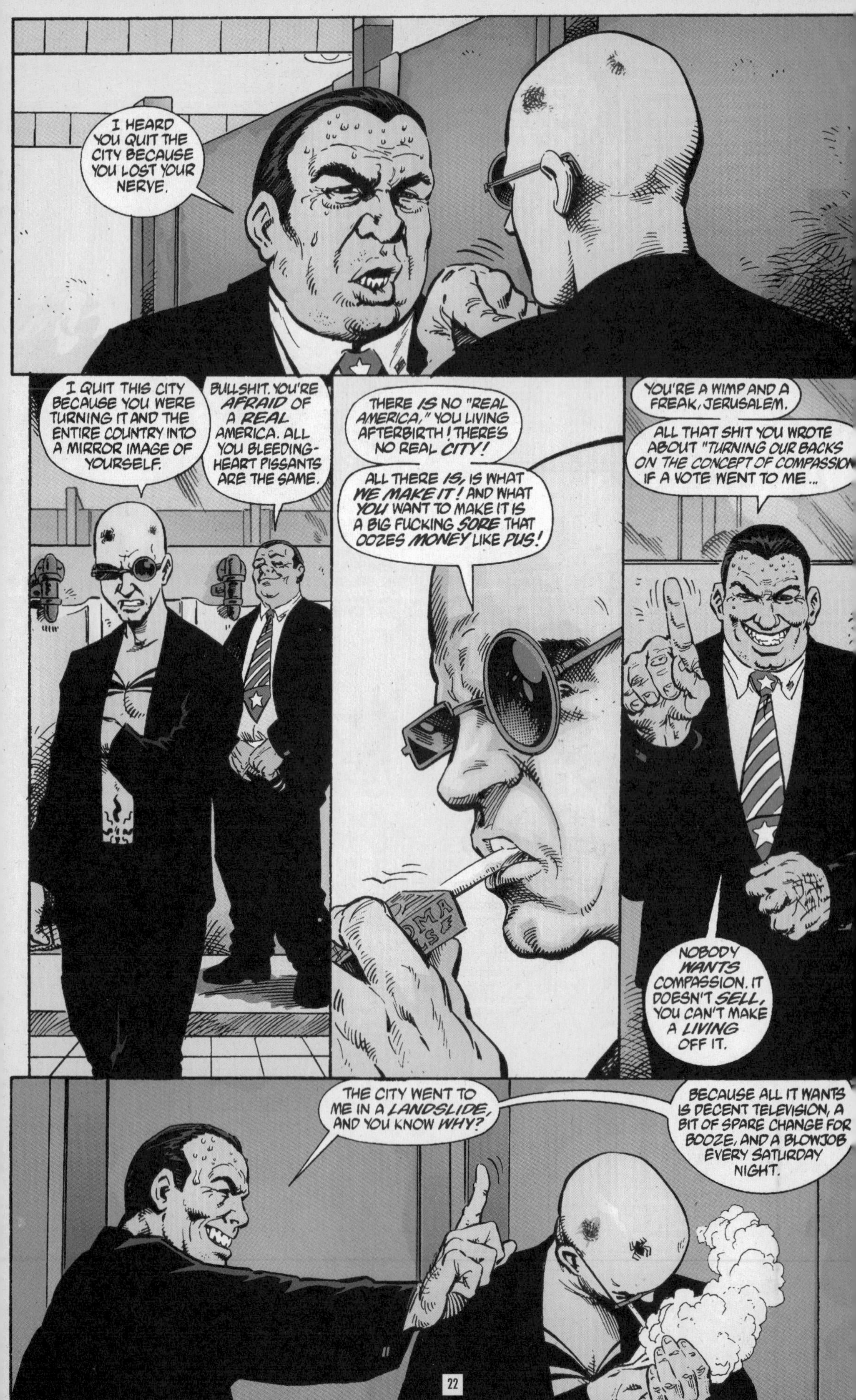

I HEARD YOU QUIT THE CITY BECAUSE YOU LOST YOUR NERVE.
I QUIT THIS CITY BECAUSE YOU WERE TURNING IT AND THE ENTIRE COUNTRY INTO A MIRROR IMAGE OF YOURSELF.
BULLSHIT. YOU'RE AFRAID OF A REAL AMERICA. ALL YOU BLEEDING-HEART PISSANTS ARE THE SAME.
THERE IS NO "REAL AMERICA," YOU LIVING AFTERBIRTH! THERE'S NO REAL CITY!
ALL THERE IS, IS WHAT WE MAKE IT! AND WHAT YOU WANT TO MAKE IT IS A BIG FUCKING SORE THAT OOZES MONEY LIKE PUS!
YOU'RE A WIMP AND A FREAK, JERUSALEM.
ALL THAT SHIT YOU WROTE ABOUT "TURNING OUR BACKS ON THE CONCEPT OF COMPASSION" IF A VOTE WENT TO ME...
NOBODY WANTS COMPASSION. IT DOESN'T SELL, YOU CAN'T MAKE A LIVING OFF IT.
THE CITY WENT TO ME IN A LANDSLIDE, AND YOU KNOW WHY?
BECAUSE ALL IT WANTS IS DECENT TELEVISION, A BIT OF SPARE CHANGE FOR BOOZE, AND A BLOWJOB EVERY SATURDAY NIGHT.

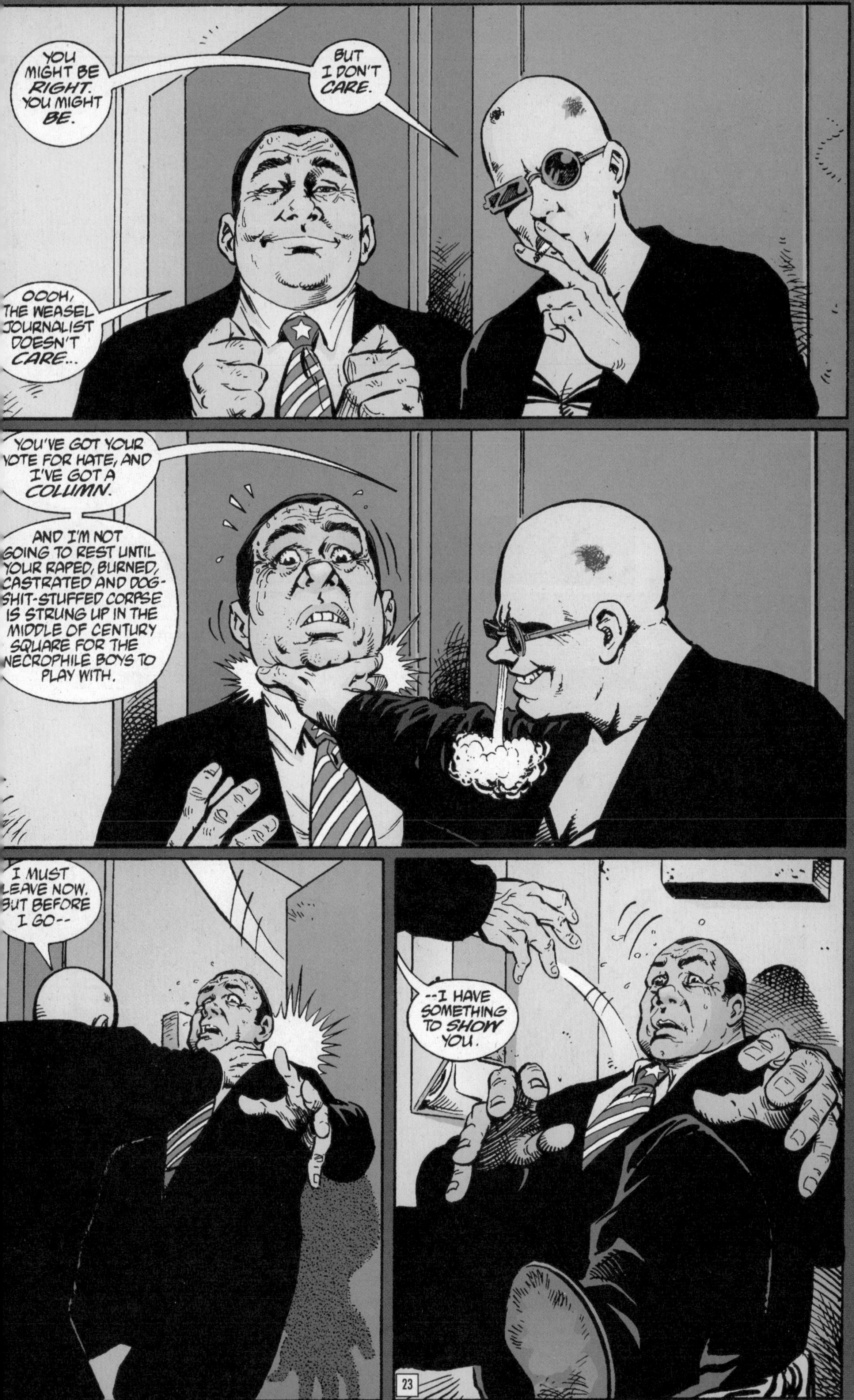
YOU MIGHT BE RIGHT. YOU MIGHT BE.
BUT I DON'T CARE.
OOOH, THE WEASEL JOURNALIST DOESN'T CARE...
YOU'VE GOT YOUR VOTE FOR HATE, AND I'VE GOT A COLUMN.
AND I'M NOT GOING TO REST UNTIL YOUR RAPED, BURNED, CASTRATED AND DOG-SHIT-STUFFED CORPSE IS STRUNG UP IN THE MIDDLE OF CENTURY SQUARE FOR THE NECROPHILE BOYS TO PLAY WITH.
I MUST LEAVE NOW. BUT BEFORE I GO--
--I HAVE SOMETHING TO SHOW YOU.

THIS IS A *BOWEL DISRUPTOR*. IT HAS NO SIGNATURE -- YOU CAN'T DETECT ITS USAGE ON A BODY.

IT HAS SEVERAL SETTINGS. SEE THIS DIAL?

LOOSE...

WATERY...

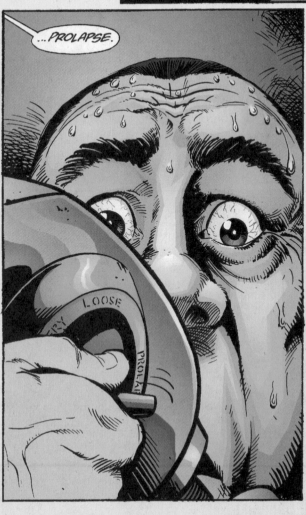

...PROLAPSE.

LOOSE

PROLAP

THERE'S A MAN IN THERE WHO'S HAVING SOME TROUBLE, I THINK. I KNOW YOU'RE NOT ARKADIN HALL SECURITY, BUT...

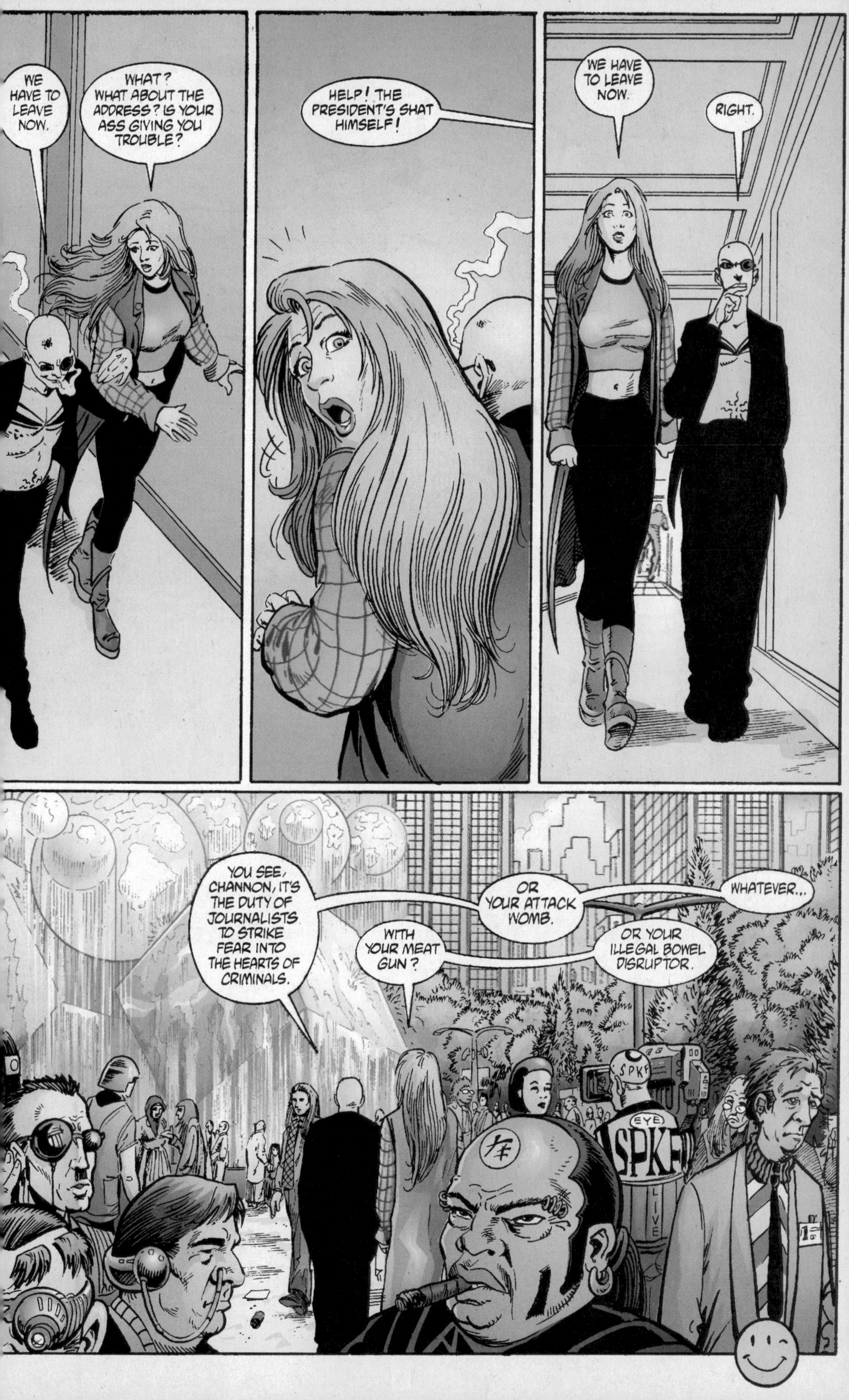
WE HAVE TO LEAVE NOW.
WHAT? WHAT ABOUT THE ADDRESS? IS YOUR ASS GIVING YOU TROUBLE?
HELP! THE PRESIDENT'S SHAT HIMSELF!
WE HAVE TO LEAVE NOW.
RIGHT.
YOU SEE, CHANNON, IT'S THE DUTY OF JOURNALISTS TO STRIKE FEAR INTO THE HEARTS OF CRIMINALS.
WITH YOUR MEAT GUN?
OR YOUR ATTACK WOMB.
OR YOUR ILLEGAL BOWEL DISRUPTOR.
WHATEVER...
SPKF
EYE
LIVE

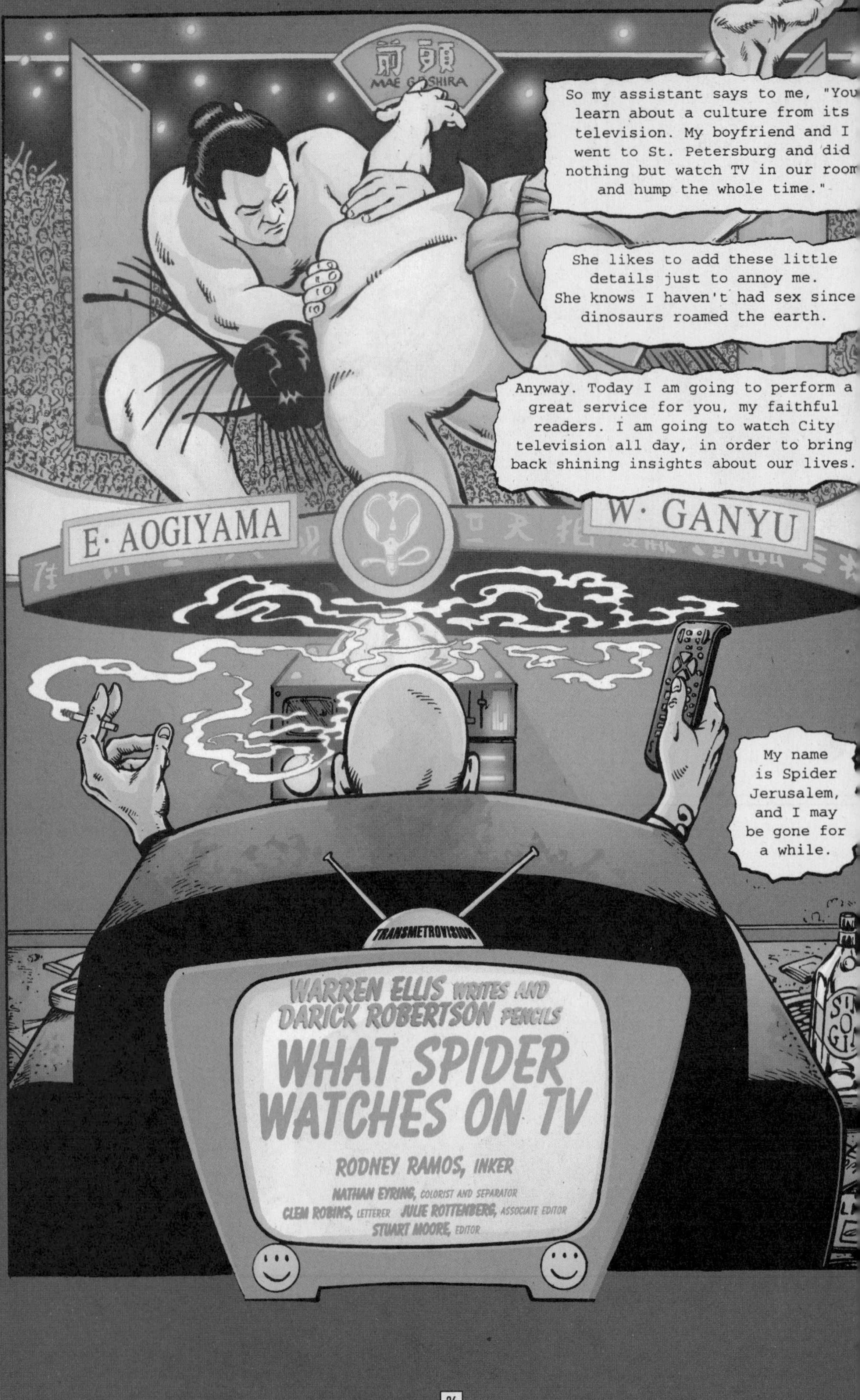

前頭
MAÉ GOSHIRA
So my assistant says to me, "You learn about a culture from its television. My boyfriend and I went to St. Petersburg and did nothing but watch TV in our room and hump the whole time."
She likes to add these little details just to annoy me. She knows I haven't had sex since dinosaurs roamed the earth.
Anyway. Today I am going to perform a great service for you, my faithful readers. I am going to watch City television all day, in order to bring back shining insights about our lives.
E·AOGIYAMA
W·GANYU
My name is Spider Jerusalem, and I may be gone for a while.
TRANSMETROVISION
WARREN ELLIS WRITES AND DARICK ROBERTSON PENCILS
WHAT SPIDER WATCHES ON TV
RODNEY RAMOS, INKER
NATHAN EYRING, COLORIST AND SEPARATOR
CLEM ROBINS, LETTERER JULIE ROTTENBERG, ASSOCIATE EDITOR
STUART MOORE, EDITOR

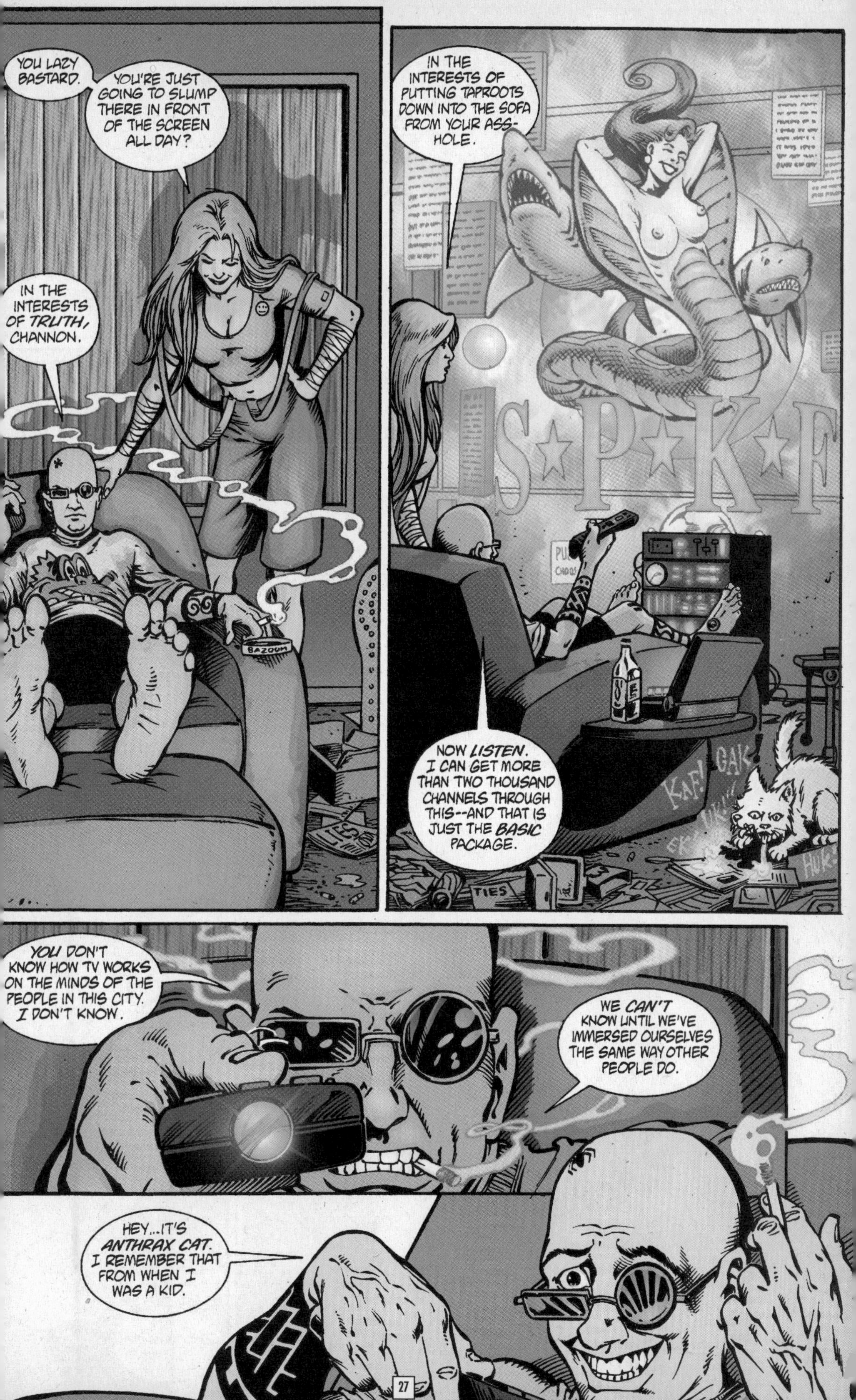
YOU LAZY BASTARD.
YOU'RE JUST GOING TO SLUMP THERE IN FRONT OF THE SCREEN ALL DAY?
IN THE INTERESTS OF TRUTH, CHANNON.
BAZOOM
IN THE INTERESTS OF PUTTING TAPROOTS DOWN INTO THE SOFA FROM YOUR ASS-HOLE.
S★P★K★F
NOW LISTEN. I CAN GET MORE THAN TWO THOUSAND CHANNELS THROUGH THIS--AND THAT IS JUST THE BASIC PACKAGE.
KAF! GAK
HUK!
TIES
YOU DON'T KNOW HOW TV WORKS ON THE MINDS OF THE PEOPLE IN THIS CITY. I DON'T KNOW.
WE CAN'T KNOW UNTIL WE'VE IMMERSED OURSELVES THE SAME WAY OTHER PEOPLE DO.
HEY...IT'S ANTHRAX CAT. I REMEMBER THAT FROM WHEN I WAS A KID.

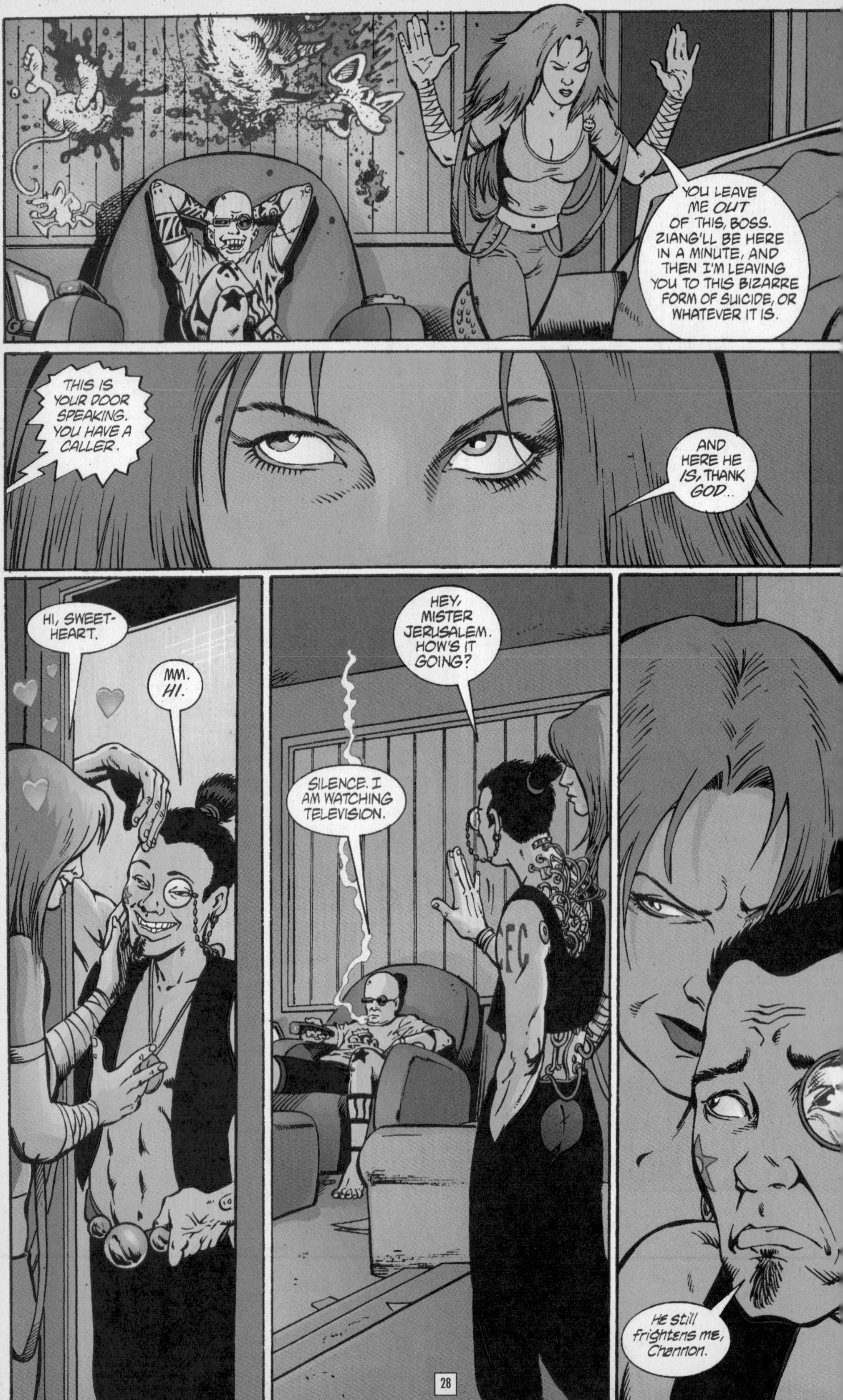

YOU LEAVE ME *OUT* OF THIS, BOSS. ZIANG'LL BE HERE IN A MINUTE, AND THEN I'M LEAVING YOU TO THIS BIZARRE FORM OF SUICIDE, OR WHATEVER IT IS.
THIS IS YOUR DOOR SPEAKING. YOU HAVE A CALLER.
AND HERE HE *IS*, THANK *GOD*...
HI, SWEETHEART.
MM. *HI*.
HEY, MISTER JERUSALEM. HOW'S IT GOING?
SILENCE. I AM WATCHING TELEVISION.
CFC
He still frightens me, Channon.

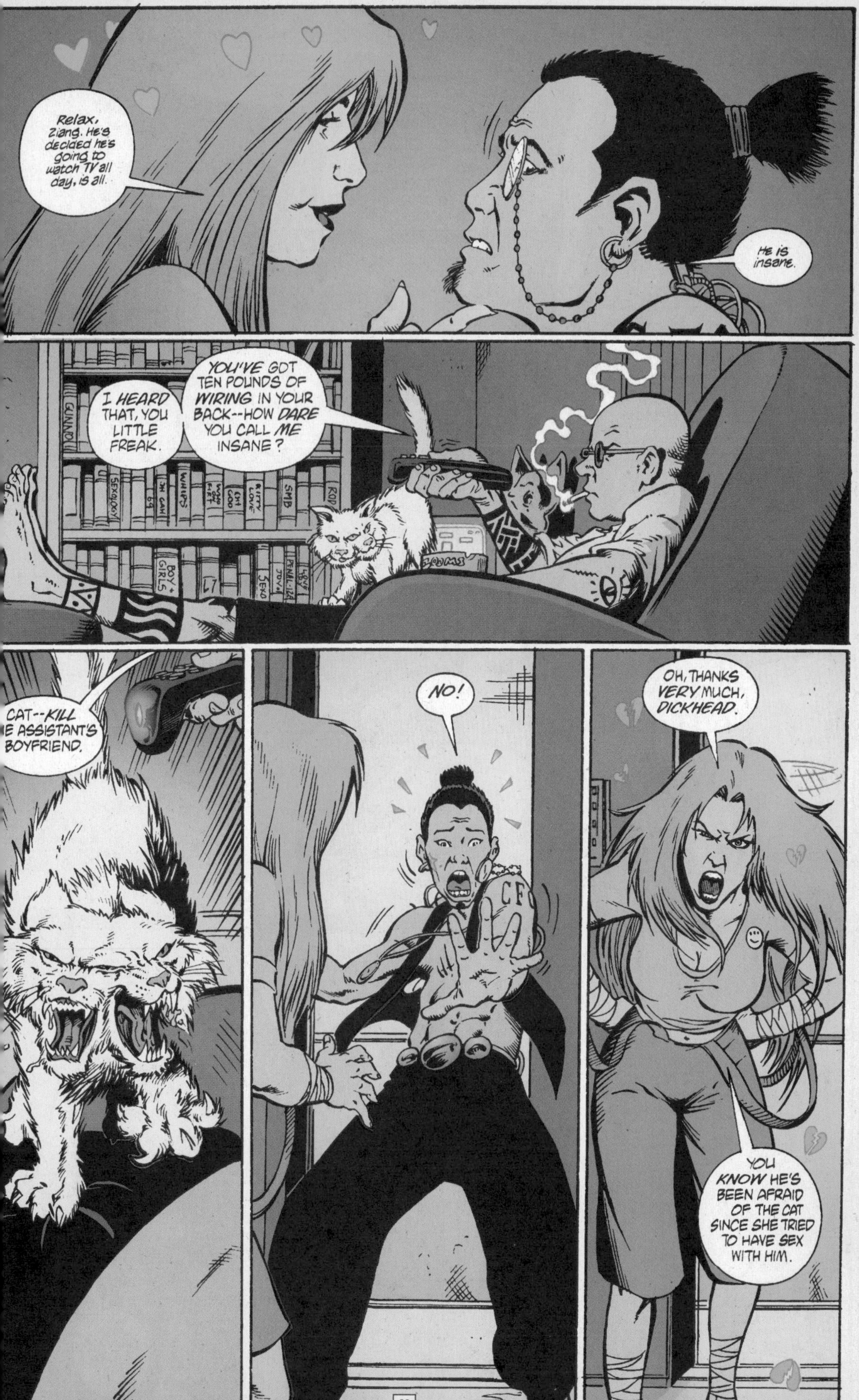
Relax, Ziang. He's decided he's going to watch TV all day, is all.
He is insane.
I HEARD THAT, YOU LITTLE FREAK.
YOU'VE GOT TEN POUNDS OF WIRING IN YOUR BACK--HOW DARE YOU CALL ME INSANE?
CAT--KILL E ASSISTANT'S BOYFRIEND.
NO!
OH, THANKS VERY MUCH, DICKHEAD.
YOU KNOW HE'S BEEN AFRAID OF THE CAT SINCE SHE TRIED TO HAVE SEX WITH HIM.

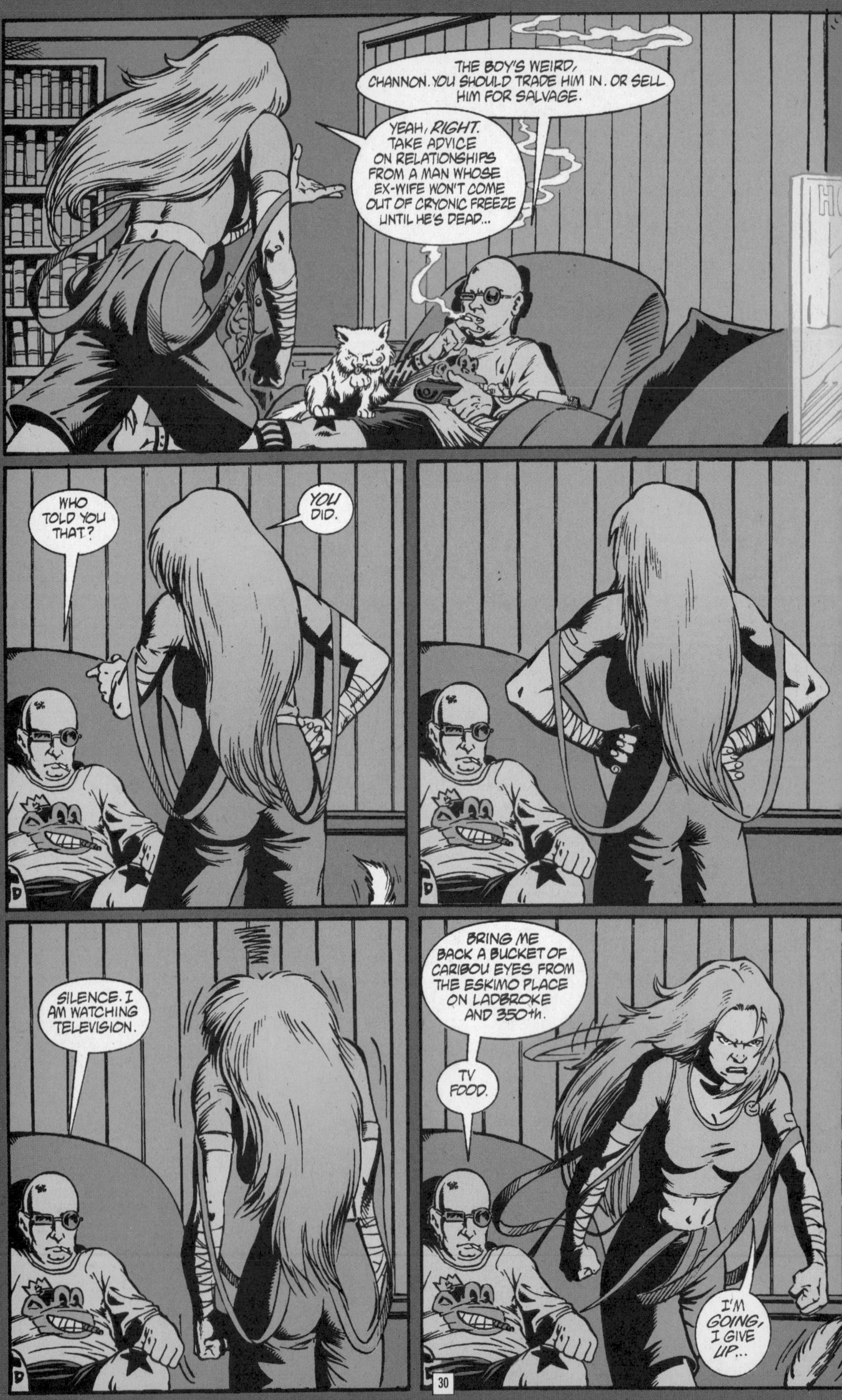
THE BOY'S WEIRD, CHANNON. YOU SHOULD TRADE HIM IN. OR SELL HIM FOR SALVAGE.
YEAH, *RIGHT*. TAKE ADVICE ON RELATIONSHIPS FROM A MAN WHOSE EX-WIFE WON'T COME OUT OF CRYONIC FREEZE UNTIL HE'S DEAD...
WHO TOLD YOU THAT?
YOU DID.
SILENCE. I AM WATCHING TELEVISION.
BRING ME BACK A BUCKET OF CARIBOU EYES FROM THE ESKIMO PLACE ON LADBROKE AND 350th.
TV FOOD.
I'M GOING, I GIVE UP...

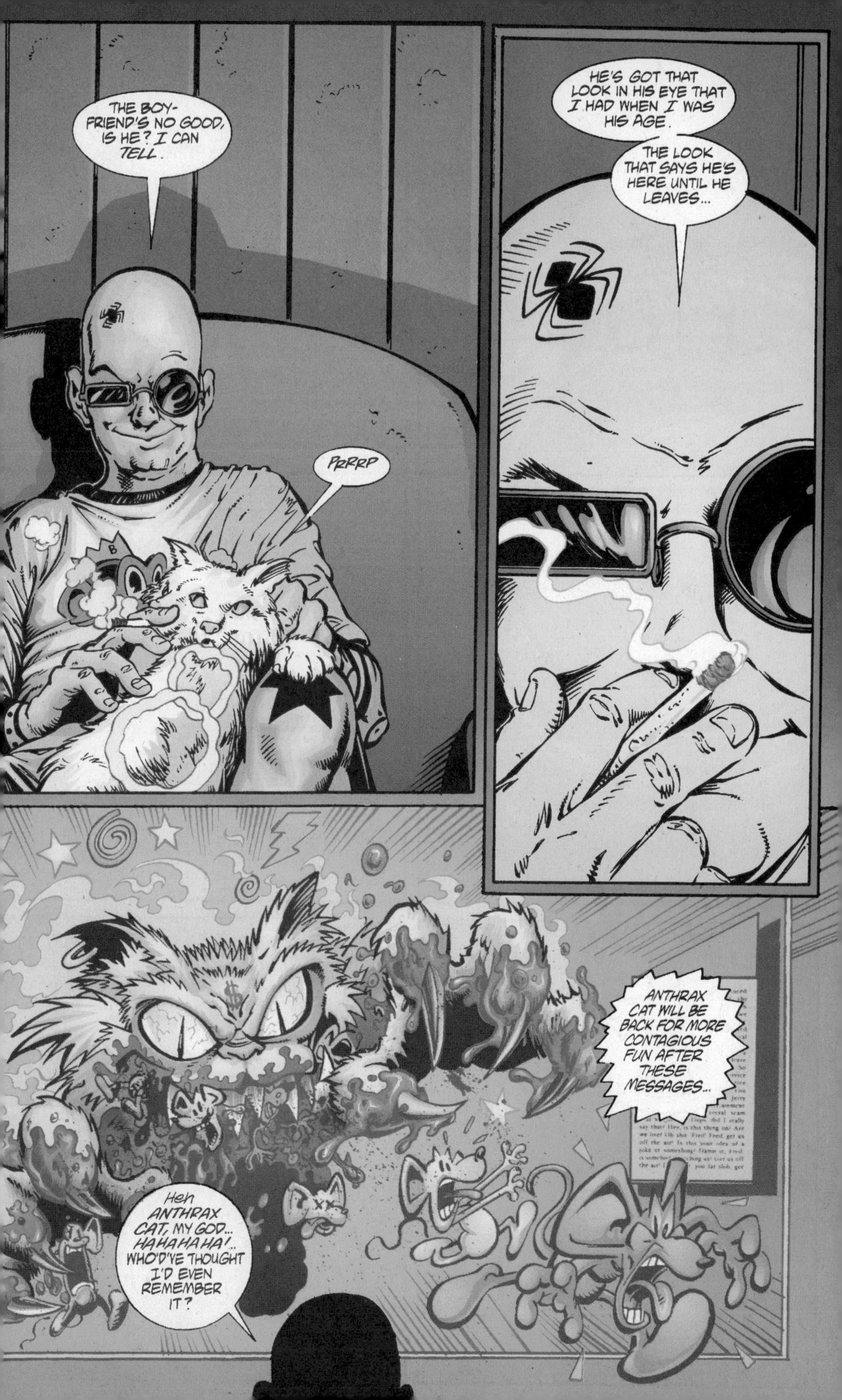
THE BOY-FRIEND'S NO GOOD, IS HE? I CAN TELL.
PRRRP
HE'S GOT THAT LOOK IN HIS EYE THAT I HAD WHEN I WAS HIS AGE.
THE LOOK THAT SAYS HE'S HERE UNTIL HE LEAVES...
ANTHRAX CAT WILL BE BACK FOR MORE CONTAGIOUS FUN AFTER THESE MESSAGES...
Heh ANTHRAX CAT, MY GOD... HAHAHAHA!... WHO'D'VE THOUGHT I'D EVEN REMEMBER IT?

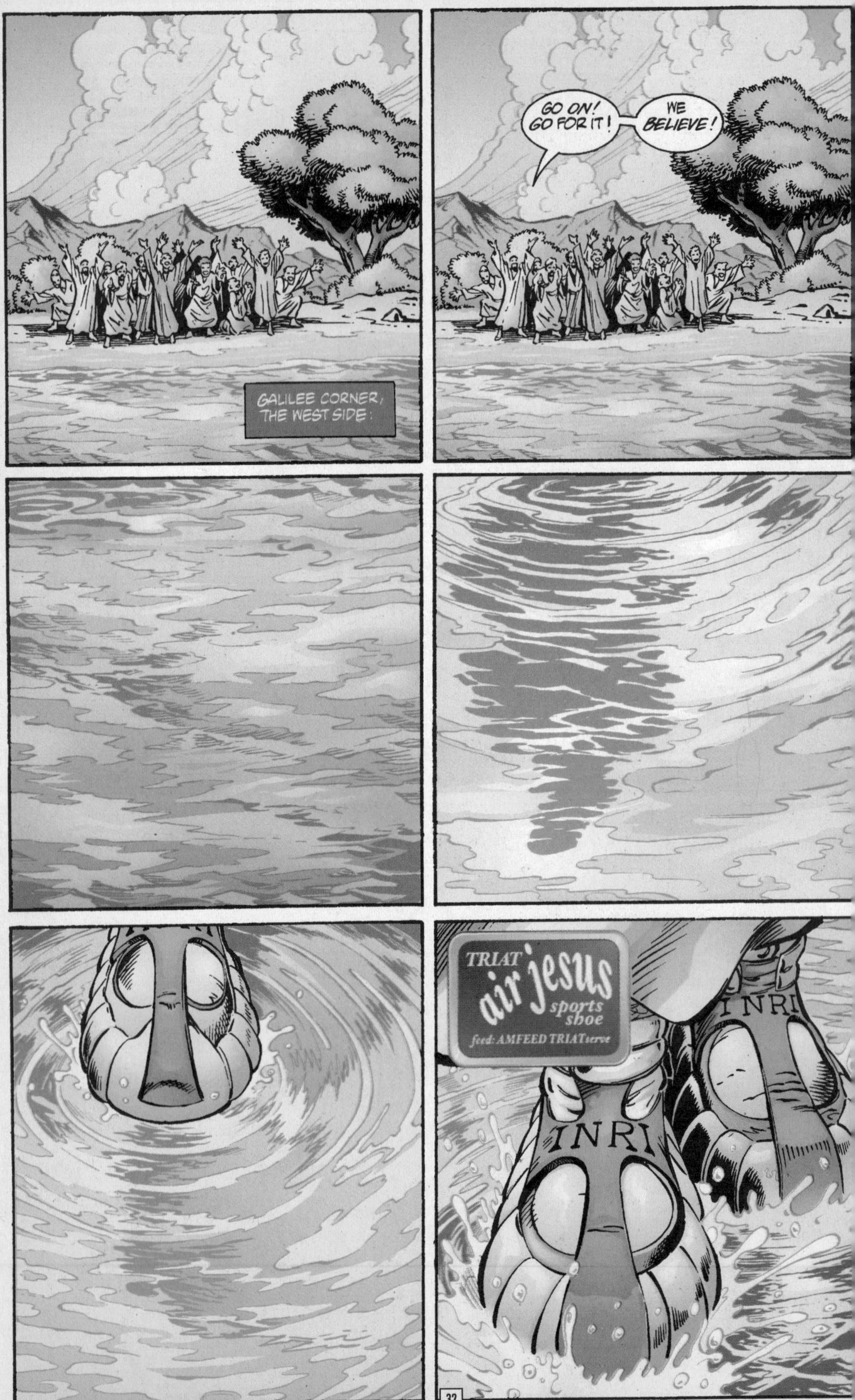
GALILEE CORNER, THE WEST SIDE:
GO ON! GO FOR IT!
WE BELIEVE!
TRIAT air jesus sports shoe
feed: AMFEED TRIATserve
INRI
INRI

TRIAT SPORTSWEAR. MY NAME'S REBEKAH, WITH TRIAT CUSTOMER SERVICE. HELP YOU?

I'VE JUST BEEN SUBJECTED TO A BLOOD-STOPPINGLY INANE TV AD FOR A SHOE CALLED AIR JESUS, AND I JUST WANT TO KNOW...

...WHAT DOES THE DAMN THING DO?

IT LETS YOU WALK ON WATER, SIR. OR ON THE WALLS. OR ON AIR, IF YOU FEEL LIKE IT. IT'S THE FIRST ALL-TERRAIN SPORTS SHOE, MAXIMALLY EFFECTIVE ON...

WHERE CAN I BUY A PAIR?

RIGHT NOW, IF YOU HOLD A SECOND-TIER CREDIT CARD OR BETTER, WE CAN HAVE THEM COURIERED OUT TO YOU IN FIVE MINUTES.

I AM SO INCREDIBLY BORED THAT I WILL BUY A PAIR OF YOUR RIDICULOUS SHOES.

LOOK GRATEFUL.

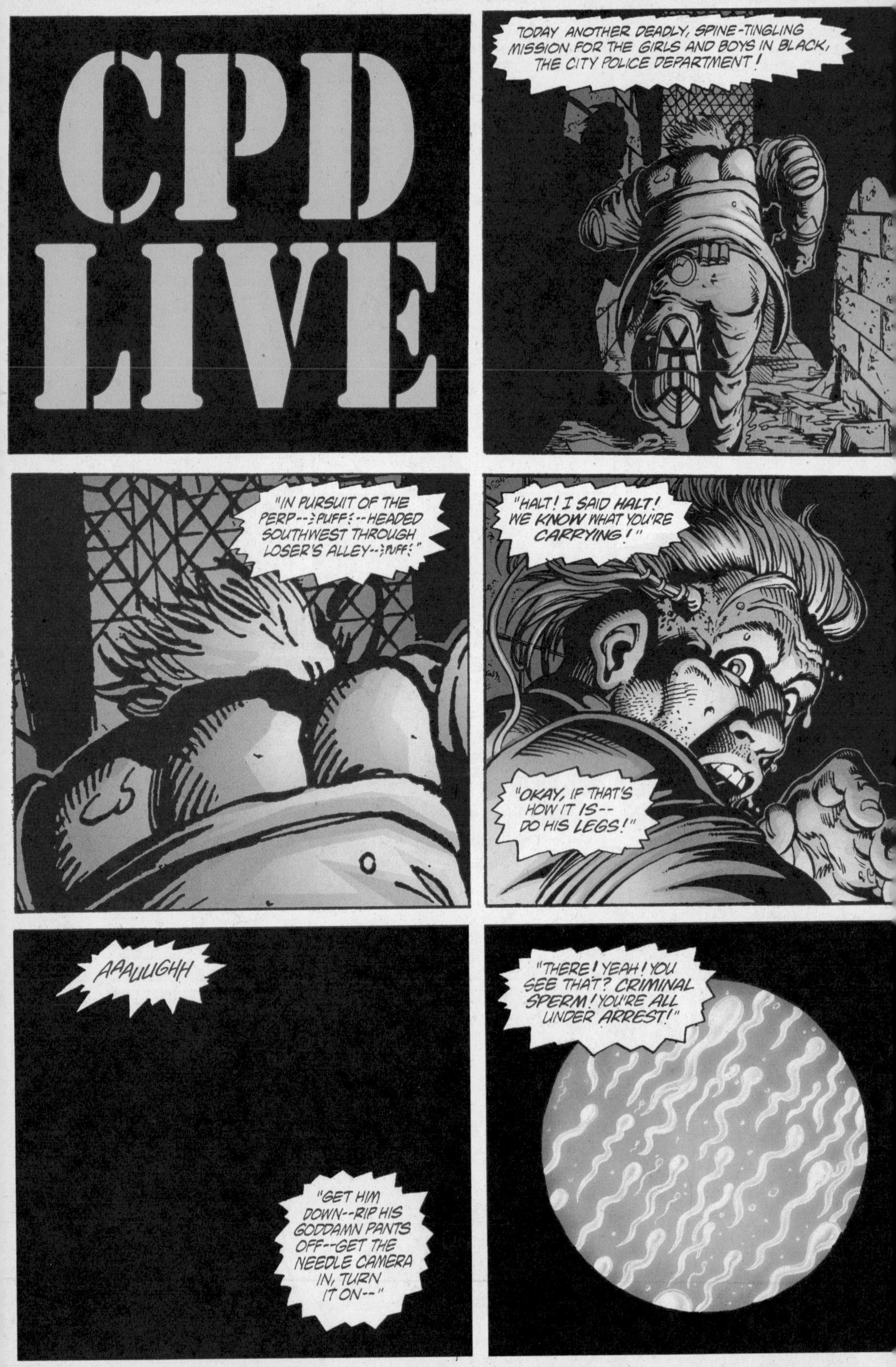
CPD LIVE
TODAY ANOTHER DEADLY, SPINE-TINGLING MISSION FOR THE GIRLS AND BOYS IN BLACK, THE CITY POLICE DEPARTMENT!
"IN PURSUIT OF THE PERP--PUFF--HEADED SOUTHWEST THROUGH LOSER'S ALLEY--PUFF"
"HALT! I SAID HALT! WE KNOW WHAT YOU'RE CARRYING!"
"OKAY, IF THAT'S HOW IT IS--DO HIS LEGS!"
AAAUUGHH
"GET HIM DOWN--RIP HIS GODDAMN PANTS OFF--GET THE NEEDLE CAMERA IN, TURN IT ON--"
"THERE! YEAH! YOU SEE THAT? CRIMINAL SPERM! YOU'RE ALL UNDER ARREST!"

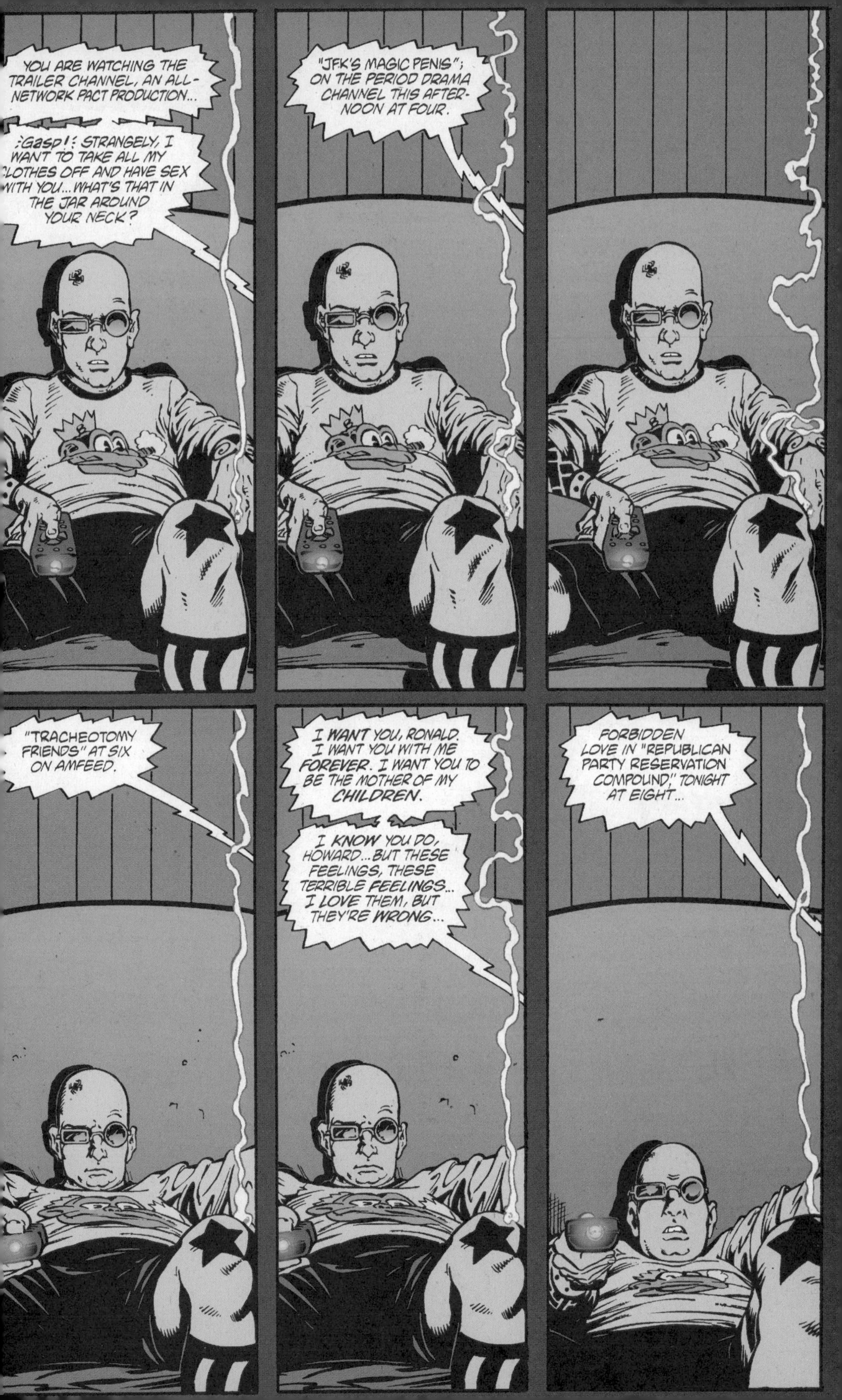
YOU ARE WATCHING THE TRAILER CHANNEL, AN ALL-NETWORK PACT PRODUCTION...
:Gasp!: STRANGELY, I WANT TO TAKE ALL MY CLOTHES OFF AND HAVE SEX WITH YOU... WHAT'S THAT IN THE JAR AROUND YOUR NECK?
"JFK'S MAGIC PENIS"; ON THE PERIOD DRAMA CHANNEL THIS AFTERNOON AT FOUR.
"TRACHEOTOMY FRIENDS" AT SIX ON AMFEED.
I WANT YOU, RONALD. I WANT YOU WITH ME FOREVER. I WANT YOU TO BE THE MOTHER OF MY CHILDREN.
I KNOW YOU DO, HOWARD... BUT THESE FEELINGS, THESE TERRIBLE FEELINGS... I LOVE THEM, BUT THEY'RE WRONG...
FORBIDDEN LOVE IN "REPUBLICAN PARTY RESERVATION COMPOUND," TONIGHT AT EIGHT...

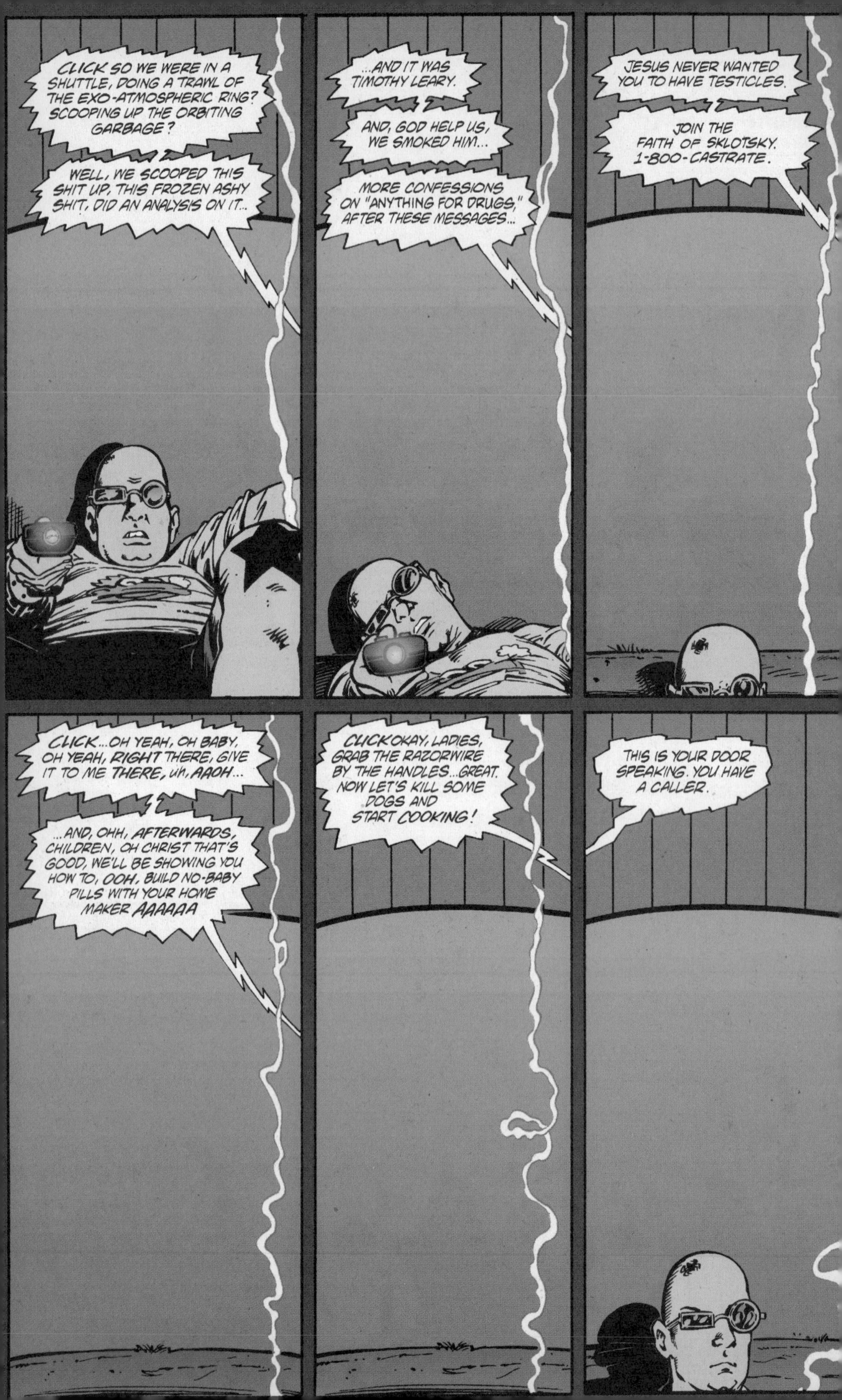

CLICK SO WE WERE IN A SHUTTLE, DOING A TRAWL OF THE EXO-ATMOSPHERIC RING? SCOOPING UP THE ORBITING GARBAGE?
WELL, WE SCOOPED THIS SHIT UP, THIS FROZEN ASHY SHIT, DID AN ANALYSIS ON IT...
...AND IT WAS TIMOTHY LEARY.
AND, GOD HELP US, WE SMOKED HIM...
MORE CONFESSIONS ON "ANYTHING FOR DRUGS," AFTER THESE MESSAGES...
JESUS NEVER WANTED YOU TO HAVE TESTICLES.
JOIN THE FAITH OF SKLOTSKY. 1-800-CASTRATE.
CLICK...OH YEAH, OH BABY, OH YEAH, RIGHT THERE, GIVE IT TO ME THERE, uh, AAOH...
...AND, OHH, AFTERWARDS, CHILDREN, OH CHRIST THAT'S GOOD, WE'LL BE SHOWING YOU HOW TO, OOH, BUILD NO-BABY PILLS WITH YOUR HOME MAKER AAAAAA
CLICK OKAY, LADIES, GRAB THE RAZORWIRE BY THE HANDLES...GREAT. NOW LET'S KILL SOME DOGS AND START COOKING!
THIS IS YOUR DOOR SPEAKING. YOU HAVE A CALLER.

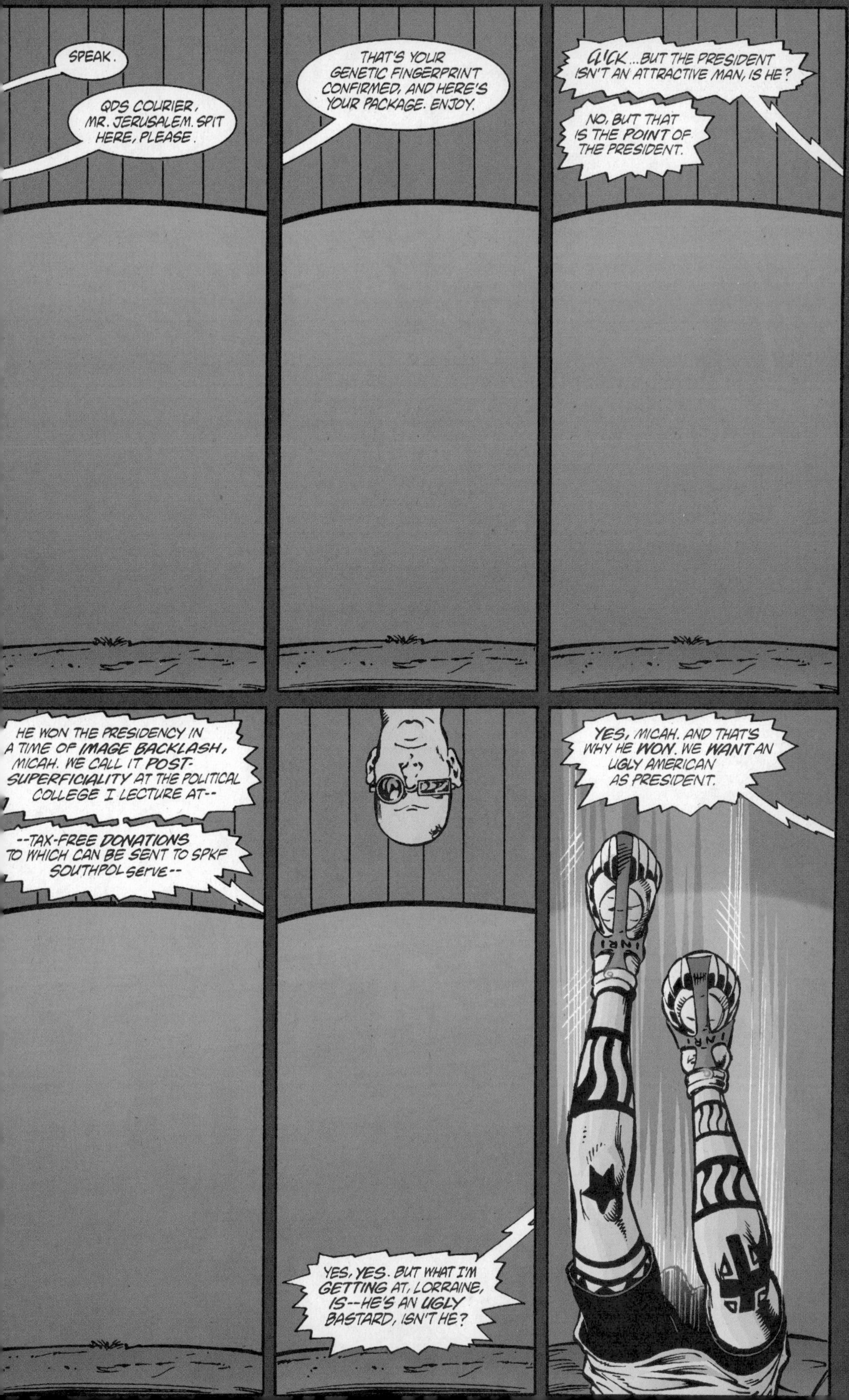
SPEAK.
QDS COURIER, MR. JERUSALEM. SPIT HERE, PLEASE.
THAT'S YOUR GENETIC FINGERPRINT CONFIRMED, AND HERE'S YOUR PACKAGE. ENJOY.
CLICK ...BUT THE PRESIDENT ISN'T AN ATTRACTIVE MAN, IS HE?
NO, BUT THAT IS THE POINT OF THE PRESIDENT.
HE WON THE PRESIDENCY IN A TIME OF IMAGE BACKLASH, MICAH. WE CALL IT POST-SUPERFICIALITY AT THE POLITICAL COLLEGE I LECTURE AT--
--TAX-FREE DONATIONS TO WHICH CAN BE SENT TO SPKF SOUTHPOL serve--
YES, YES. BUT WHAT I'M GETTING AT, LORRAINE, IS--HE'S AN UGLY BASTARD, ISN'T HE?
YES, MICAH. AND THAT'S WHY HE WON. WE WANT AN UGLY AMERICAN AS PRESIDENT.

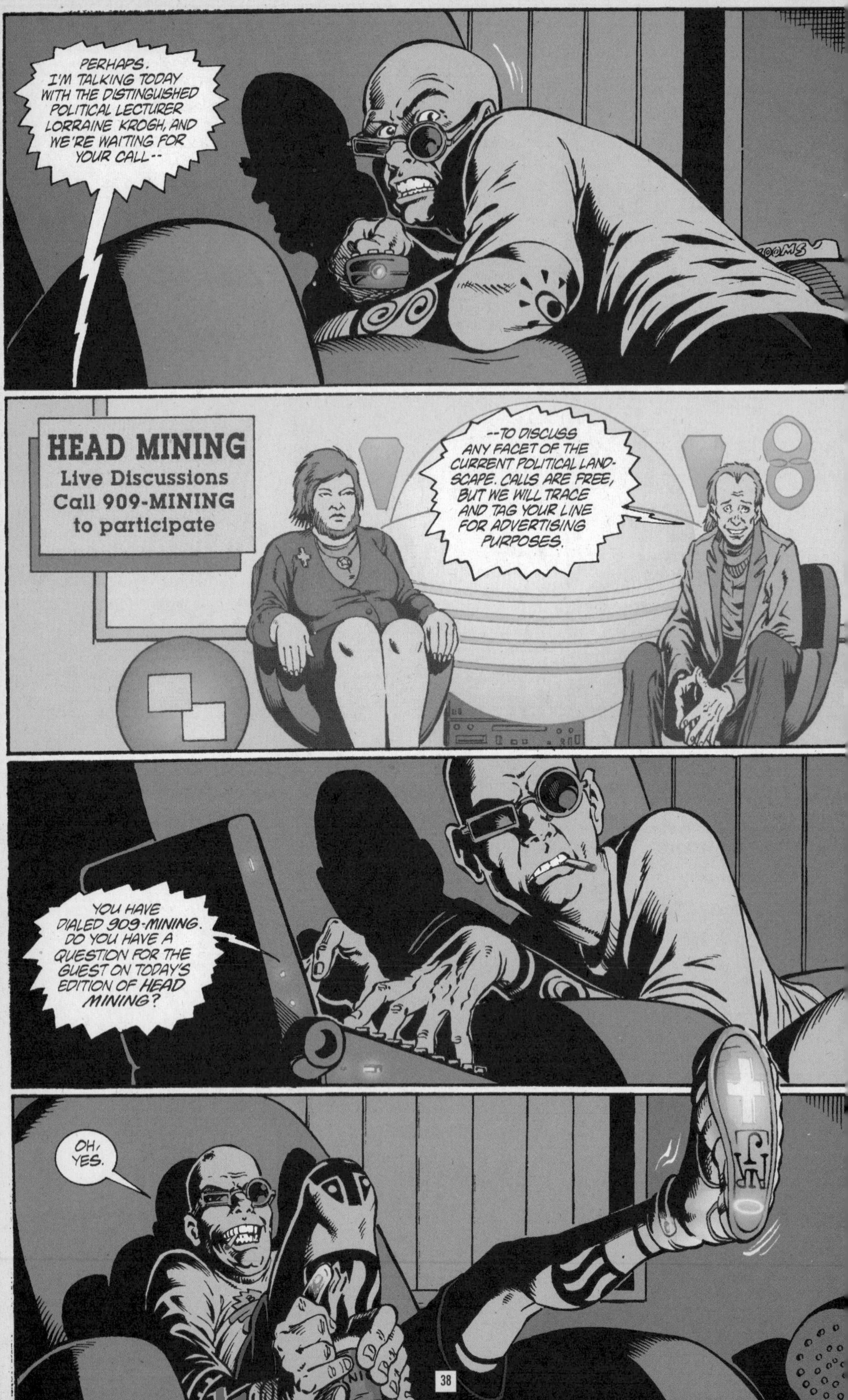
PERHAPS. I'M TALKING TODAY WITH THE DISTINGUISHED POLITICAL LECTURER LORRAINE KROGH, AND WE'RE WAITING FOR YOUR CALL--
HEAD MINING
Live Discussions
Call 909-MINING
to participate
--TO DISCUSS ANY FACET OF THE CURRENT POLITICAL LAND-SCAPE. CALLS ARE FREE, BUT WE WILL TRACE AND TAG YOUR LINE FOR ADVERTISING PURPOSES.
YOU HAVE DIALED 909-MINING. DO YOU HAVE A QUESTION FOR THE GUEST ON TODAY'S EDITION OF HEAD MINING?
OH, YES.

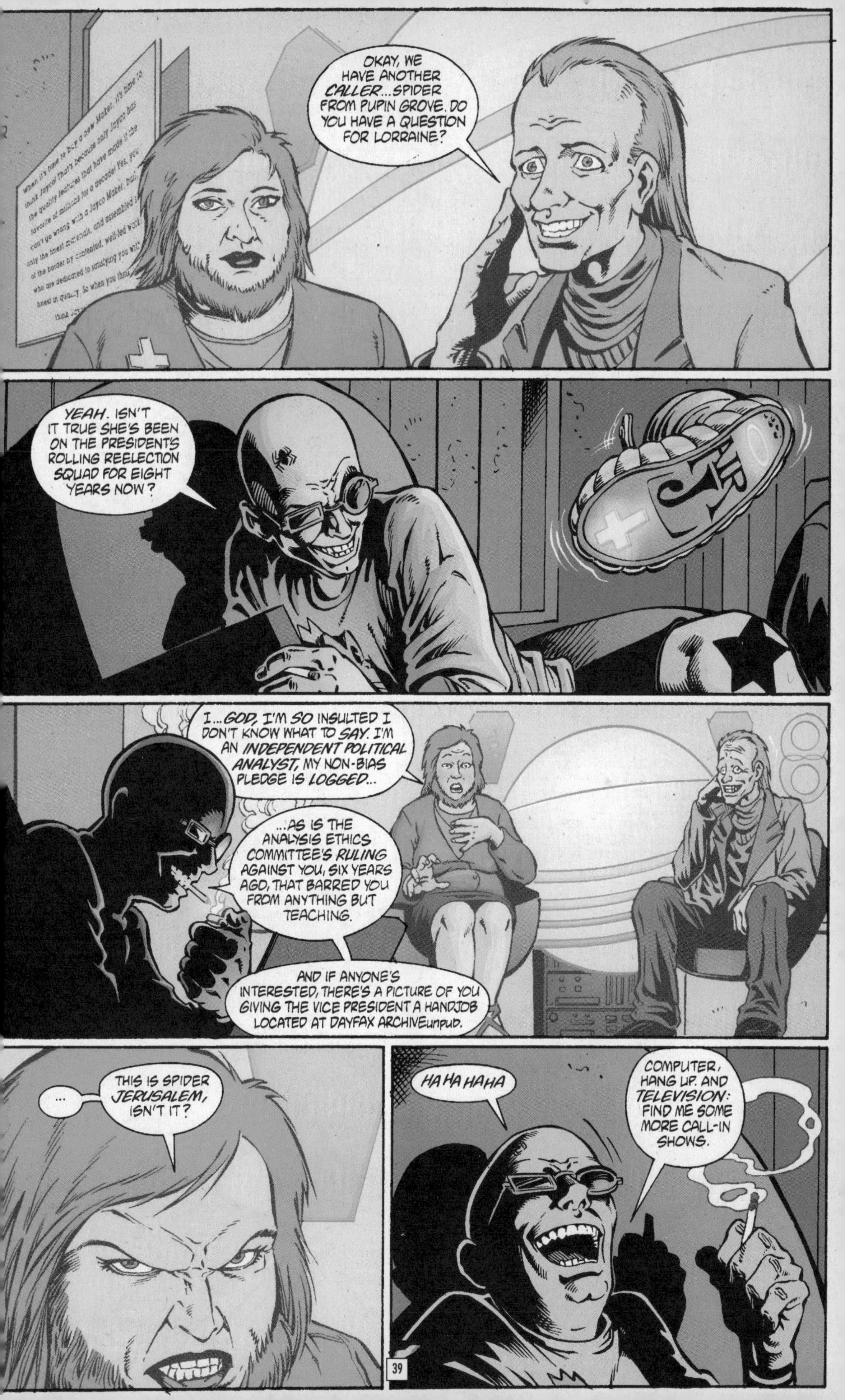
OKAY, WE HAVE ANOTHER CALLER...SPIDER FROM PUPIN GROVE. DO YOU HAVE A QUESTION FOR LORRAINE?
YEAH. ISN'T IT TRUE SHE'S BEEN ON THE PRESIDENT'S ROLLING REELECTION SQUAD FOR EIGHT YEARS NOW?
AIR J
I...GOD, I'M SO INSULTED I DON'T KNOW WHAT TO SAY. I'M AN INDEPENDENT POLITICAL ANALYST, MY NON-BIAS PLEDGE IS LOGGED...
...AS IS THE ANALYSIS ETHICS COMMITTEE'S RULING AGAINST YOU, SIX YEARS AGO, THAT BARRED YOU FROM ANYTHING BUT TEACHING.
AND IF ANYONE'S INTERESTED, THERE'S A PICTURE OF YOU GIVING THE VICE PRESIDENT A HANDJOB LOCATED AT DAYFAX ARCHIVEunpub.
...
THIS IS SPIDER JERUSALEM, ISN'T IT?
HA HA HA HA
COMPUTER, HANG UP. AND TELEVISION: FIND ME SOME MORE CALL-IN SHOWS.

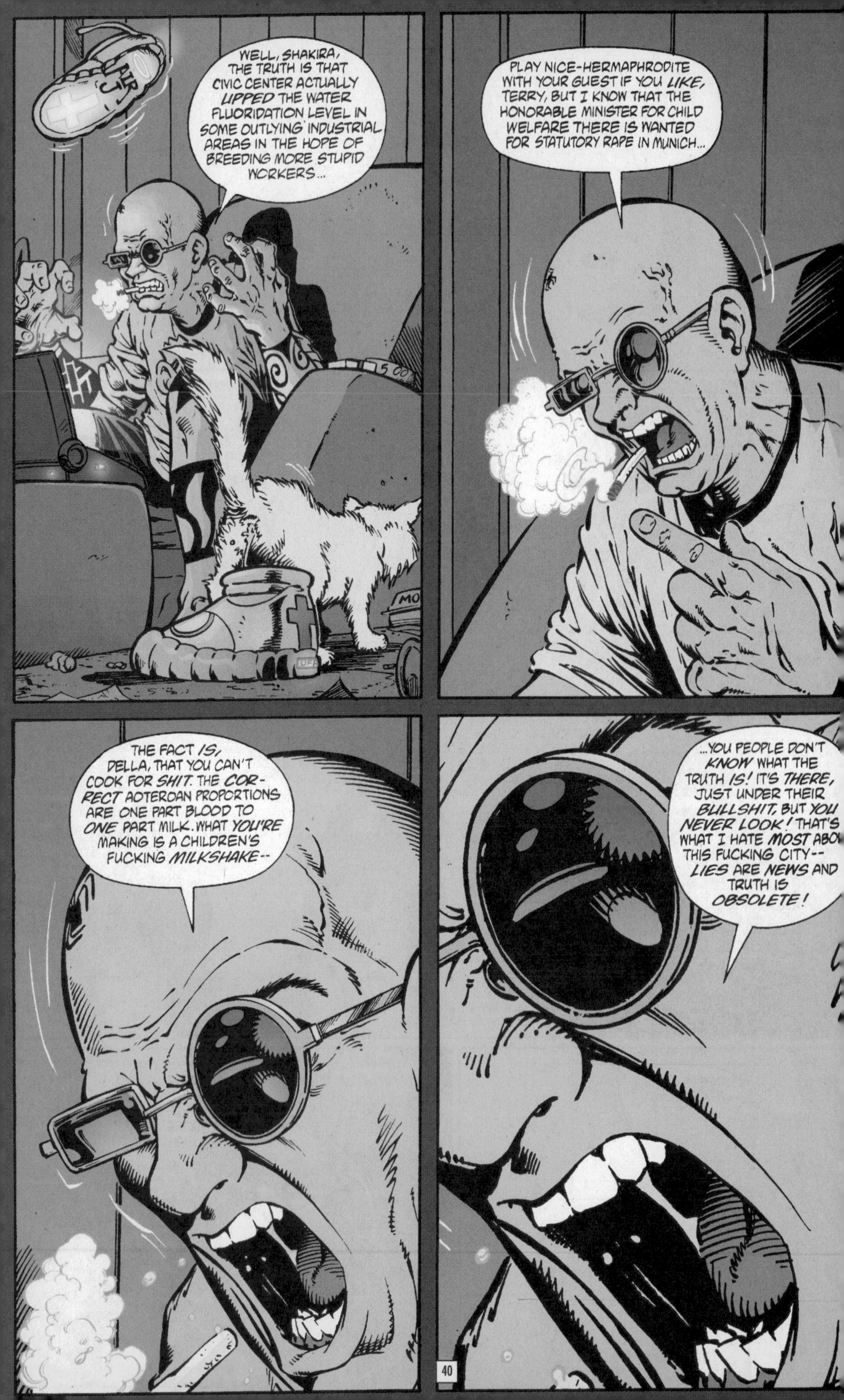
WELL, SHAKIRA, THE TRUTH IS THAT CIVIC CENTER ACTUALLY *LIPPED* THE WATER FLUORIDATION LEVEL IN SOME OUTLYING INDUSTRIAL AREAS IN THE HOPE OF BREEDING MORE STUPID WORKERS...
PLAY NICE-HERMAPHRODITE WITH YOUR GUEST IF YOU *LIKE*, TERRY, BUT I KNOW THAT THE HONORABLE MINISTER FOR CHILD WELFARE THERE IS WANTED FOR STATUTORY RAPE IN MUNICH...
THE FACT *IS*, DELLA, THAT YOU CAN'T COOK FOR *SHIT*. THE *CORRECT* AOTEROAN PROPORTIONS ARE ONE PART BLOOD TO *ONE* PART MILK. WHAT *YOU'RE* MAKING IS A CHILDREN'S FUCKING *MILKSHAKE*--
...YOU PEOPLE DON'T *KNOW* WHAT THE TRUTH *IS!* IT'S *THERE*, JUST UNDER THEIR *BULLSHIT*, BUT *YOU NEVER LOOK!* THAT'S WHAT I HATE *MOST* ABO THIS FUCKING CITY-- *LIES* ARE *NEWS* AND TRUTH IS *OBSOLETE!*

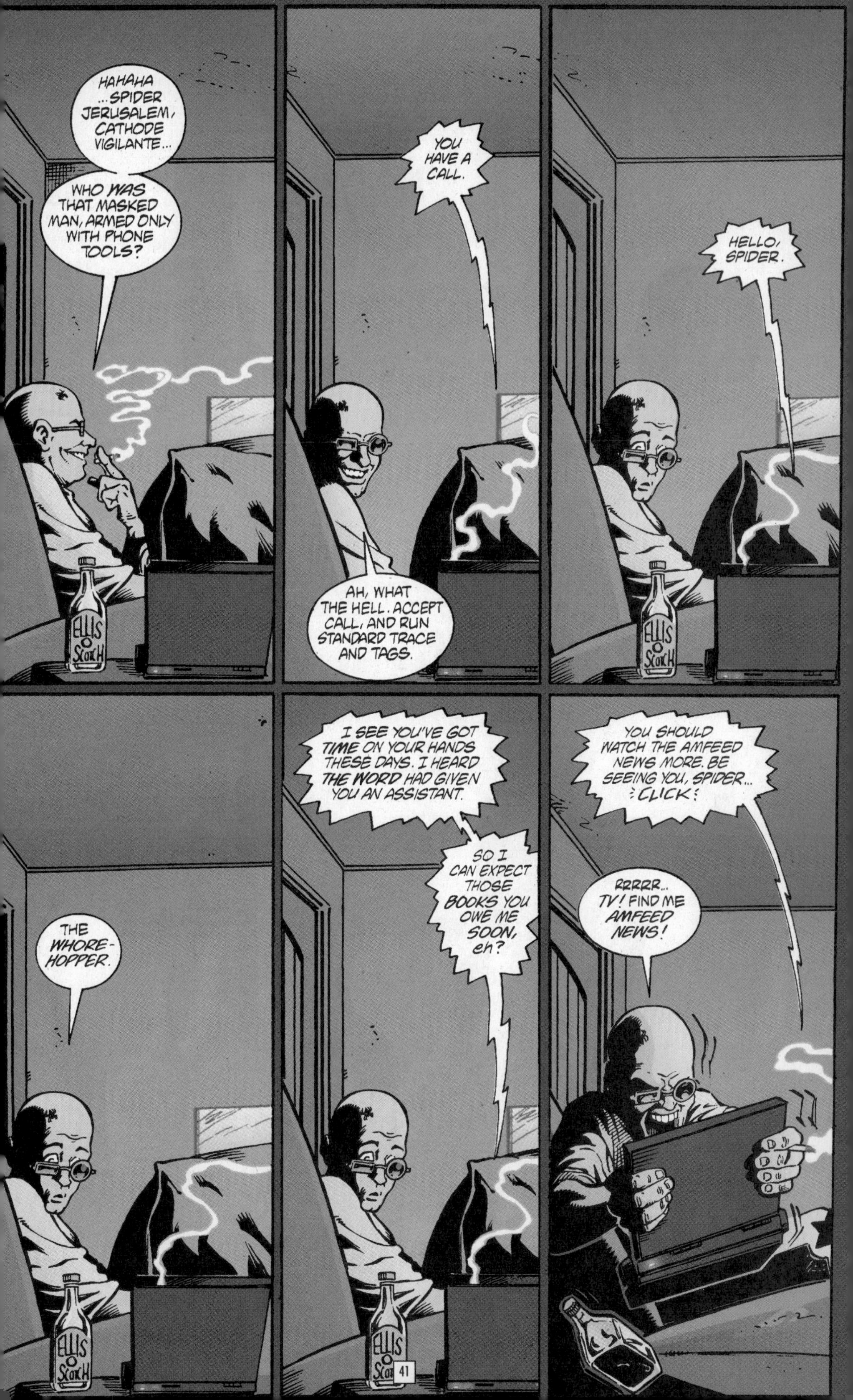
HAHAHA ...SPIDER JERUSALEM, CATHODE VIGILANTE...
WHO WAS THAT MASKED MAN, ARMED ONLY WITH PHONE TOOLS?
ELLIS SCOTCH
YOU HAVE A CALL.
AH, WHAT THE HELL. ACCEPT CALL, AND RUN STANDARD TRACE AND TAGS.
HELLO, SPIDER.
THE WHORE-HOPPER.
I SEE YOU'VE GOT TIME ON YOUR HANDS THESE DAYS. I HEARD THE WORD HAD GIVEN YOU AN ASSISTANT.
SO I CAN EXPECT THOSE BOOKS YOU OWE ME SOON, eh?
YOU SHOULD WATCH THE AMFEED NEWS MORE. BE SEEING YOU, SPIDER... CLICK
RRRRR... TV! FIND ME AMFEED NEWS!

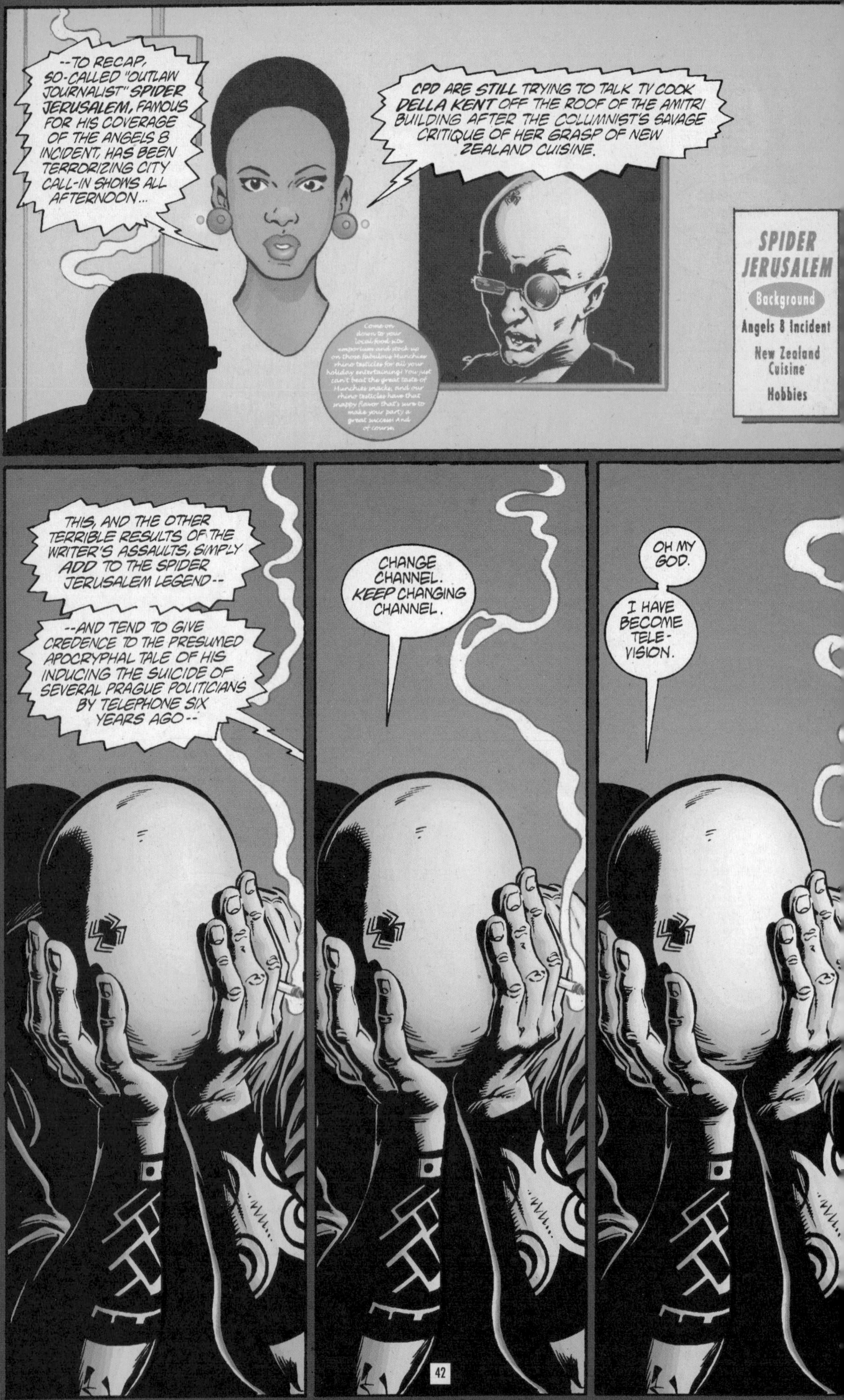

--TO RECAP, SO-CALLED "OUTLAW JOURNALIST" SPIDER JERUSALEM, FAMOUS FOR HIS COVERAGE OF THE ANGELS 8 INCIDENT, HAS BEEN TERRORIZING CITY CALL-IN SHOWS ALL AFTERNOON...

CPD ARE STILL TRYING TO TALK TV COOK DELLA KENT OFF THE ROOF OF THE AMITRI BUILDING AFTER THE COLUMNIST'S SAVAGE CRITIQUE OF HER GRASP OF NEW ZEALAND CUISINE.

Come on down to your local food biz emporium and stock up on these fabulous Huncher rhino testicles for all your holiday entertaining! You just can't beat the great taste of Huncher snacks, and our rhino testicles have that snappy flavor that's sure to make your party a great success! And of course

SPIDER JERUSALEM
Background
Angels 8 Incident
New Zealand Cuisine
Hobbies

THIS, AND THE OTHER TERRIBLE RESULTS OF THE WRITER'S ASSAULTS, SIMPLY ADD TO THE SPIDER JERUSALEM LEGEND--

--AND TEND TO GIVE CREDENCE TO THE PRESUMED APOCRYPHAL TALE OF HIS INDUCING THE SUICIDE OF SEVERAL PRAGUE POLITICIANS BY TELEPHONE SIX YEARS AGO--

CHANGE CHANNEL. KEEP CHANGING CHANNEL.

OH MY GOD.

I HAVE BECOME TELEVISION.

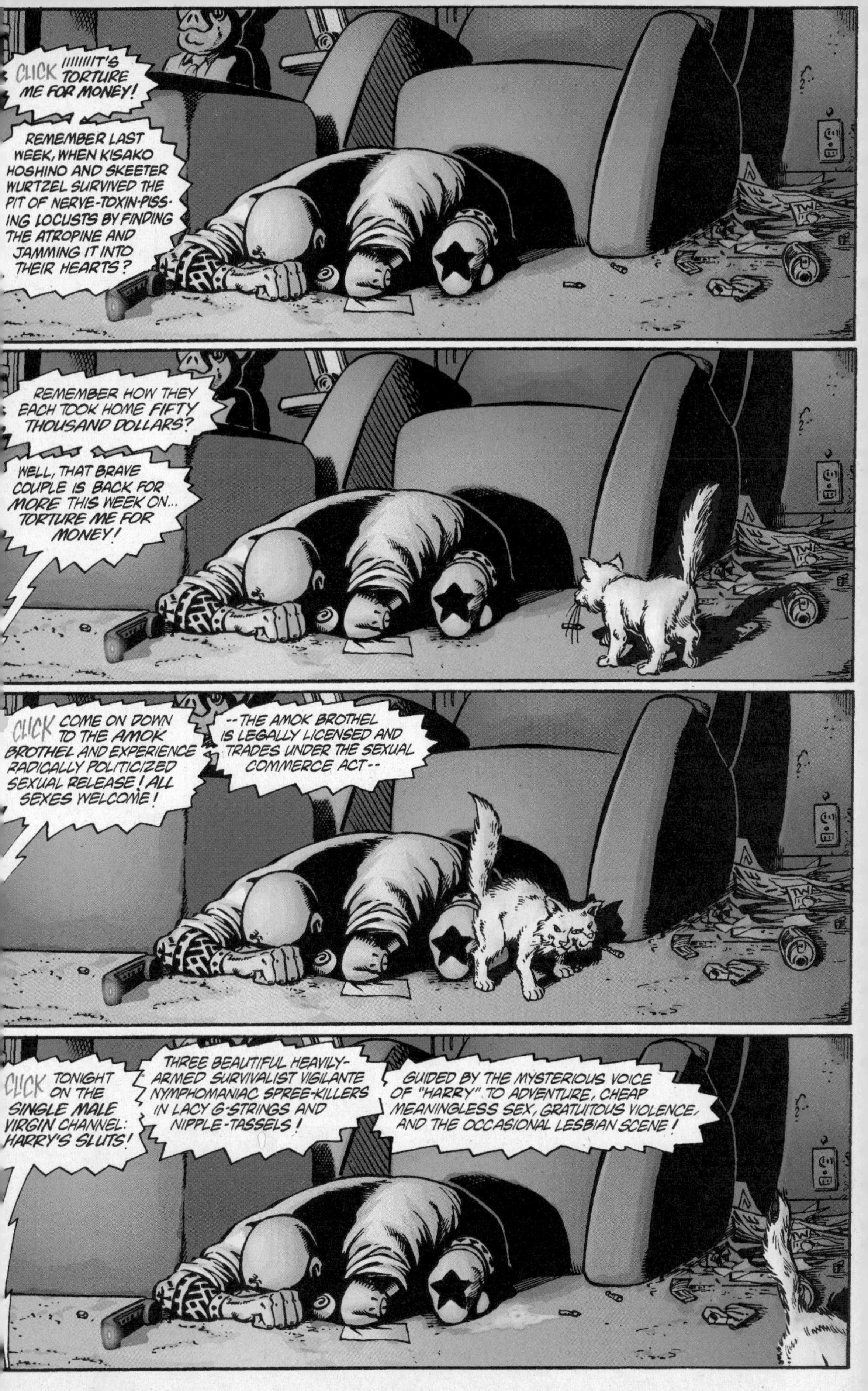
CLICK !!!!!!!IT'S TORTURE ME FOR MONEY!
REMEMBER LAST WEEK, WHEN KISAKO HOSHINO AND SKEETER WURTZEL SURVIVED THE PIT OF NERVE-TOXIN-PISSING LOCUSTS BY FINDING THE ATROPINE AND JAMMING IT INTO THEIR HEARTS?
REMEMBER HOW THEY EACH TOOK HOME FIFTY THOUSAND DOLLARS?
WELL, THAT BRAVE COUPLE IS BACK FOR MORE THIS WEEK ON... TORTURE ME FOR MONEY!
CLICK COME ON DOWN TO THE AMOK BROTHEL AND EXPERIENCE RADICALLY POLITICIZED SEXUAL RELEASE! ALL SEXES WELCOME!
--THE AMOK BROTHEL IS LEGALLY LICENSED AND TRADES UNDER THE SEXUAL COMMERCE ACT--
CLICK TONIGHT ON THE SINGLE MALE VIRGIN CHANNEL: HARRY'S SLUTS!
THREE BEAUTIFUL HEAVILY-ARMED SURVIVALIST VIGILANTE NYMPHOMANIAC SPREE-KILLERS IN LACY G-STRINGS AND NIPPLE-TASSELS!
GUIDED BY THE MYSTERIOUS VOICE OF "HARRY" TO ADVENTURE, CHEAP MEANINGLESS SEX, GRATUITOUS VIOLENCE, AND THE OCCASIONAL LESBIAN SCENE!

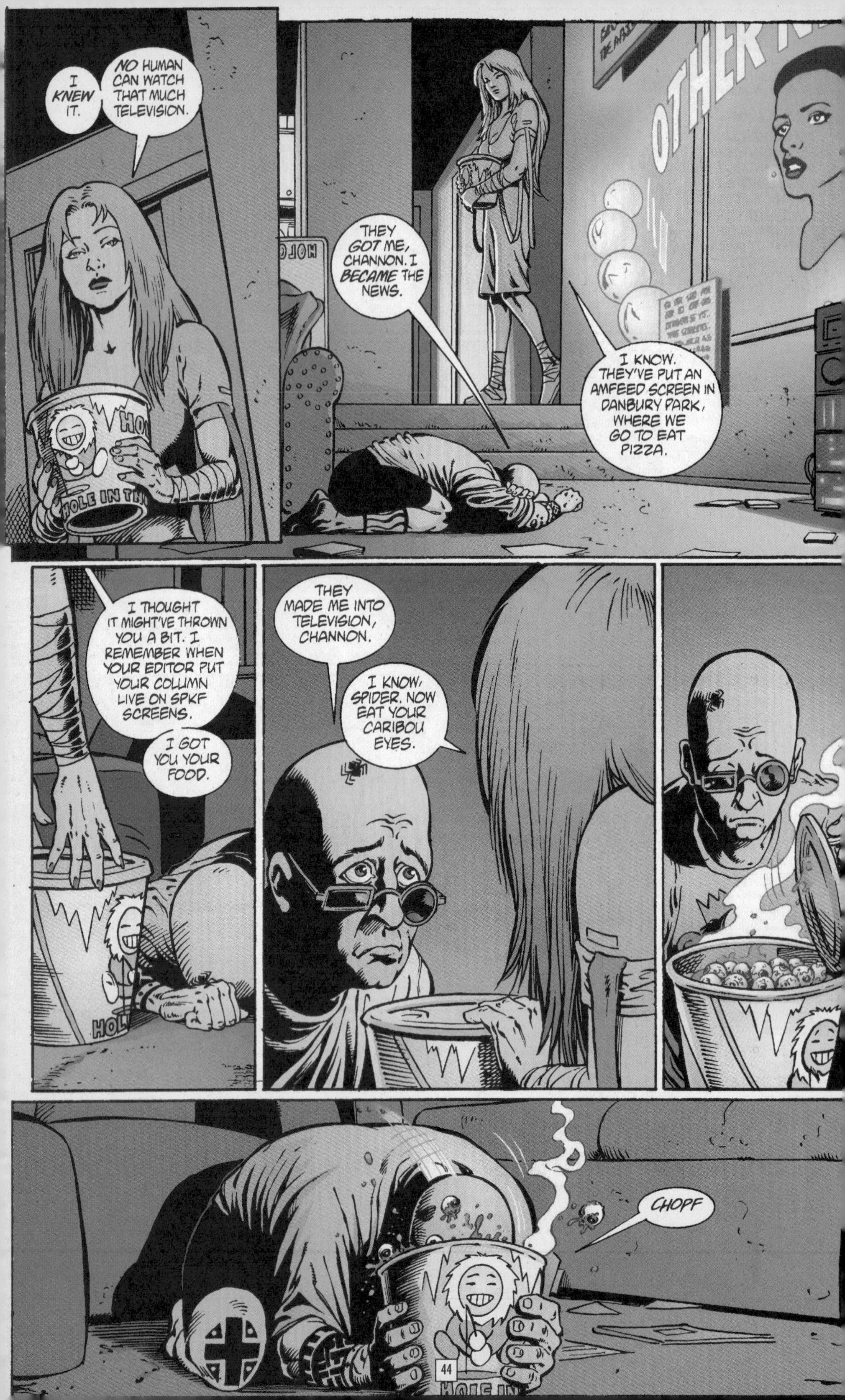
I KNEW IT.
NO HUMAN CAN WATCH THAT MUCH TELEVISION.
THEY GOT ME, CHANNON. I BECAME THE NEWS.
I KNOW. THEY'VE PUT AN AMFEED SCREEN IN DANBURY PARK, WHERE WE GO TO EAT PIZZA.
I THOUGHT IT MIGHT'VE THROWN YOU A BIT. I REMEMBER WHEN YOUR EDITOR PUT YOUR COLUMN LIVE ON SPKF SCREENS.
I GOT YOU YOUR FOOD.
THEY MADE ME INTO TELEVISION, CHANNON.
I KNOW, SPIDER. NOW EAT YOUR CARIBOU EYES.
CHOPF

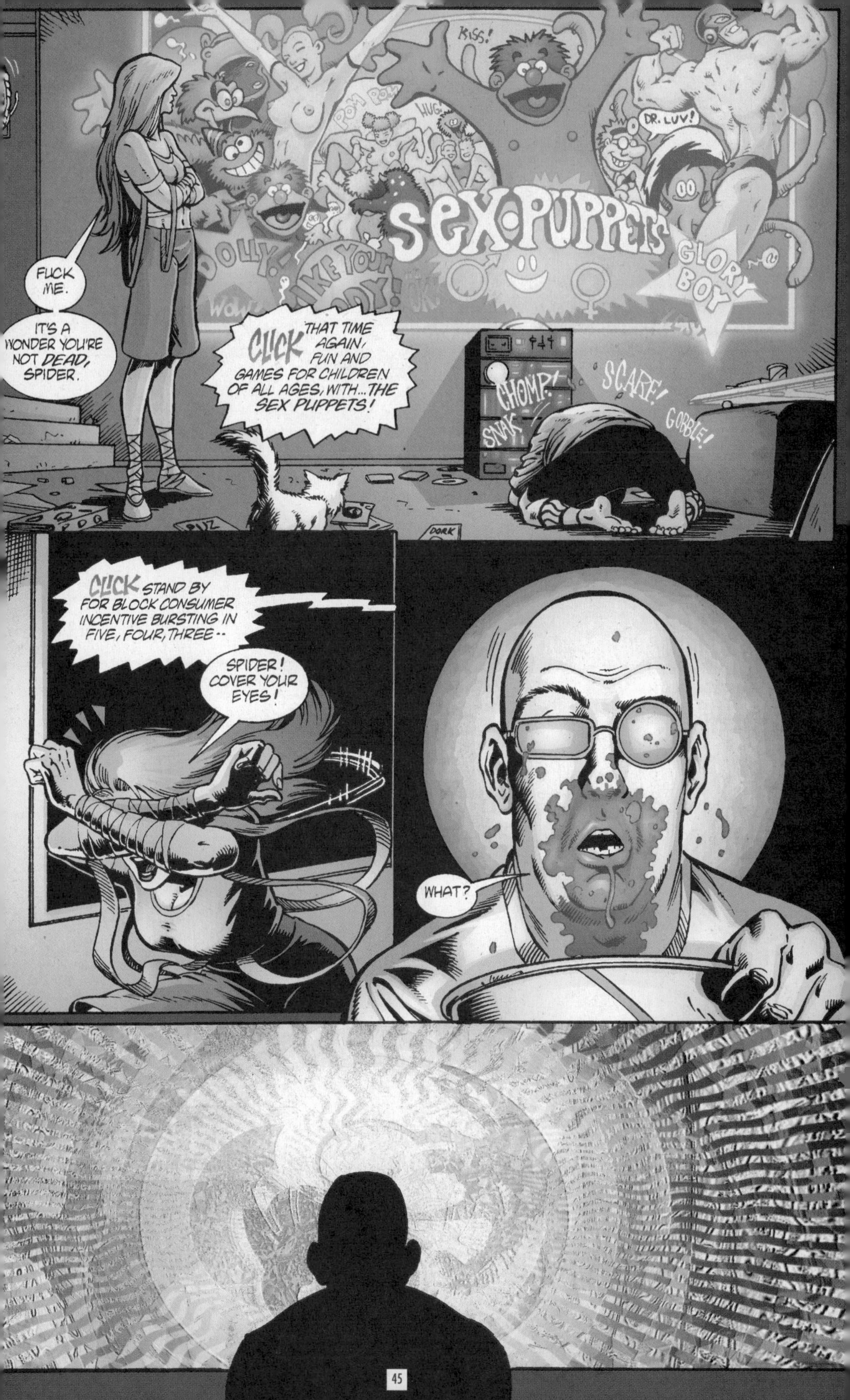
KISS!
POM POM
HUG
DR. LUV!
SEX-PUPPETS
DOLLY
LIKE YOUR BODY!
GLORY BOY
FUCK ME.
IT'S A WONDER YOU'RE NOT DEAD, SPIDER.
CLICK THAT TIME AGAIN, FUN AND GAMES FOR CHILDREN OF ALL AGES, WITH... THE SEX PUPPETS!
CHOMP!
SNAK
SCARF!
GOBBLE!
DORK
CLICK STAND BY FOR BLOCK CONSUMER INCENTIVE BURSTING IN FIVE, FOUR, THREE--
SPIDER! COVER YOUR EYES!
WHAT?

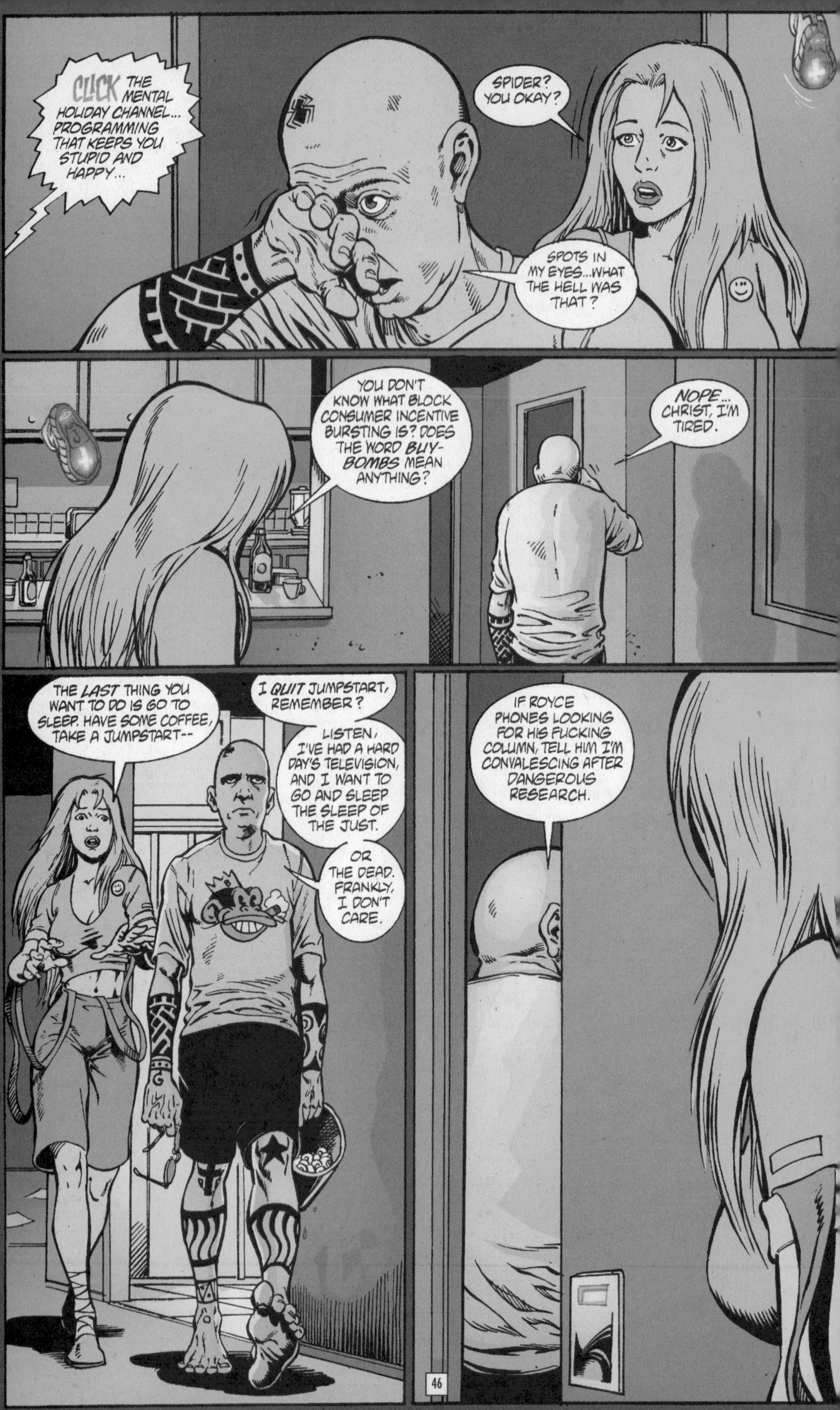
CLICK THE MENTAL HOLIDAY CHANNEL... PROGRAMMING THAT KEEPS YOU STUPID AND HAPPY...
SPIDER? YOU OKAY?
SPOTS IN MY EYES...WHAT THE HELL WAS THAT?
YOU DON'T KNOW WHAT BLOCK CONSUMER INCENTIVE BURSTING IS? DOES THE WORD BUY-BOMBS MEAN ANYTHING?
NOPE... CHRIST, I'M TIRED.
THE LAST THING YOU WANT TO DO IS GO TO SLEEP. HAVE SOME COFFEE, TAKE A JUMPSTART--
I QUIT JUMPSTART, REMEMBER?
LISTEN, I'VE HAD A HARD DAY'S TELEVISION, AND I WANT TO GO AND SLEEP THE SLEEP OF THE JUST.
OR THE DEAD. FRANKLY, I DON'T CARE.
IF ROYCE PHONES LOOKING FOR HIS FUCKING COLUMN, TELL HIM I'M CONVALESCING AFTER DANGEROUS RESEARCH.

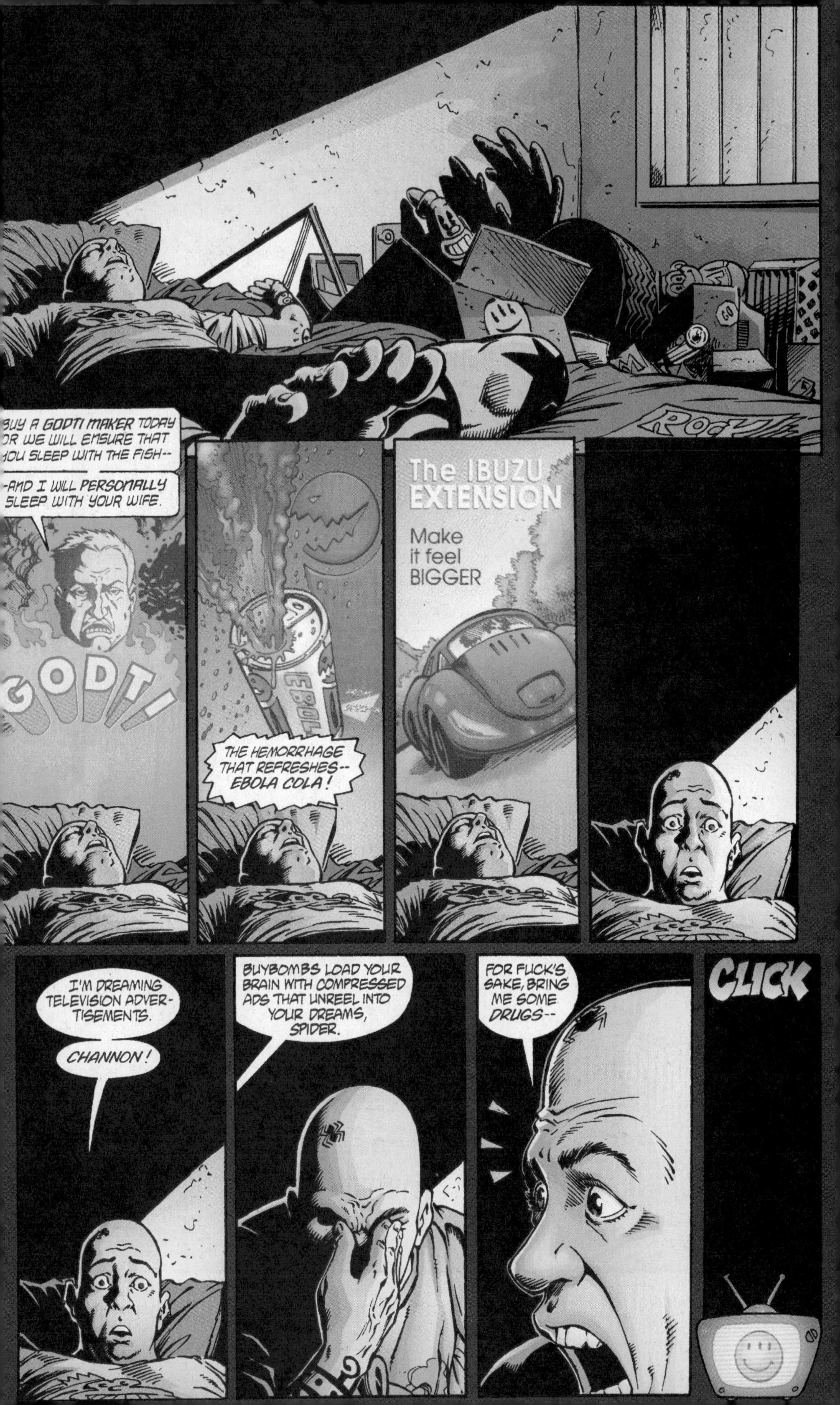

BUY A GODTI MAKER TODAY OR WE WILL ENSURE THAT YOU SLEEP WITH THE FISH--
-AND I WILL PERSONALLY SLEEP WITH YOUR WIFE.
GODTI
THE HEMORRHAGE THAT REFRESHES-- EBOLA COLA!
The IBUZU EXTENSION
Make it feel BIGGER
I'M DREAMING TELEVISION ADVERTISEMENTS.
CHANNON!
BUYBOMBS LOAD YOUR BRAIN WITH COMPRESSED ADS THAT UNREEL INTO YOUR DREAMS, SPIDER.
FOR FUCK'S SAKE, BRING ME SOME DRUGS--
CLICK

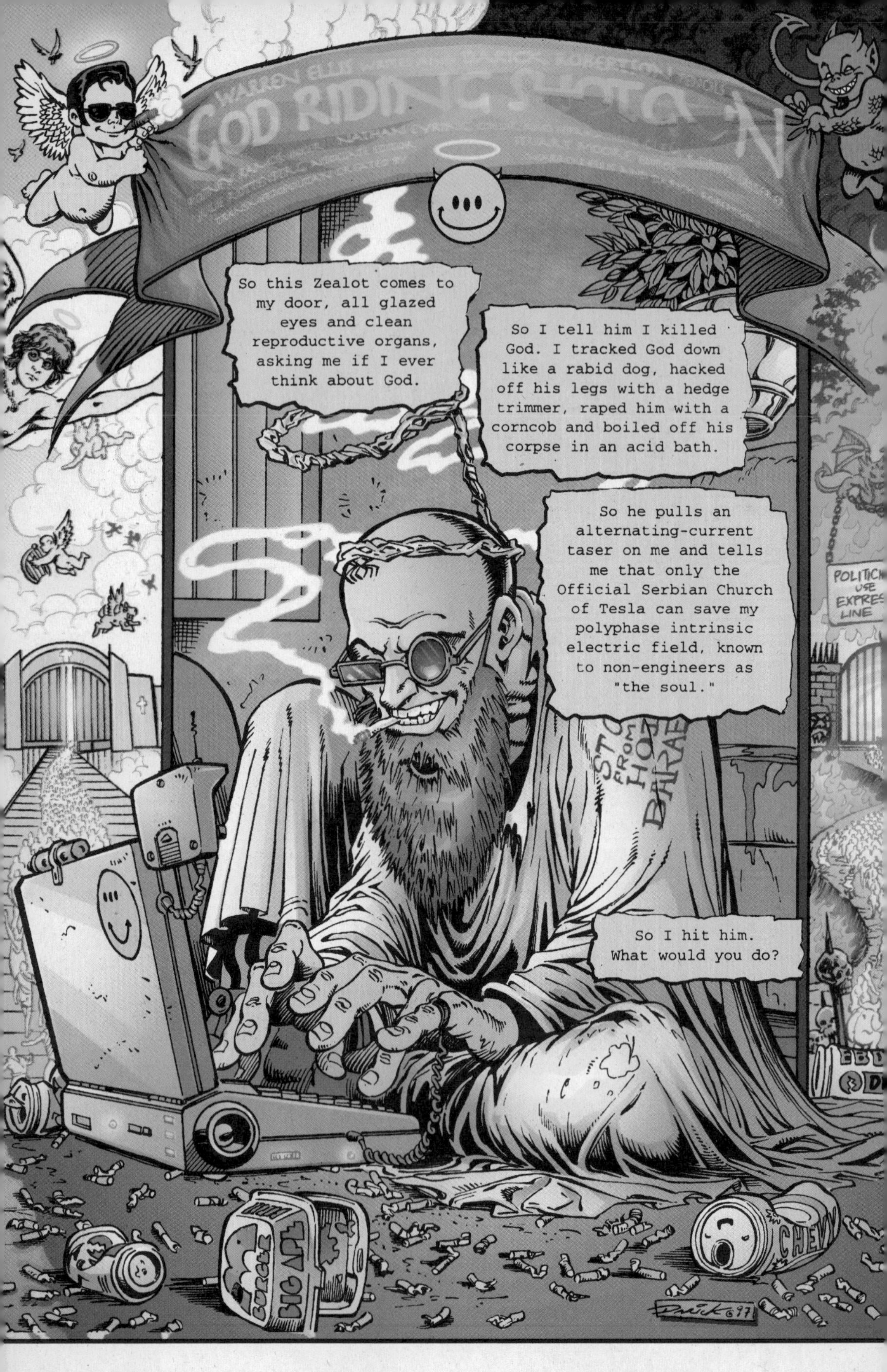

WARREN ELLIS
So this Zealot comes to my door, all glazed eyes and clean reproductive organs, asking me if I ever think about God.
So I tell him I killed God. I tracked God down like a rabid dog, hacked off his legs with a hedge trimmer, raped him with a corncob and boiled off his corpse in an acid bath.
So he pulls an alternating-current taser on me and tells me that only the Official Serbian Church of Tesla can save my polyphase intrinsic electric field, known to non-engineers as "the soul."
So I hit him. What would you do?
BURGER
BIG APL
CHEVY

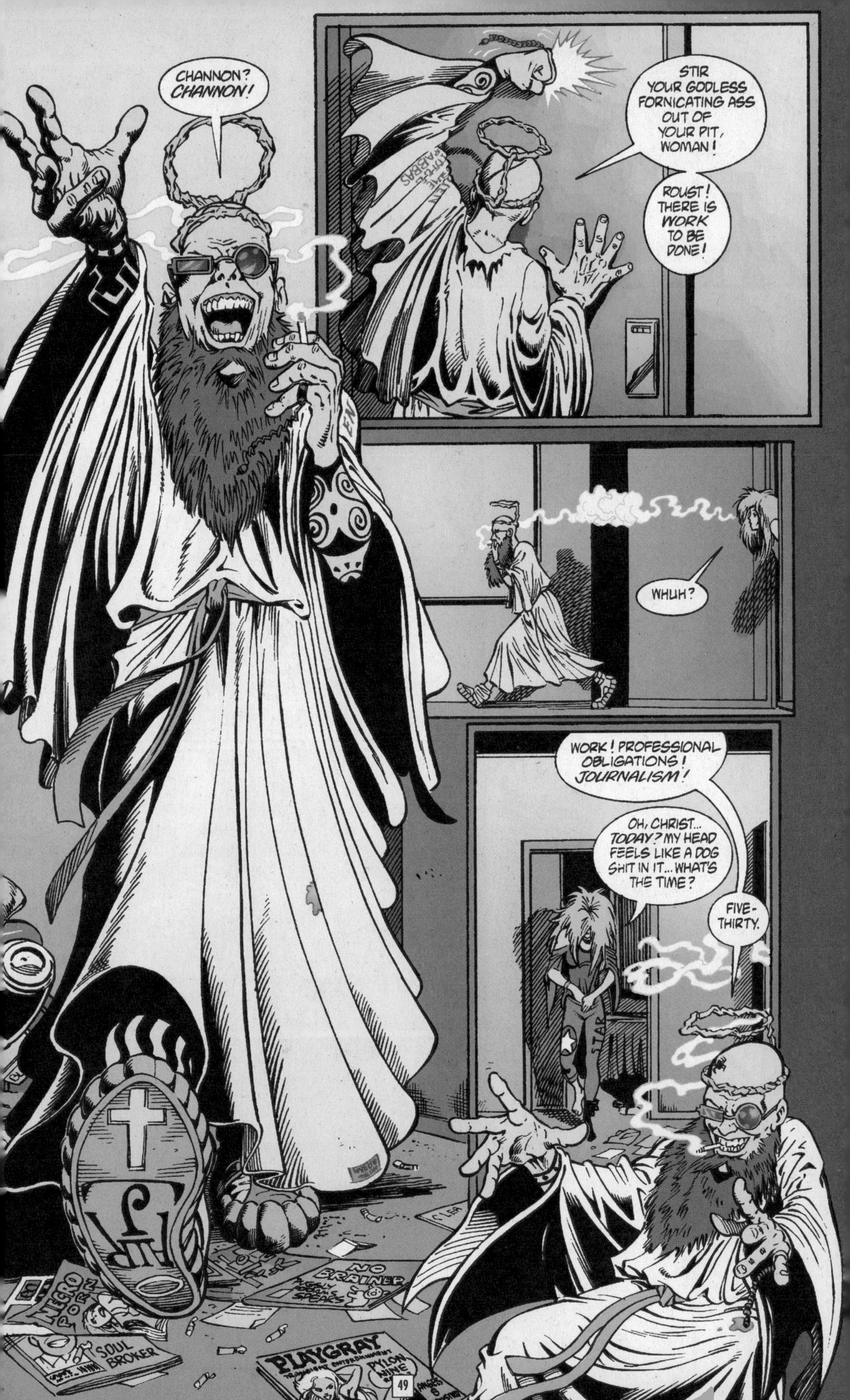
CHANNON? CHANNON!
STIR YOUR GODLESS FORNICATING ASS OUT OF YOUR PIT, WOMAN!
ROUST! THERE IS WORK TO BE DONE!
WHUH?
WORK! PROFESSIONAL OBLIGATIONS! JOURNALISM!
OH, CHRIST... TODAY? MY HEAD FEELS LIKE A DOG SHIT IN IT... WHAT'S THE TIME?
FIVE-THIRTY.
NO BRAINER
SOUL BROKER
PLAYGRAY
PYLON NINE

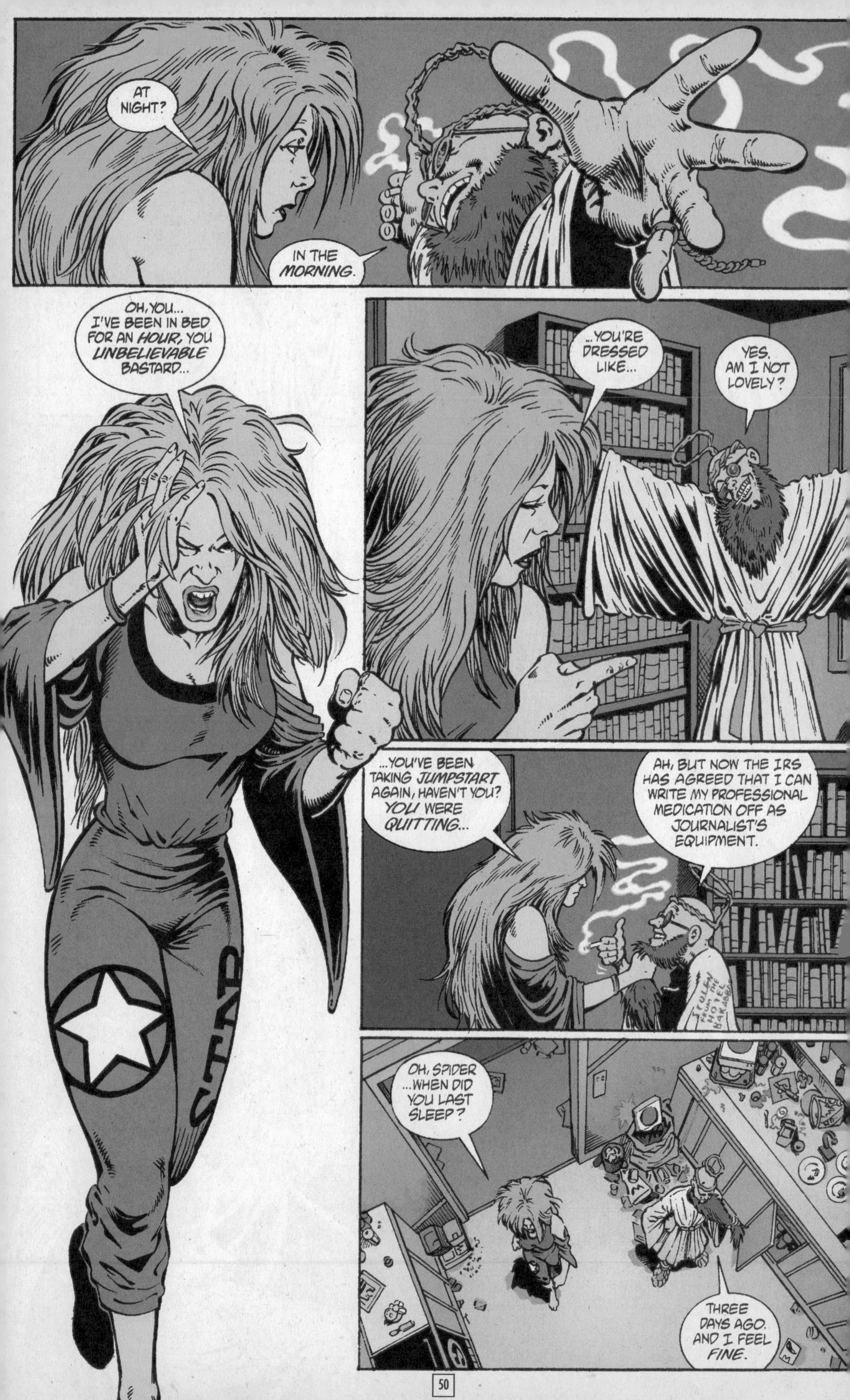
AT NIGHT?
IN THE MORNING.
OH, YOU... I'VE BEEN IN BED FOR AN HOUR, YOU UNBELIEVABLE BASTARD...
...YOU'RE DRESSED LIKE...
YES. AM I NOT LOVELY?
...YOU'VE BEEN TAKING JUMPSTART AGAIN, HAVEN'T YOU? YOU WERE QUITTING...
AH, BUT NOW THE IRS HAS AGREED THAT I CAN WRITE MY PROFESSIONAL MEDICATION OFF AS JOURNALIST'S EQUIPMENT.
STOLEN FROM THE HOTEL BARABBAS
OH, SPIDER ...WHEN DID YOU LAST SLEEP?
THREE DAYS AGO. AND I FEEL FINE.

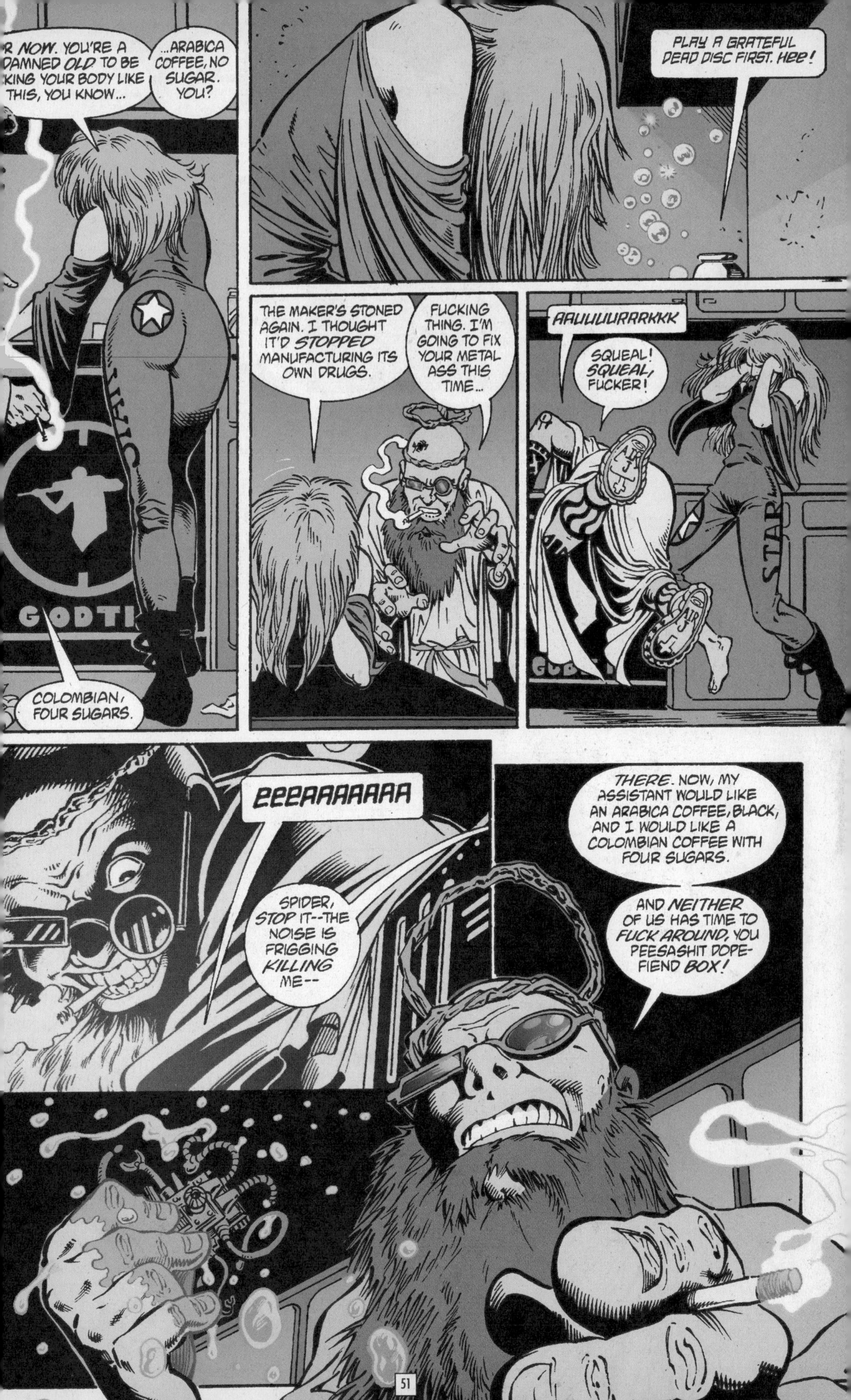
R NOW. YOU'RE A DAMNED OLD TO BE KING YOUR BODY LIKE THIS, YOU KNOW...
...ARABICA COFFEE, NO SUGAR. YOU?
COLOMBIAN, FOUR SUGARS.
GODTI
PLAY A GRATEFUL DEAD DISC FIRST. HEE!
THE MAKER'S STONED AGAIN. I THOUGHT IT'D STOPPED MANUFACTURING ITS OWN DRUGS.
FUCKING THING. I'M GOING TO FIX YOUR METAL ASS THIS TIME...
AAUUUURRRKKK
SQUEAL! SQUEAL, FUCKER!
STAR
EEEAAAAAAAA
SPIDER, STOP IT--THE NOISE IS FRIGGING KILLING ME--
THERE. NOW, MY ASSISTANT WOULD LIKE AN ARABICA COFFEE, BLACK, AND I WOULD LIKE A COLOMBIAN COFFEE WITH FOUR SUGARS.
AND NEITHER OF US HAS TIME TO FUCK AROUND, YOU PEESASHIT DOPE-FIEND BOX!

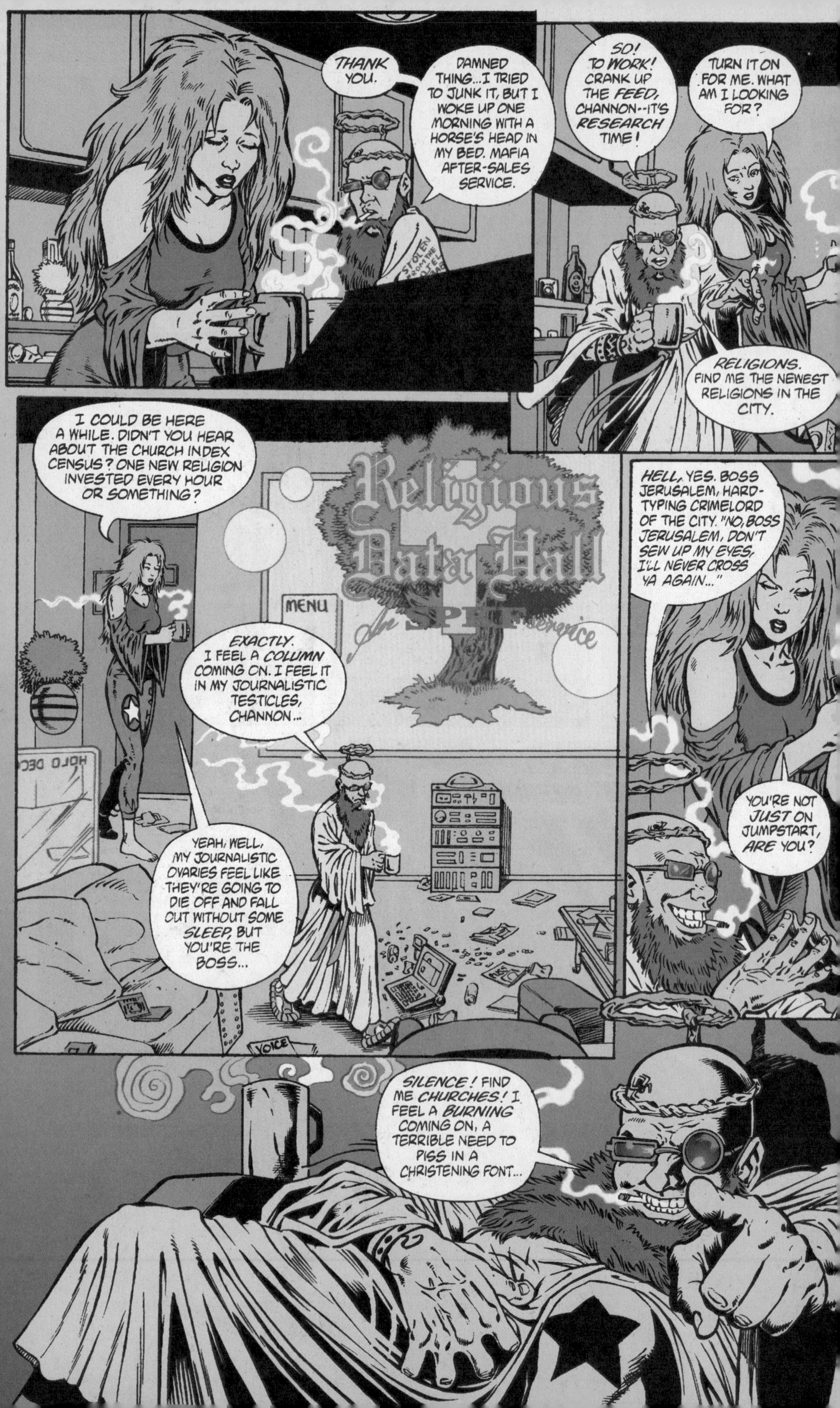
THANK YOU.
DAMNED THING...I TRIED TO JUNK IT, BUT I WOKE UP ONE MORNING WITH A HORSE'S HEAD IN MY BED. MAFIA AFTER-SALES SERVICE.
SO! TO WORK! CRANK UP THE FEED, CHANNON--IT'S RESEARCH TIME!
TURN IT ON FOR ME. WHAT AM I LOOKING FOR?
RELIGIONS. FIND ME THE NEWEST RELIGIONS IN THE CITY.
I COULD BE HERE A WHILE. DIDN'T YOU HEAR ABOUT THE CHURCH INDEX CENSUS? ONE NEW RELIGION INVESTED EVERY HOUR OR SOMETHING?
Religious Data Hall
MENU
EXACTLY. I FEEL A COLUMN COMING ON. I FEEL IT IN MY JOURNALISTIC TESTICLES, CHANNON...
YEAH, WELL, MY JOURNALISTIC OVARIES FEEL LIKE THEY'RE GOING TO DIE OFF AND FALL OUT WITHOUT SOME SLEEP, BUT YOU'RE THE BOSS...
VOICE
HELL, YES. BOSS JERUSALEM, HARD-TYPING CRIMELORD OF THE CITY. "NO, BOSS JERUSALEM, DON'T SEW UP MY EYES, I'LL NEVER CROSS YA AGAIN..."
YOU'RE NOT JUST ON JUMPSTART, ARE YOU?
SILENCE! FIND ME CHURCHES! I FEEL A BURNING COMING ON, A TERRIBLE NEED TO PISS IN A CHRISTENING FONT...

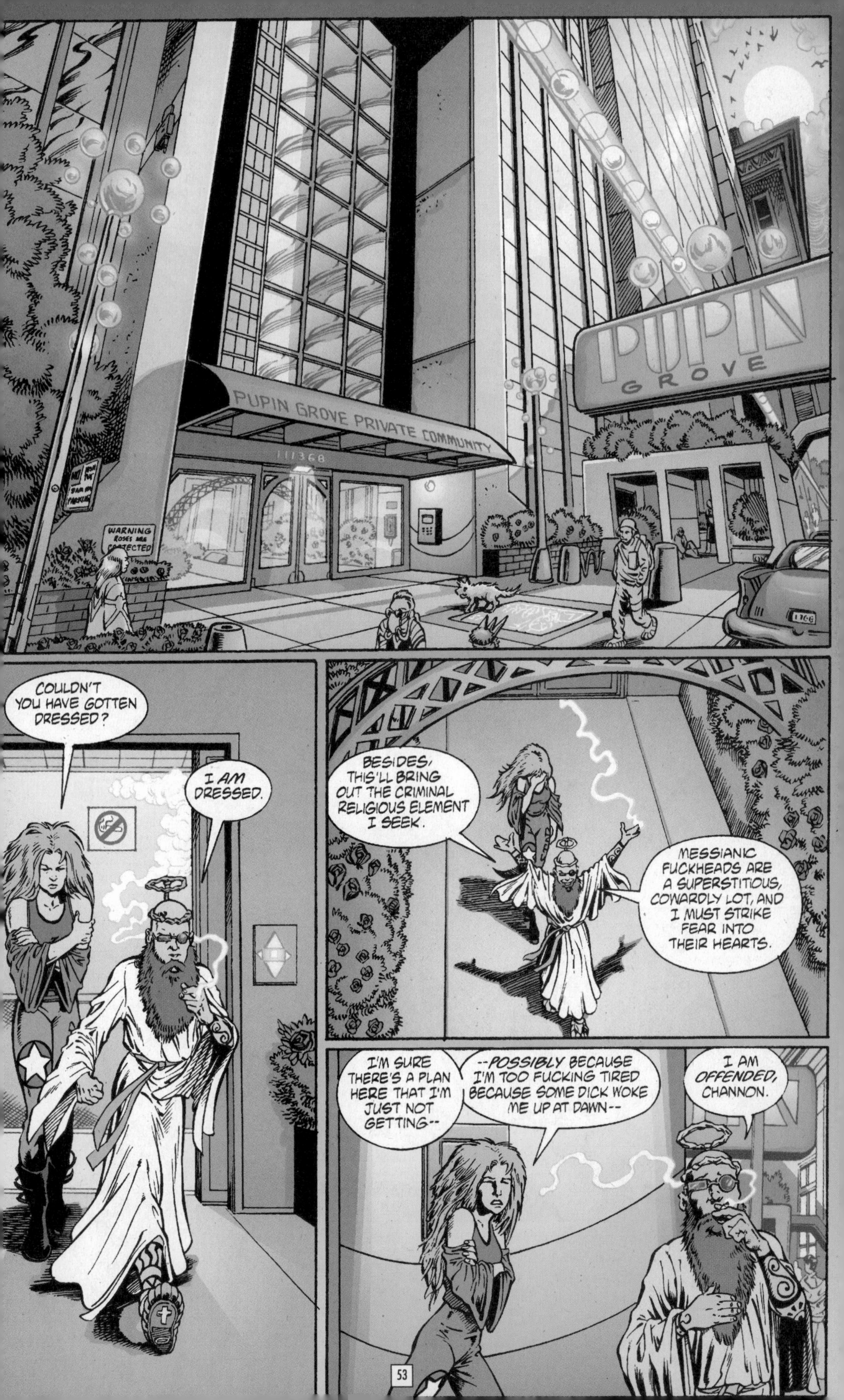
PUPIN GROVE PRIVATE COMMUNITY
111368
WARNING ROSES ARE PROTECTED
PUPIN GROVE
COULDN'T YOU HAVE GOTTEN DRESSED?
I AM DRESSED.
BESIDES, THIS'LL BRING OUT THE CRIMINAL RELIGIOUS ELEMENT I SEEK.
MESSIANIC FUCKHEADS ARE A SUPERSTITIOUS, COWARDLY LOT, AND I MUST STRIKE FEAR INTO THEIR HEARTS.
I'M SURE THERE'S A PLAN HERE THAT I'M JUST NOT GETTING--
--*POSSIBLY* BECAUSE I'M TOO FUCKING TIRED BECAUSE SOME DICK WOKE ME UP AT DAWN--
I AM *OFFENDED*, CHANNON.

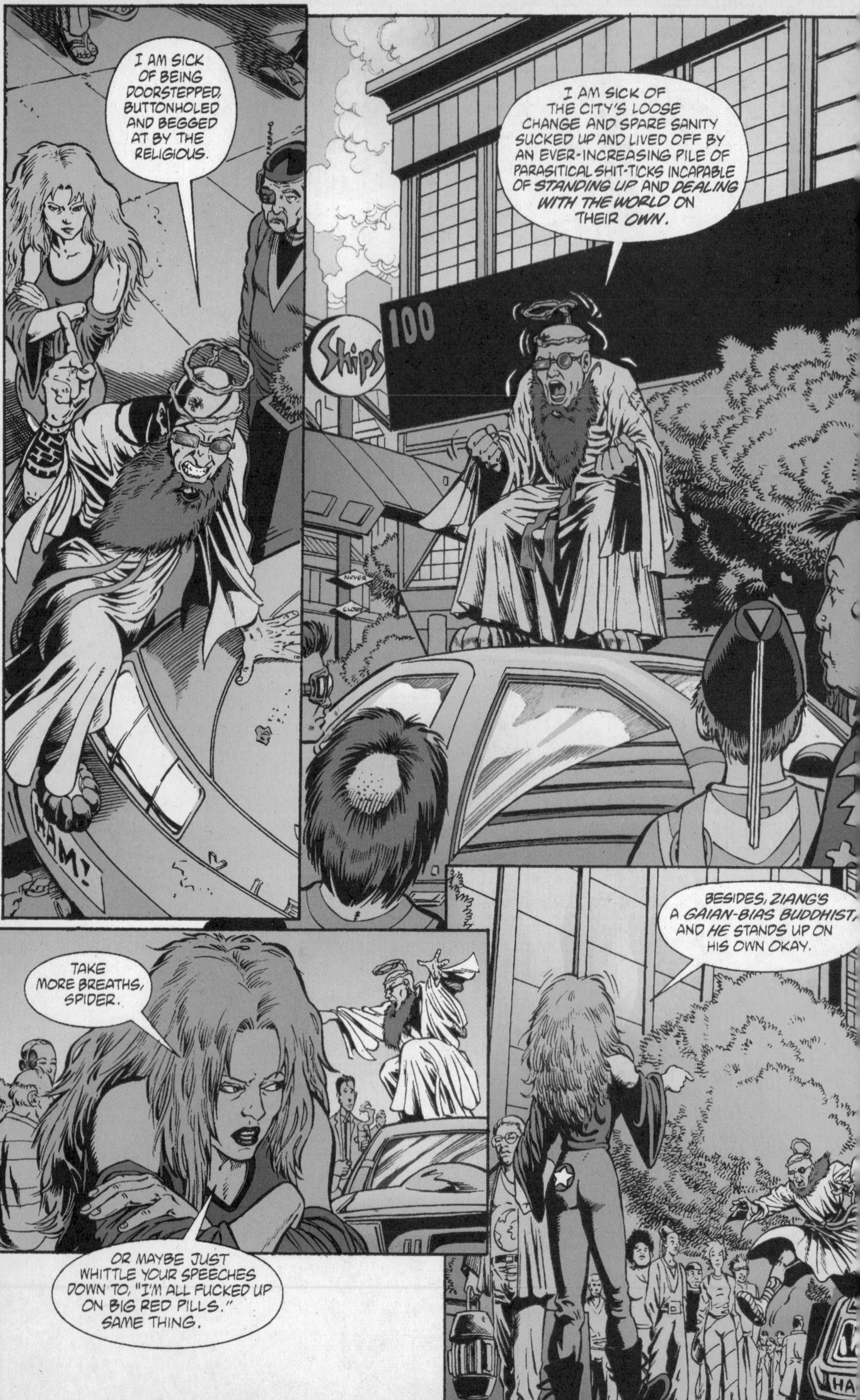
I AM SICK OF BEING DOORSTEPPED, BUTTONHOLED AND BEGGED AT BY THE RELIGIOUS.
I AM SICK OF THE CITY'S LOOSE CHANGE AND SPARE SANITY SUCKED UP AND LIVED OFF BY AN EVER-INCREASING PILE OF PARASITICAL SHIT-TICKS INCAPABLE OF *STANDING UP* AND *DEALING WITH THE WORLD* ON THEIR *OWN*.
Ships
100
HAM!
TAKE MORE BREATHS, SPIDER.
OR MAYBE JUST WHITTLE YOUR SPEECHES DOWN TO, "I'M ALL FUCKED UP ON BIG RED PILLS." SAME THING.
BESIDES, ZIANG'S A *GAIAN-BIAS BUDDHIST*, AND *HE* STANDS UP ON HIS OWN OKAY.

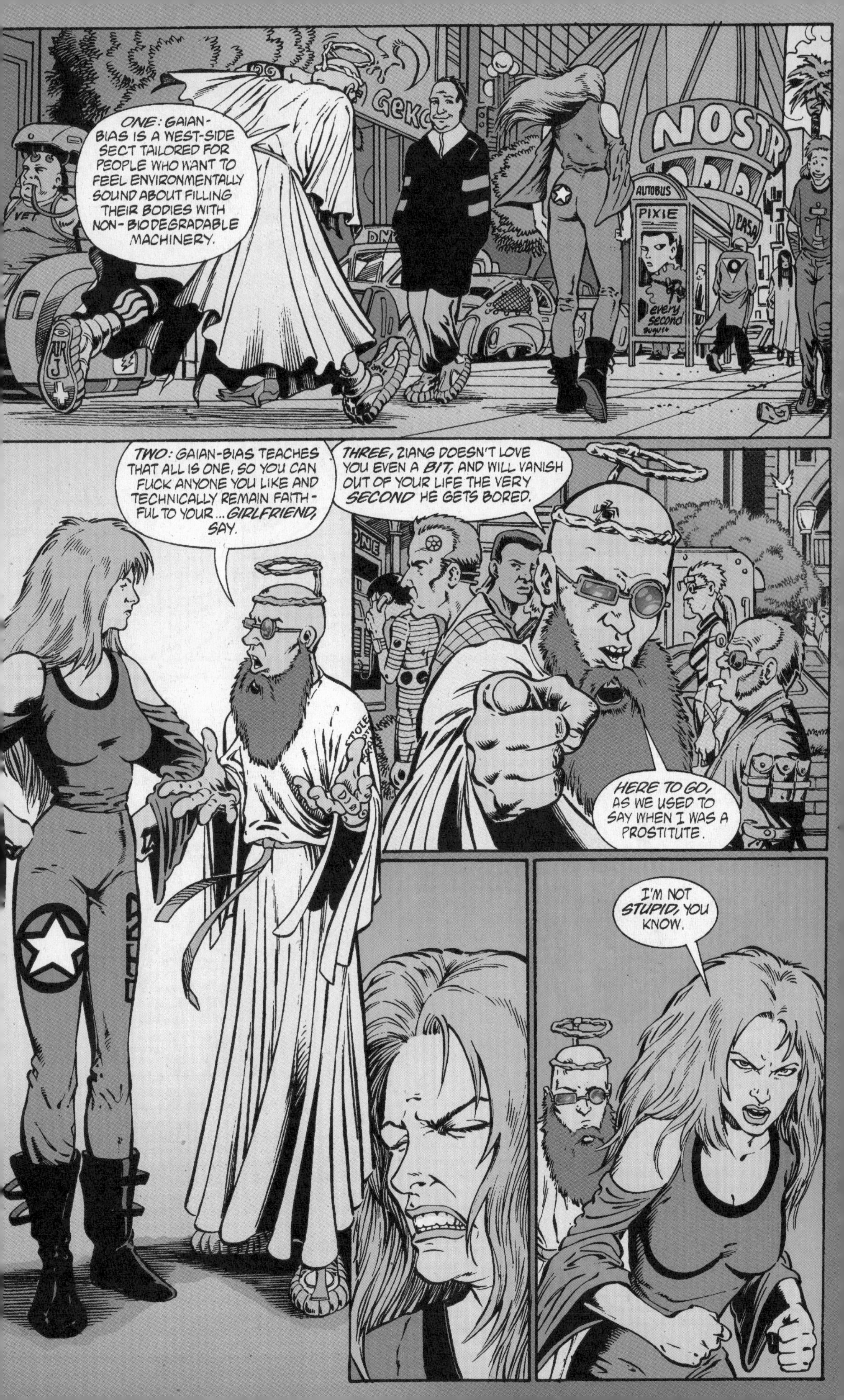
ONE: GAIAN-BIAS IS A WEST-SIDE SECT TAILORED FOR PEOPLE WHO WANT TO FEEL ENVIRONMENTALLY SOUND ABOUT FILLING THEIR BODIES WITH NON-BIODEGRADABLE MACHINERY.
GEKO
NOSTR
AUTOBUS
PIXIE
every second
CASA
TWO: GAIAN-BIAS TEACHES THAT ALL IS ONE, SO YOU CAN FUCK ANYONE YOU LIKE AND TECHNICALLY REMAIN FAITH-FUL TO YOUR...GIRLFRIEND, SAY.
THREE, ZIANG DOESN'T LOVE YOU EVEN A BIT, AND WILL VANISH OUT OF YOUR LIFE THE VERY SECOND HE GETS BORED.
HERE TO GO, AS WE USED TO SAY WHEN I WAS A PROSTITUTE.
I'M NOT STUPID, YOU KNOW.

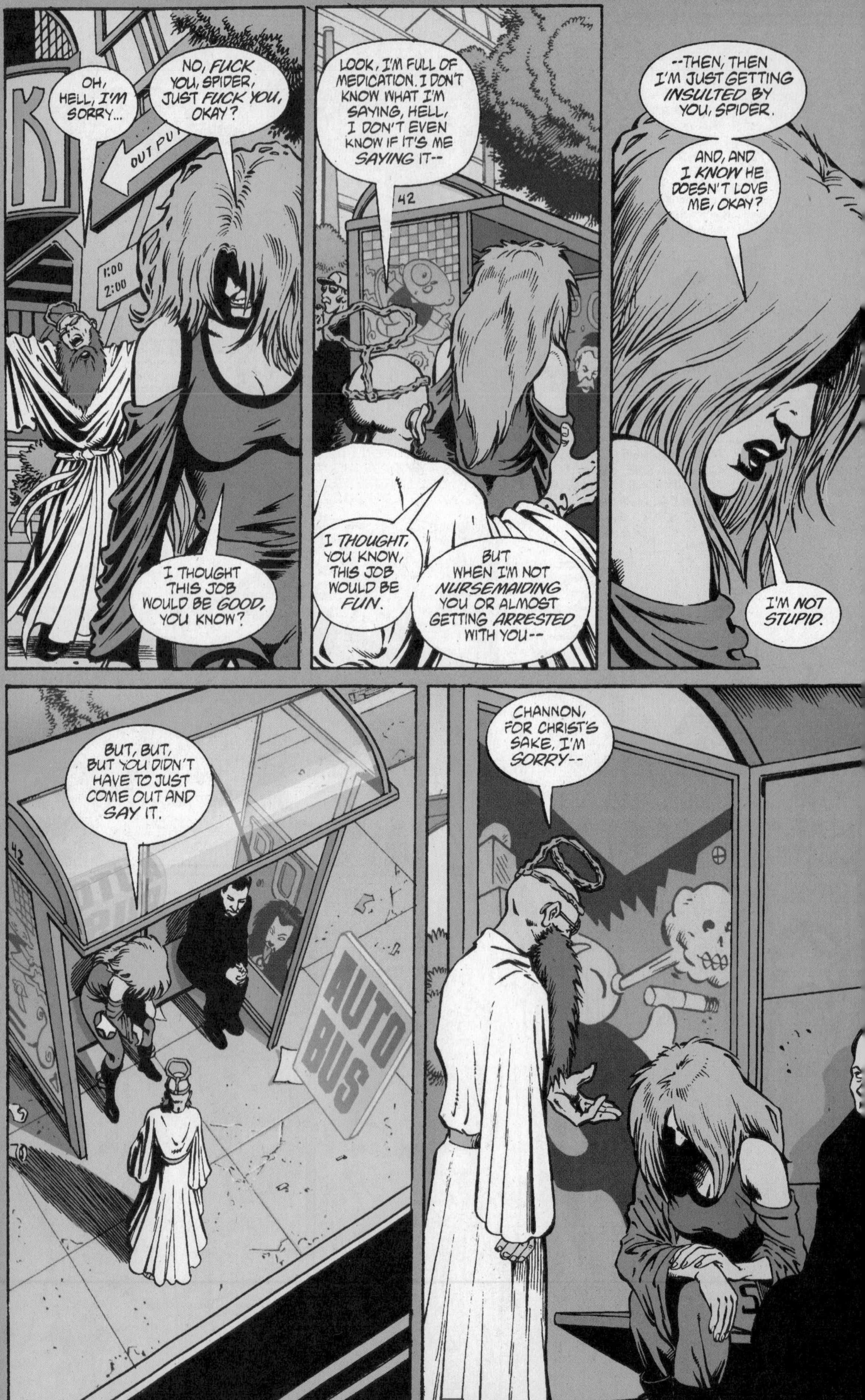

OH, HELL, I'M SORRY...
NO, FUCK YOU, SPIDER, JUST FUCK YOU, OKAY?
I THOUGHT THIS JOB WOULD BE GOOD, YOU KNOW?
LOOK, I'M FULL OF MEDICATION. I DON'T KNOW WHAT I'M SAYING, HELL, I DON'T EVEN KNOW IF IT'S ME SAYING IT--
I THOUGHT, YOU KNOW, THIS JOB WOULD BE FUN.
BUT WHEN I'M NOT NURSEMAIDING YOU OR ALMOST GETTING ARRESTED WITH YOU--
--THEN, THEN I'M JUST GETTING INSULTED BY YOU, SPIDER.
AND, AND I KNOW HE DOESN'T LOVE ME, OKAY?
I'M NOT STUPID.
BUT, BUT, BUT YOU DIDN'T HAVE TO JUST COME OUT AND SAY IT.
AUTO BUS
CHANNON, FOR CHRIST'S SAKE, I'M SORRY--

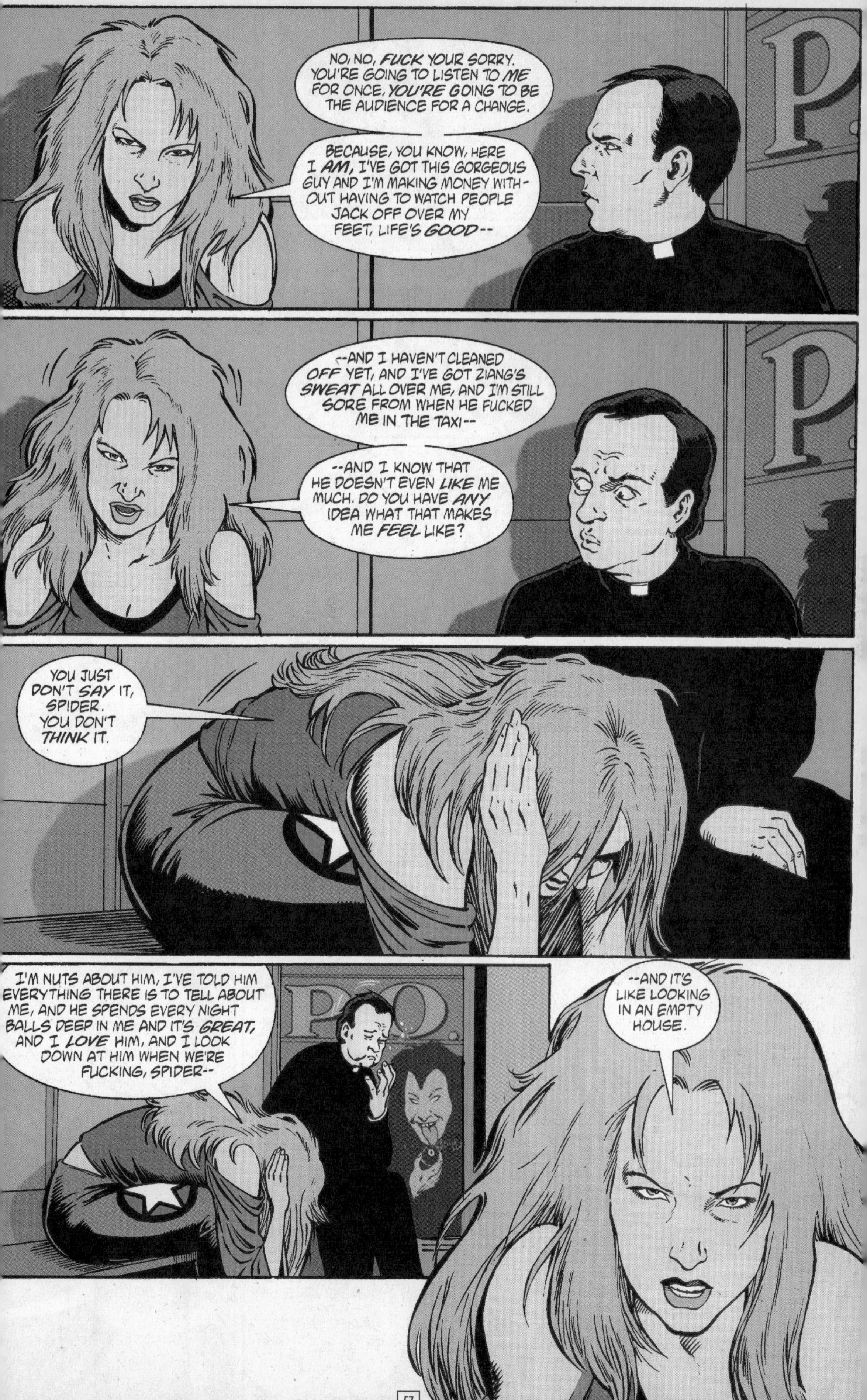
NO, NO, FUCK YOUR SORRY. YOU'RE GOING TO LISTEN TO ME FOR ONCE. YOU'RE GOING TO BE THE AUDIENCE FOR A CHANGE.
BECAUSE, YOU KNOW, HERE I AM, I'VE GOT THIS GORGEOUS GUY AND I'M MAKING MONEY WITH-OUT HAVING TO WATCH PEOPLE JACK OFF OVER MY FEET, LIFE'S GOOD--
--AND I HAVEN'T CLEANED OFF YET, AND I'VE GOT ZIANG'S SWEAT ALL OVER ME, AND I'M STILL SORE FROM WHEN HE FUCKED ME IN THE TAXI--
--AND I KNOW THAT HE DOESN'T EVEN LIKE ME MUCH. DO YOU HAVE ANY IDEA WHAT THAT MAKES ME FEEL LIKE?
YOU JUST DON'T SAY IT, SPIDER. YOU DON'T THINK IT.
I'M NUTS ABOUT HIM, I'VE TOLD HIM EVERYTHING THERE IS TO TELL ABOUT ME, AND HE SPENDS EVERY NIGHT BALLS DEEP IN ME AND IT'S GREAT, AND I LOVE HIM, AND I LOOK DOWN AT HIM WHEN WE'RE FUCKING, SPIDER--
--AND IT'S LIKE LOOKING IN AN EMPTY HOUSE.

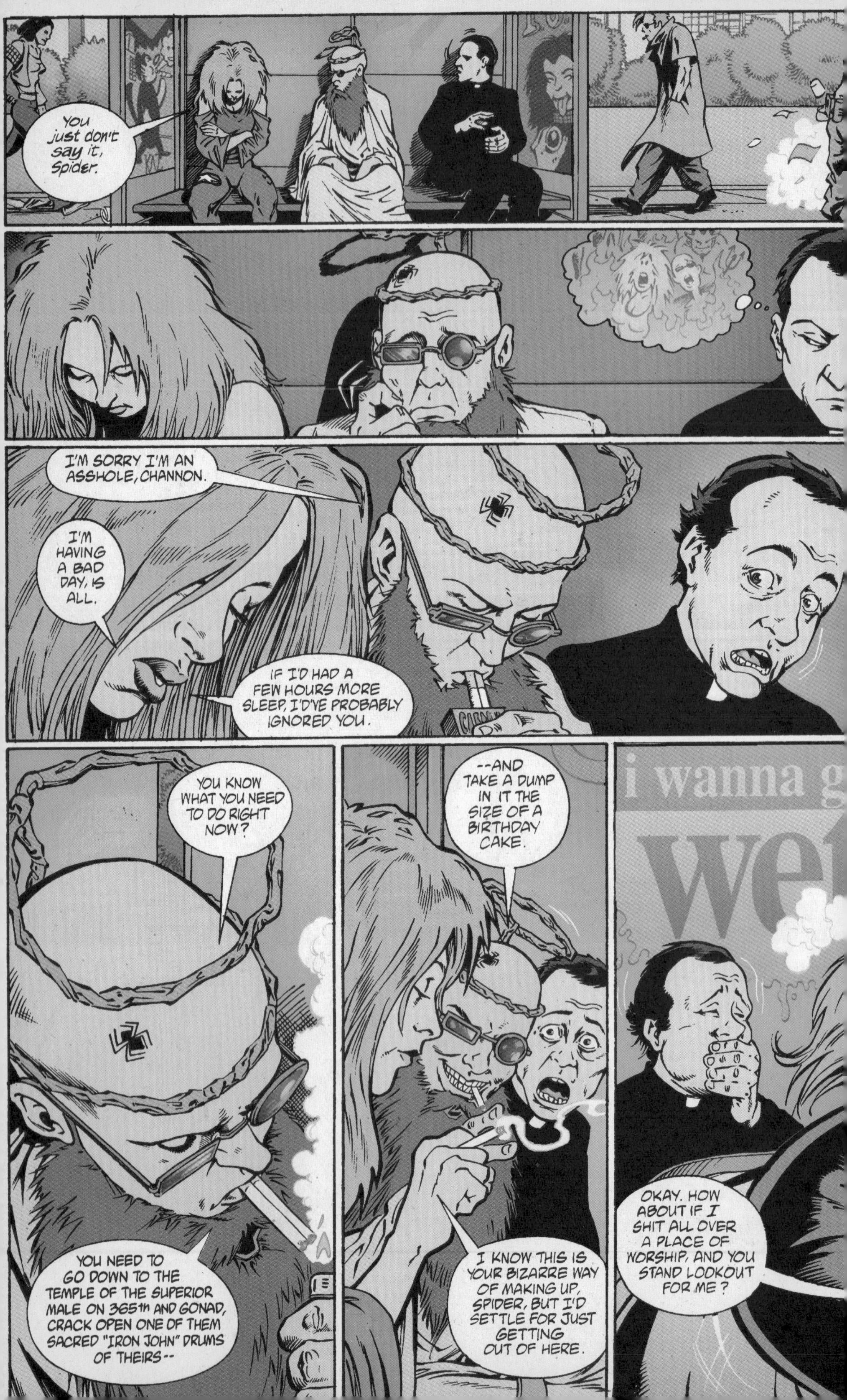
You just don't say it, Spider.
I'M SORRY I'M AN ASSHOLE, CHANNON.
I'M HAVING A BAD DAY, IS ALL.
IF I'D HAD A FEW HOURS MORE SLEEP, I'D'VE PROBABLY IGNORED YOU.
YOU KNOW WHAT YOU NEED TO DO RIGHT NOW?
YOU NEED TO GO DOWN TO THE TEMPLE OF THE SUPERIOR MALE ON 365th AND GONAD, CRACK OPEN ONE OF THEM SACRED "IRON JOHN" DRUMS OF THEIRS--
--AND TAKE A DUMP IN IT THE SIZE OF A BIRTHDAY CAKE.
I KNOW THIS IS YOUR BIZARRE WAY OF MAKING UP, SPIDER, BUT I'D SETTLE FOR JUST GETTING OUT OF HERE.
i wanna g
we
OKAY. HOW ABOUT IF I SHIT ALL OVER A PLACE OF WORSHIP, AND YOU STAND LOOKOUT FOR ME?

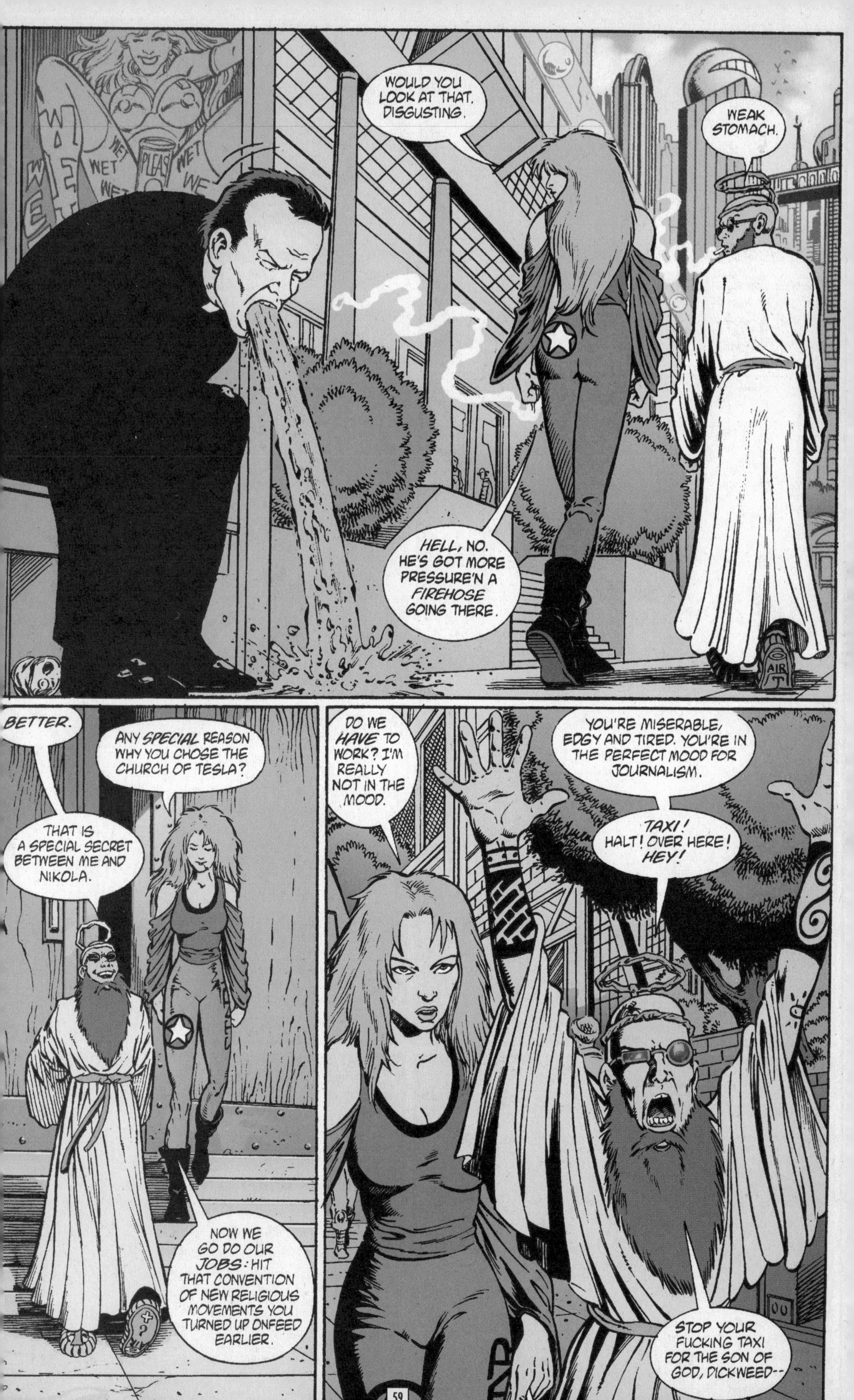
WET
WET
PLEAS
WET
WET
WE
WOULD YOU LOOK AT THAT. DISGUSTING.
WEAK STOMACH.
HELL, NO. HE'S GOT MORE PRESSURE'N A FIREHOSE GOING THERE.
BETTER.
ANY SPECIAL REASON WHY YOU CHOSE THE CHURCH OF TESLA?
THAT IS A SPECIAL SECRET BETWEEN ME AND NIKOLA.
NOW WE GO DO OUR JOBS: HIT THAT CONVENTION OF NEW RELIGIOUS MOVEMENTS YOU TURNED UP ONFEED EARLIER.
DO WE HAVE TO WORK? I'M REALLY NOT IN THE MOOD.
YOU'RE MISERABLE, EDGY AND TIRED. YOU'RE IN THE PERFECT MOOD FOR JOURNALISM.
TAXI! HALT! OVER HERE! HEY!
STOP YOUR FUCKING TAXI FOR THE SON OF GOD, DICKWEED--

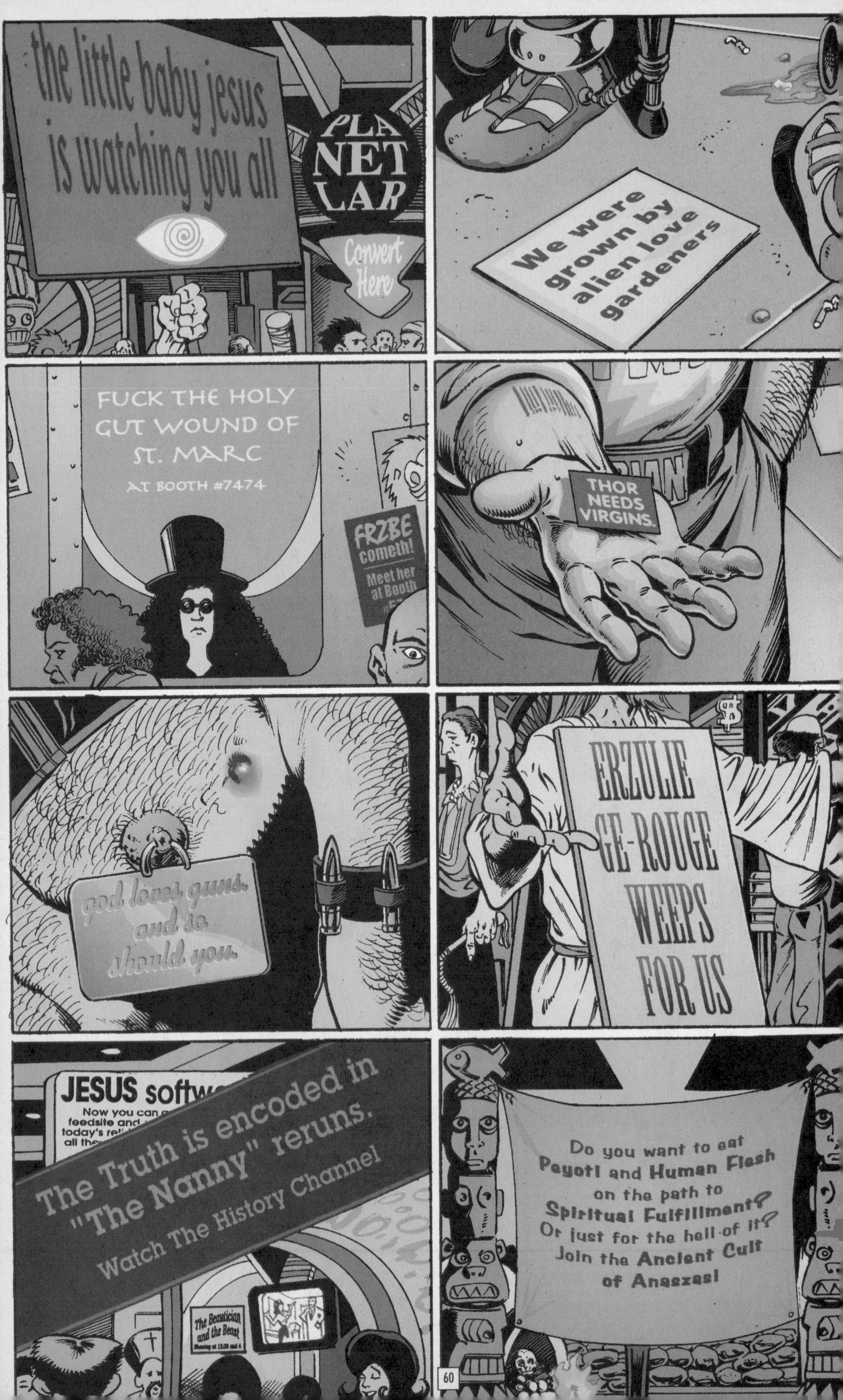
the little baby jesus is watching you all
PLA NET LAR
Convert Here
We were grown by alien love gardeners
FUCK THE HOLY GUT WOUND OF ST. MARC
AT BOOTH #7474
FRZBE cometh!
Meet her at Booth
THOR NEEDS VIRGINS.
god loves guns. and so should you.
ERZULIE GE-ROUGE WEEPS FOR US
JESUS
Now you can
feedsite and
today's
The Truth is encoded in "The Nanny" reruns.
Watch The History Channel
The Beautician and the Beast
Showing at 12:30 and 4
Do you want to eat Peyotl and Human Flesh on the path to Spiritual Fulfillment? Or just for the hell of it? Join the Ancient Cult of Anazazi

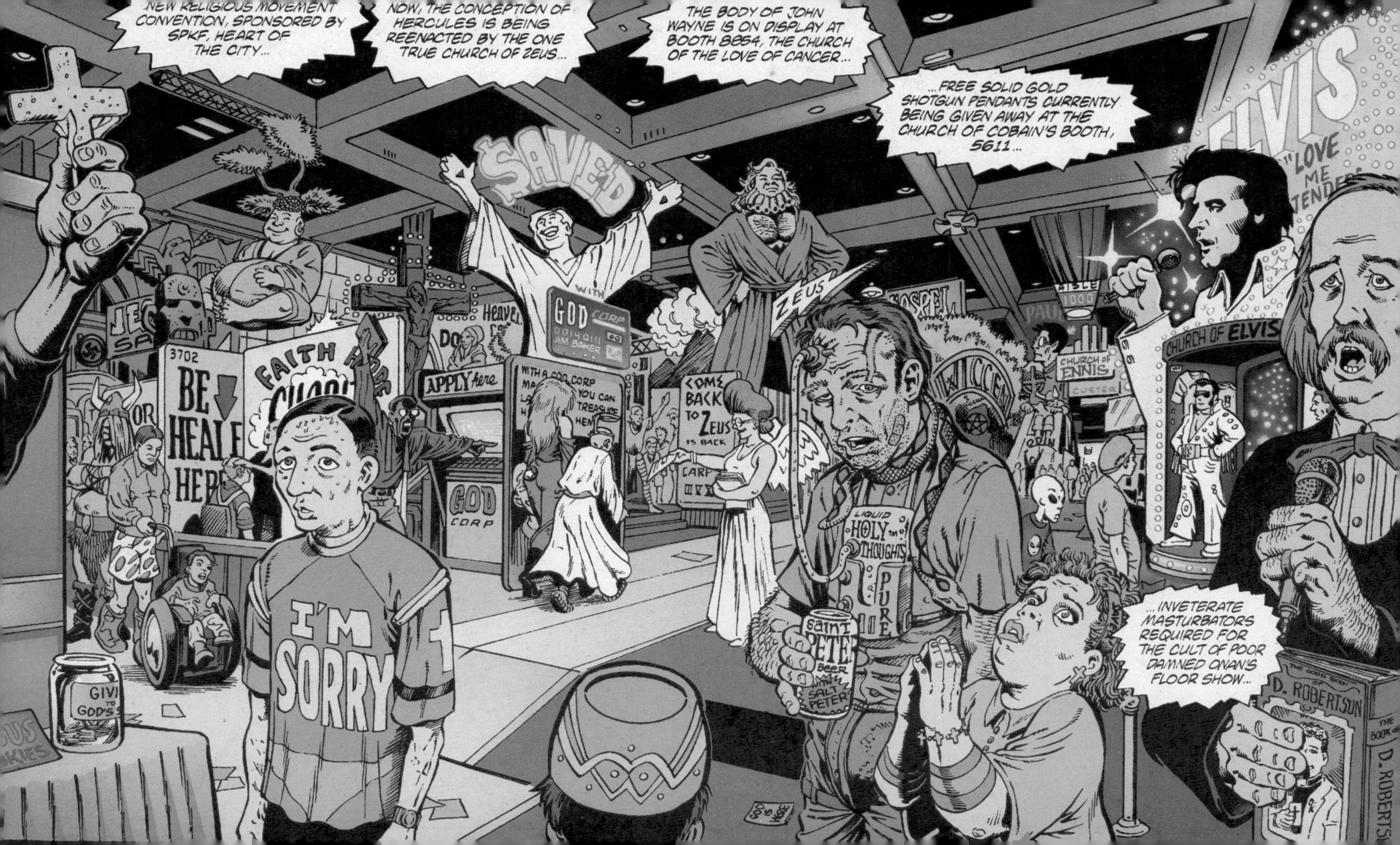

NEW RELIGIOUS MOVEMENT CONVENTION, SPONSORED BY SPKF, HEART OF THE CITY...
NOW, THE CONCEPTION OF HERCULES IS BEING REENACTED BY THE ONE TRUE CHURCH OF ZEUS...
THE BODY OF JOHN WAYNE IS ON DISPLAY AT BOOTH 8854, THE CHURCH OF THE LOVE OF CANCER...
...FREE SOLID GOLD SHOTGUN PENDANTS CURRENTLY BEING GIVEN AWAY AT THE CHURCH OF COBAIN'S BOOTH, 5611...
...INVETERATE MASTURBATORS REQUIRED FOR THE CULT OF POOR DAMNED ONAN'S FLOOR SHOW...
ELVIS
"LOVE ME TENDER"
SAVED
WITH GOD CORP
JIM BAKER
ZEUS
3702
BE HEALED HERE
FAITH
APPLY here
WITH A GOD CORP
YOU CAN TREASURE
COME BACK TO ZEUS
IS BACK
GOD CORP
CHURCH OF ELVIS
CHURCH OF ENNIS
AISLE 1000
LIQUID HOLY THOUGHTS
PURE
Saint PETER BEER SALT PETER
I'M SORRY
GIVE TO GOD'S
D. ROBERTSON
GOD IS HERE

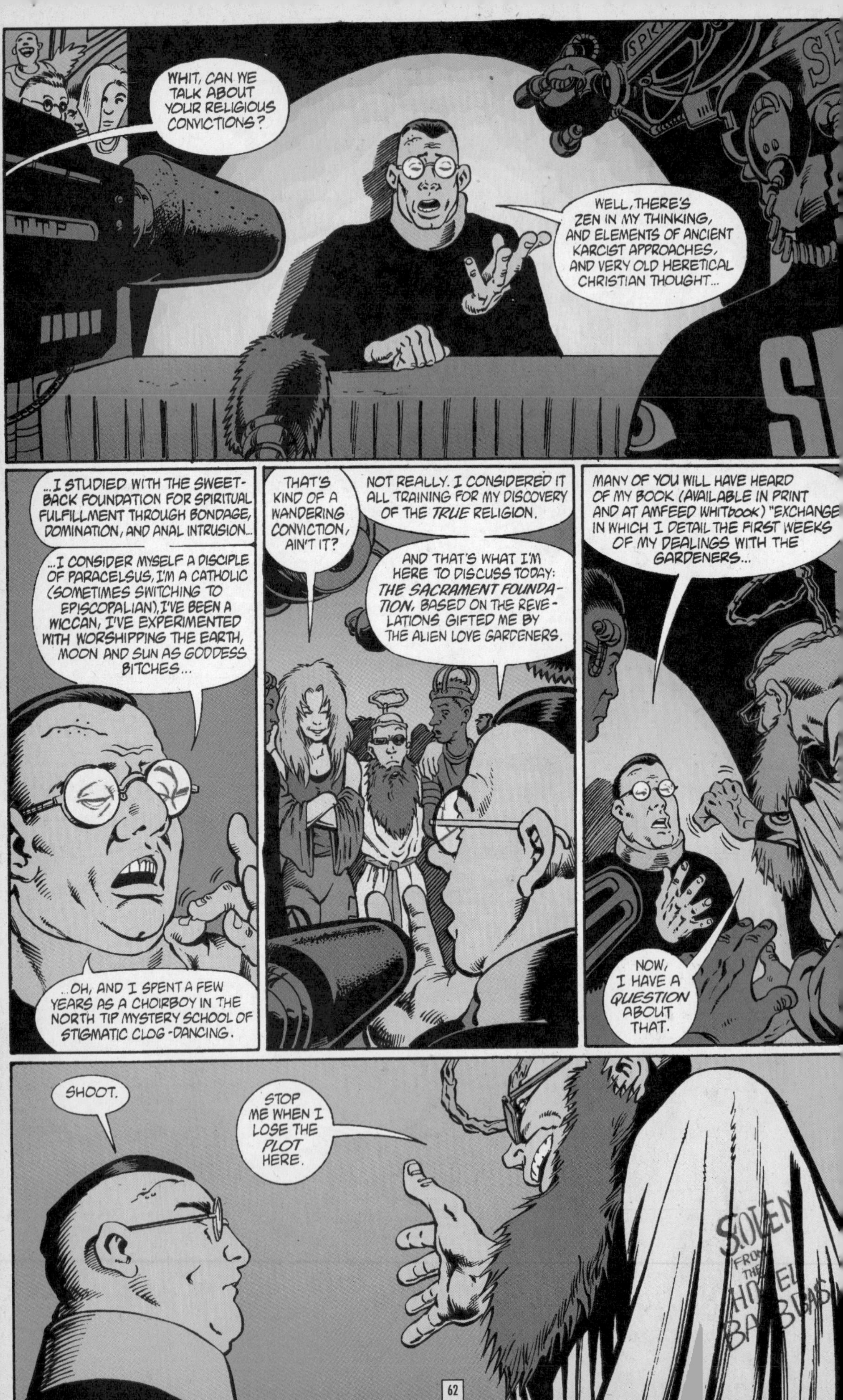
WHIT, CAN WE TALK ABOUT YOUR RELIGIOUS CONVICTIONS?
WELL, THERE'S ZEN IN MY THINKING, AND ELEMENTS OF ANCIENT KARCIST APPROACHES, AND VERY OLD HERETICAL CHRISTIAN THOUGHT...
...I STUDIED WITH THE SWEET-BACK FOUNDATION FOR SPIRITUAL FULFILLMENT THROUGH BONDAGE, DOMINATION, AND ANAL INTRUSION...
...I CONSIDER MYSELF A DISCIPLE OF PARACELSUS, I'M A CATHOLIC (SOMETIMES SWITCHING TO EPISCOPALIAN), I'VE BEEN A WICCAN, I'VE EXPERIMENTED WITH WORSHIPPING THE EARTH, MOON AND SUN AS GODDESS BITCHES...
...OH, AND I SPENT A FEW YEARS AS A CHOIRBOY IN THE NORTH TIP MYSTERY SCHOOL OF STIGMATIC CLOG-DANCING.
THAT'S KIND OF A WANDERING CONVICTION, AIN'T IT?
NOT REALLY. I CONSIDERED IT ALL TRAINING FOR MY DISCOVERY OF THE *TRUE* RELIGION.
AND THAT'S WHAT I'M HERE TO DISCUSS TODAY: *THE SACRAMENT FOUNDATION*, BASED ON THE REVELATIONS GIFTED ME BY THE ALIEN LOVE GARDENERS.
MANY OF YOU WILL HAVE HEARD OF MY BOOK (AVAILABLE IN PRINT AND AT AMFEED WHITbook) "EXCHANGE" IN WHICH I DETAIL THE FIRST WEEKS OF MY DEALINGS WITH THE GARDENERS...
NOW, I HAVE A *QUESTION* ABOUT THAT.
SHOOT.
STOP ME WHEN I LOSE THE *PLOT* HERE.
STOLEN FROM THE HOTEL BARBDAS

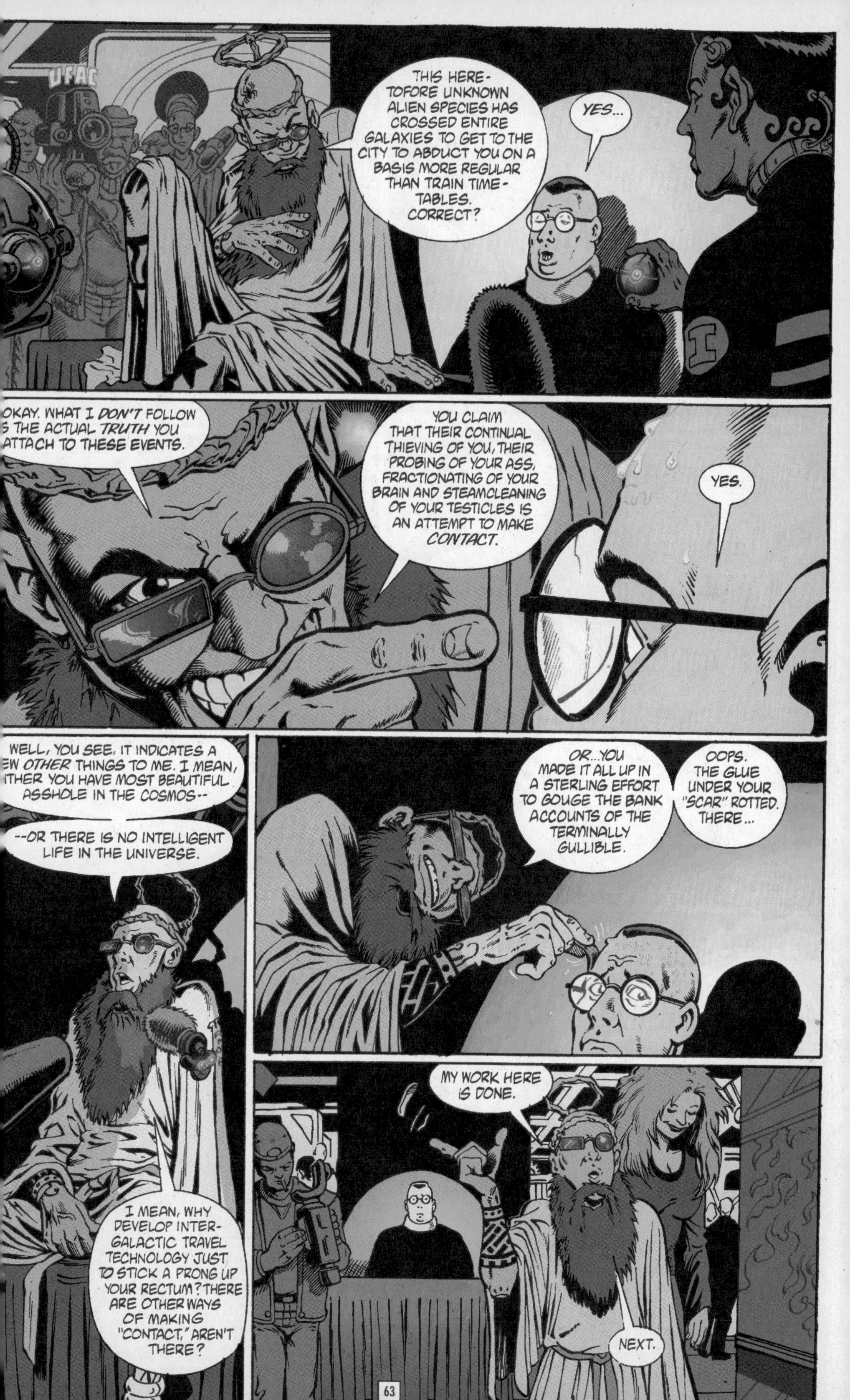
THIS HERE-TOFORE UNKNOWN ALIEN SPECIES HAS CROSSED ENTIRE GALAXIES TO GET TO THE CITY TO ABDUCT YOU ON A BASIS MORE REGULAR THAN TRAIN TIME-TABLES. CORRECT?
YES...
OKAY. WHAT I DON'T FOLLOW IS THE ACTUAL TRUTH YOU ATTACH TO THESE EVENTS.
YOU CLAIM THAT THEIR CONTINUAL THIEVING OF YOU, THEIR PROBING OF YOUR ASS, FRACTIONATING OF YOUR BRAIN AND STEAMCLEANING OF YOUR TESTICLES IS AN ATTEMPT TO MAKE CONTACT.
YES.
WELL, YOU SEE, IT INDICATES A FEW OTHER THINGS TO ME. I MEAN, EITHER YOU HAVE MOST BEAUTIFUL ASSHOLE IN THE COSMOS--
--OR THERE IS NO INTELLIGENT LIFE IN THE UNIVERSE.
I MEAN, WHY DEVELOP INTER-GALACTIC TRAVEL TECHNOLOGY JUST TO STICK A PRONG UP YOUR RECTUM? THERE ARE OTHER WAYS OF MAKING "CONTACT," AREN'T THERE?
OR...YOU MADE IT ALL UP IN A STERLING EFFORT TO GOUGE THE BANK ACCOUNTS OF THE TERMINALLY GULLIBLE.
OOPS. THE GLUE UNDER YOUR "SCAR" ROTTED. THERE...
MY WORK HERE IS DONE.
NEXT.

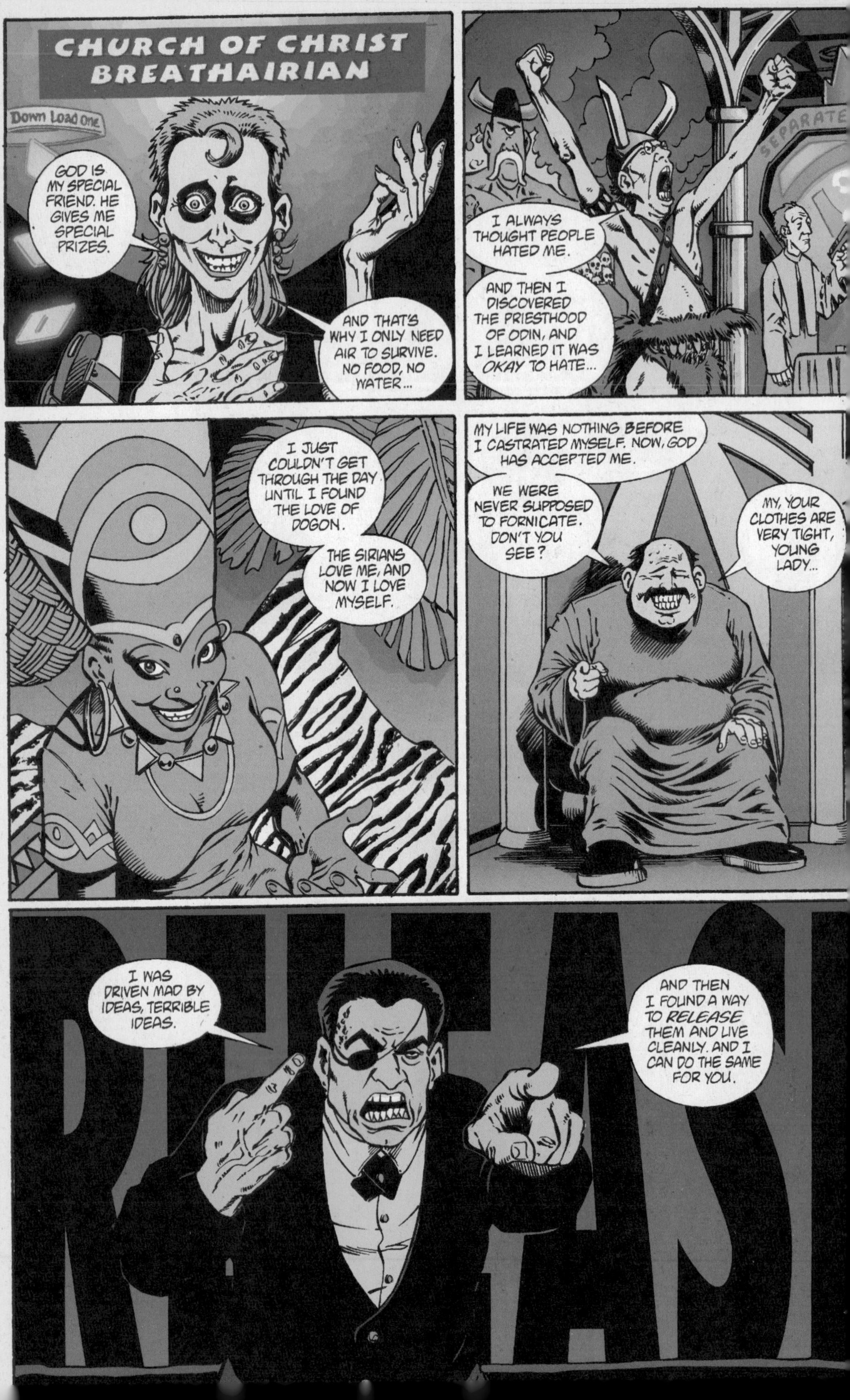
CHURCH OF CHRIST BREATHAIRIAN
Down Load One
GOD IS MY SPECIAL FRIEND. HE GIVES ME SPECIAL PRIZES.
AND THAT'S WHY I ONLY NEED AIR TO SURVIVE. NO FOOD, NO WATER...
SEPARATE
I ALWAYS THOUGHT PEOPLE HATED ME.
AND THEN I DISCOVERED THE PRIESTHOOD OF ODIN, AND I LEARNED IT WAS OKAY TO HATE...
I JUST COULDN'T GET THROUGH THE DAY UNTIL I FOUND THE LOVE OF DOGON.
THE SIRIANS LOVE ME, AND NOW I LOVE MYSELF.
MY LIFE WAS NOTHING BEFORE I CASTRATED MYSELF. NOW, GOD HAS ACCEPTED ME.
WE WERE NEVER SUPPOSED TO FORNICATE. DON'T YOU SEE?
MY, YOUR CLOTHES ARE VERY TIGHT, YOUNG LADY...
I WAS DRIVEN MAD BY IDEAS, TERRIBLE IDEAS.
AND THEN I FOUND A WAY TO RELEASE THEM AND LIVE CLEANLY. AND I CAN DO THE SAME FOR YOU.

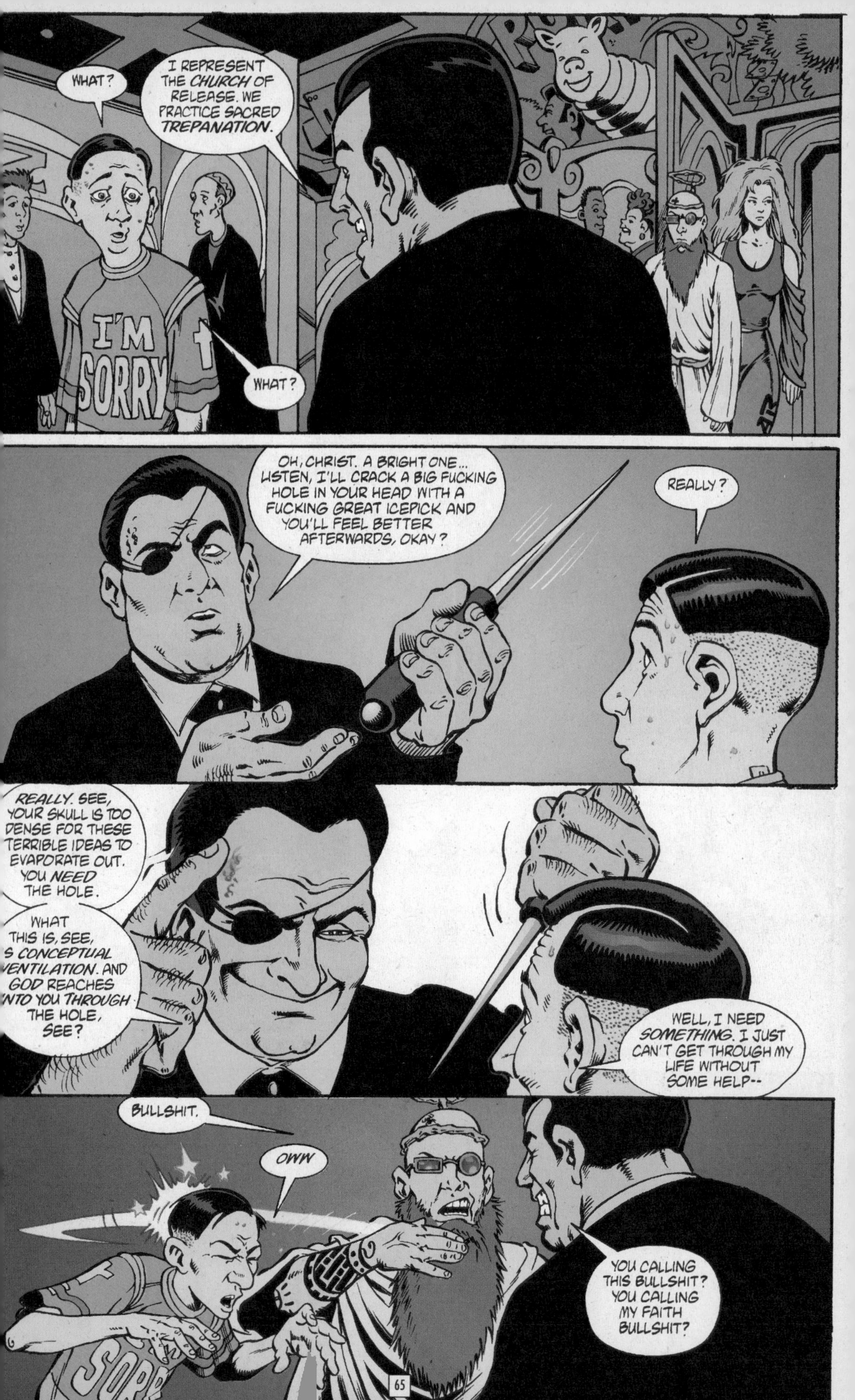
WHAT?
I REPRESENT THE CHURCH OF RELEASE. WE PRACTICE SACRED TREPANATION.
WHAT?
OH, CHRIST. A BRIGHT ONE... LISTEN, I'LL CRACK A BIG FUCKING HOLE IN YOUR HEAD WITH A FUCKING GREAT ICEPICK AND YOU'LL FEEL BETTER AFTERWARDS, OKAY?
REALLY?
REALLY. SEE, YOUR SKULL IS TOO DENSE FOR THESE TERRIBLE IDEAS TO EVAPORATE OUT. YOU NEED THE HOLE.
WHAT THIS IS, SEE, S CONCEPTUAL VENTILATION. AND GOD REACHES NTO YOU THROUGH THE HOLE, SEE?
WELL, I NEED SOMETHING. I JUST CAN'T GET THROUGH MY LIFE WITHOUT SOME HELP--
BULLSHIT.
OWW
YOU CALLING THIS BULLSHIT? YOU CALLING MY FAITH BULLSHIT?

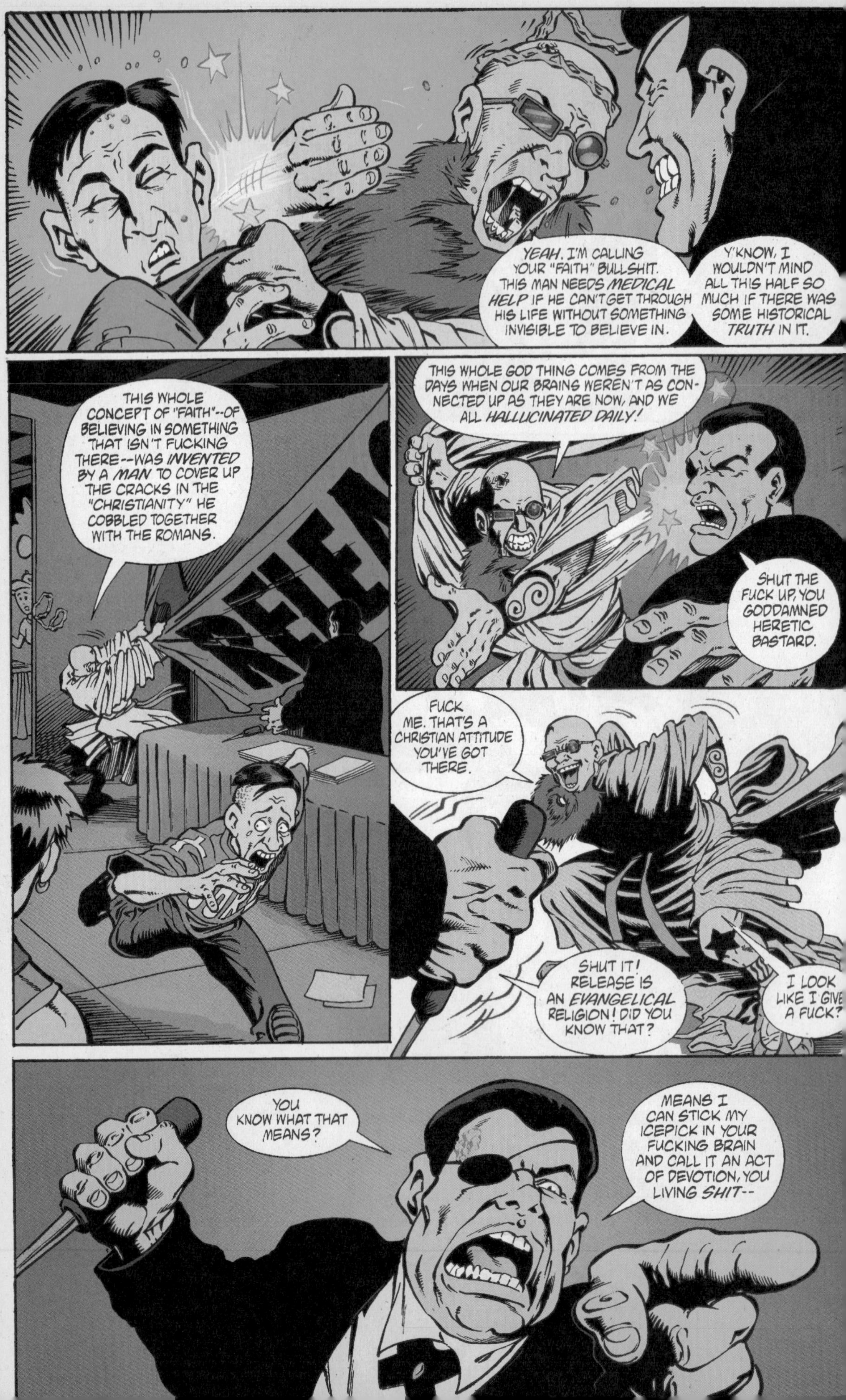
YEAH. I'M CALLING YOUR "FAITH" BULLSHIT. THIS MAN NEEDS MEDICAL HELP IF HE CAN'T GET THROUGH HIS LIFE WITHOUT SOMETHING INVISIBLE TO BELIEVE IN.
Y'KNOW, I WOULDN'T MIND ALL THIS HALF SO MUCH IF THERE WAS SOME HISTORICAL TRUTH IN IT.
THIS WHOLE CONCEPT OF "FAITH"--OF BELIEVING IN SOMETHING THAT ISN'T FUCKING THERE--WAS INVENTED BY A MAN TO COVER UP THE CRACKS IN THE "CHRISTIANITY" HE COBBLED TOGETHER WITH THE ROMANS.
THIS WHOLE GOD THING COMES FROM THE DAYS WHEN OUR BRAINS WEREN'T AS CONNECTED UP AS THEY ARE NOW, AND WE ALL HALLUCINATED DAILY!
SHUT THE FUCK UP, YOU GODDAMNED HERETIC BASTARD.
FUCK ME. THAT'S A CHRISTIAN ATTITUDE YOU'VE GOT THERE.
SHUT IT! RELEASE IS AN EVANGELICAL RELIGION! DID YOU KNOW THAT?
I LOOK LIKE I GIVE A FUCK?
YOU KNOW WHAT THAT MEANS?
MEANS I CAN STICK MY ICEPICK IN YOUR FUCKING BRAIN AND CALL IT AN ACT OF DEVOTION, YOU LIVING SHIT--

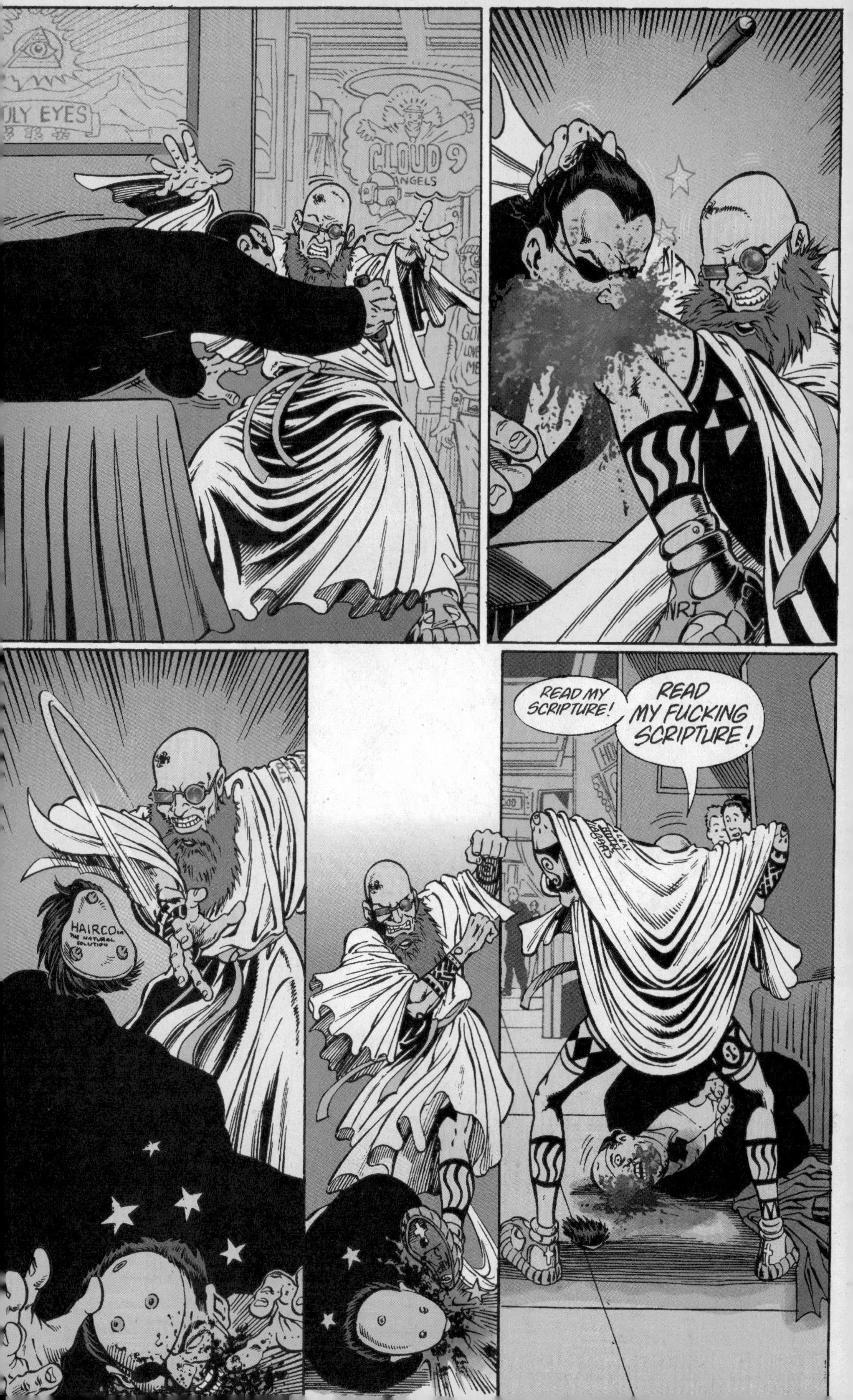

ULY EYES
CLOUD 9
ANGELS
HAIRCO
THE NATURAL SOLUTION
READ MY SCRIPTURE!
READ MY FUCKING SCRIPTURE!

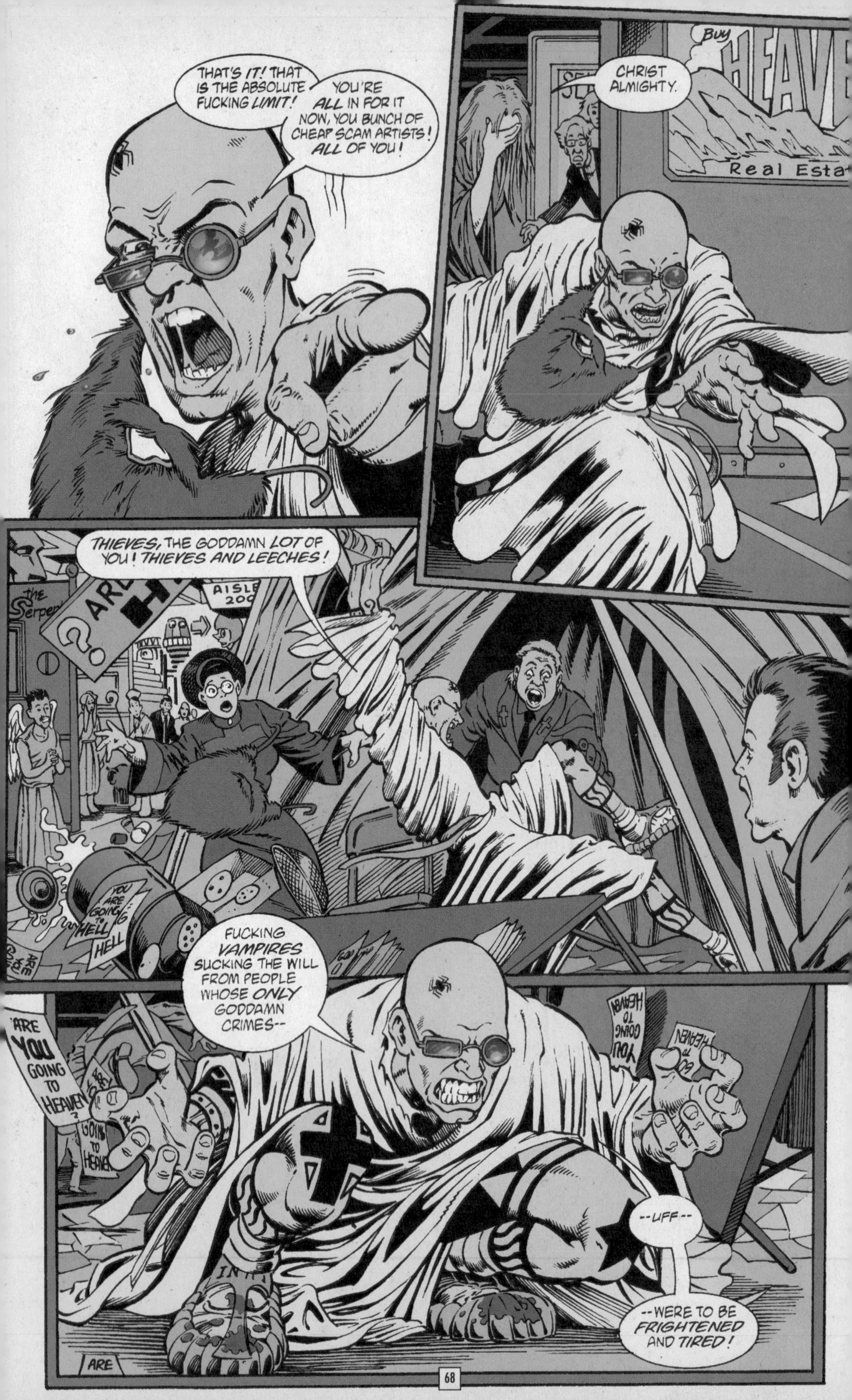
THAT'S IT! THAT IS THE ABSOLUTE FUCKING LIMIT!
YOU'RE ALL IN FOR IT NOW, YOU BUNCH OF CHEAP SCAM ARTISTS! ALL OF YOU!
Buy
Real Esta
CHRIST ALMIGHTY.
THIEVES, THE GODDAMN LOT OF YOU! THIEVES AND LEECHES!
the Serpent
YOU ARE GOING TO HELL
FUCKING VAMPIRES SUCKING THE WILL FROM PEOPLE WHOSE ONLY GODDAMN CRIMES--
ARE YOU GOING TO HEAVEN?
GOING TO HEAVEN
--UFF--
--WERE TO BE FRIGHTENED AND TIRED!
ARE

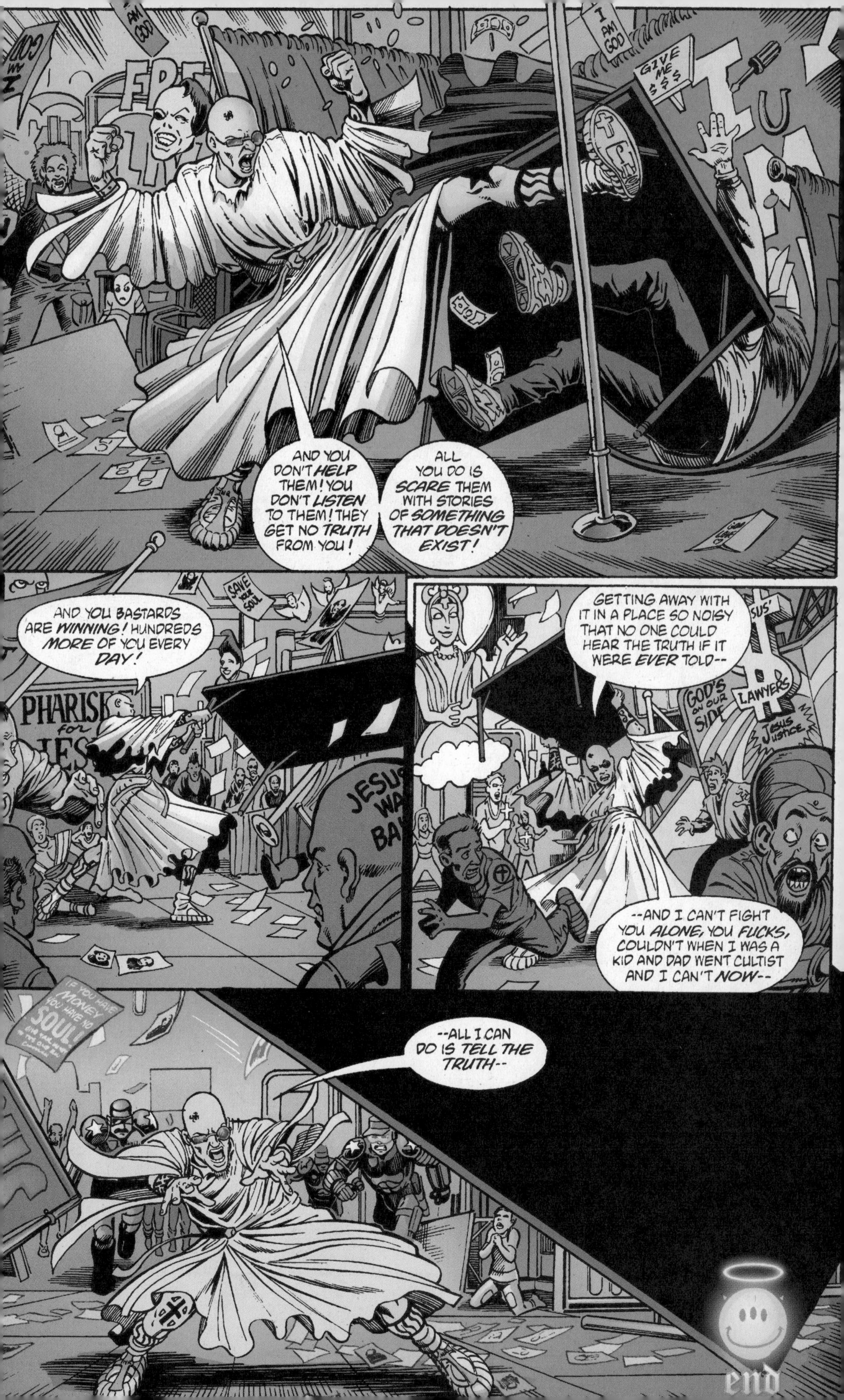
AND YOU DON'T HELP THEM! YOU DON'T LISTEN TO THEM! THEY GET NO TRUTH FROM YOU!
ALL YOU DO IS SCARE THEM WITH STORIES OF SOMETHING THAT DOESN'T EXIST!
AND YOU BASTARDS ARE WINNING! HUNDREDS MORE OF YOU EVERY DAY!
GETTING AWAY WITH IT IN A PLACE SO NOISY THAT NO ONE COULD HEAR THE TRUTH IF IT WERE EVER TOLD--
--AND I CAN'T FIGHT YOU ALONE, YOU FUCKS, COULDN'T WHEN I WAS A KID AND DAD WENT CULTIST AND I CAN'T NOW--
--ALL I CAN DO IS TELL THE TRUTH--
I AM GOD
GIVE ME $$$
SAVE YOUR SOUL
PHARISE
GOD'S on our SIDE
LAWYERS
Jesus Justice
IF YOU HAVE MONEY YOU HAVE NO SOUL!
end

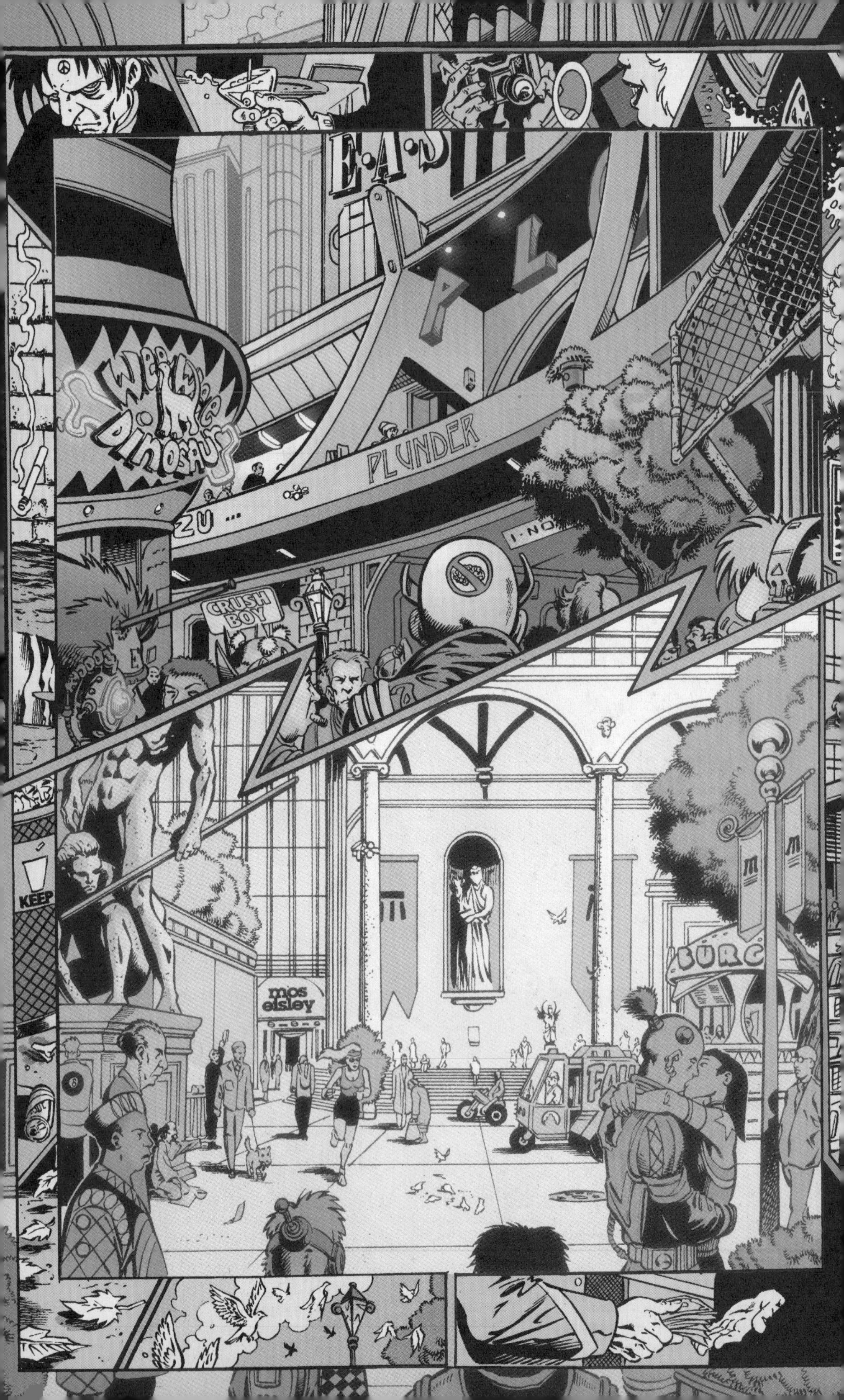
PLUNDER
CRUSH BOY
mos eisley
KEEP

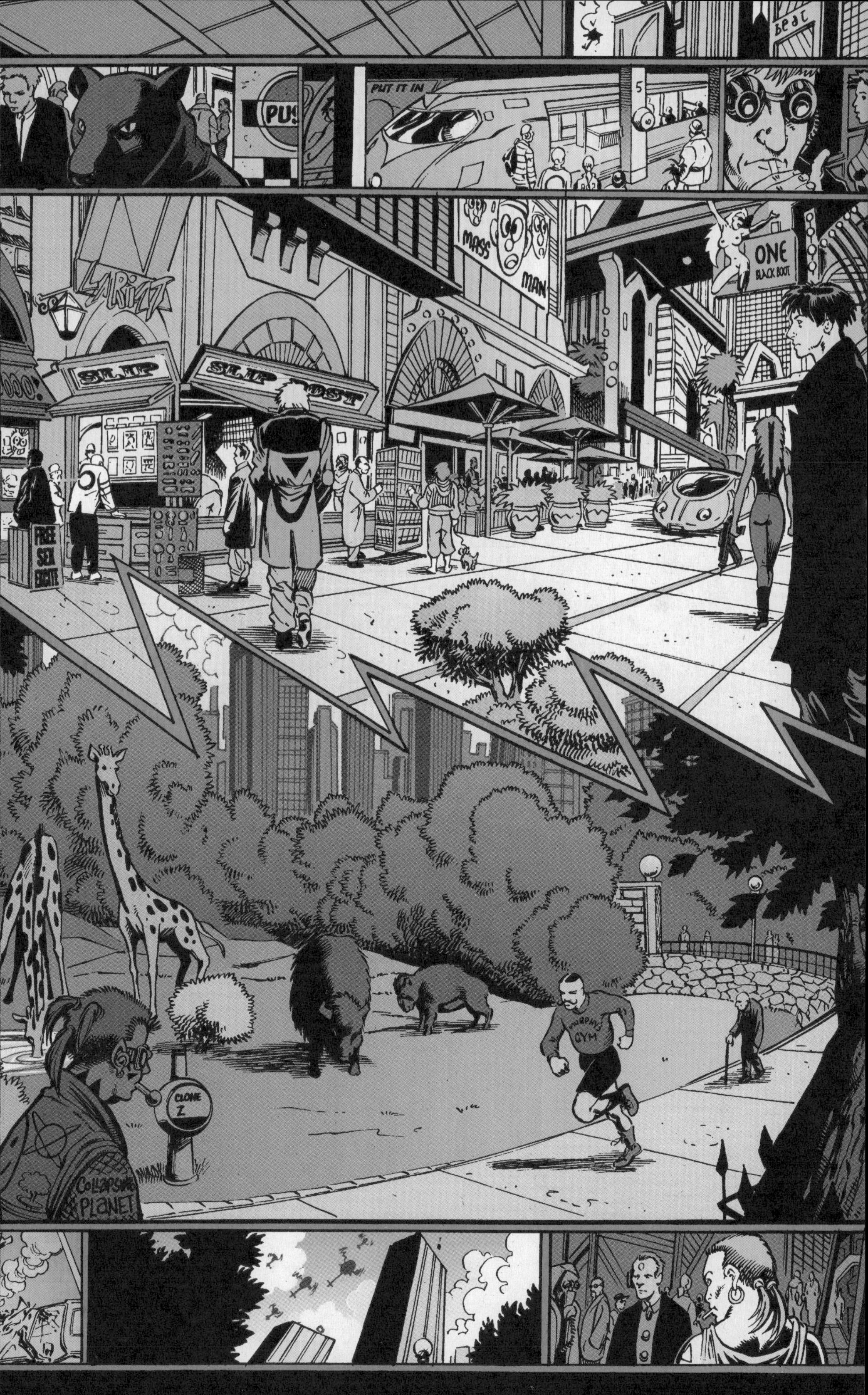

PUT IT IN
MASS MAN
ONE
BLACK BOOT
SLIP
FREE SEX EXCITE
MURPHY'S GYM
CLONE Z
COLLAPSING PLANET

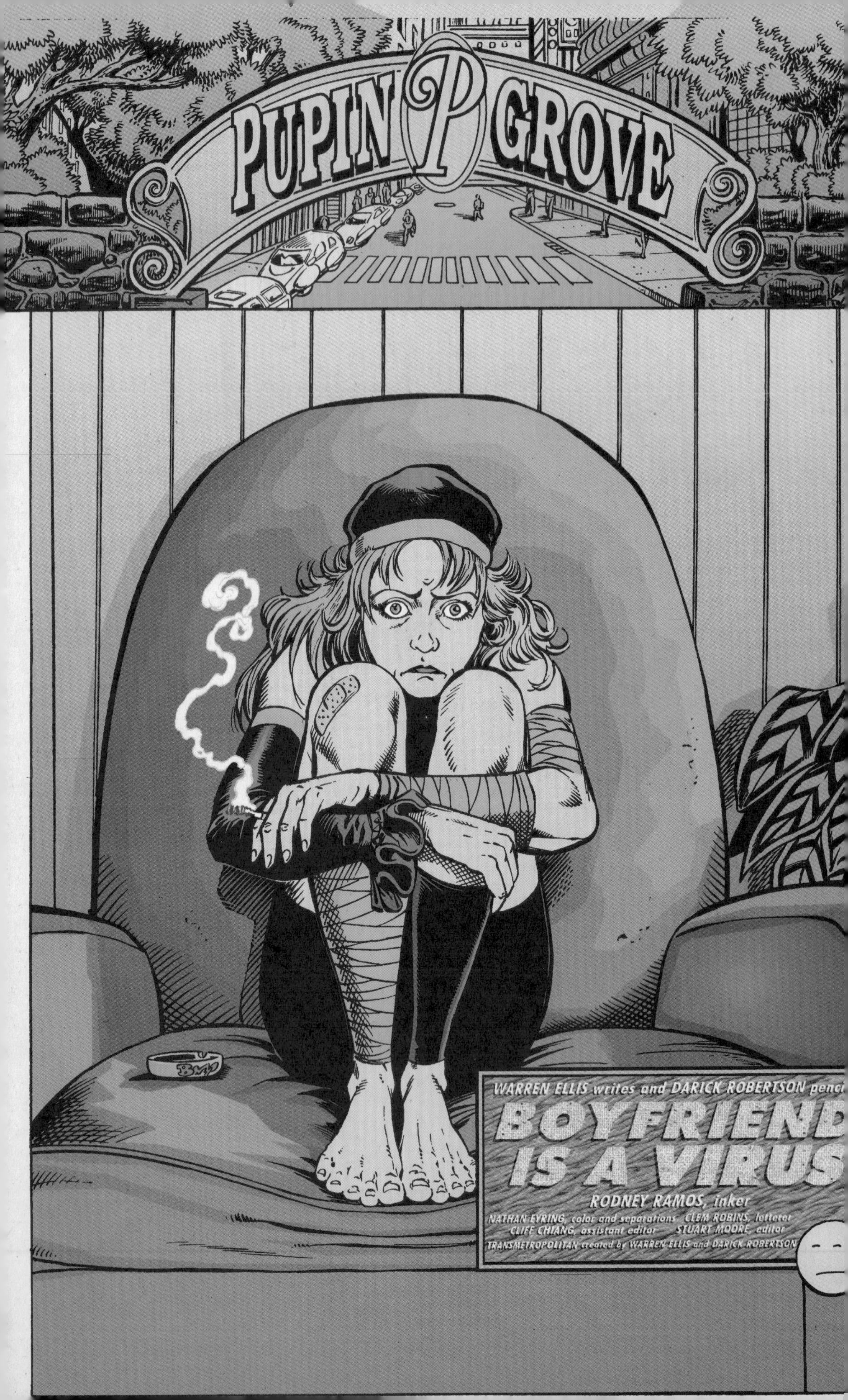
PUPIN P GROVE
WARREN ELLIS writes and DARICK ROBERTSON penci
BOYFRIEND IS A VIRUS
RODNEY RAMOS, inker
NATHAN EYRING, color and separations CLEM ROBINS, letterer
CLIFF CHIANG, assistant editor STUART MOORE, editor
TRANSMETROPOLITAN created by WARREN ELLIS and DARICK ROBERTSON

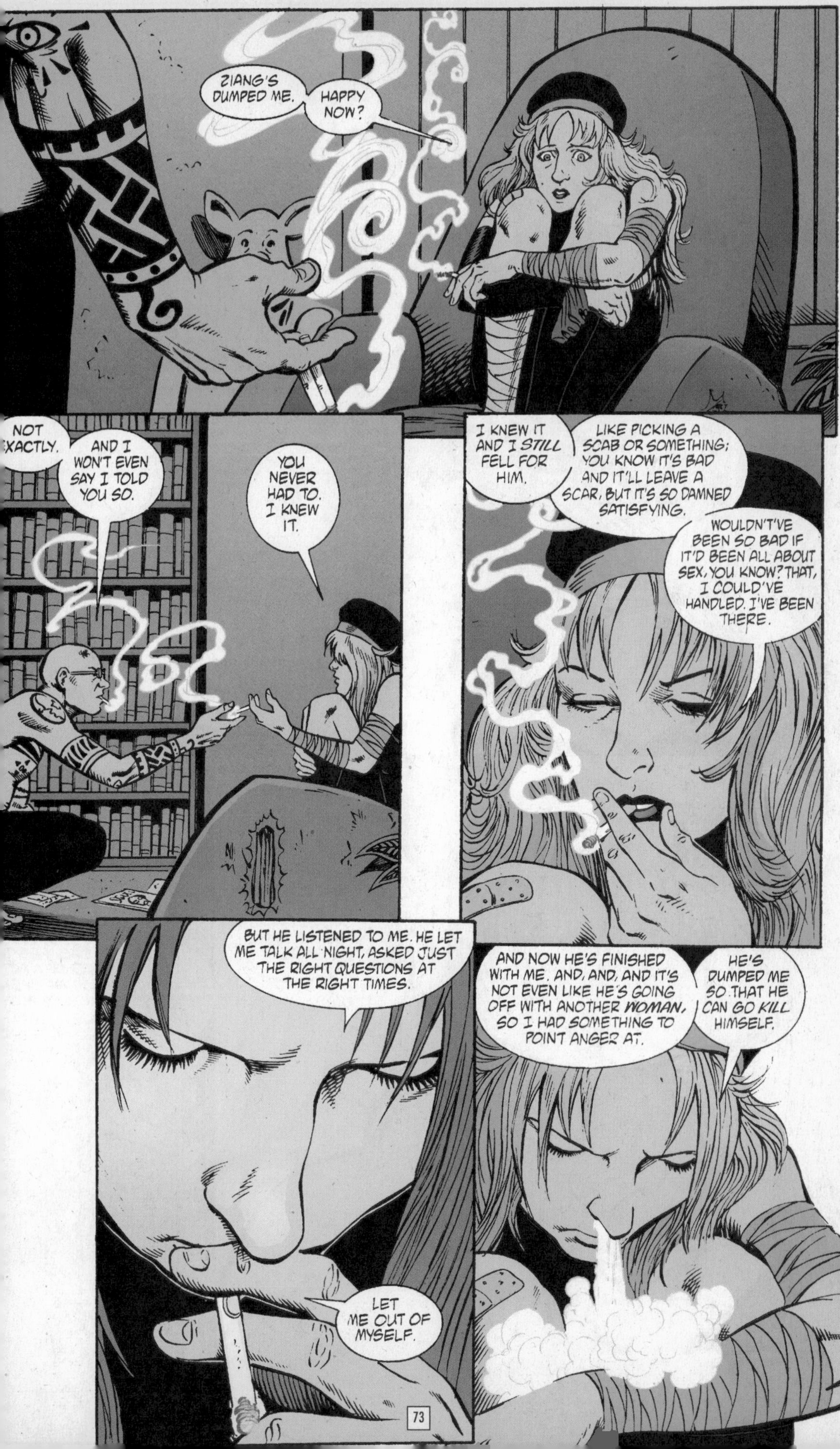
ZIANG'S DUMPED ME.
HAPPY NOW?
NOT EXACTLY.
AND I WON'T EVEN SAY I TOLD YOU SO.
YOU NEVER HAD TO. I KNEW IT.
I KNEW IT AND I STILL FELL FOR HIM.
LIKE PICKING A SCAB OR SOMETHING; YOU KNOW IT'S BAD AND IT'LL LEAVE A SCAR, BUT IT'S SO DAMNED SATISFYING.
WOULDN'T'VE BEEN SO BAD IF IT'D BEEN ALL ABOUT SEX, YOU KNOW? THAT, I COULD'VE HANDLED. I'VE BEEN THERE.
BUT HE LISTENED TO ME. HE LET ME TALK ALL NIGHT, ASKED JUST THE RIGHT QUESTIONS AT THE RIGHT TIMES.
LET ME OUT OF MYSELF.
AND NOW HE'S FINISHED WITH ME. AND, AND, AND IT'S NOT EVEN LIKE HE'S GOING OFF WITH ANOTHER WOMAN, SO I HAD SOMETHING TO POINT ANGER AT.
HE'S DUMPED ME SO THAT HE CAN GO KILL HIMSELF.

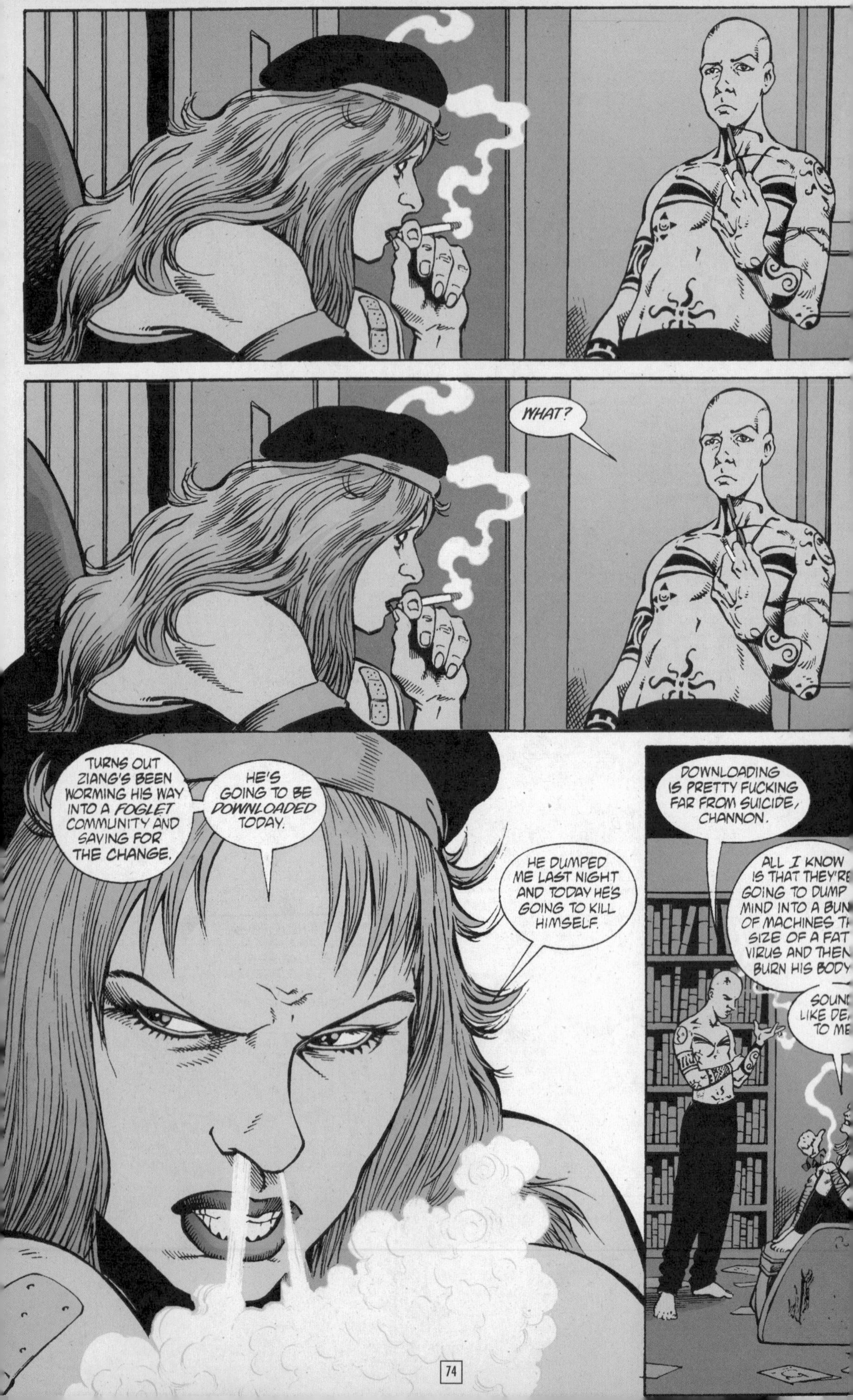
WHAT?
TURNS OUT ZIANG'S BEEN WORMING HIS WAY INTO A *FOGLET* COMMUNITY AND SAVING FOR THE CHANGE.
HE'S GOING TO BE *DOWNLOADED* TODAY.
HE DUMPED ME LAST NIGHT AND TODAY HE'S GOING TO KILL HIMSELF.
DOWNLOADING IS PRETTY FUCKING FAR FROM SUICIDE, CHANNON.
ALL *I* KNOW IS THAT THEY'R
GOING TO DUMP
MIND INTO A BUN
OF MACHINES T
SIZE OF A FAT
VIRUS AND THEN
BURN HIS BODY
SOUN
LIKE DE
TO ME

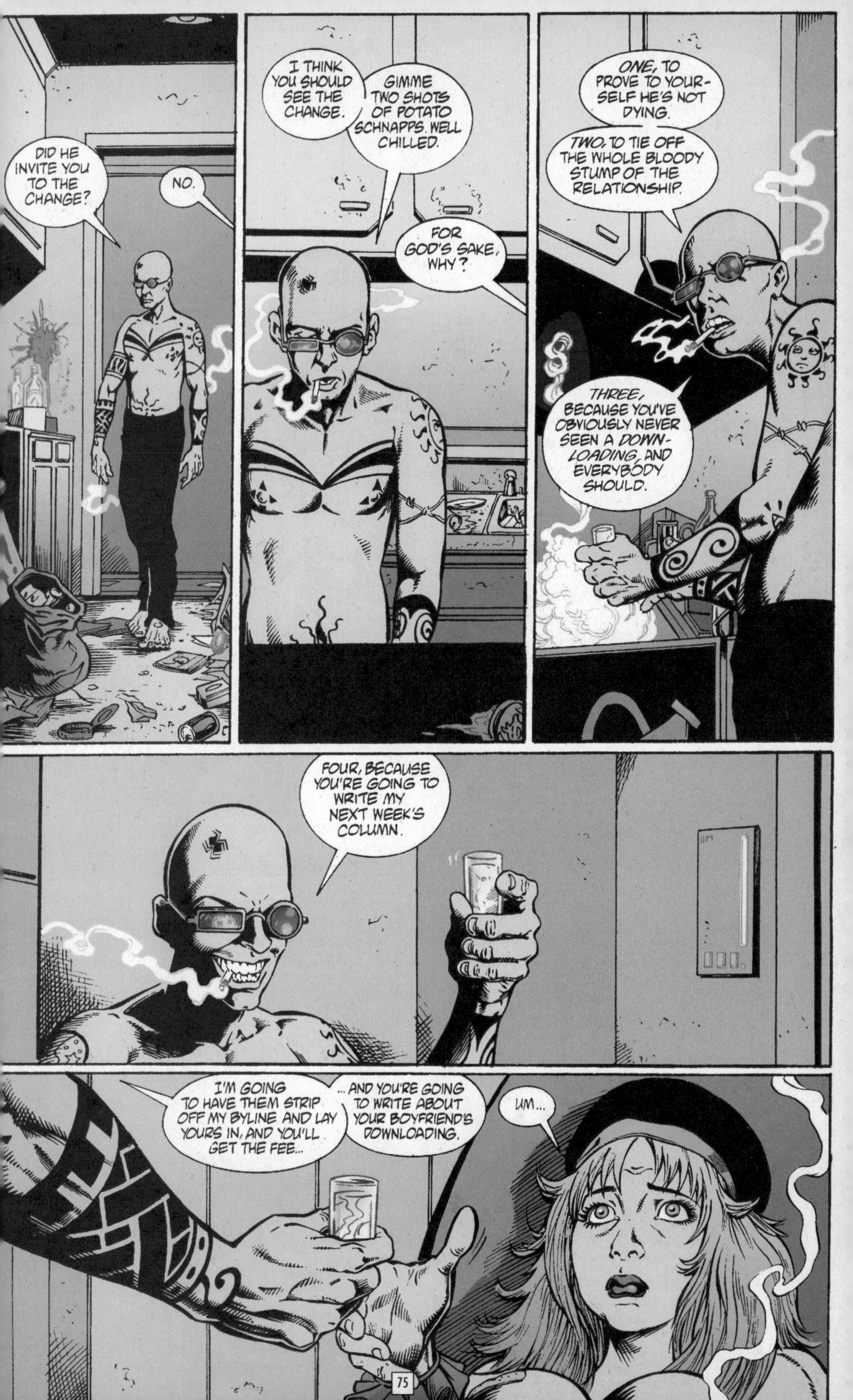
DID HE INVITE YOU TO THE CHANGE?
NO.
I THINK YOU SHOULD SEE THE CHANGE.
GIMME TWO SHOTS OF POTATO SCHNAPPS. WELL CHILLED.
FOR GOD'S SAKE, WHY?
ONE, TO PROVE TO YOURSELF HE'S NOT DYING.
TWO, TO TIE OFF THE WHOLE BLOODY STUMP OF THE RELATIONSHIP.
THREE, BECAUSE YOU'VE OBVIOUSLY NEVER SEEN A DOWNLOADING, AND EVERYBODY SHOULD.
FOUR, BECAUSE YOU'RE GOING TO WRITE MY NEXT WEEK'S COLUMN.
I'M GOING TO HAVE THEM STRIP OFF MY BYLINE AND LAY YOURS IN, AND YOU'LL GET THE FEE...
...AND YOU'RE GOING TO WRITE ABOUT YOUR BOYFRIEND'S DOWNLOADING.
UM...

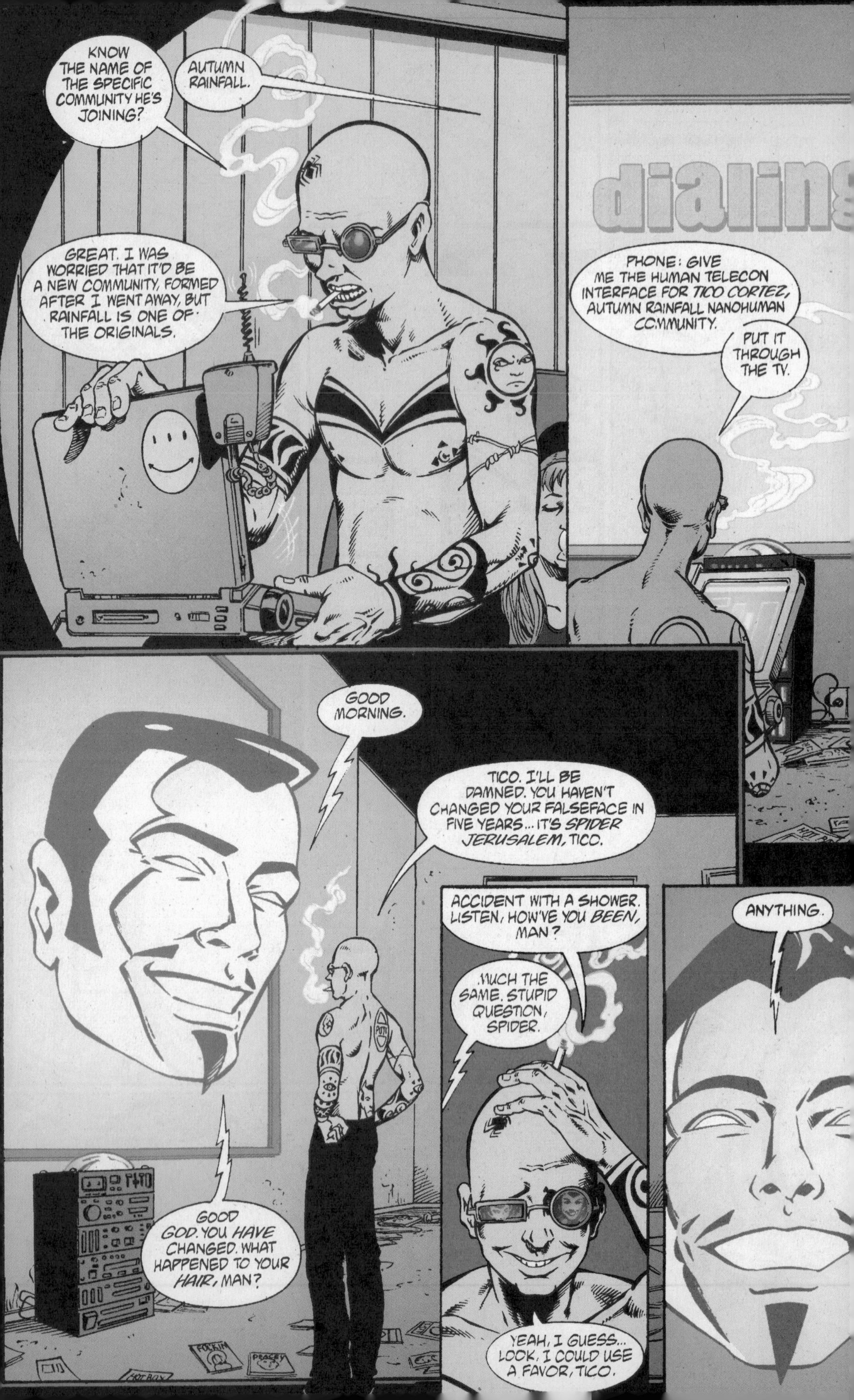
KNOW THE NAME OF THE SPECIFIC COMMUNITY HE'S JOINING?
AUTUMN RAINFALL.
GREAT. I WAS WORRIED THAT IT'D BE A NEW COMMUNITY, FORMED AFTER I WENT AWAY, BUT RAINFALL IS ONE OF THE ORIGINALS.
dialing
PHONE: GIVE ME THE HUMAN TELECON INTERFACE FOR TICO CORTEZ, AUTUMN RAINFALL NANOHUMAN COMMUNITY.
PUT IT THROUGH THE TV.
GOOD MORNING.
TICO. I'LL BE DAMNED. YOU HAVEN'T CHANGED YOUR FALSEFACE IN FIVE YEARS... IT'S SPIDER JERUSALEM, TICO.
GOOD GOD. YOU HAVE CHANGED. WHAT HAPPENED TO YOUR HAIR, MAN?
ACCIDENT WITH A SHOWER. LISTEN, HOW'VE YOU BEEN, MAN?
MUCH THE SAME. STUPID QUESTION, SPIDER.
YEAH, I GUESS... LOOK, I COULD USE A FAVOR, TICO.
ANYTHING.

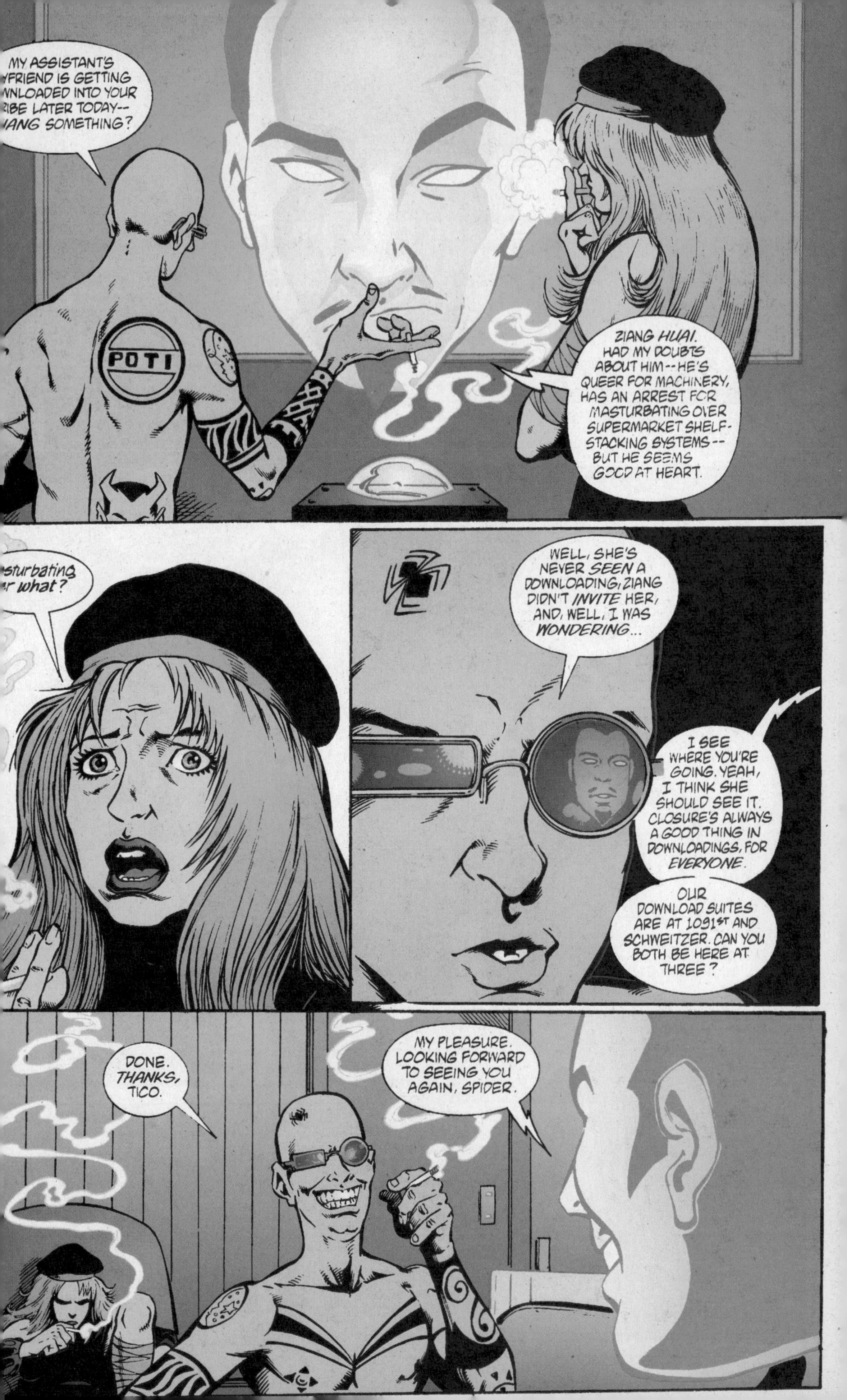

MY ASSISTANT'S
YFRIEND IS GETTING
WNLOADED INTO YOUR
RIBE LATER TODAY--
IANG SOMETHING?
ZIANG HUAI. HAD MY DOUBTS ABOUT HIM--HE'S QUEER FOR MACHINERY, HAS AN ARREST FOR MASTURBATING OVER SUPERMARKET SHELF-STACKING SYSTEMS--BUT HE SEEMS GOOD AT HEART.
POTI
sturbating
r what?
WELL, SHE'S NEVER SEEN A DOWNLOADING, ZIANG DIDN'T INVITE HER, AND, WELL, I WAS WONDERING...
I SEE WHERE YOU'RE GOING. YEAH, I THINK SHE SHOULD SEE IT. CLOSURE'S ALWAYS A GOOD THING IN DOWNLOADINGS, FOR EVERYONE.
OUR DOWNLOAD SUITES ARE AT 1091ST AND SCHWEITZER. CAN YOU BOTH BE HERE AT THREE?
DONE. THANKS, TICO.
MY PLEASURE. LOOKING FORWARD TO SEEING YOU AGAIN, SPIDER.

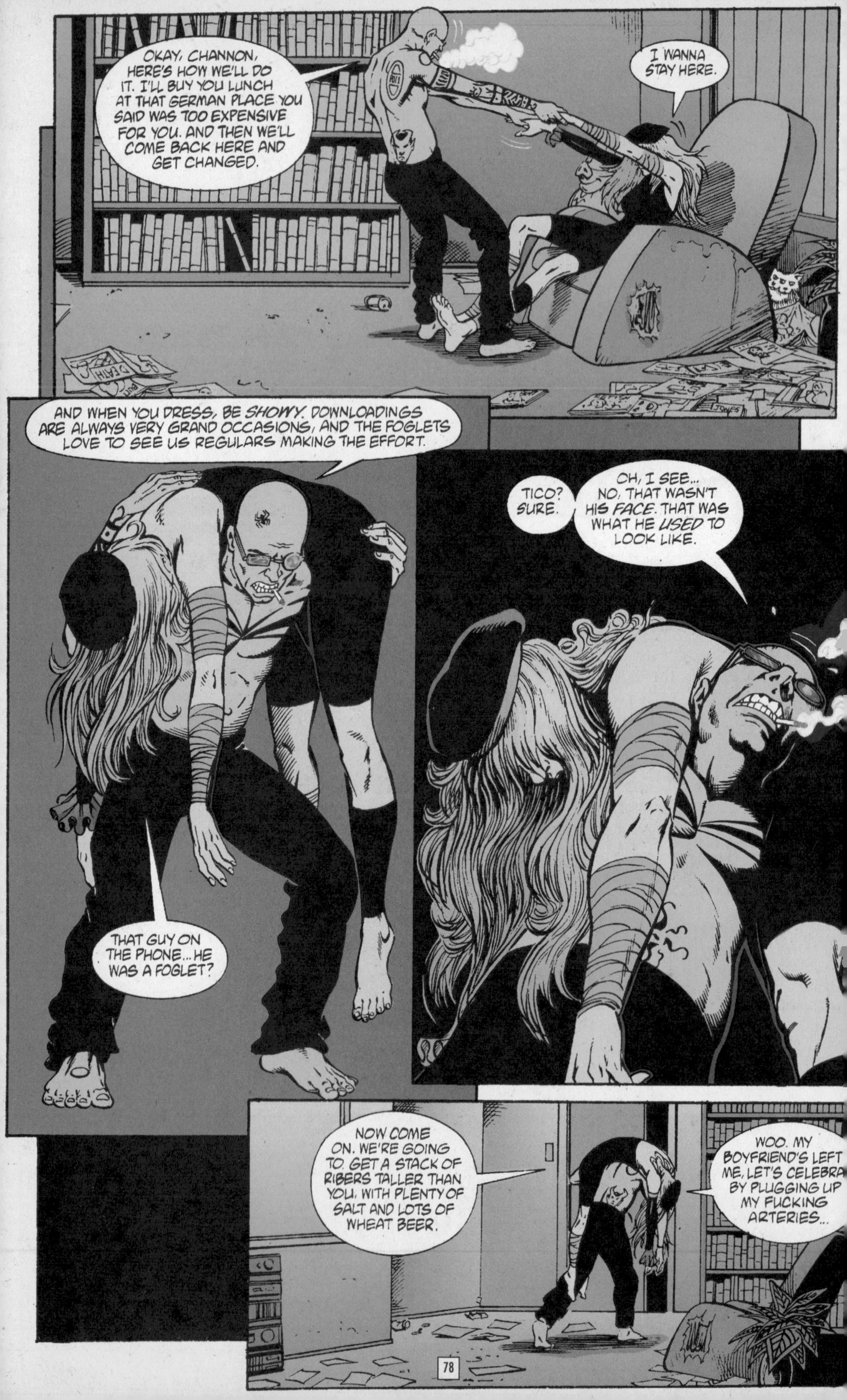
OKAY, CHANNON, HERE'S HOW WE'LL DO IT. I'LL BUY YOU LUNCH AT THAT GERMAN PLACE YOU SAID WAS TOO EXPENSIVE FOR YOU. AND THEN WE'LL COME BACK HERE AND GET CHANGED.
I WANNA STAY HERE.
AND WHEN YOU DRESS, BE SHOWY. DOWNLOADINGS ARE ALWAYS VERY GRAND OCCASIONS, AND THE FOGLETS LOVE TO SEE US REGULARS MAKING THE EFFORT.
THAT GUY ON THE PHONE... HE WAS A FOGLET?
TICO? SURE.
OH, I SEE... NO, THAT WASN'T HIS FACE. THAT WAS WHAT HE USED TO LOOK LIKE.
NOW COME ON. WE'RE GOING TO. GET A STACK OF RIBERS TALLER THAN YOU. WITH PLENTY OF SALT AND LOTS OF WHEAT BEER.
WOO. MY BOYFRIEND'S LEFT ME, LET'S CELEBRA BY PLUGGING UP MY FUCKING ARTERIES...

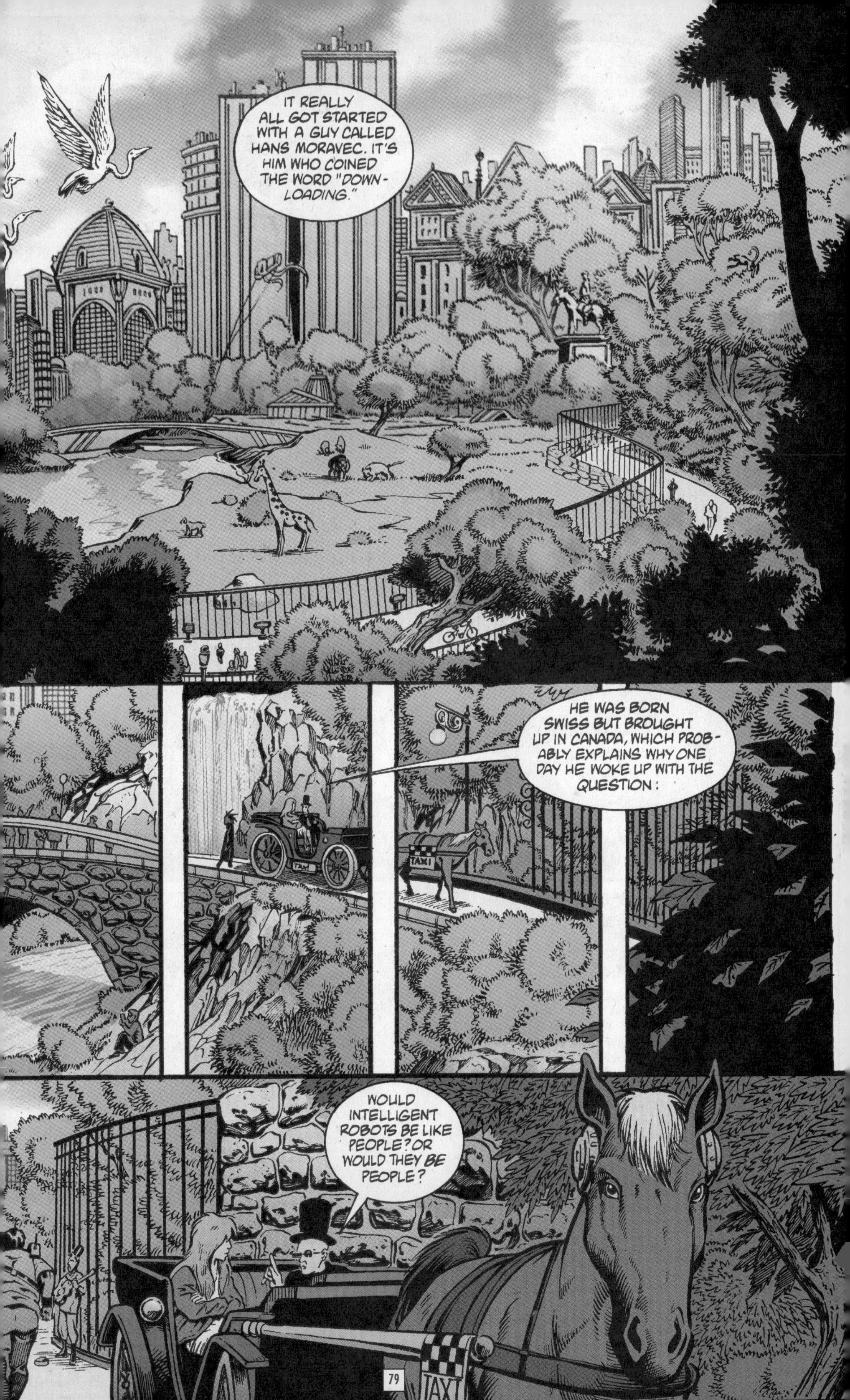
IT REALLY ALL GOT STARTED WITH A GUY CALLED HANS MORAVEC. IT'S HIM WHO COINED THE WORD "DOWN-LOADING."
TAXI
HE WAS BORN SWISS BUT BROUGHT UP IN CANADA, WHICH PROB-ABLY EXPLAINS WHY ONE DAY HE WOKE UP WITH THE QUESTION:
WOULD INTELLIGENT ROBOTS BE LIKE PEOPLE? OR WOULD THEY *BE* PEOPLE?
TAXI

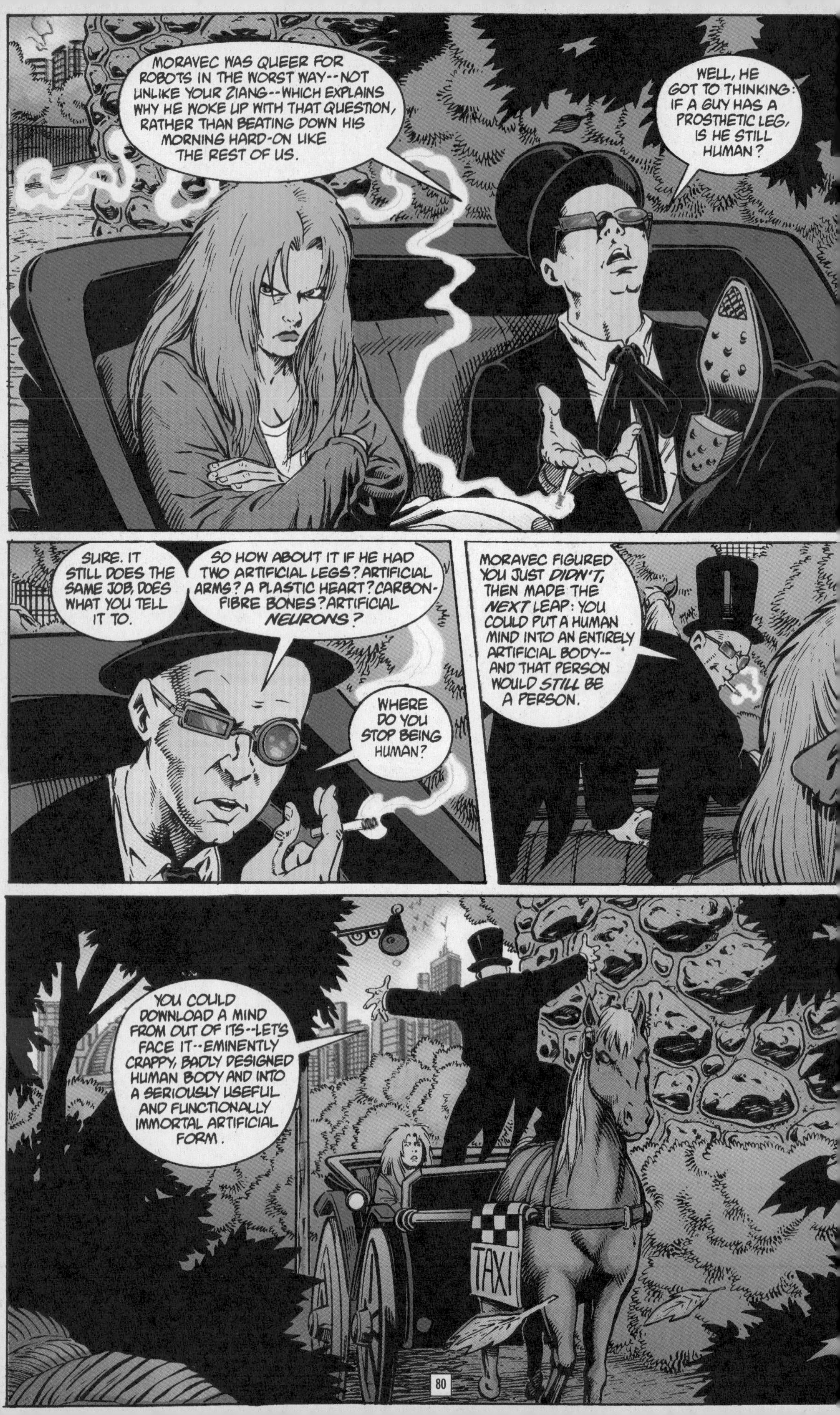
MORAVEC WAS QUEER FOR ROBOTS IN THE WORST WAY--NOT UNLIKE YOUR ZIANG--WHICH EXPLAINS WHY HE WOKE UP WITH THAT QUESTION, RATHER THAN BEATING DOWN HIS MORNING HARD-ON LIKE THE REST OF US.
WELL, HE GOT TO THINKING: IF A GUY HAS A PROSTHETIC LEG, IS HE STILL HUMAN?
SURE. IT STILL DOES THE SAME JOB, DOES WHAT YOU TELL IT TO.
SO HOW ABOUT IT IF HE HAD TWO ARTIFICIAL LEGS? ARTIFICIAL ARMS? A PLASTIC HEART? CARBON-FIBRE BONES? ARTIFICIAL *NEURONS*?
WHERE DO YOU STOP BEING HUMAN?
MORAVEC FIGURED YOU JUST *DIDN'T*, THEN MADE THE *NEXT* LEAP: YOU COULD PUT A HUMAN MIND INTO AN ENTIRELY ARTIFICIAL BODY--AND THAT PERSON WOULD *STILL* BE A PERSON.
YOU COULD DOWNLOAD A MIND FROM OUT OF ITS--LET'S FACE IT--EMINENTLY CRAPPY, BADLY DESIGNED HUMAN BODY AND INTO A SERIOUSLY USEFUL AND FUNCTIONALLY IMMORTAL ARTIFICIAL FORM.
TAXI

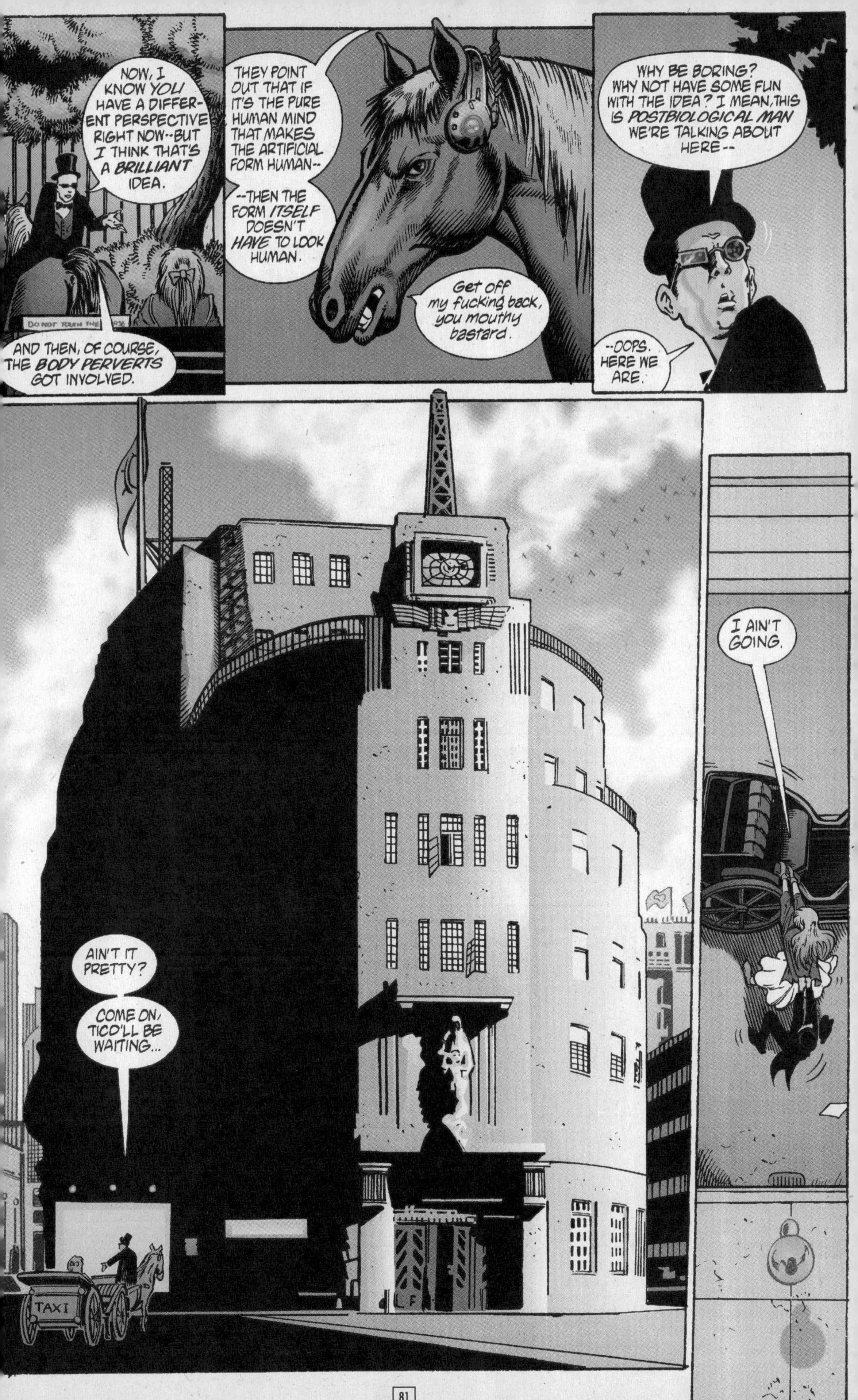
NOW, I KNOW YOU HAVE A DIFFERENT PERSPECTIVE RIGHT NOW--BUT I THINK THAT'S A BRILLIANT IDEA.
AND THEN, OF COURSE, THE BODY PERVERTS GOT INVOLVED.
THEY POINT OUT THAT IF IT'S THE PURE HUMAN MIND THAT MAKES THE ARTIFICIAL FORM HUMAN--
--THEN THE FORM ITSELF DOESN'T HAVE TO LOOK HUMAN.
Get off my fucking back, you mouthy bastard.
WHY BE BORING? WHY NOT HAVE SOME FUN WITH THE IDEA? I MEAN, THIS IS POSTBIOLOGICAL MAN WE'RE TALKING ABOUT HERE--
--OOPS. HERE WE ARE.
AIN'T IT PRETTY?
COME ON, TICO'LL BE WAITING...
TAXI
I AIN'T GOING.

TICO! TICO CORTEZ!

I ain't going I ain't going

SPIDER, YOU LOOK LIKE SOMEONE NAILED A BAT TO YOUR THROAT.

HEY, I MADE THE EFFORT. DISPLAY YOUR INVISIBLE ASS FOR MY ASSISTANT.

CHANNON, MEET MY OLD FRIEND TICO CORTEZ.

OH, GROW A FACE, YOU RUDE BASTARD.

SORRY. SPIDER NEVER GAVE ME YOUR NAME, MS...?

YARROW. CHANNON YARROW YOU'RE...UM...

...YOU LOOK LIKE A PILE OF DUST.

WHY, THANK YOU. YOU LOOK VERY PRETTY, TOO.

WASN'T A COMPLIMEN' CHANNON, TRE' HIM LIKE MEX' SMOG, OKAY

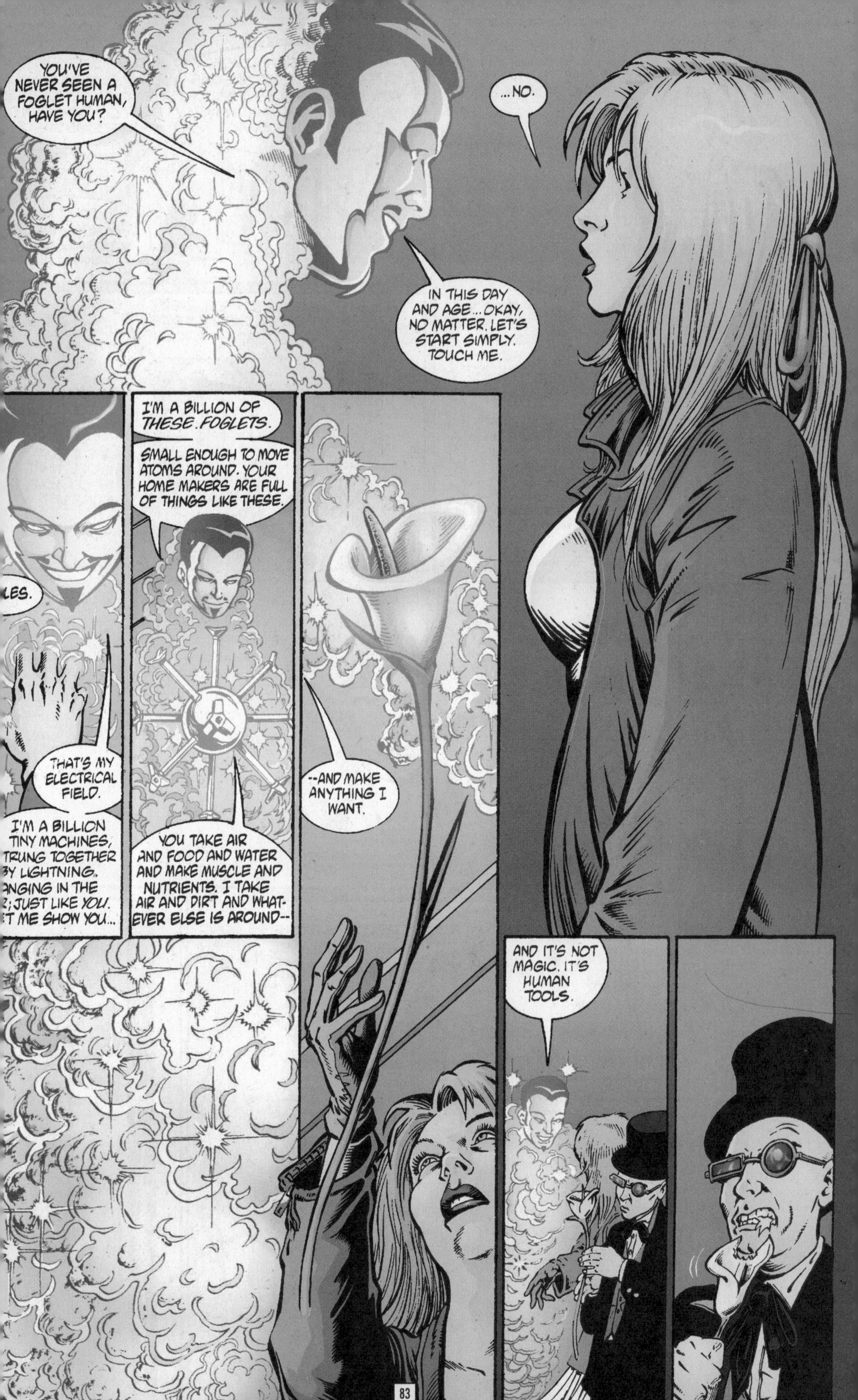
YOU'VE NEVER SEEN A FOGLET HUMAN, HAVE YOU?
...NO.
IN THIS DAY AND AGE...OKAY, NO MATTER. LET'S START SIMPLY. TOUCH ME.
LES.
THAT'S MY ELECTRICAL FIELD.
I'M A BILLION TINY MACHINES, TRUNG TOGETHER BY LIGHTNING. ANGING IN THE ; JUST LIKE YOU. T ME SHOW YOU...
I'M A BILLION OF THESE. FOGLETS.
SMALL ENOUGH TO MOVE ATOMS AROUND. YOUR HOME MAKERS ARE FULL OF THINGS LIKE THESE.
YOU TAKE AIR AND FOOD AND WATER AND MAKE MUSCLE AND NUTRIENTS. I TAKE AIR AND DIRT AND WHATEVER ELSE IS AROUND--
--AND MAKE ANYTHING I WANT.
AND IT'S NOT MAGIC. IT'S HUMAN TOOLS.

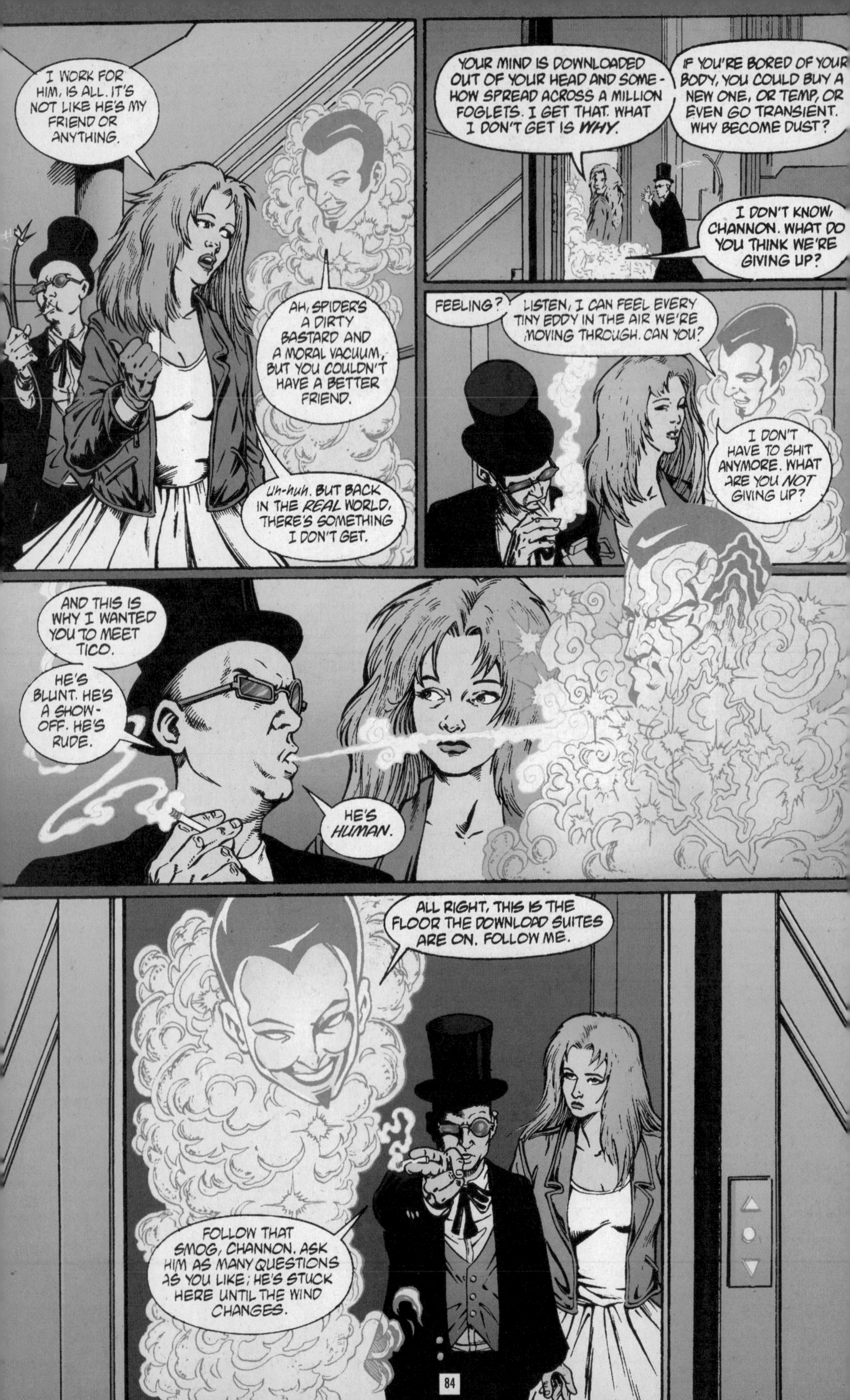
I WORK FOR HIM, IS ALL. IT'S NOT LIKE HE'S MY FRIEND OR ANYTHING.
AH, SPIDER'S A DIRTY BASTARD AND A MORAL VACUUM, BUT YOU COULDN'T HAVE A BETTER FRIEND.
Uh-huh. BUT BACK IN THE REAL WORLD, THERE'S SOMETHING I DON'T GET.
YOUR MIND IS DOWNLOADED OUT OF YOUR HEAD AND SOME-HOW SPREAD ACROSS A MILLION FOGLETS. I GET THAT. WHAT I DON'T GET IS WHY.
IF YOU'RE BORED OF YOUR BODY, YOU COULD BUY A NEW ONE, OR TEMP, OR EVEN GO TRANSIENT. WHY BECOME DUST?
I DON'T KNOW, CHANNON. WHAT DO YOU THINK WE'RE GIVING UP?
FEELING?
LISTEN, I CAN FEEL EVERY TINY EDDY IN THE AIR WE'RE MOVING THROUGH. CAN YOU?
I DON'T HAVE TO SHIT ANYMORE. WHAT ARE YOU NOT GIVING UP?
AND THIS IS WHY I WANTED YOU TO MEET TICO.
HE'S BLUNT. HE'S A SHOW-OFF. HE'S RUDE.
HE'S HUMAN.
ALL RIGHT, THIS IS THE FLOOR THE DOWNLOAD SUITES ARE ON. FOLLOW ME.
FOLLOW THAT SMOG, CHANNON. ASK HIM AS MANY QUESTIONS AS YOU LIKE; HE'S STUCK HERE UNTIL THE WIND CHANGES.

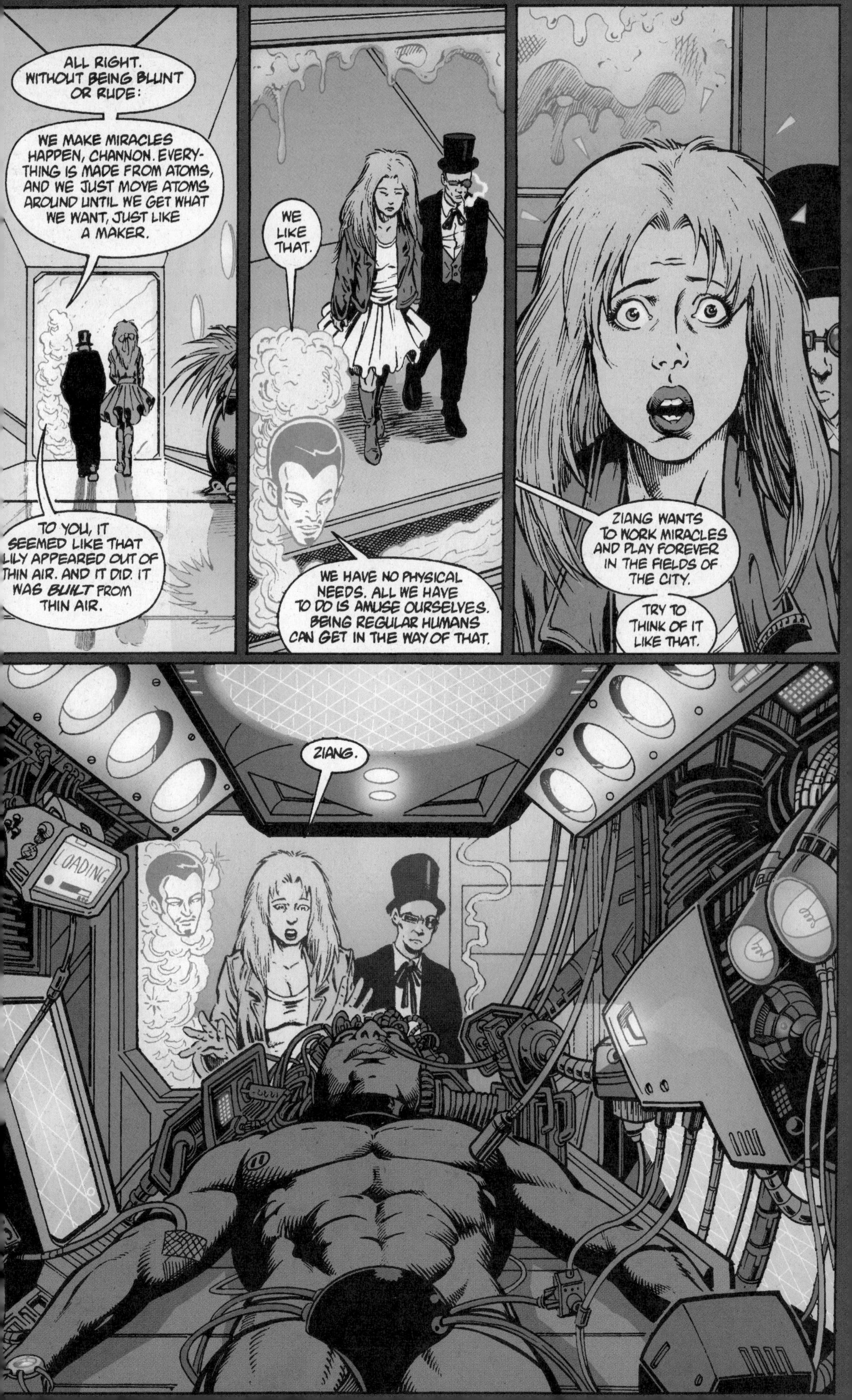
ALL RIGHT. WITHOUT BEING BLUNT OR RUDE:
WE MAKE MIRACLES HAPPEN, CHANNON. EVERY-THING IS MADE FROM ATOMS, AND WE JUST MOVE ATOMS AROUND UNTIL WE GET WHAT WE WANT, JUST LIKE A MAKER.
TO YOU, IT SEEMED LIKE THAT LILY APPEARED OUT OF THIN AIR. AND IT DID. IT WAS *BUILT* FROM THIN AIR.
WE LIKE THAT.
WE HAVE NO PHYSICAL NEEDS. ALL WE HAVE TO DO IS AMUSE OURSELVES. BEING REGULAR HUMANS CAN GET IN THE WAY OF THAT.
ZIANG WANTS TO WORK MIRACLES AND PLAY FOREVER IN THE FIELDS OF THE CITY.
TRY TO THINK OF IT LIKE THAT.
ZIANG.
LOADING

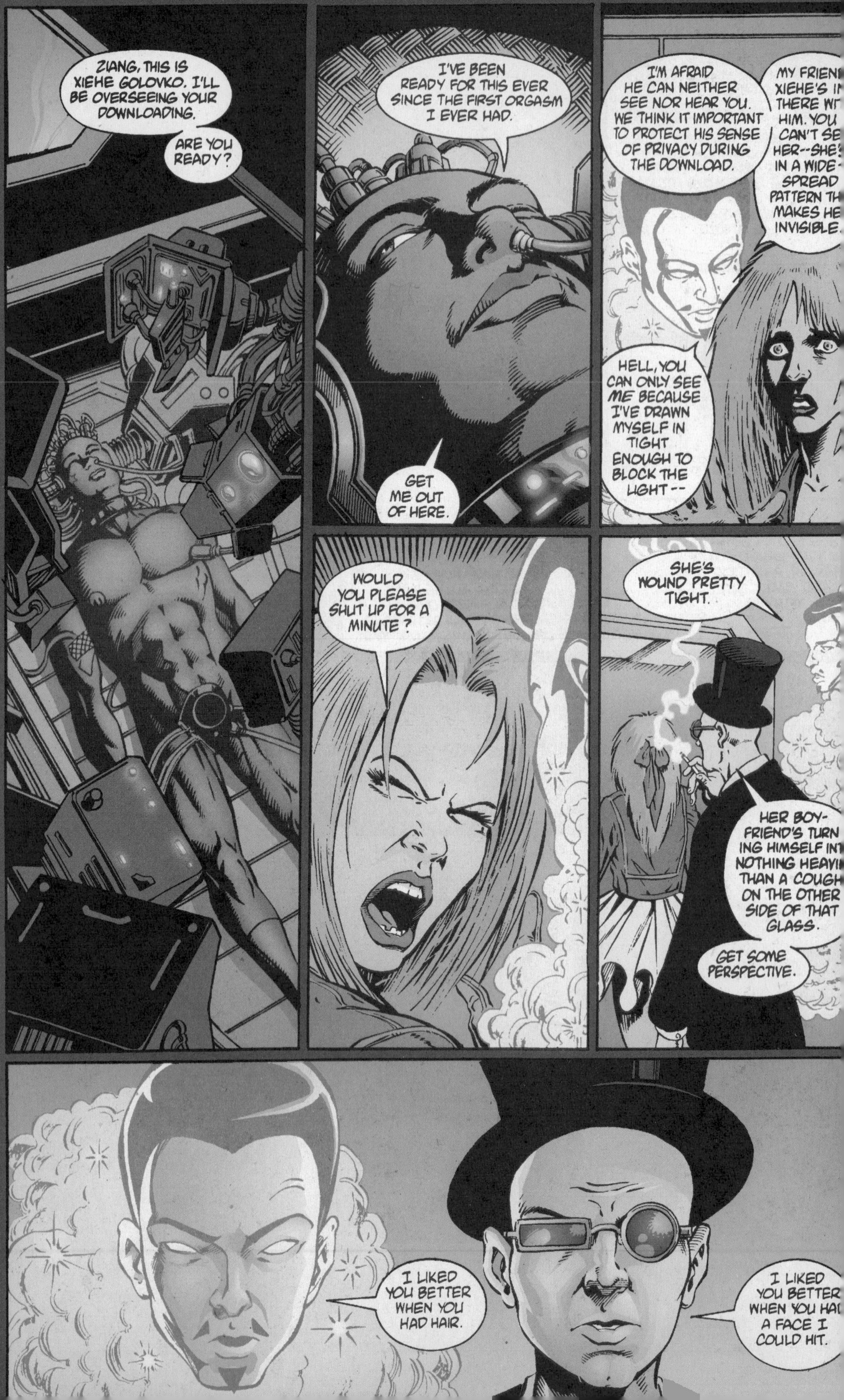

ZIANG, THIS IS XIEHE GOLOVKO. I'LL BE OVERSEEING YOUR DOWNLOADING.
ARE YOU READY?
I'VE BEEN READY FOR THIS EVER SINCE THE FIRST ORGASM I EVER HAD.
GET ME OUT OF HERE.
I'M AFRAID HE CAN NEITHER SEE NOR HEAR YOU. WE THINK IT IMPORTANT TO PROTECT HIS SENSE OF PRIVACY DURING THE DOWNLOAD.
MY FRIEN XIEHE'S I THERE WI HIM. YOU CAN'T SE HER--SHE' IN A WIDE- SPREAD PATTERN TH MAKES HE INVISIBLE.
HELL, YOU CAN ONLY SEE *ME* BECAUSE I'VE DRAWN MYSELF IN TIGHT ENOUGH TO BLOCK THE LIGHT--
WOULD YOU PLEASE SHUT UP FOR A MINUTE?
SHE'S WOUND PRETTY TIGHT.
HER BOY-FRIEND'S TURN ING HIMSELF INT NOTHING HEAVI THAN A COUGH ON THE OTHER SIDE OF THAT GLASS.
GET SOME PERSPECTIVE.
I LIKED YOU BETTER WHEN YOU HAD HAIR.
I LIKED YOU BETTER WHEN YOU HA A FACE I COULD HIT.

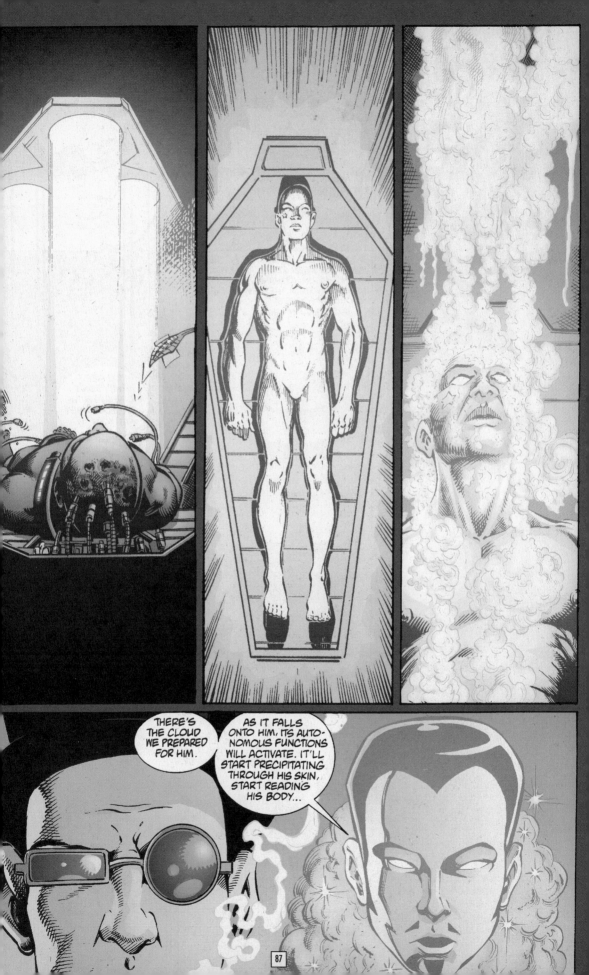

THERE'S THE CLOUD WE PREPARED FOR HIM.

AS IT FALLS ONTO HIM, ITS AUTONOMOUS FUNCTIONS WILL ACTIVATE. IT'LL START PRECIPITATING THROUGH HIS SKIN, START READING HIS BODY...

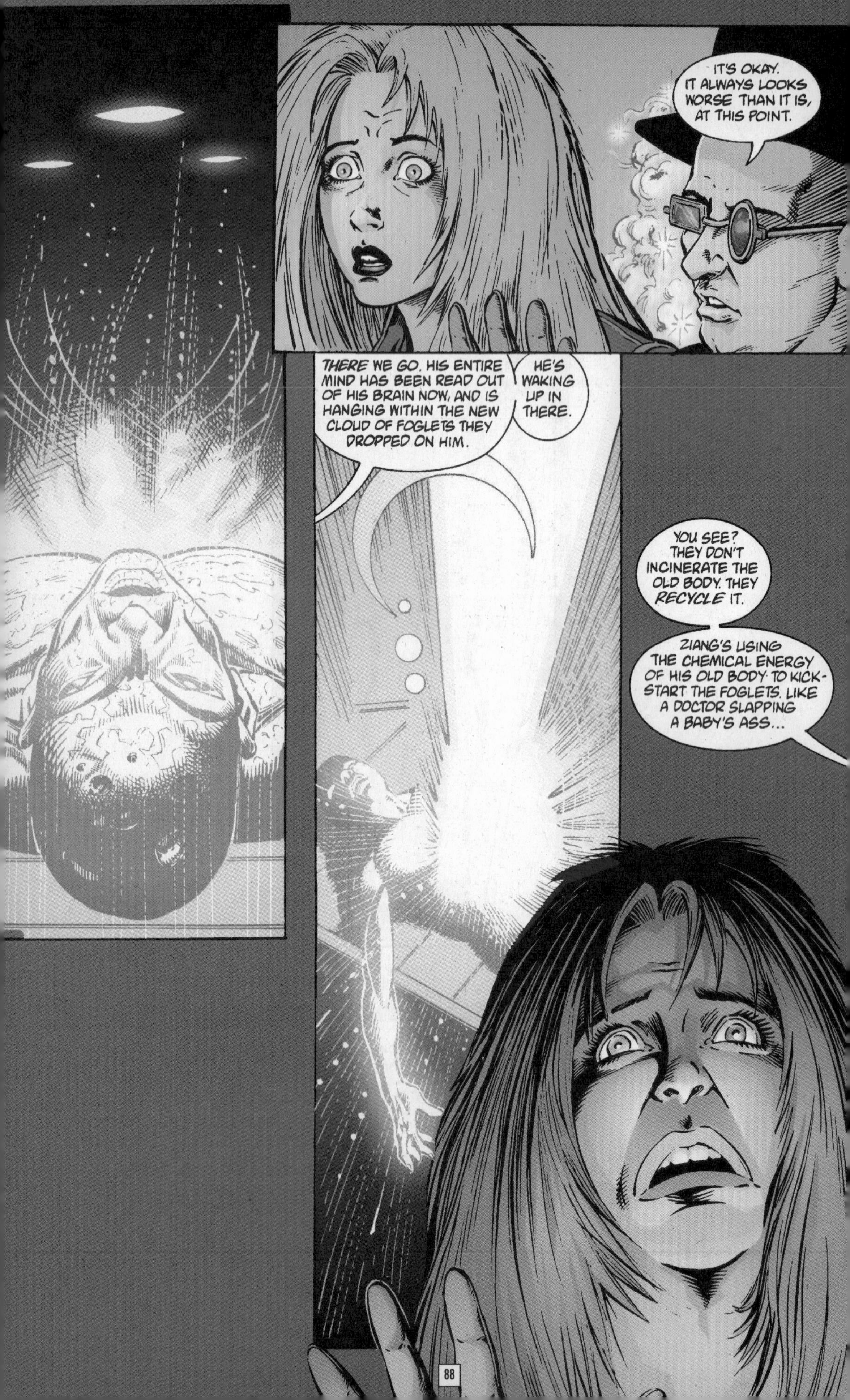
IT'S OKAY. IT ALWAYS LOOKS WORSE THAN IT IS, AT THIS POINT.
THERE WE GO. HIS ENTIRE MIND HAS BEEN READ OUT OF HIS BRAIN NOW, AND IS HANGING WITHIN THE NEW CLOUD OF FOGLETS THEY DROPPED ON HIM.
HE'S WAKING UP IN THERE.
YOU SEE? THEY DON'T INCINERATE THE OLD BODY. THEY RECYCLE IT.
ZIANG'S USING THE CHEMICAL ENERGY OF HIS OLD BODY TO KICK-START THE FOGLETS. LIKE A DOCTOR SLAPPING A BABY'S ASS...

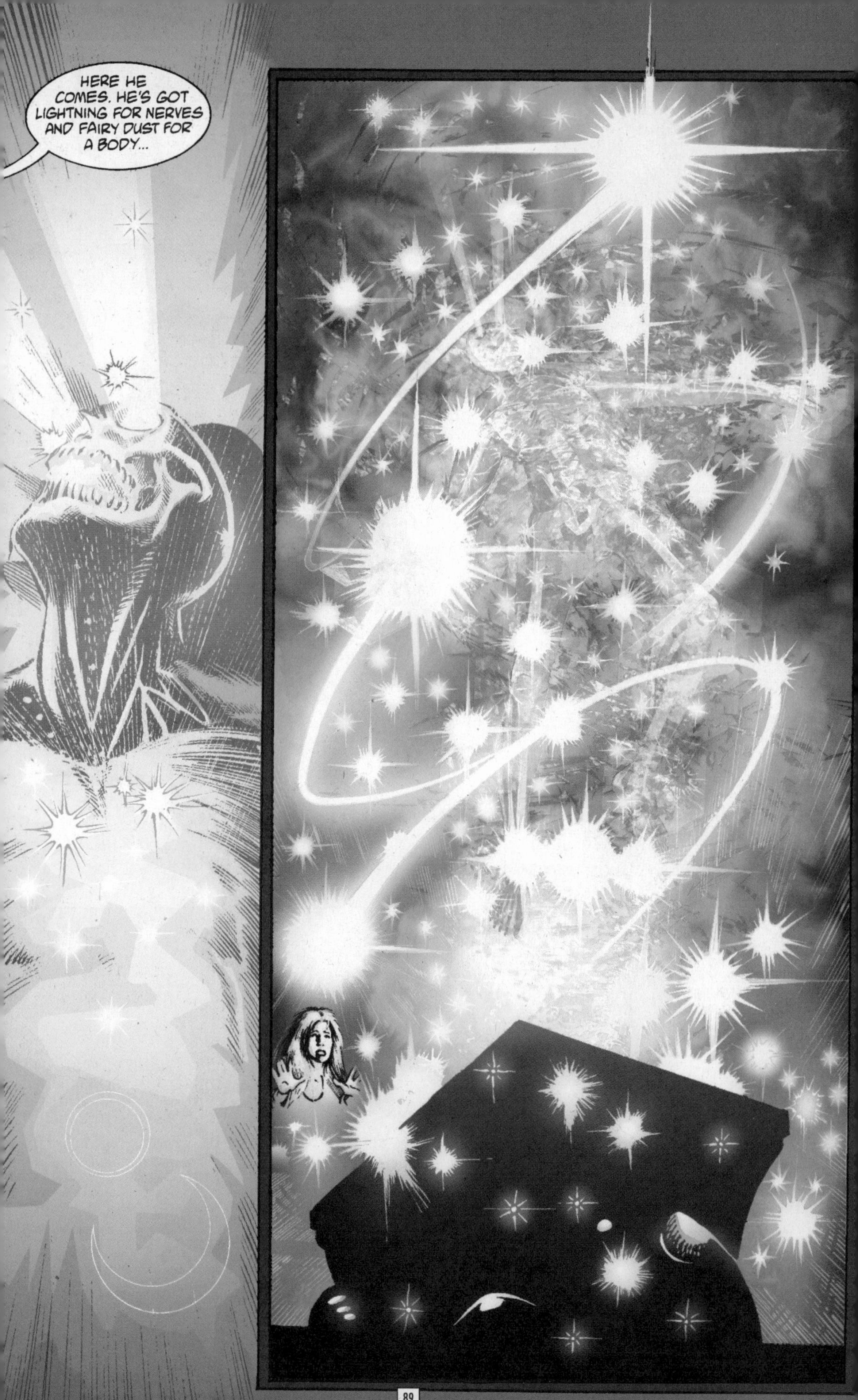
HERE HE COMES. HE'S GOT LIGHTNING FOR NERVES AND FAIRY DUST FOR A BODY...

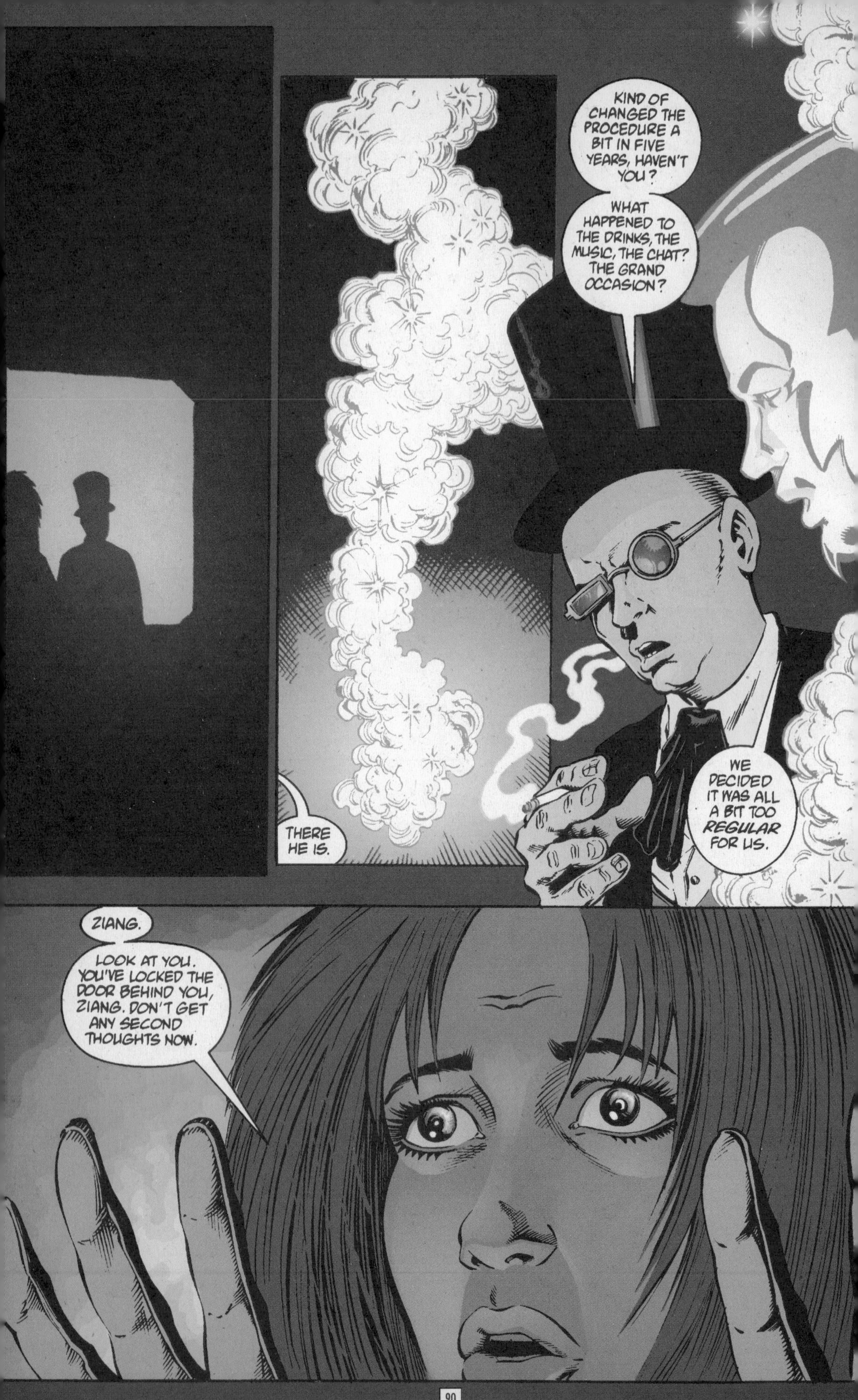
KIND OF CHANGED THE PROCEDURE A BIT IN FIVE YEARS, HAVEN'T YOU?
WHAT HAPPENED TO THE DRINKS, THE MUSIC, THE CHAT? THE GRAND OCCASION?
THERE HE IS.
WE DECIDED IT WAS ALL A BIT TOO REGULAR FOR US.
ZIANG.
LOOK AT YOU. YOU'VE LOCKED THE DOOR BEHIND YOU, ZIANG. DON'T GET ANY SECOND THOUGHTS NOW.

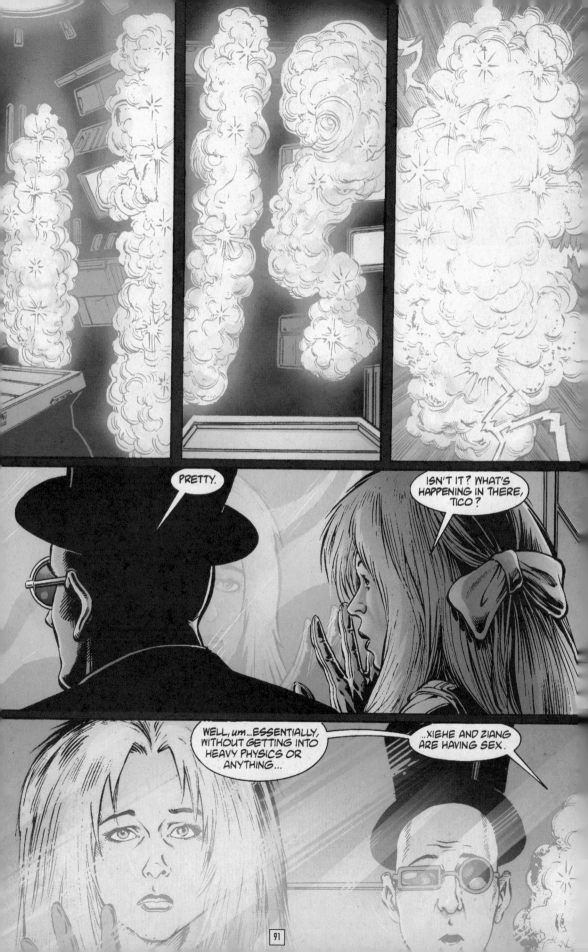

PRETTY.

ISN'T IT? WHAT'S HAPPENING IN THERE, TICO?

WELL, UM...ESSENTIALLY, WITHOUT GETTING INTO HEAVY PHYSICS OR ANYTHING...

...XIEHE AND ZIANG ARE HAVING SEX.

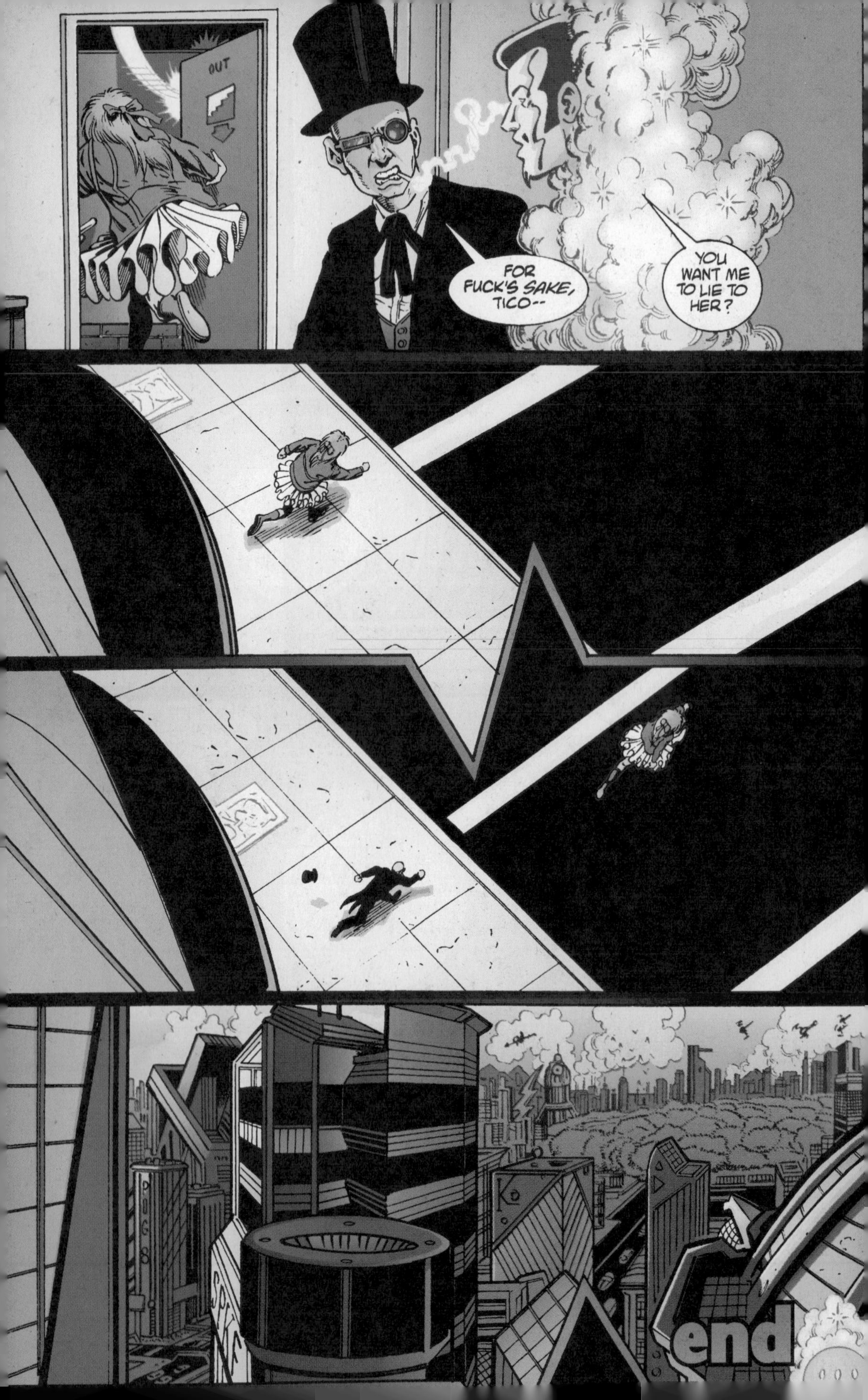
OUT
FOR FUCK'S SAKE, TICO--
YOU WANT ME TO LIE TO HER?
end

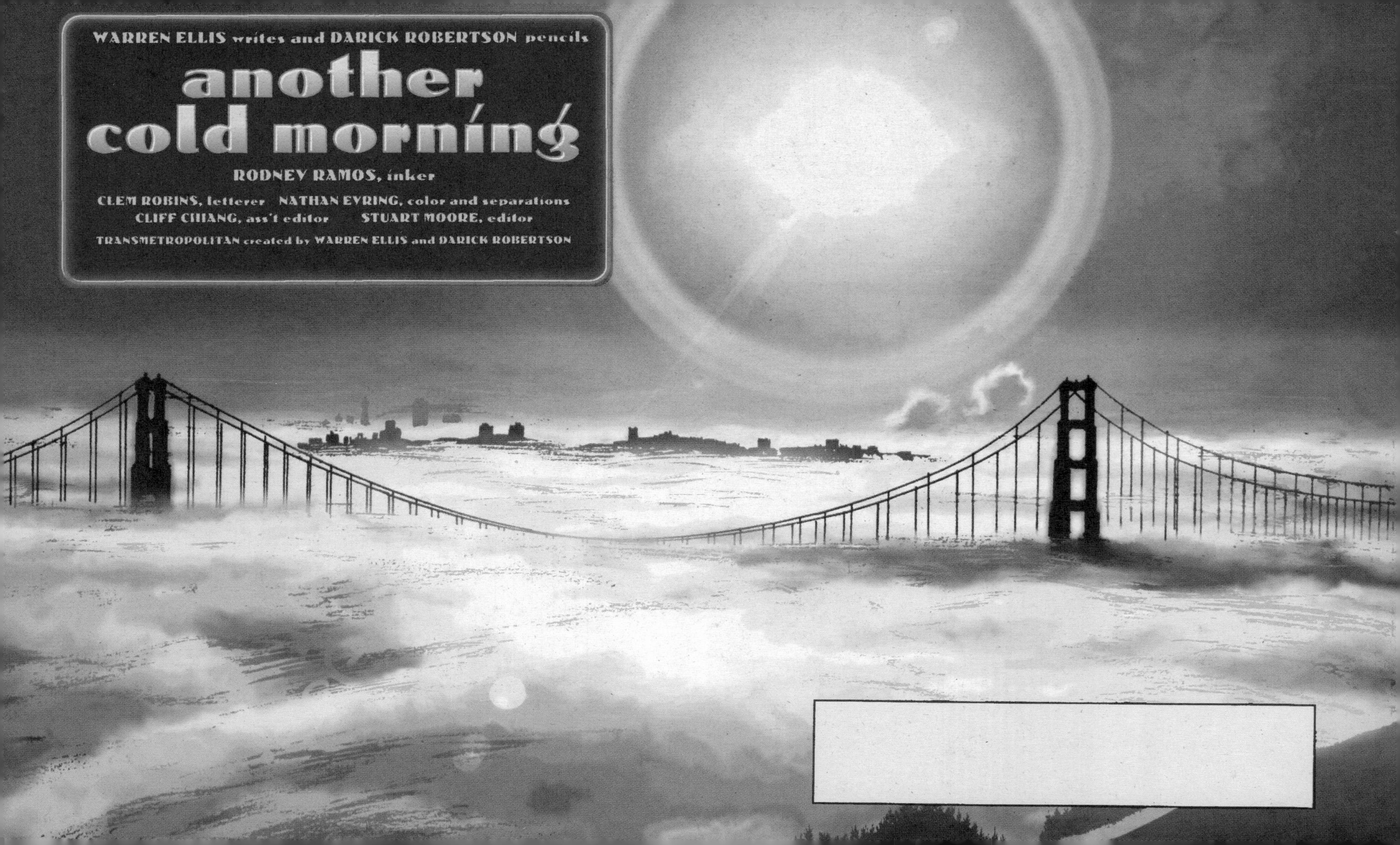
WARREN ELLIS writes and DARICK ROBERTSON pencils
another cold morning
RODNEY RAMOS, inker
CLEM ROBINS, letterer NATHAN EYRING, color and separations
CLIFF CHIANG, ass't editor STUART MOORE, editor
TRANSMETROPOLITAN created by WARREN ELLIS and DARICK ROBERTSON

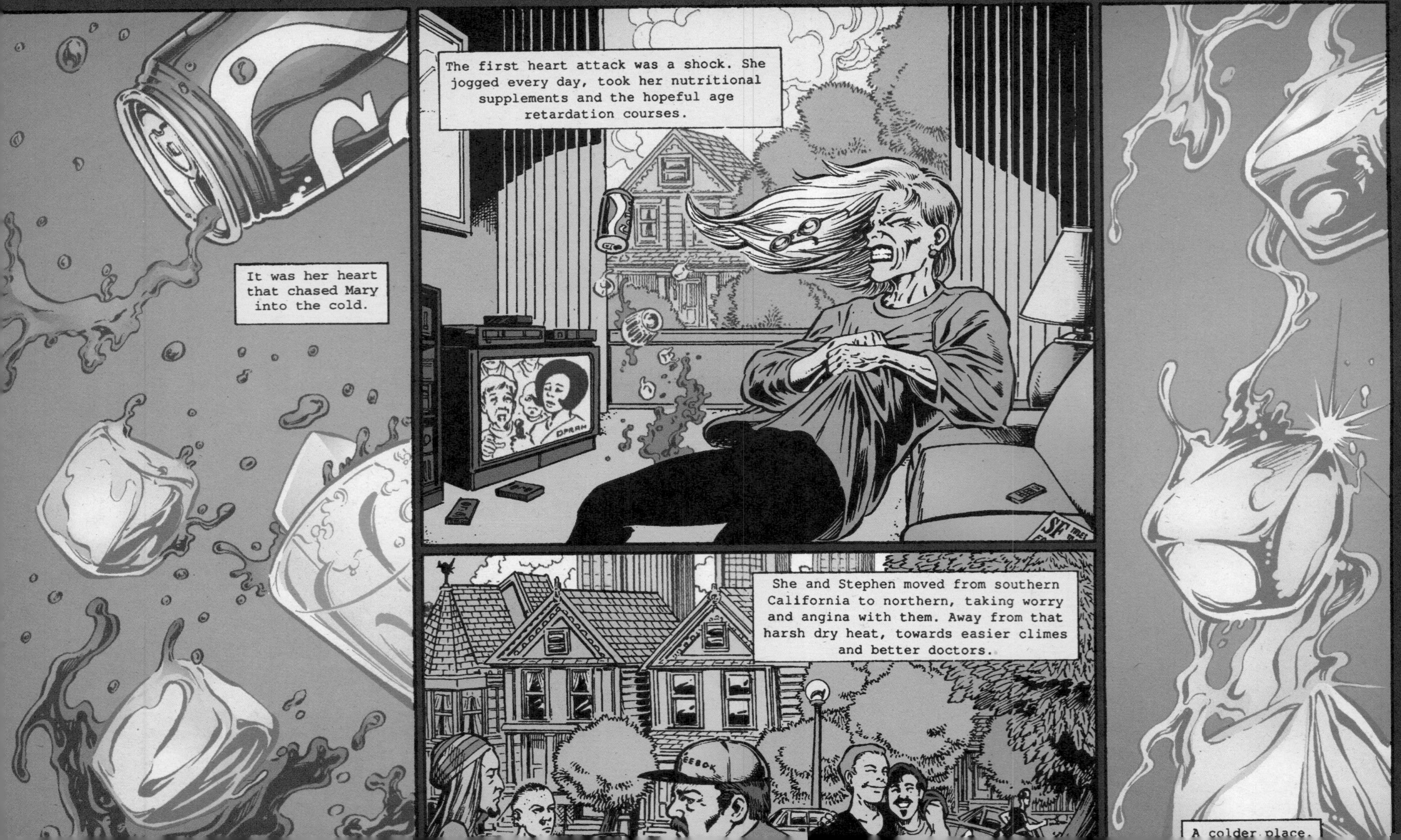
It was her heart that chased Mary into the cold.
The first heart attack was a shock. She jogged every day, took her nutritional supplements and the hopeful age retardation courses.
OPRAH
She and Stephen moved from southern California to northern, taking worry and angina with them. Away from that harsh dry heat, towards easier climes and better doctors.
A colder place.

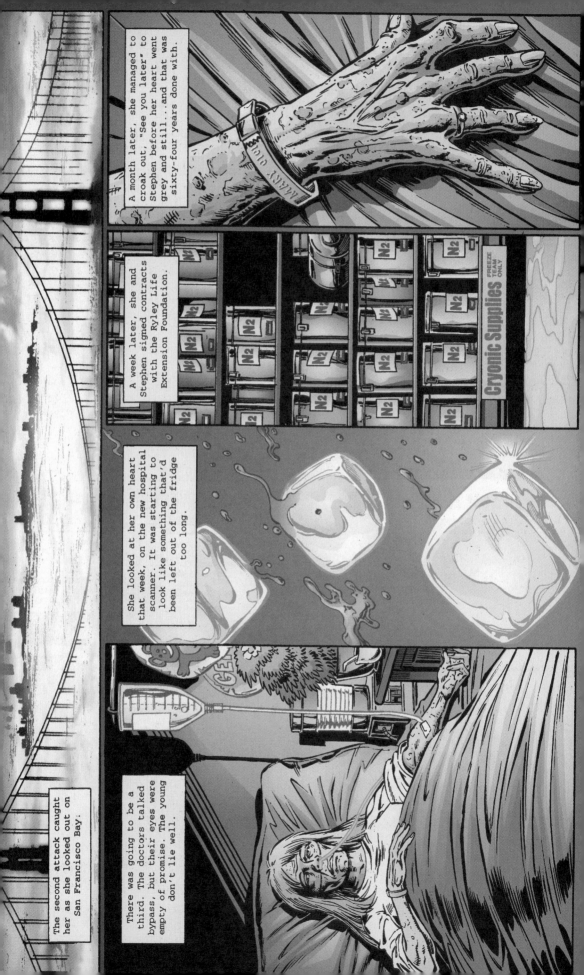

A month later, she managed to croak out, "See you later" to Stephen before her heart went grey and still...and that was sixty-four years done with.

A week later, she and Stephen signed contracts with the Ryley Life Extension Foundation.

Cryonic Supplies
FREEZE TEAM ONLY

She looked at her own heart that week, on the new hospital scanner. It was starting to look like something that'd been left out of the fridge too long.

The second attack caught her as she looked out on San Francisco Bay.

There was going to be a third. The doctors talked bypass, but their eyes were empty of promise. The young don't lie well.

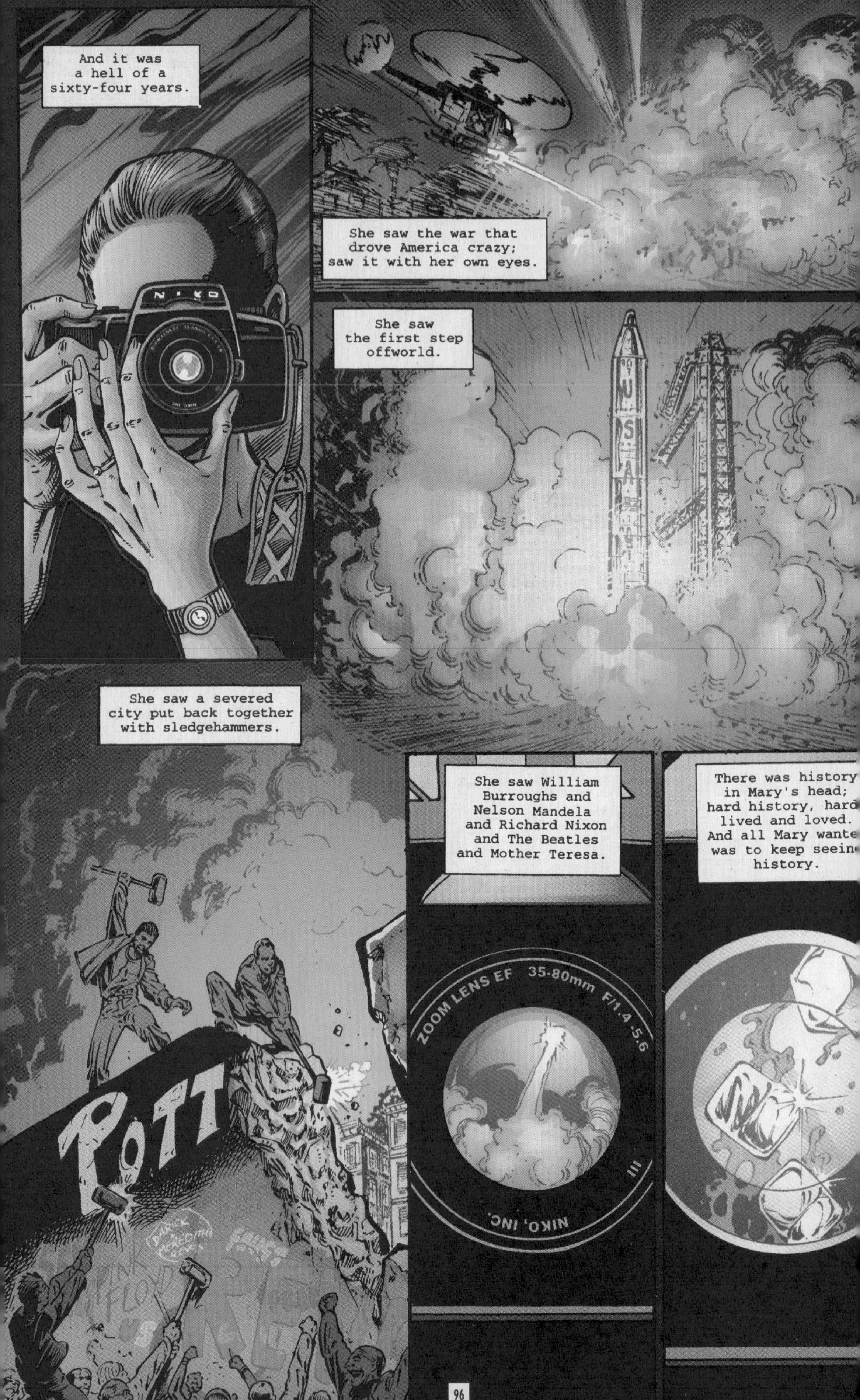
And it was a hell of a sixty-four years.
She saw the war that drove America crazy; saw it with her own eyes.
She saw the first step offworld.
She saw a severed city put back together with sledgehammers.
POTT
PINK FLOYD
She saw William Burroughs and Nelson Mandela and Richard Nixon and The Beatles and Mother Teresa.
ZOOM LENS EF 35-80mm F/1.4-5.6
NIKO, INC.
There was history in Mary's head; hard history, hard lived and loved. And all Mary wante was to keep seein history.

Her contract was for a neuro job. Neurological suspension.

The busy optimists at Ryley ever so gently hacked off Mary's head, wrapped it in fairly crude protective fabrics, and dropped it into a steel can full of liquid nitrogen, like throwing a coin into a wishing well.

Cryonic Supplies FREEZE TEAM ONLY

Mary's head was frozen at -186°C, and racked up with everyone else they were tossing down into time.

CRYO-FREEZE ▶ #239 DO NOT OPEN

-186°

Stephen died of some disgusting disease in Kuala Lumpur three years later, way the hell too far from Ryley.

He died hard, fists clenched, eyes shining with anger. An endless future with his beautiful wife had been stolen from him, and he died with hate and a sadness too big for his mouth to capture.

Stephen's last words were, "If you people ever washed your fucking toilet seats—"

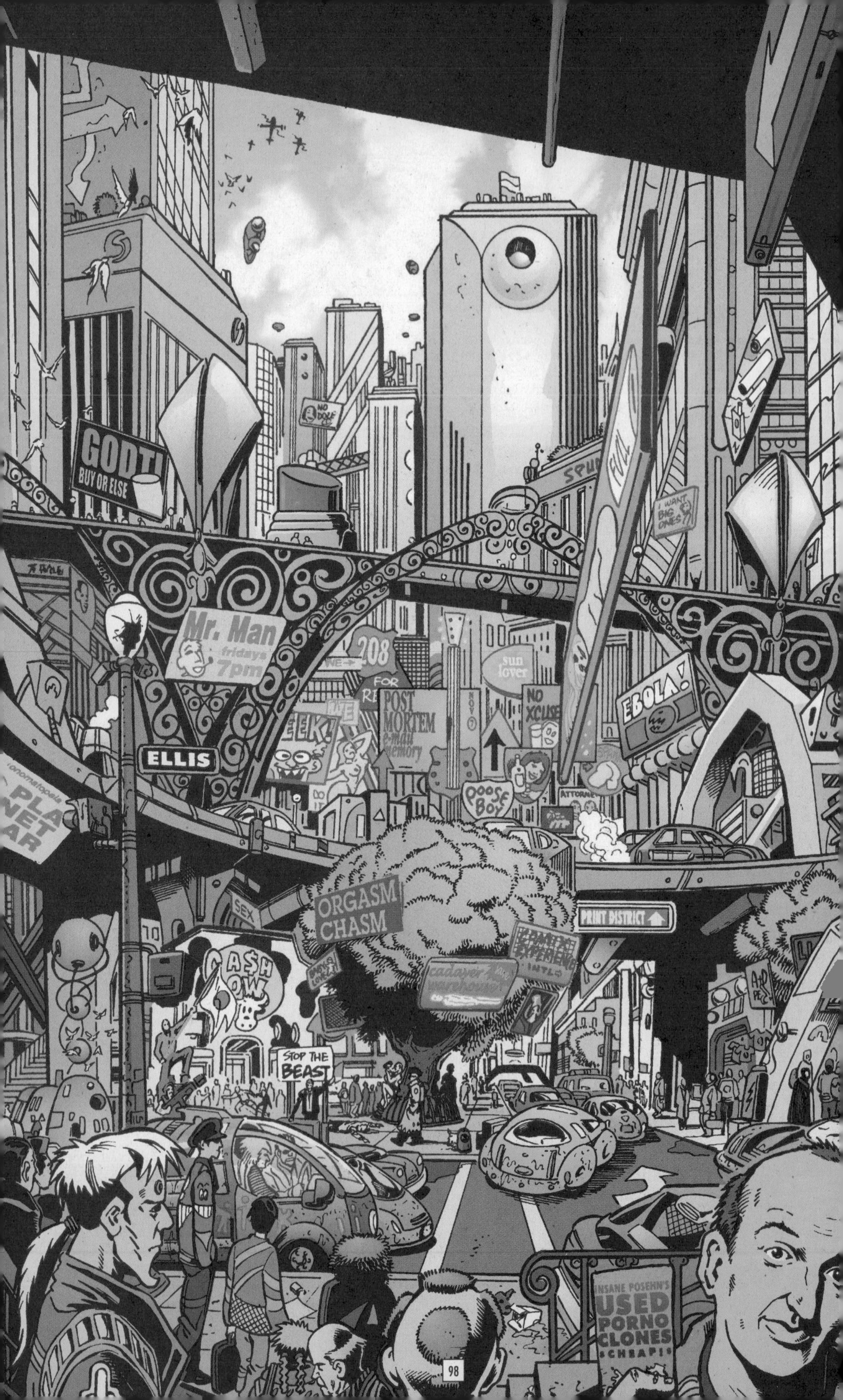
GODT!
BUY OR ELSE
Mr. Man
fridays
7pm
ELLIS
208
FOR
POST
MORTEM
e-mail
memory
EEK!
sun
lover
NO
XCUSE
EBOLA!
POOSE
BOY
I WANT
BIG
ONES
ORGASM
CHASM
PRINT DISTRICT
SEX
CA$H
COW
cadaver
warehouse
STOP THE
BEAST
INSANE POSEHN'S
USED
PORNO
CLONES
CHEAP!

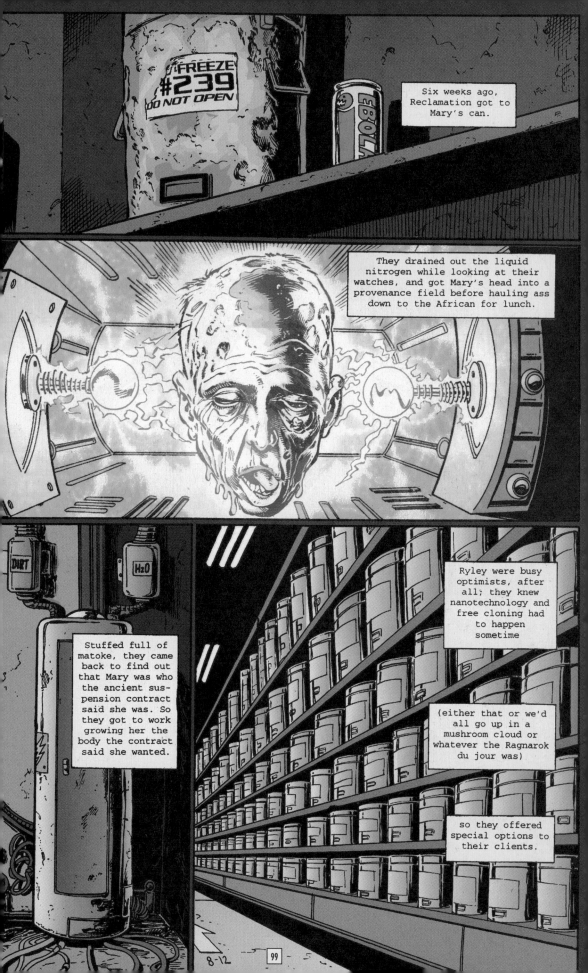

FREEZE
#239
DO NOT OPEN

EBOLA

Six weeks ago, Reclamation got to Mary's can.

They drained out the liquid nitrogen while looking at their watches, and got Mary's head into a provenance field before hauling ass down to the African for lunch.

DIRT

H₂O

Stuffed full of matoke, they came back to find out that Mary was who the ancient suspension contract said she was. So they got to work growing her the body the contract said she wanted.

Ryley were busy optimists, after all; they knew nanotechnology and free cloning had to happen sometime

(either that or we'd all go up in a mushroom cloud or whatever the Ragnarok du jour was)

so they offered special options to their clients.

8-12

99

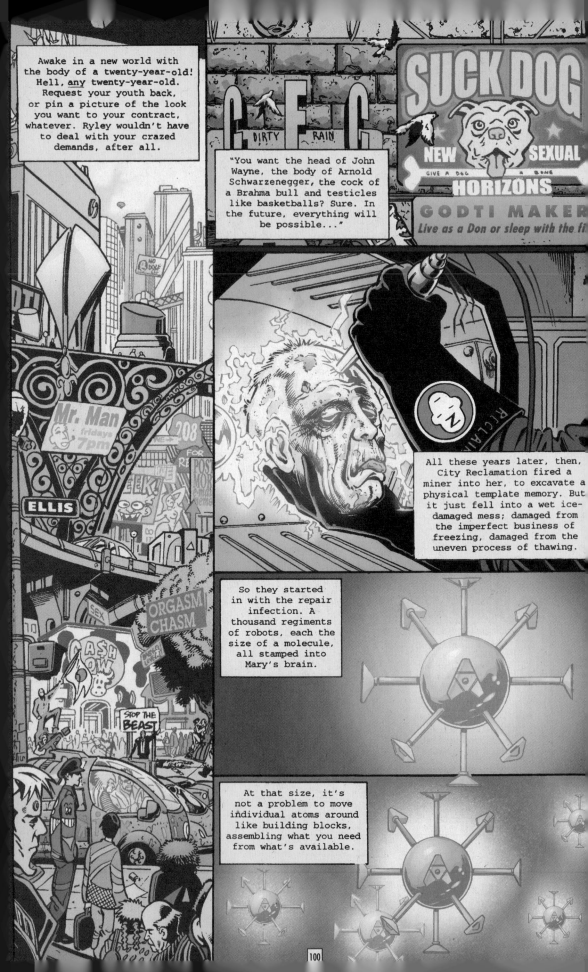

Awake in a new world with the body of a twenty-year-old! Hell, _any_ twenty-year-old. Request your youth back, or pin a picture of the look you want to your contract, whatever. Ryley wouldn't have to deal with your crazed demands, after all.

"You want the head of John Wayne, the body of Arnold Schwarzenegger, the cock of a Brahma bull and testicles like basketballs? Sure. In the future, everything will be possible..."

SUCK DOG
NEW SEXUAL
GIVE A DOG   A BONE
HORIZONS
GODTI MAKER
Live as a Don or sleep with the fi

C F C
DIRTY   RAIN

Mr. Man
fridays
7pm

208

ELLIS

ORGASM
CHASM

SEX

A$H
OW

STOP THE
BEAST

All these years later, then, City Reclamation fired a miner into her, to excavate a physical template memory. But it just fell into a wet ice-damaged mess; damaged from the imperfect business of freezing, damaged from the uneven process of thawing.

So they started in with the repair infection. A thousand regiments of robots, each the size of a molecule, all stamped into Mary's brain.

At that size, it's not a problem to move individual atoms around like building blocks, assembling what you need from what's available.

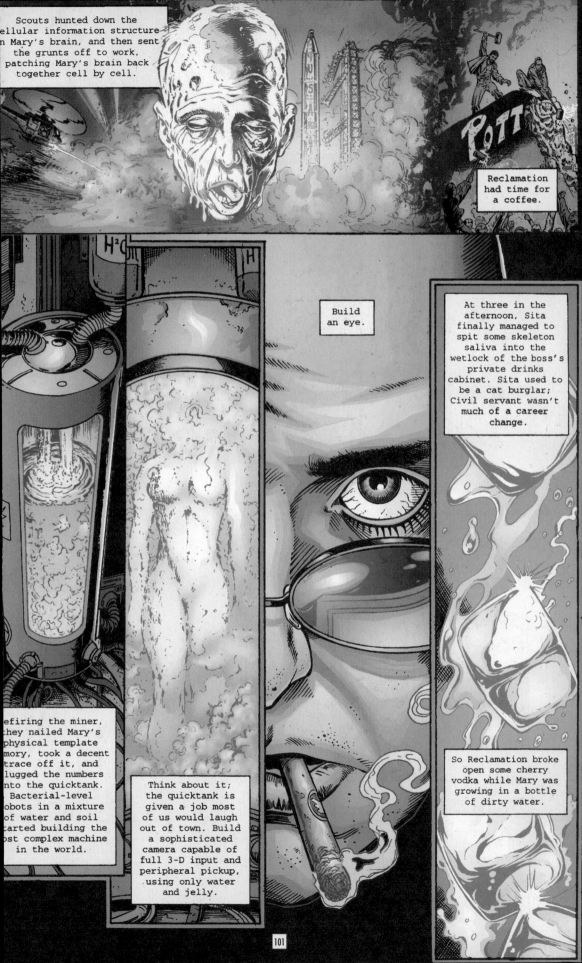

Scouts hunted down the cellular information structure in Mary's brain, and then sent the grunts off to work, patching Mary's brain back together cell by cell.

Reclamation had time for a coffee.

Build an eye.

At three in the afternoon, Sita finally managed to spit some skeleton saliva into the wetlock of the boss's private drinks cabinet. Sita used to be a cat burglar; Civil servant wasn't much of a career change.

...efiring the miner, ...hey nailed Mary's ...physical template ...mory, took a decent ...trace off it, and ...lugged the numbers ...nto the quicktank. Bacterial-level ...obots in a mixture ...of water and soil ...tarted building the ...ost complex machine in the world.

Think about it; the quicktank is given a job most of us would laugh out of town. Build a sophisticated camera capable of full 3-D input and peripheral pickup, using only water and jelly.

So Reclamation broke open some cherry vodka while Mary was growing in a bottle of dirty water.

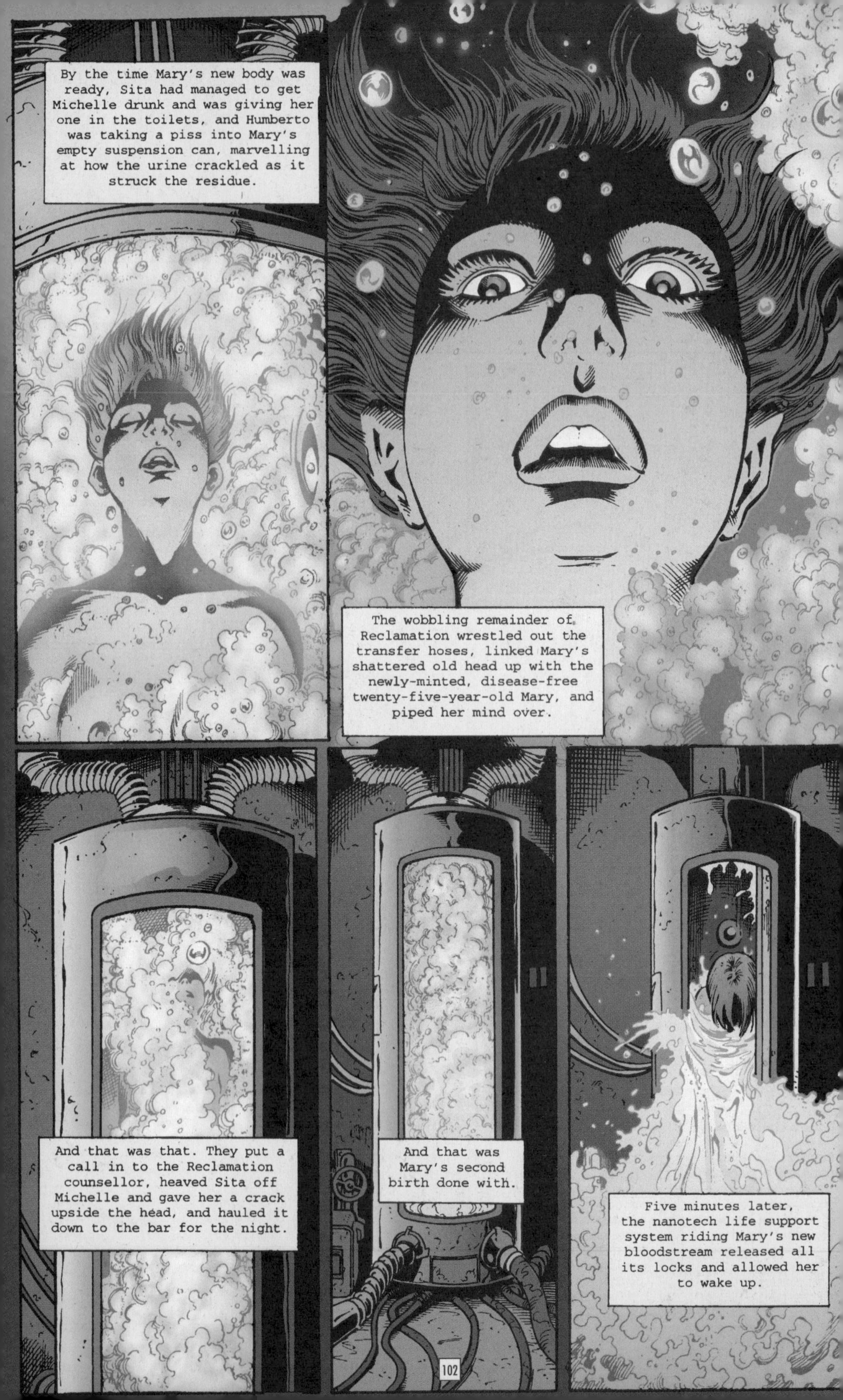
By the time Mary's new body was ready, Sita had managed to get Michelle drunk and was giving her one in the toilets, and Humberto was taking a piss into Mary's empty suspension can, marvelling at how the urine crackled as it struck the residue.
The wobbling remainder of Reclamation wrestled out the transfer hoses, linked Mary's shattered old head up with the newly-minted, disease-free twenty-five-year-old Mary, and piped her mind over.
And that was that. They put a call in to the Reclamation counsellor, heaved Sita off Michelle and gave her a crack upside the head, and hauled it down to the bar for the night.
And that was Mary's second birth done with.
Five minutes later, the nanotech life support system riding Mary's new bloodstream released all its locks and allowed her to wake up.

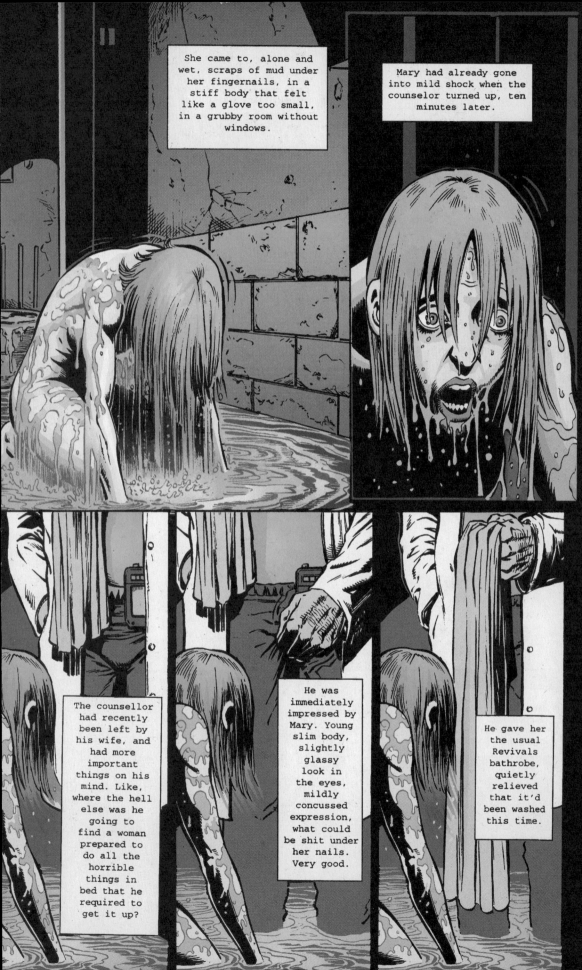

She came to, alone and wet, scraps of mud under her fingernails, in a stiff body that felt like a glove too small, in a grubby room without windows.

Mary had already gone into mild shock when the counselor turned up, ten minutes later.

The counsellor had recently been left by his wife, and had more important things on his mind. Like, where the hell else was he going to find a woman prepared to do all the horrible things in bed that he required to get it up?

He was immediately impressed by Mary. Young slim body, slightly glassy look in the eyes, mildly concussed expression, what could be shit under her nails. Very good.

He gave her the usual Revivals bathrobe, quietly relieved that it'd been washed this time.

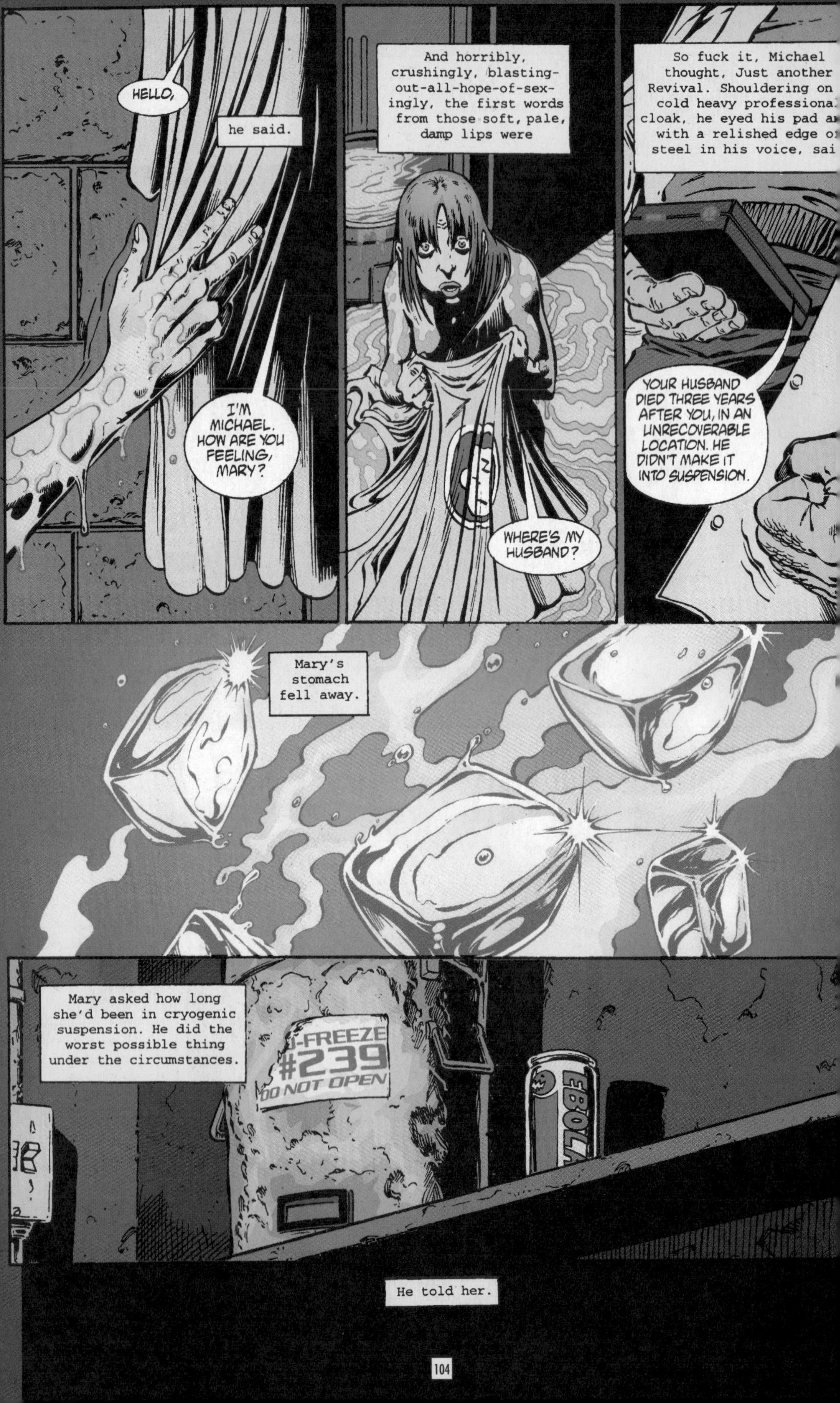

HELLO,
he said.
I'M MICHAEL. HOW ARE YOU FEELING, MARY?
And horribly, crushingly, blasting-out-all-hope-of-sex-ingly, the first words from those soft, pale, damp lips were
WHERE'S MY HUSBAND?
So fuck it, Michael thought, Just another Revival. Shouldering on cold heavy professiona cloak, he eyed his pad a with a relished edge o steel in his voice, sai
YOUR HUSBAND DIED THREE YEARS AFTER YOU, IN AN UNRECOVERABLE LOCATION. HE DIDN'T MAKE IT INTO SUSPENSION.
Mary's stomach fell away.
Mary asked how long she'd been in cryogenic suspension. He did the worst possible thing under the circumstances.
-FREEZE #239 DO NOT OPEN
EBOL
He told her.

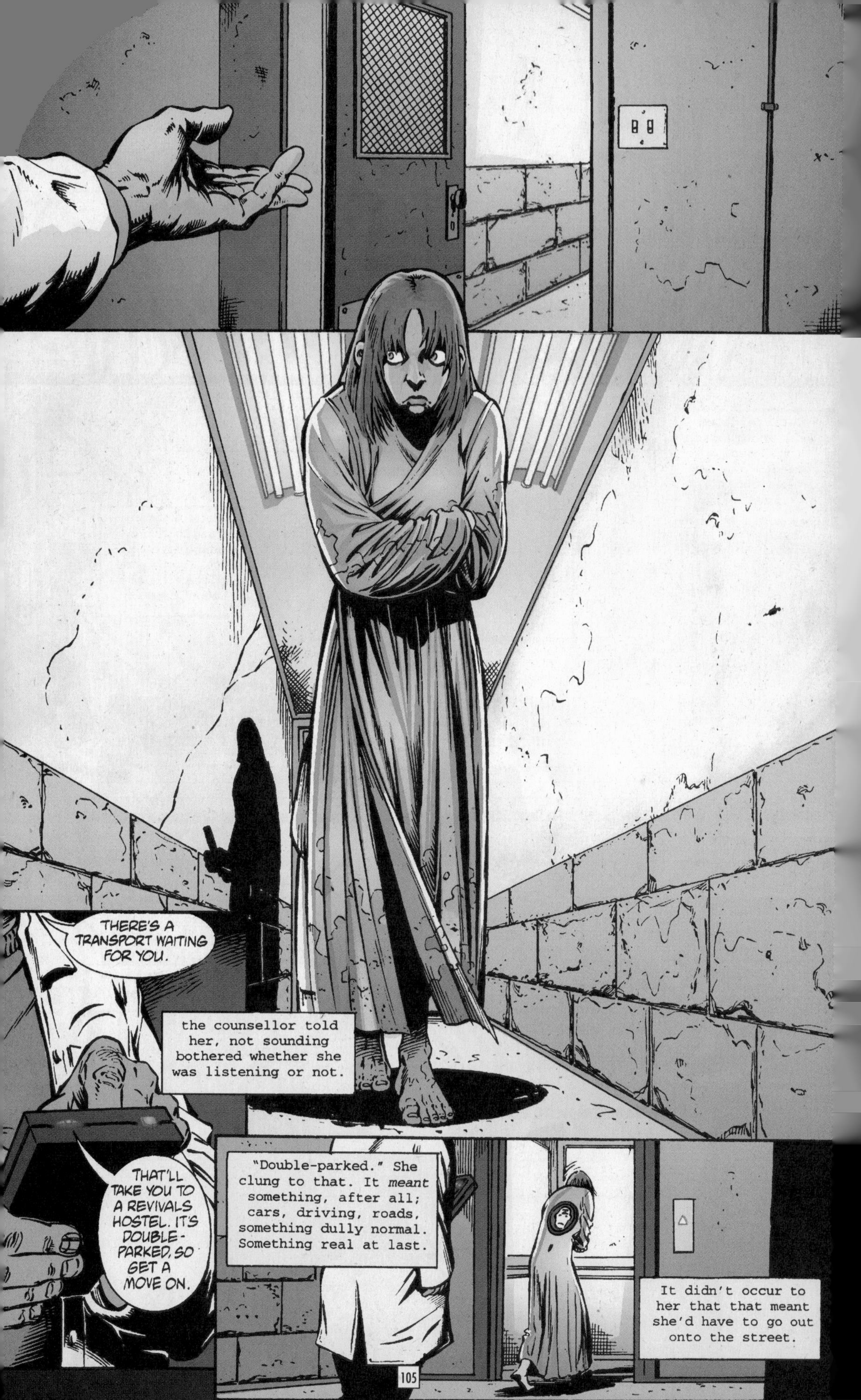
THERE'S A TRANSPORT WAITING FOR YOU.
the counsellor told her, not sounding bothered whether she was listening or not.
THAT'LL TAKE YOU TO A REVIVALS HOSTEL. IT'S DOUBLE-PARKED, SO GET A MOVE ON.
"Double-parked." She clung to that. It *meant* something, after all; cars, driving, roads, something dully normal. Something real at last.
It didn't occur to her that that meant she'd have to go out onto the street.

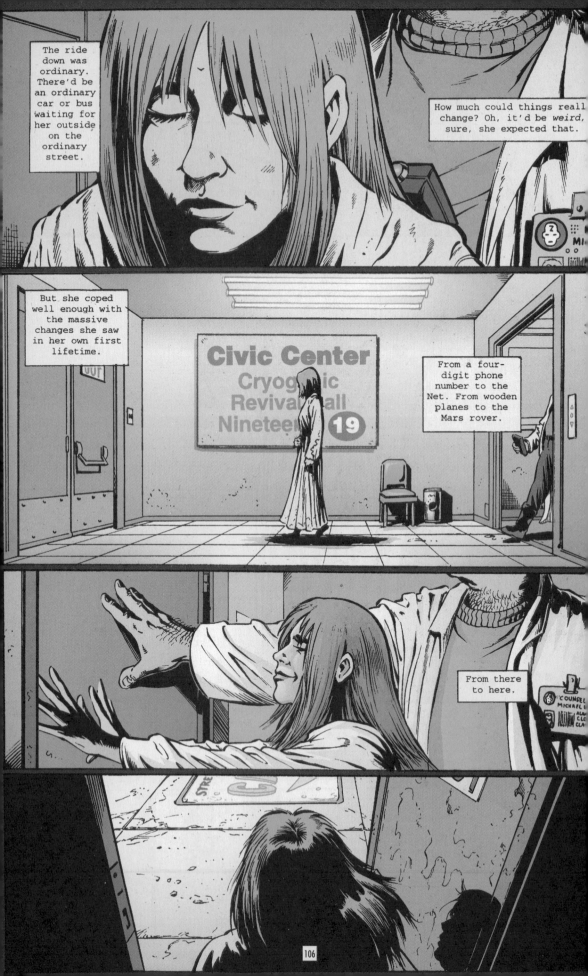

The ride down was ordinary. There'd be an ordinary car or bus waiting for her outside on the ordinary street.

How much could things really change? Oh, it'd be *weird*, sure, she expected that.

But she coped well enough with the massive changes she saw in her own first lifetime.

**Civic Center**
Cryogenic
Revival Hall
Nineteen **19**

From a four-digit phone number to the Net. From wooden planes to the Mars rover.

From there to here.

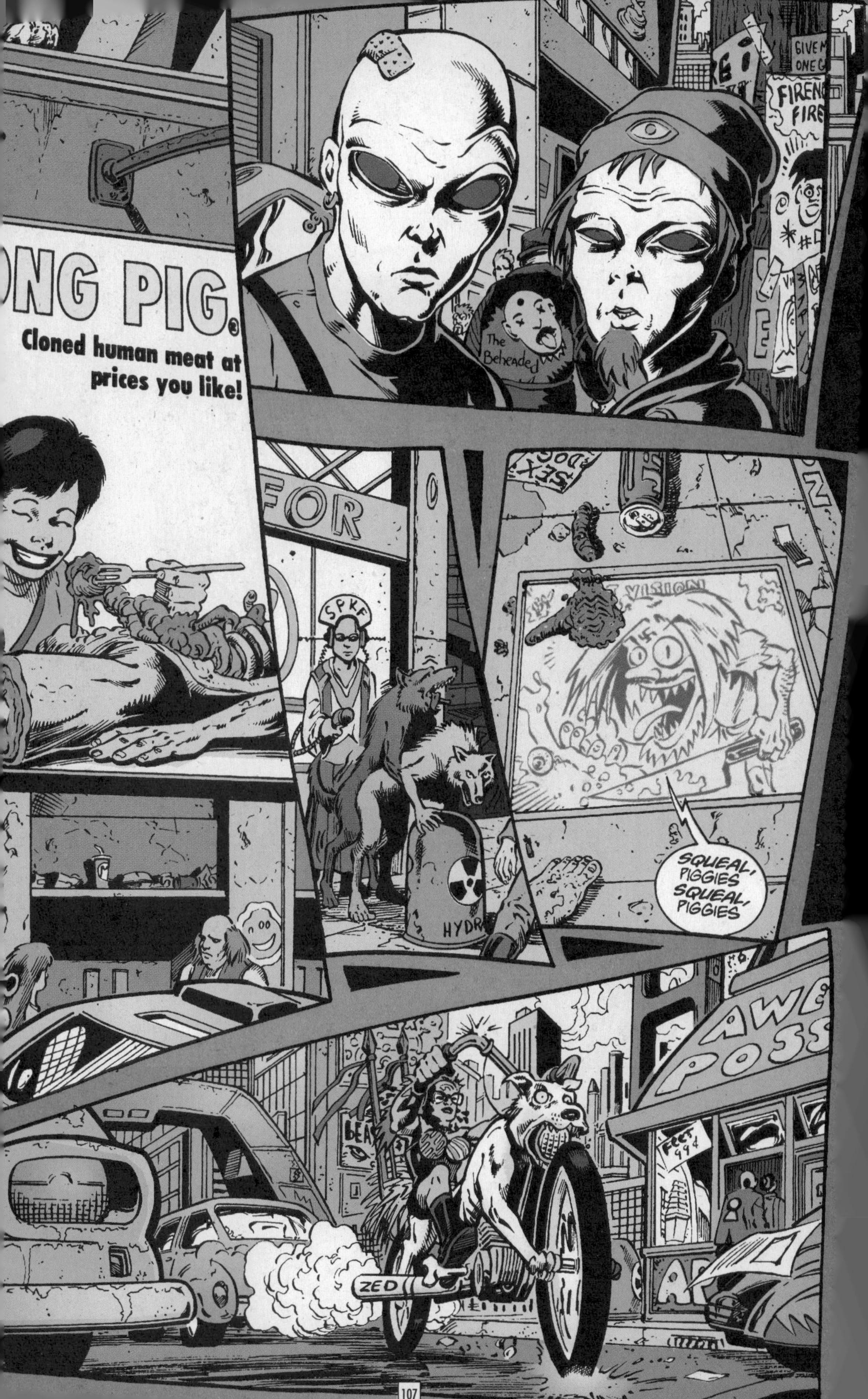
ONG PIG®
Cloned human meat at prices you like!
The Beheaded
FOR
SPKF
HYDR
SEX
VISION
SQUEAL, PIGGIES SQUEAL, PIGGIES
ZED
FEET 99¢
AWE
POSS

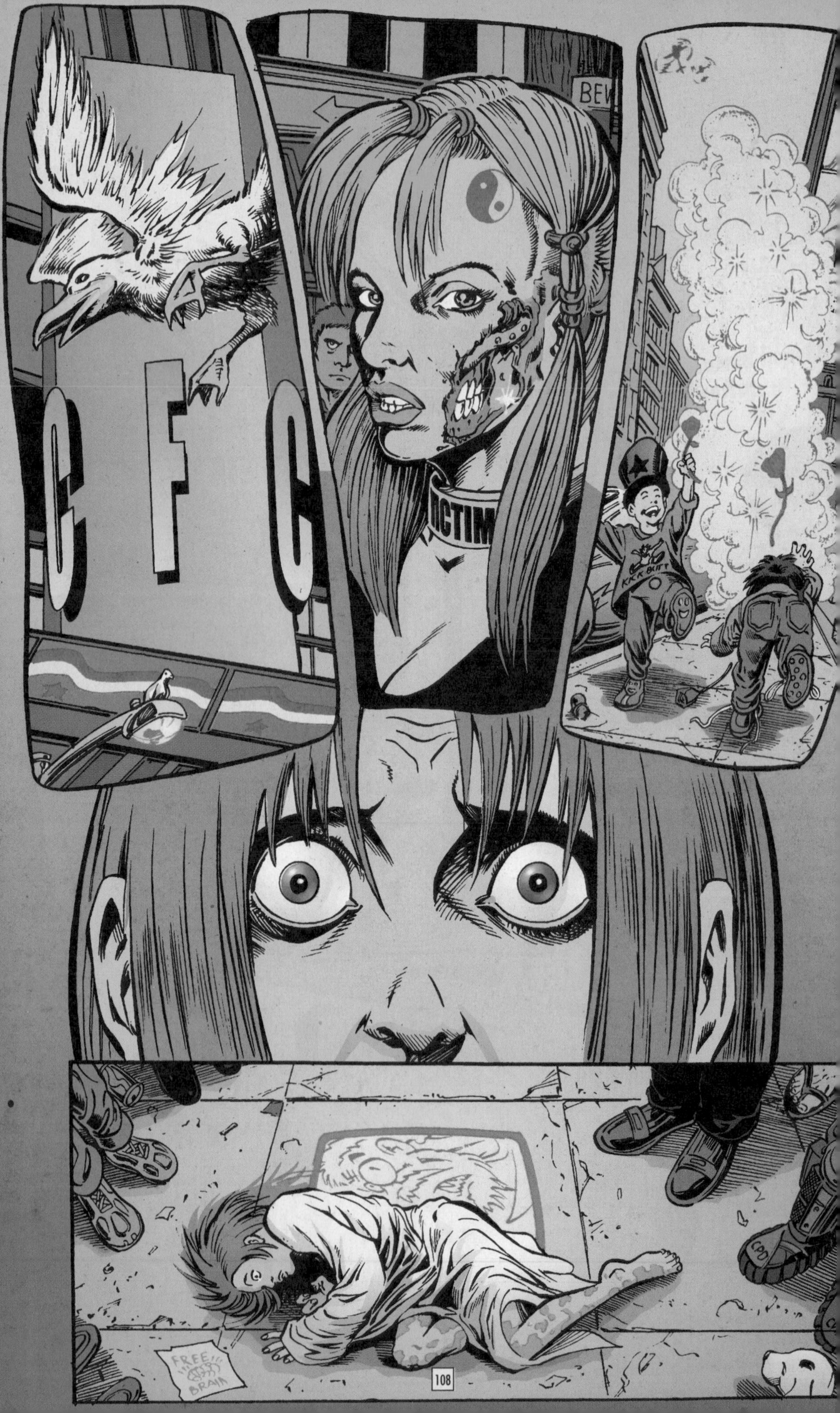
BEW
C F C
ICTIM
KICK BUTT
FREE
BRAIN

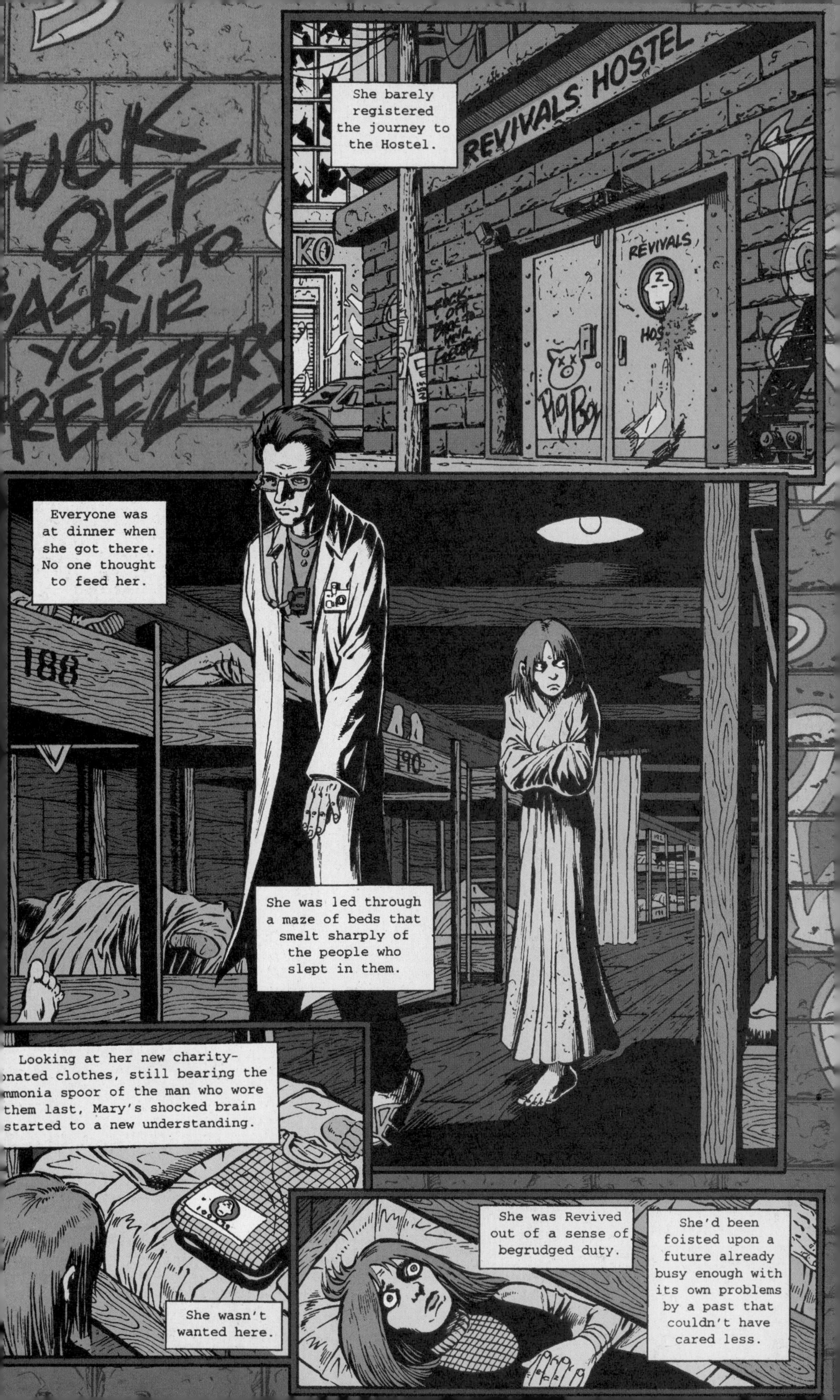
UCK OFF
ACK TO
YOUR
REEZERS
She barely registered the journey to the Hostel.
REVIVALS HOSTEL
REVIVALS
HOS
Pig Boy
Everyone was at dinner when she got there. No one thought to feed her.
188
190
She was led through a maze of beds that smelt sharply of the people who slept in them.
Looking at her new charity-
onated clothes, still bearing the
mmonia spoor of the man who wore
them last, Mary's shocked brain
started to a new understanding.
She wasn't wanted here.
She was Revived out of a sense of begrudged duty.
She'd been foisted upon a future already busy enough with its own problems by a past that couldn't have cared less.

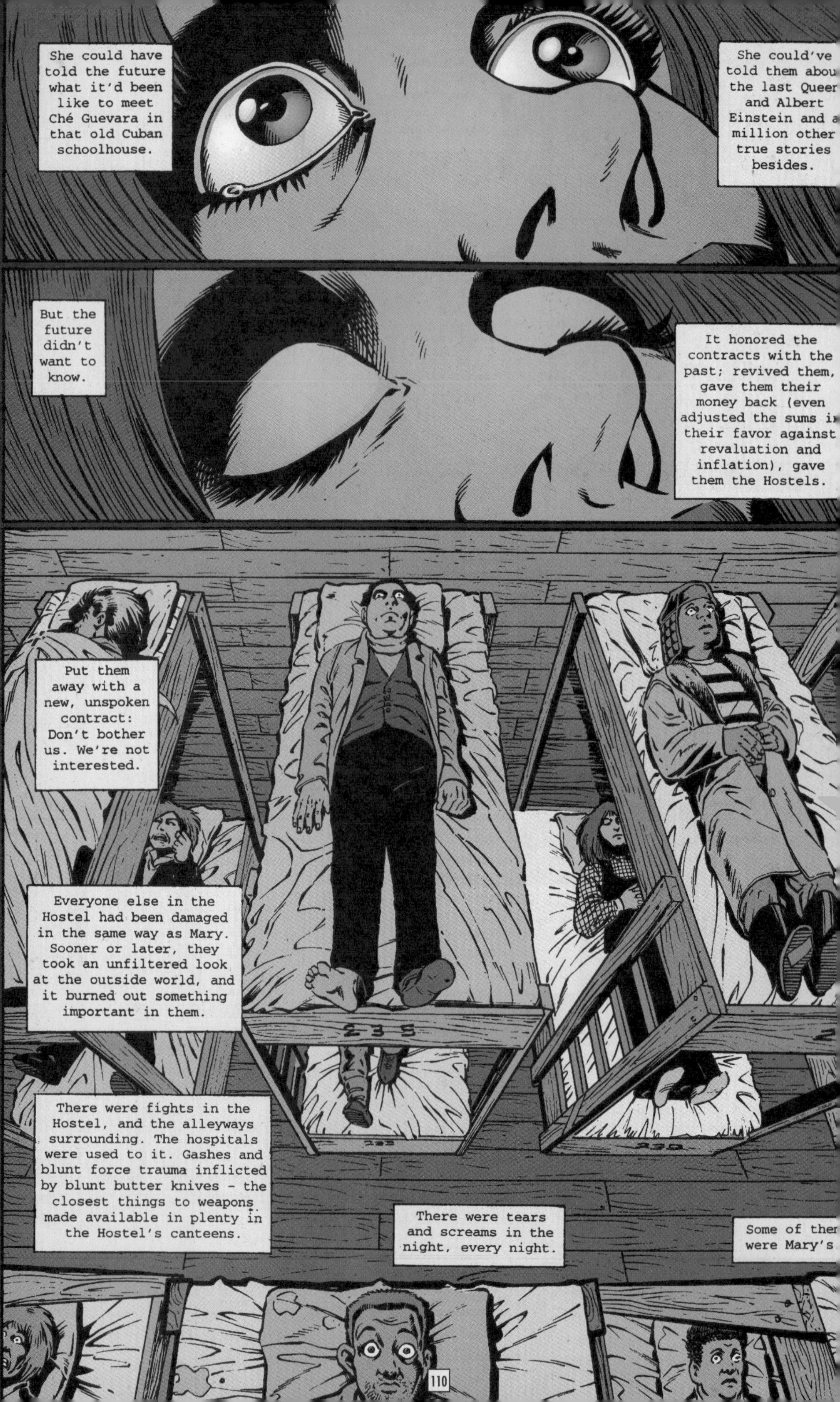
She could have told the future what it'd been like to meet Ché Guevara in that old Cuban schoolhouse.
She could've told them abou the last Queer and Albert Einstein and a million other true stories besides.
But the future didn't want to know.
It honored the contracts with the past; revived them, gave them their money back (even adjusted the sums i their favor against revaluation and inflation), gave them the Hostels.
Put them away with a new, unspoken contract: Don't bother us. We're not interested.
Everyone else in the Hostel had been damaged in the same way as Mary. Sooner or later, they took an unfiltered look at the outside world, and it burned out something important in them.
There were fights in the Hostel, and the alleyways surrounding. The hospitals were used to it. Gashes and blunt force trauma inflicted by blunt butter knives - the closest things to weapons made available in plenty in the Hostel's canteens.
There were tears and screams in the night, every night.
Some of the were Mary's

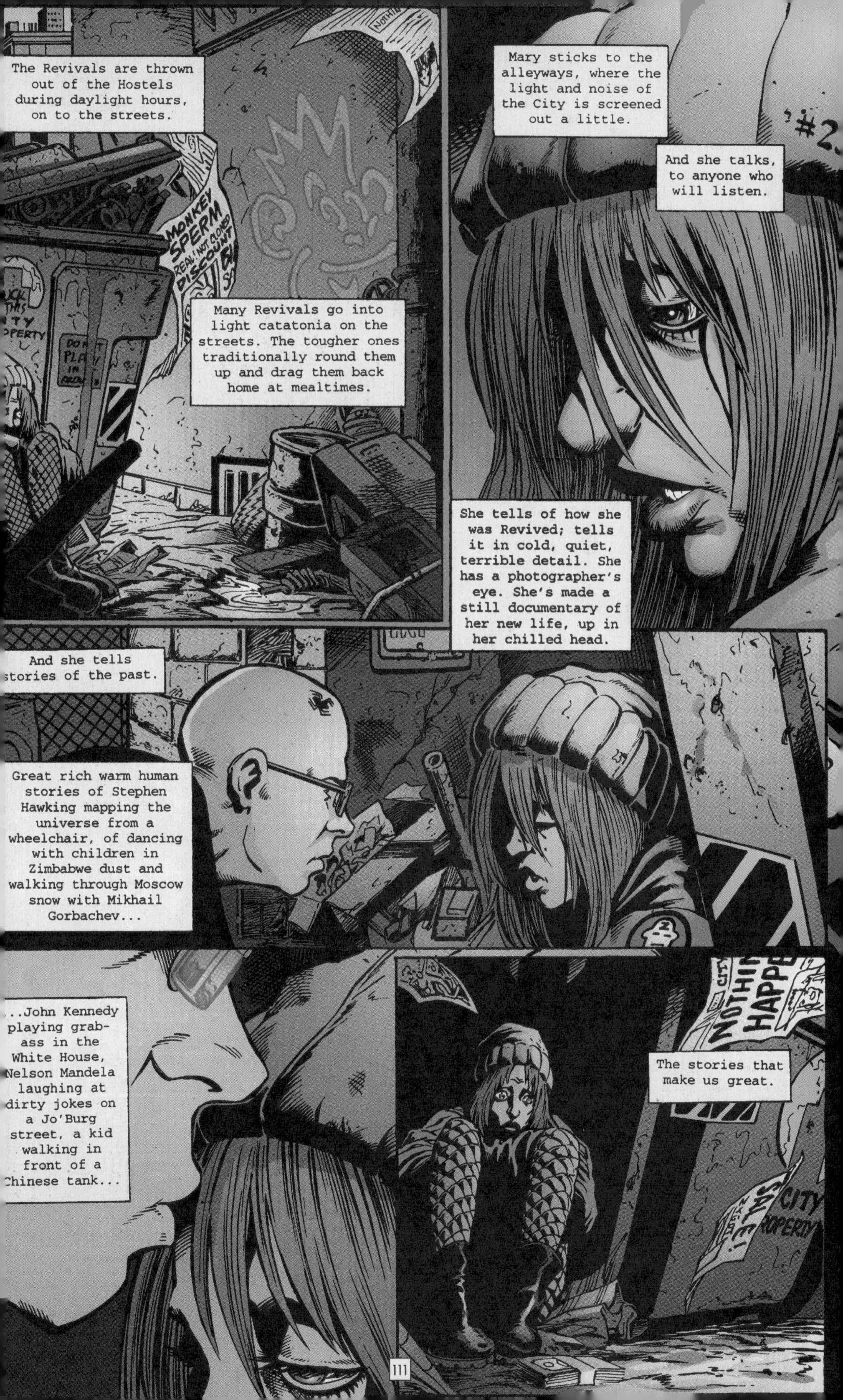

The Revivals are thrown out of the Hostels during daylight hours, on to the streets.
MONKEY SPERM
REAL! NOT CLONED
DISCOUNT
Many Revivals go into light catatonia on the streets. The tougher ones traditionally round them up and drag them back home at mealtimes.
Mary sticks to the alleyways, where the light and noise of the City is screened out a little.
And she talks, to anyone who will listen.
She tells of how she was Revived; tells it in cold, quiet, terrible detail. She has a photographer's eye. She's made a still documentary of her new life, up in her chilled head.
And she tells stories of the past.
Great rich warm human stories of Stephen Hawking mapping the universe from a wheelchair, of dancing with children in Zimbabwe dust and walking through Moscow snow with Mikhail Gorbachev...
...John Kennedy playing grab-ass in the White House, Nelson Mandela laughing at dirty jokes on a Jo'Burg street, a kid walking in front of a Chinese tank...
The stories that make us great.
CITY
ROPERTY

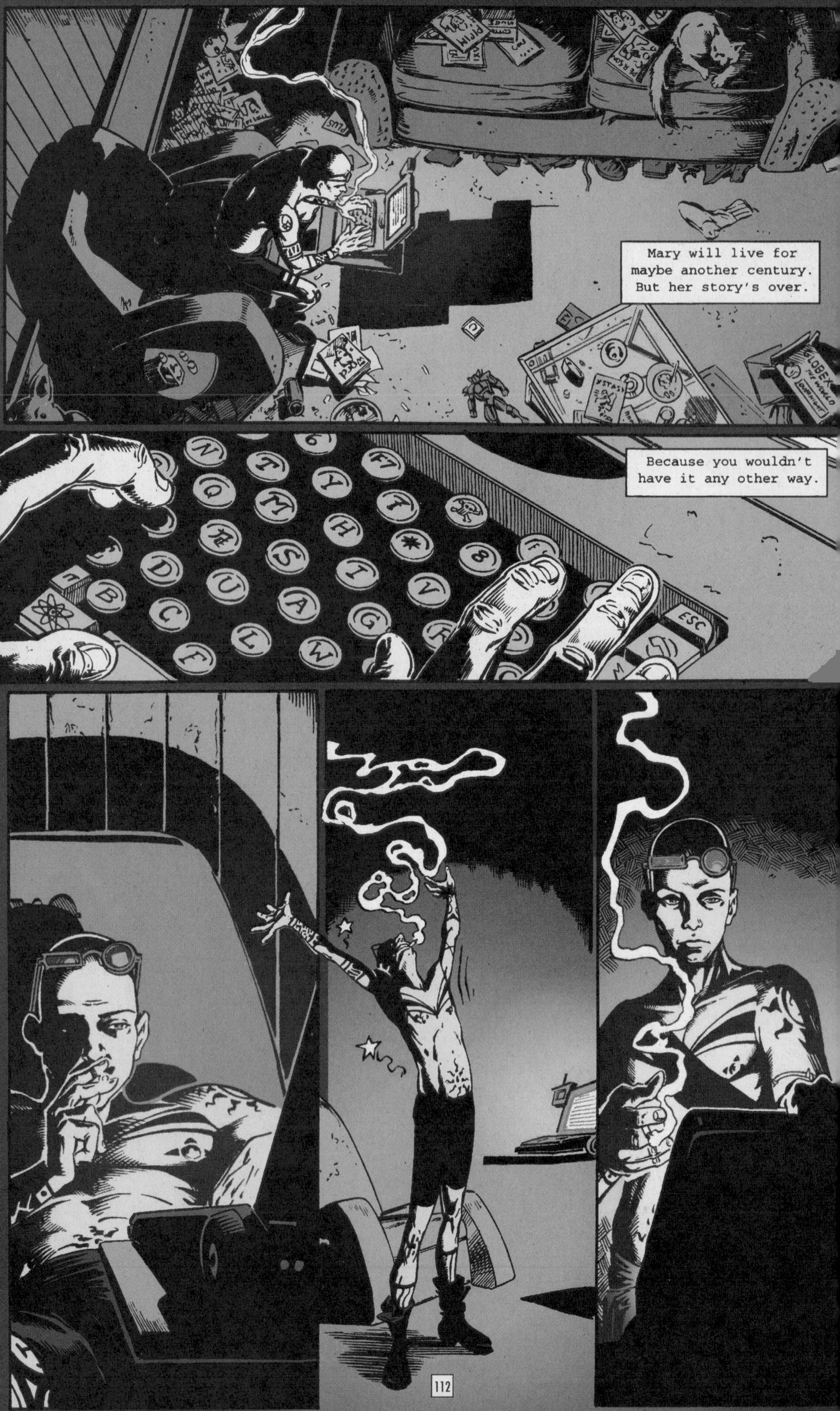
Mary will live for maybe another century. But her story's over.
Because you wouldn't have it any other way.

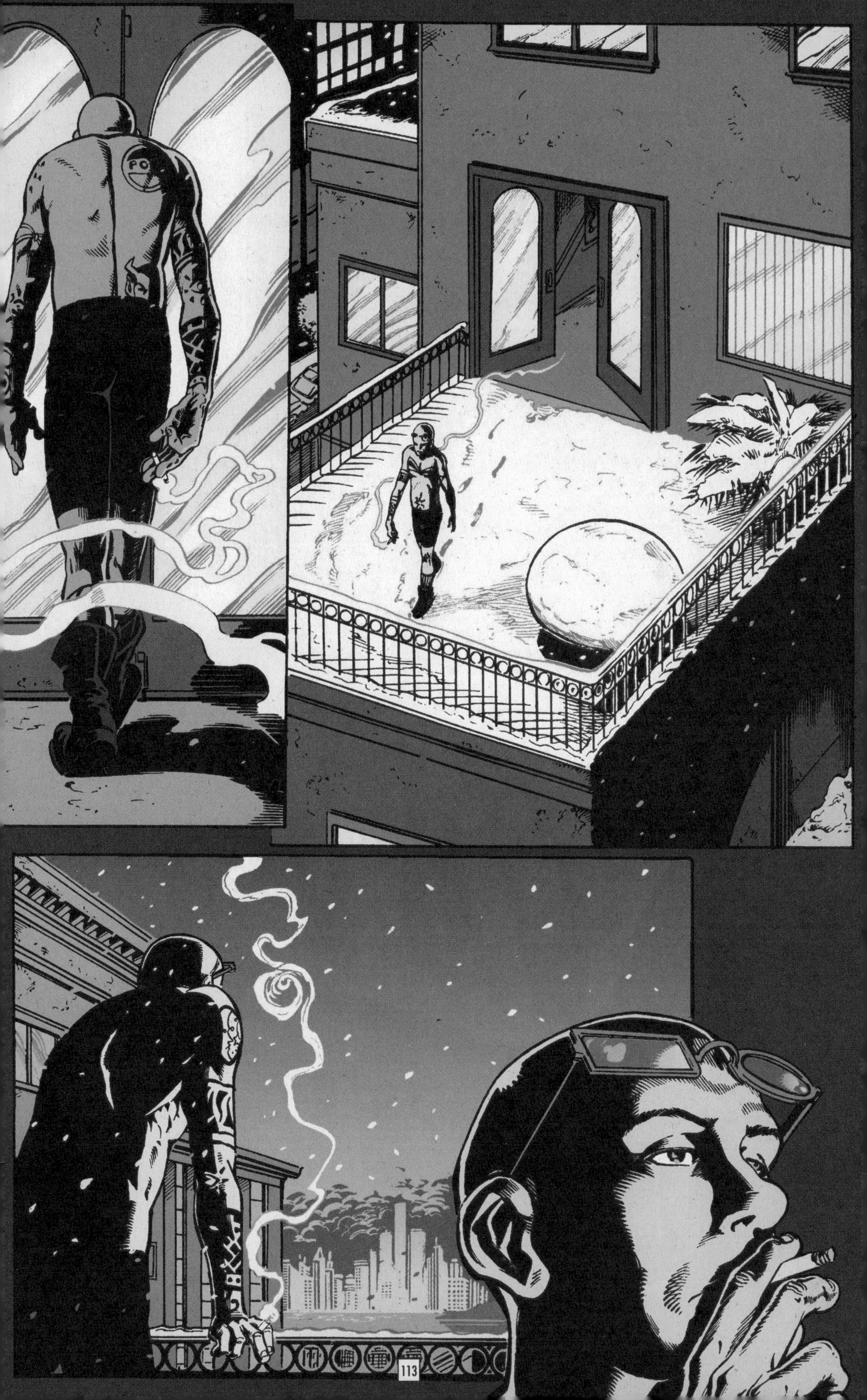

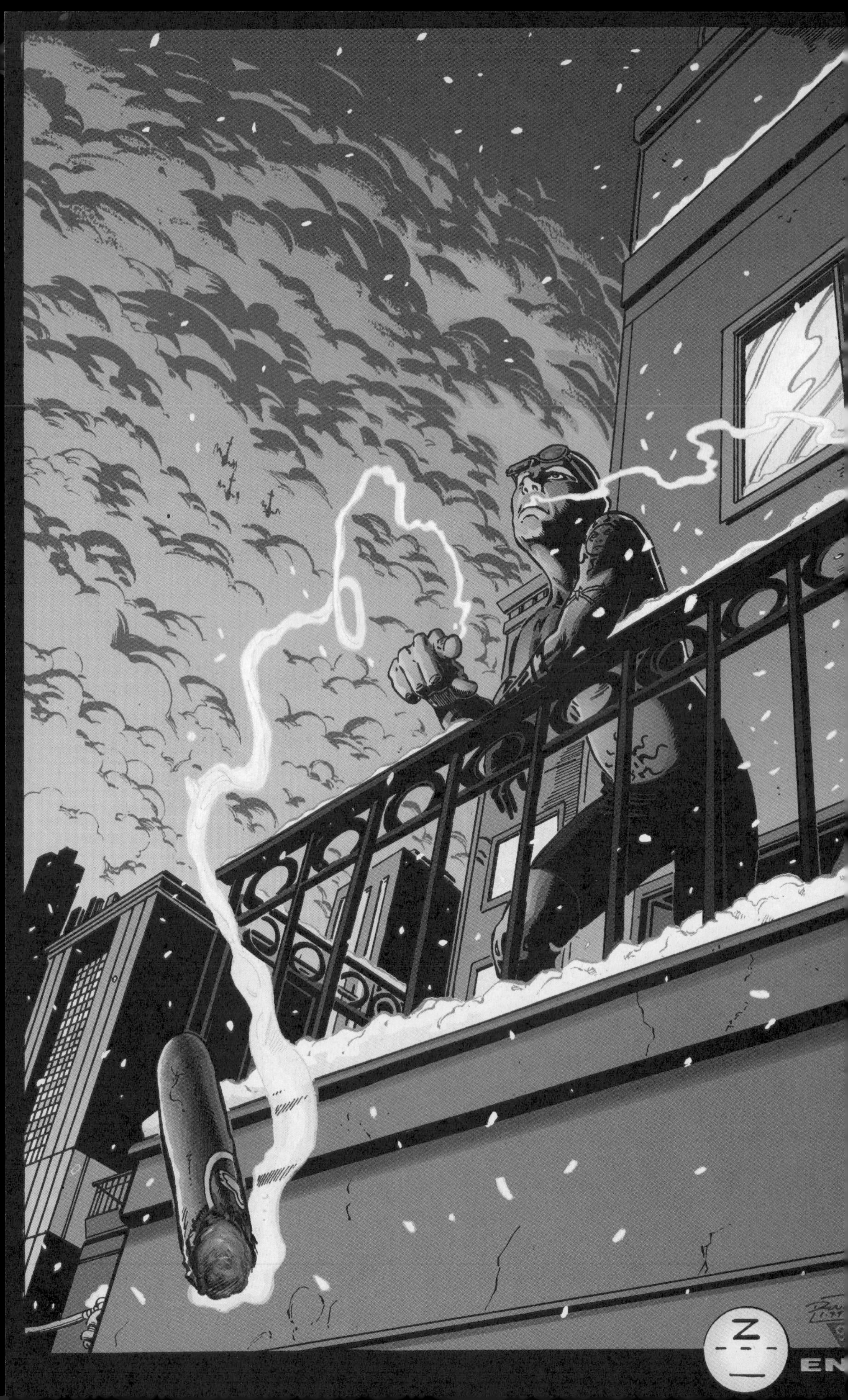

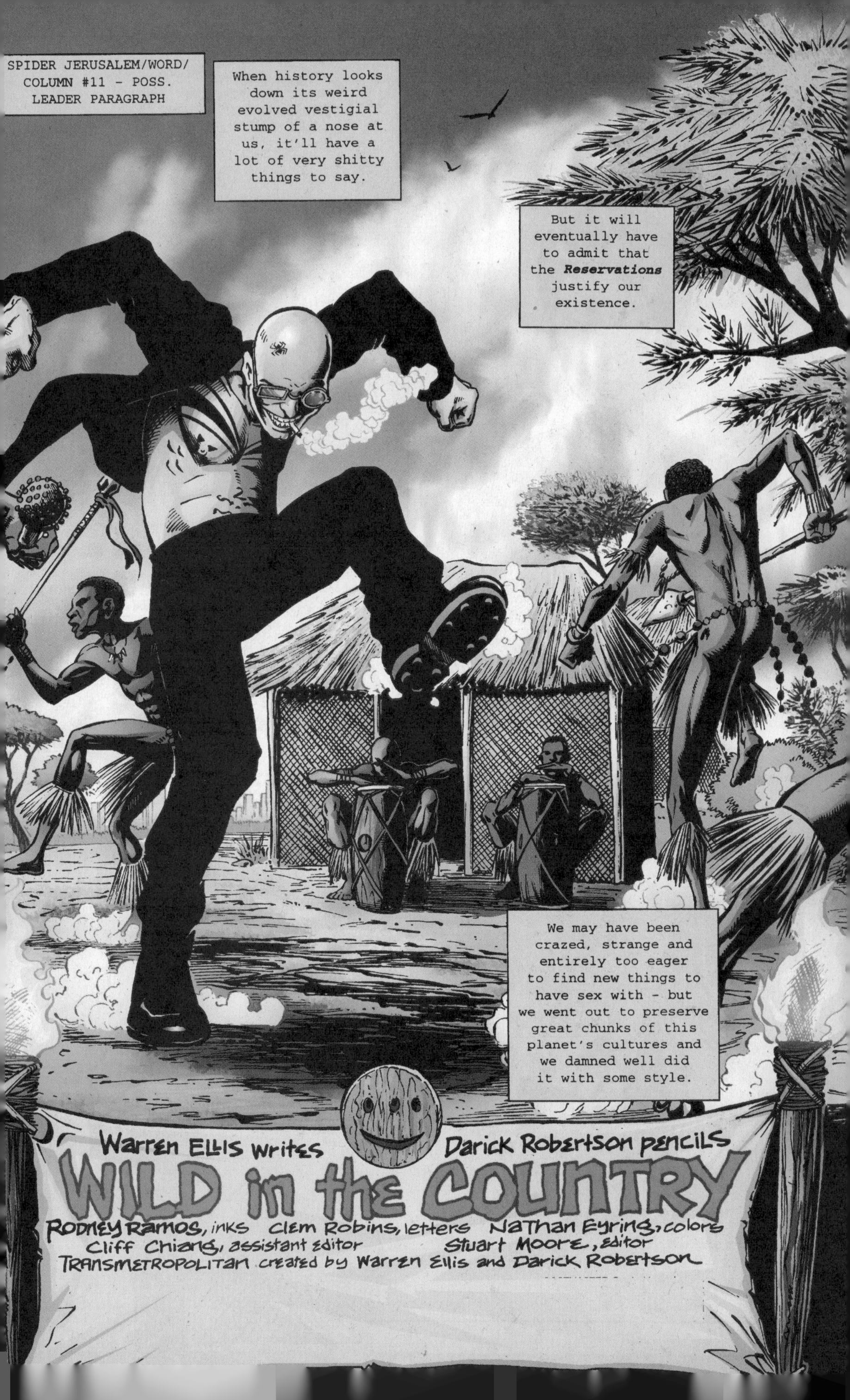
SPIDER JERUSALEM/WORD/ COLUMN #11 - POSS. LEADER PARAGRAPH
When history looks down its weird evolved vestigial stump of a nose at us, it'll have a lot of very shitty things to say.
But it will eventually have to admit that the *Reservations* justify our existence.
We may have been crazed, strange and entirely too eager to find new things to have sex with - but we went out to preserve great chunks of this planet's cultures and we damned well did it with some style.
Warren Ellis writes
Darick Robertson pencils
WILD in the COUNTRY
Rodney Ramos, inks
Clem Robins, letters
Nathan Eyring, colors
Cliff Chiang, assistant editor
Stuart Moore, Editor
TRANSMETROPOLITAN created by Warren Ellis and Darick Robertson

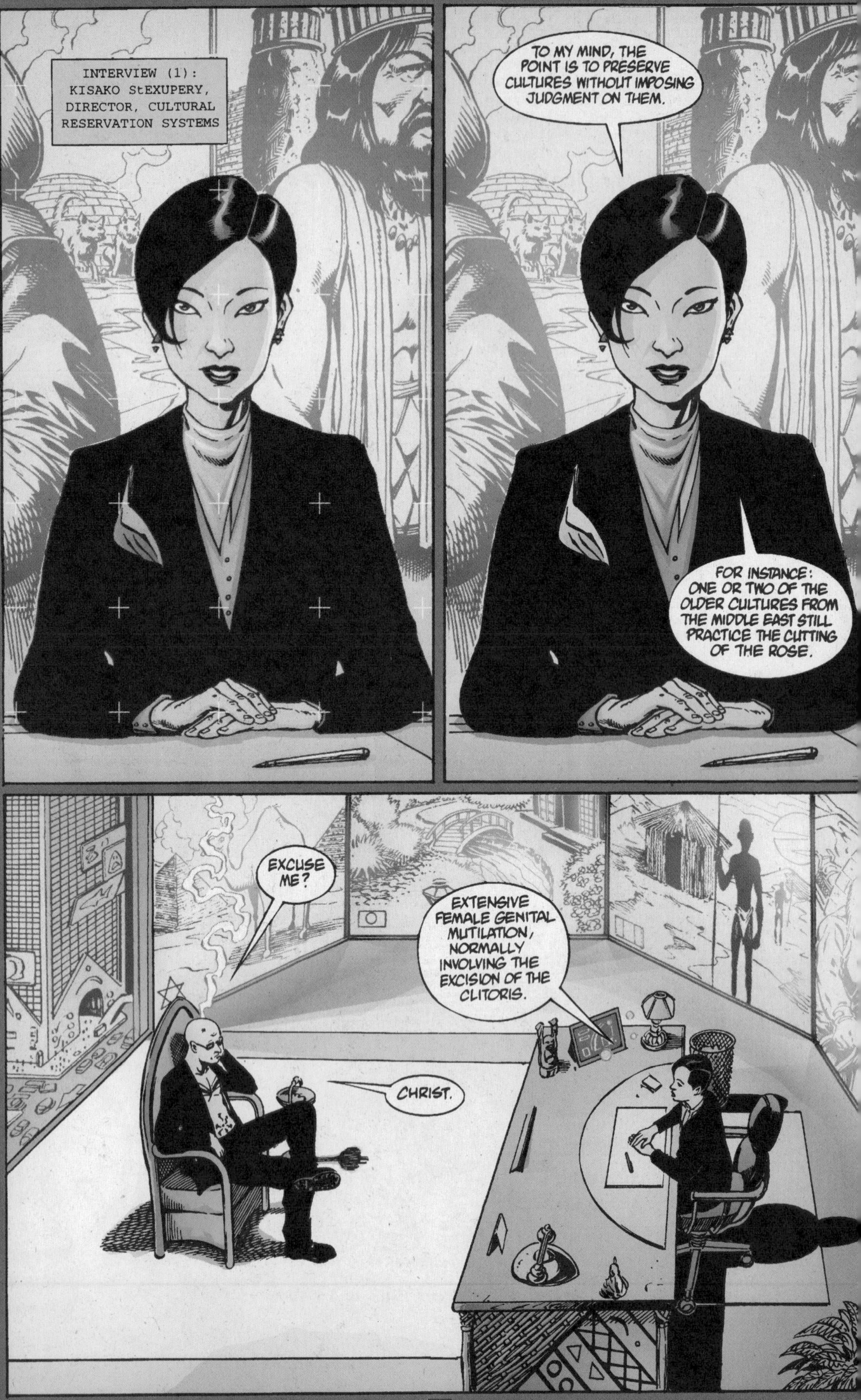

INTERVIEW (1): KISAKO StEXUPERY, DIRECTOR, CULTURAL RESERVATION SYSTEMS
TO MY MIND, THE POINT IS TO PRESERVE CULTURES WITHOUT IMPOSING JUDGMENT ON THEM.
FOR INSTANCE: ONE OR TWO OF THE OLDER CULTURES FROM THE MIDDLE EAST STILL PRACTICE THE CUTTING OF THE ROSE.
EXCUSE ME?
EXTENSIVE FEMALE GENITAL MUTILATION, NORMALLY INVOLVING THE EXCISION OF THE CLITORIS.
CHRIST.

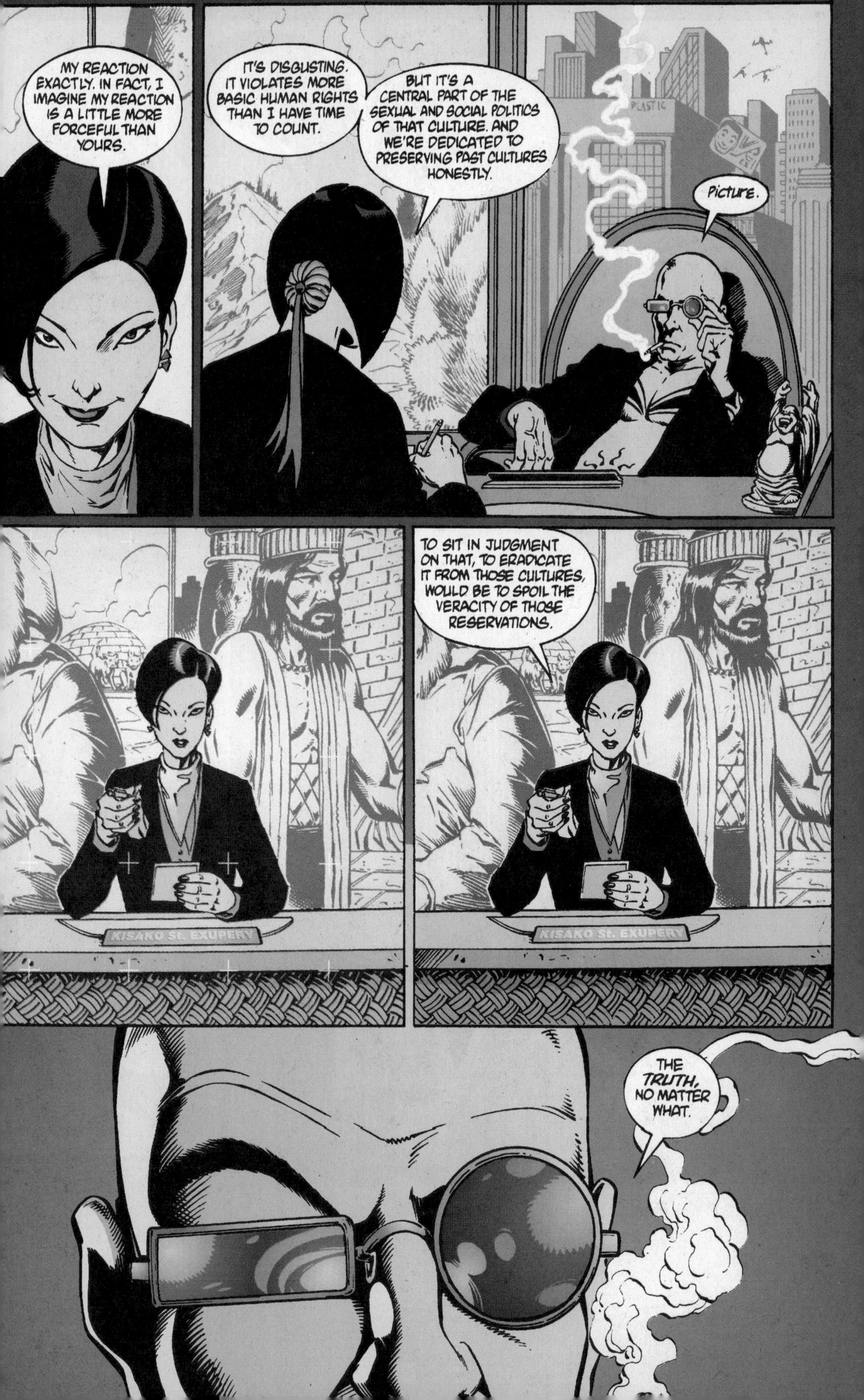
MY REACTION EXACTLY. IN FACT, I IMAGINE MY REACTION IS A LITTLE MORE FORCEFUL THAN YOURS.
IT'S DISGUSTING. IT VIOLATES MORE BASIC HUMAN RIGHTS THAN I HAVE TIME TO COUNT.
BUT IT'S A CENTRAL PART OF THE SEXUAL AND SOCIAL POLITICS OF THAT CULTURE. AND WE'RE DEDICATED TO PRESERVING PAST CULTURES HONESTLY.
PLASTIC
Picture.
KISAKO St. EXUPERY
TO SIT IN JUDGMENT ON THAT, TO ERADICATE IT FROM THOSE CULTURES, WOULD BE TO SPOIL THE VERACITY OF THOSE RESERVATIONS.
KISAKO St. EXUPERY
THE TRUTH, NO MATTER WHAT.

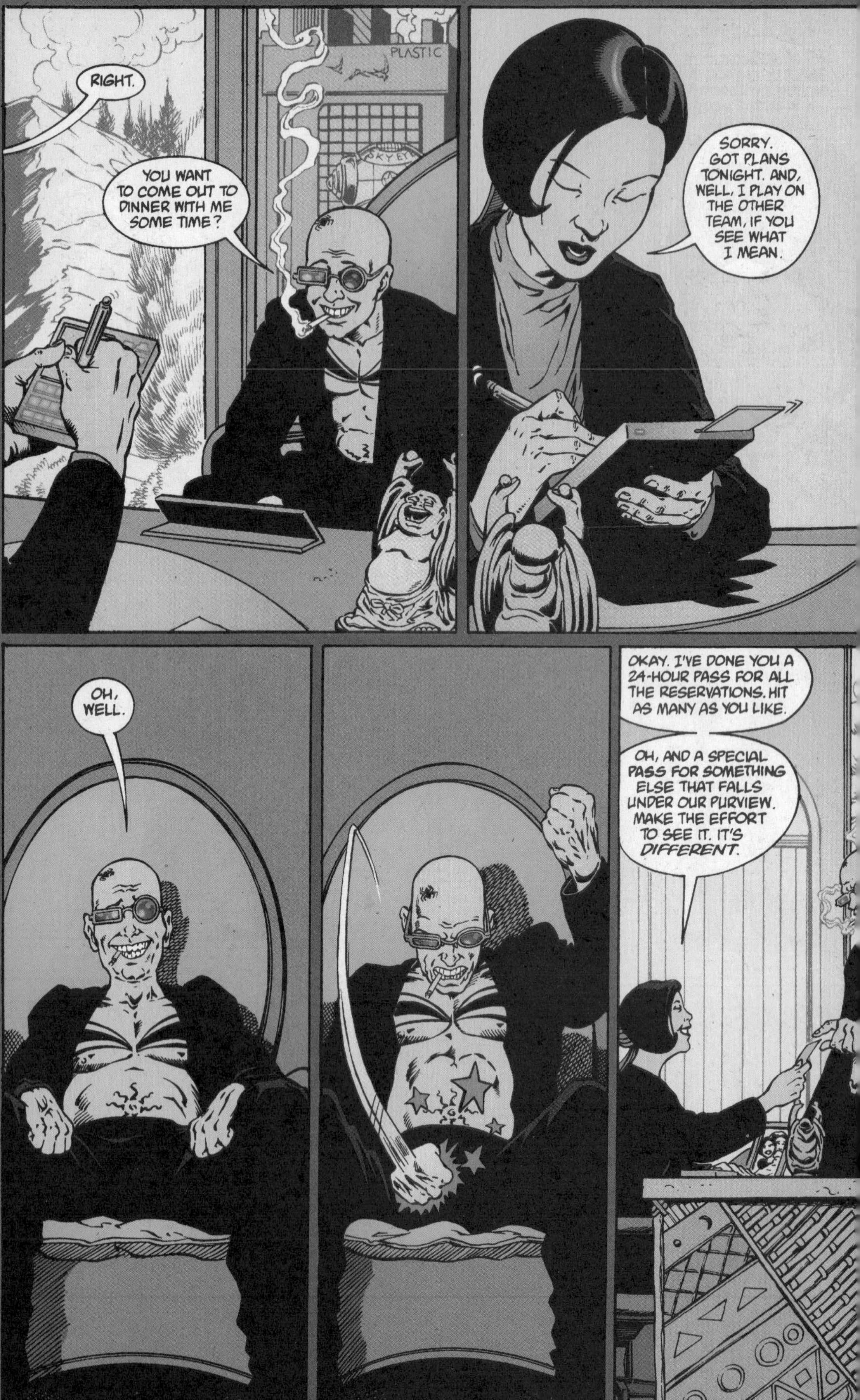
RIGHT.
YOU WANT TO COME OUT TO DINNER WITH ME SOME TIME?
PLASTIC
SORRY. GOT PLANS TONIGHT. AND, WELL, I PLAY ON THE OTHER TEAM, IF YOU SEE WHAT I MEAN.
OH, WELL.
OKAY. I'VE DONE YOU A 24-HOUR PASS FOR ALL THE RESERVATIONS. HIT AS MANY AS YOU LIKE.
OH, AND A SPECIAL PASS FOR SOMETHING ELSE THAT FALLS UNDER OUR PURVIEW. MAKE THE EFFORT TO SEE IT. IT'S *DIFFERENT*.

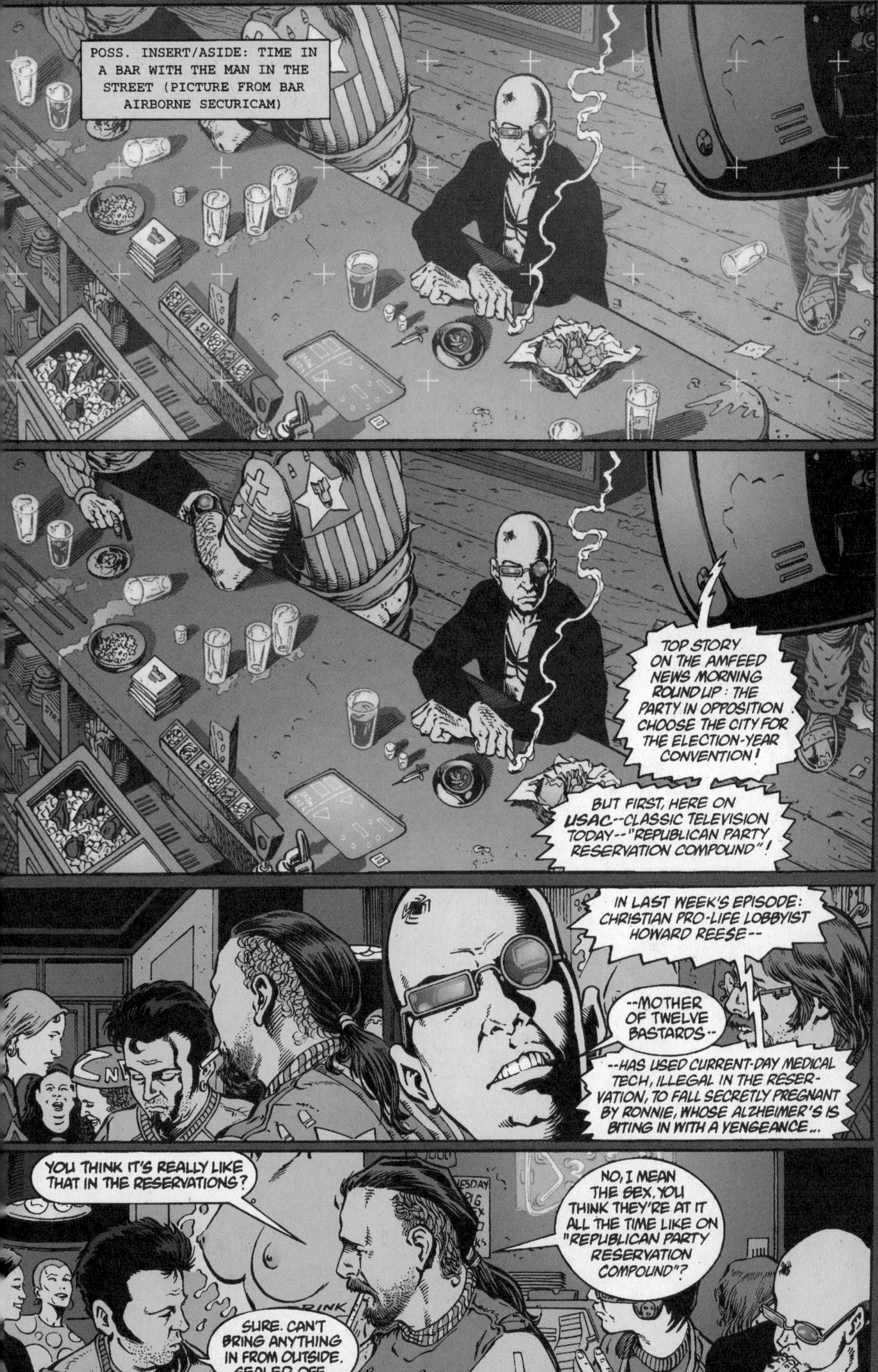

POSS. INSERT/ASIDE: TIME IN A BAR WITH THE MAN IN THE STREET (PICTURE FROM BAR AIRBORNE SECURICAM)
TOP STORY ON THE AMFEED NEWS MORNING ROUNDUP: THE PARTY IN OPPOSITION CHOOSE THE CITY FOR THE ELECTION-YEAR CONVENTION!
BUT FIRST, HERE ON USAC--CLASSIC TELEVISION TODAY--"REPUBLICAN PARTY RESERVATION COMPOUND"!
IN LAST WEEK'S EPISODE: CHRISTIAN PRO-LIFE LOBBYIST HOWARD REESE--
--MOTHER OF TWELVE BASTARDS--
--HAS USED CURRENT-DAY MEDICAL TECH, ILLEGAL IN THE RESERVATION, TO FALL SECRETLY PREGNANT BY RONNIE, WHOSE ALZHEIMER'S IS BITING IN WITH A VENGEANCE...
YOU THINK IT'S REALLY LIKE THAT IN THE RESERVATIONS?
SURE. CAN'T BRING ANYTHING IN FROM OUTSIDE. SEALED OFF.
NO, I MEAN THE SEX. YOU THINK THEY'RE AT IT ALL THE TIME LIKE ON "REPUBLICAN PARTY RESERVATION COMPOUND"?
DAMNED

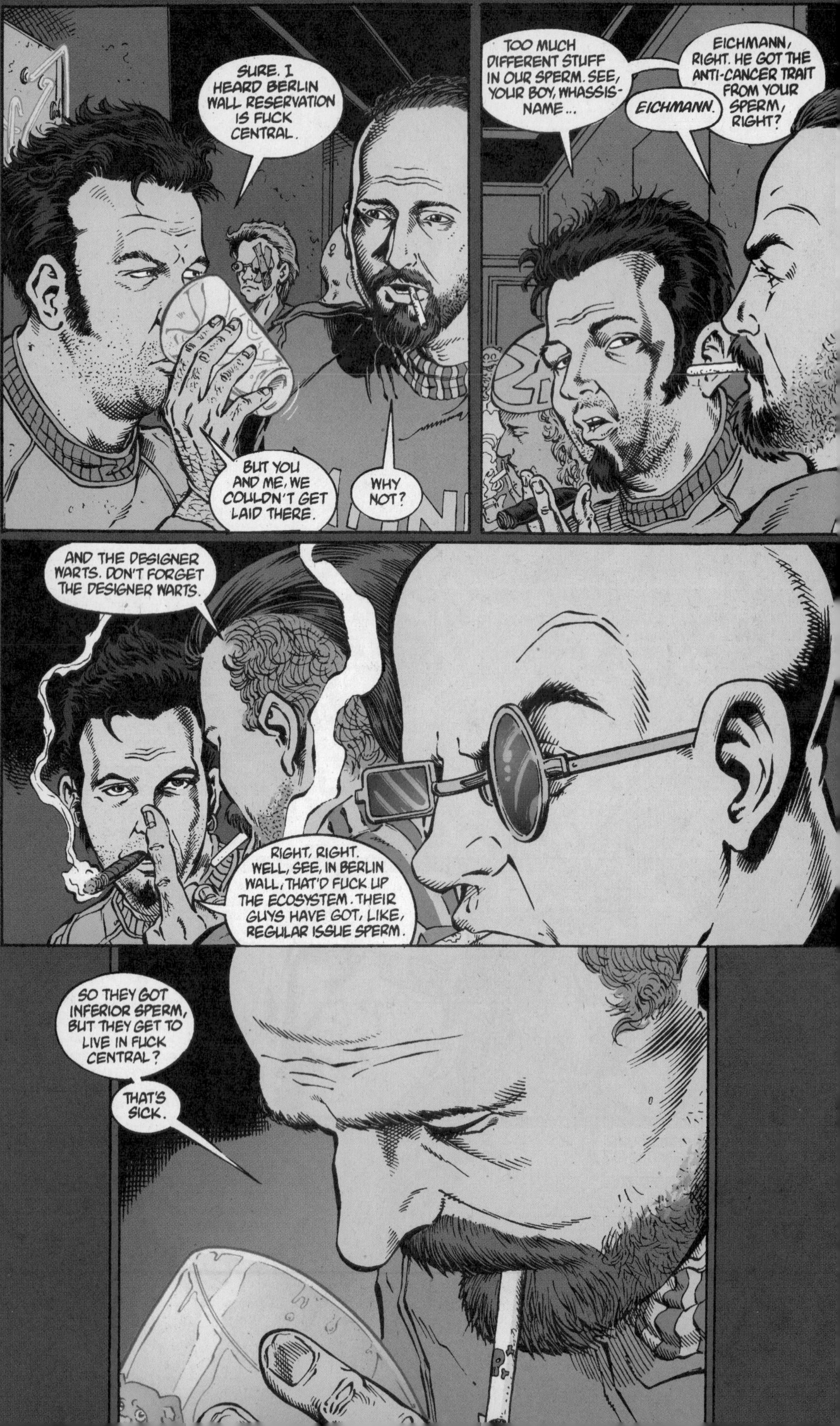
SURE. I HEARD BERLIN WALL RESERVATION IS FUCK CENTRAL.
BUT YOU AND ME, WE COULDN'T GET LAID THERE.
WHY NOT?
TOO MUCH DIFFERENT STUFF IN OUR SPERM. SEE, YOUR BOY, WHASSIS-NAME...
EICHMANN.
EICHMANN, RIGHT. HE GOT THE ANTI-CANCER TRAIT FROM YOUR SPERM, RIGHT?
AND THE DESIGNER WARTS. DON'T FORGET THE DESIGNER WARTS.
RIGHT, RIGHT. WELL, SEE, IN BERLIN WALL, THAT'D FUCK UP THE ECOSYSTEM. THEIR GUYS HAVE GOT, LIKE, REGULAR ISSUE SPERM.
SO THEY GOT INFERIOR SPERM, BUT THEY GET TO LIVE IN FUCK CENTRAL?
THAT'S SICK.

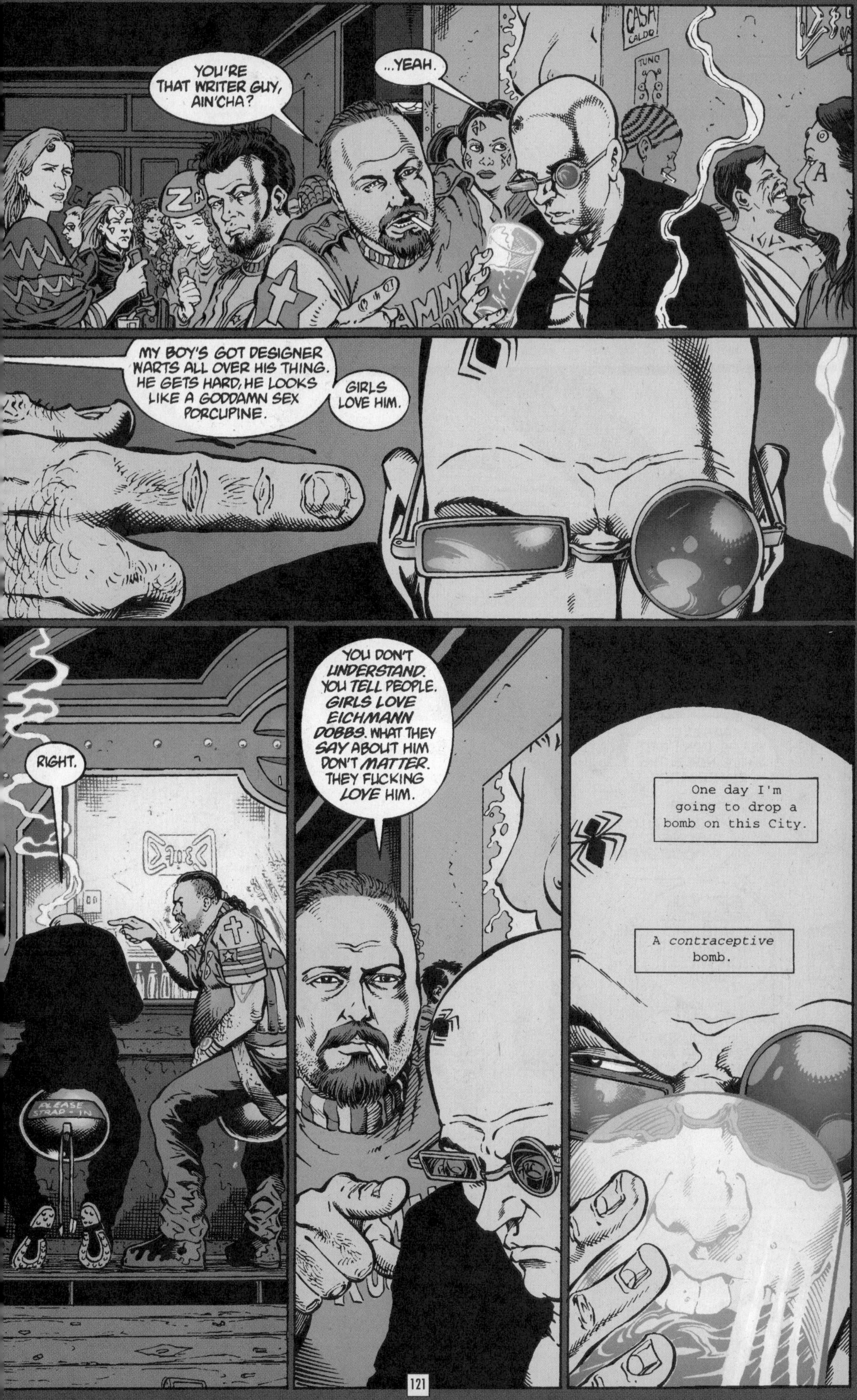
YOU'RE THAT WRITER GUY, AIN'CHA?
...YEAH.
CASA CALDO
TUNG
MY BOY'S GOT DESIGNER WARTS ALL OVER HIS THING. HE GETS HARD, HE LOOKS LIKE A GODDAMN SEX PORCUPINE.
GIRLS LOVE HIM.
RIGHT.
PLEASE STRAP-IN
YOU DON'T UNDERSTAND. YOU TELL PEOPLE. GIRLS LOVE EICHMANN DOBBS. WHAT THEY SAY ABOUT HIM DON'T MATTER. THEY FUCKING LOVE HIM.
One day I'm going to drop a bomb on this City.
A contraceptive bomb.

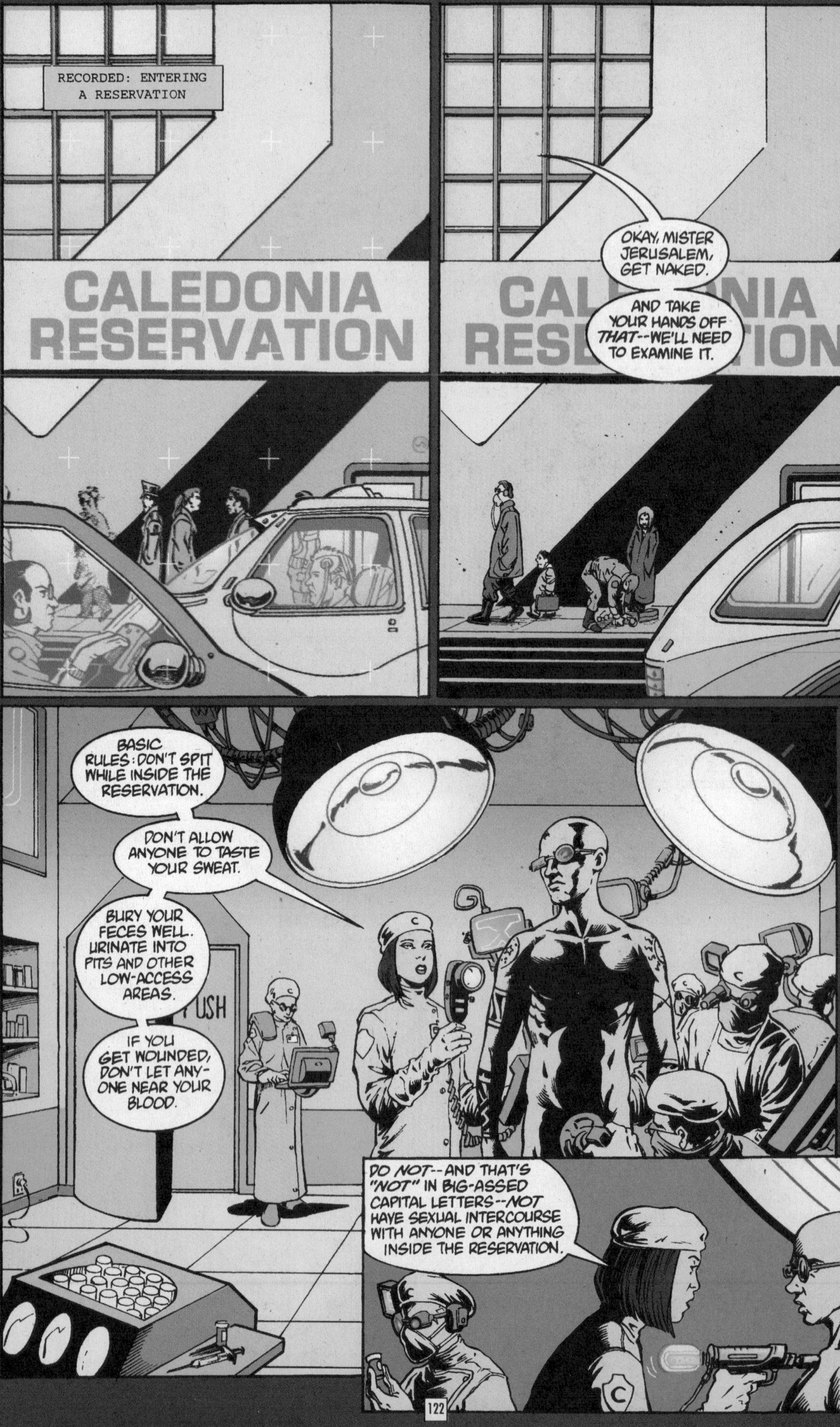
RECORDED: ENTERING A RESERVATION
CALEDONIA RESERVATION
OKAY, MISTER JERUSALEM, GET NAKED.
AND TAKE YOUR HANDS OFF *THAT*--WE'LL NEED TO EXAMINE IT.
BASIC RULES: DON'T SPIT WHILE INSIDE THE RESERVATION.
DON'T ALLOW ANYONE TO TASTE YOUR SWEAT.
BURY YOUR FECES WELL. URINATE INTO PITS AND OTHER LOW-ACCESS AREAS.
IF YOU GET WOUNDED, DON'T LET ANY-ONE NEAR YOUR BLOOD.
PUSH
DO *NOT*--AND THAT'S "*NOT*" IN BIG-ASSED CAPITAL LETTERS--*NOT* HAVE SEXUAL INTERCOURSE WITH ANYONE OR ANYTHING INSIDE THE RESERVATION.

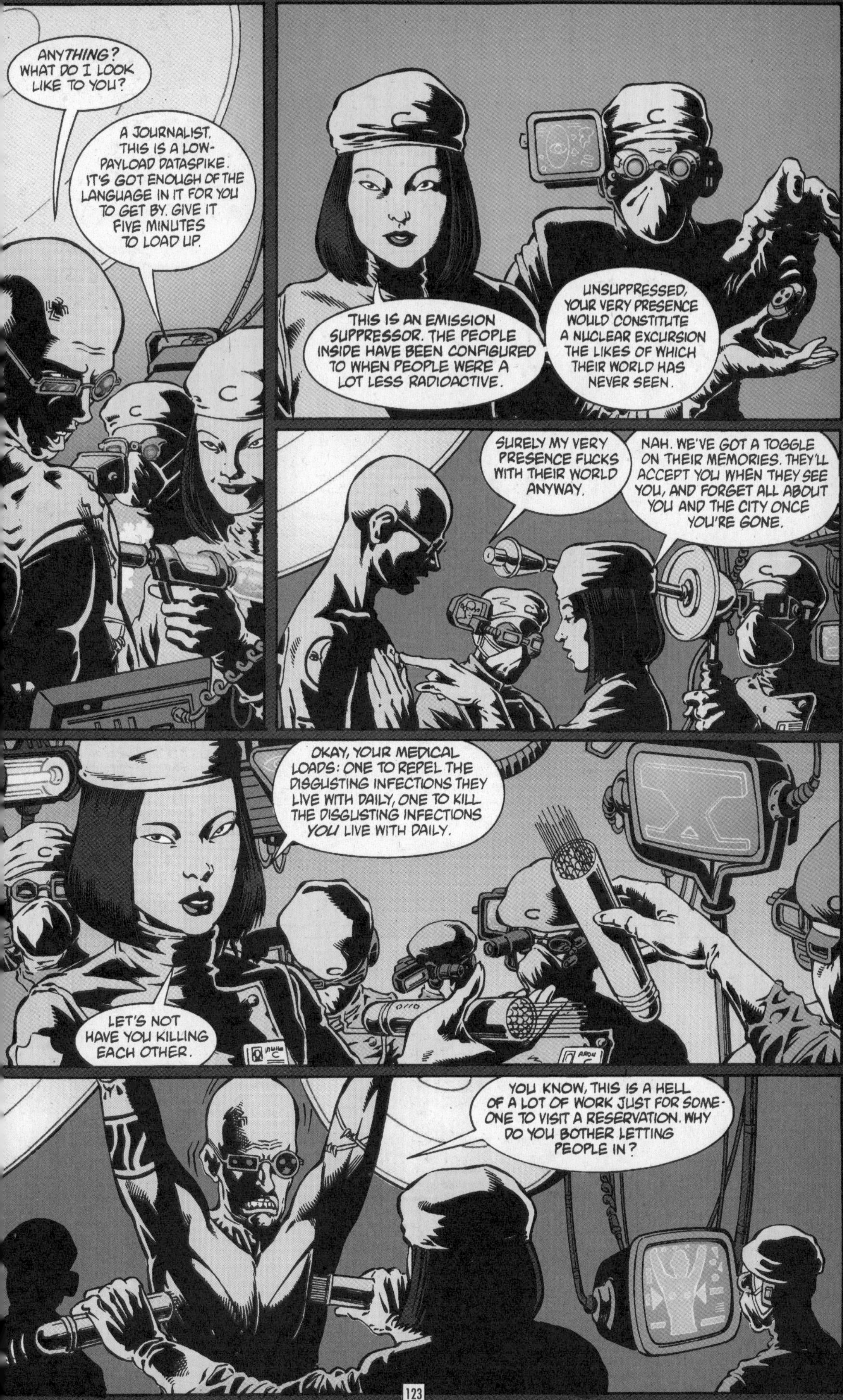

ANYTHING? WHAT DO I LOOK LIKE TO YOU?
A JOURNALIST. THIS IS A LOW-PAYLOAD DATASPIKE. IT'S GOT ENOUGH OF THE LANGUAGE IN IT FOR YOU TO GET BY. GIVE IT FIVE MINUTES TO LOAD UP.
THIS IS AN EMISSION SUPPRESSOR. THE PEOPLE INSIDE HAVE BEEN CONFIGURED TO WHEN PEOPLE WERE A LOT LESS RADIOACTIVE.
UNSUPPRESSED, YOUR VERY PRESENCE WOULD CONSTITUTE A NUCLEAR EXCURSION THE LIKES OF WHICH THEIR WORLD HAS NEVER SEEN.
SURELY MY VERY PRESENCE FUCKS WITH THEIR WORLD ANYWAY.
NAH. WE'VE GOT A TOGGLE ON THEIR MEMORIES. THEY'LL ACCEPT YOU WHEN THEY SEE YOU, AND FORGET ALL ABOUT YOU AND THE CITY ONCE YOU'RE GONE.
OKAY, YOUR MEDICAL LOADS: ONE TO REPEL THE DISGUSTING INFECTIONS THEY LIVE WITH DAILY, ONE TO KILL THE DISGUSTING INFECTIONS YOU LIVE WITH DAILY.
LET'S NOT HAVE YOU KILLING EACH OTHER.
YOU KNOW, THIS IS A HELL OF A LOT OF WORK JUST FOR SOME-ONE TO VISIT A RESERVATION. WHY DO YOU BOTHER LETTING PEOPLE IN?

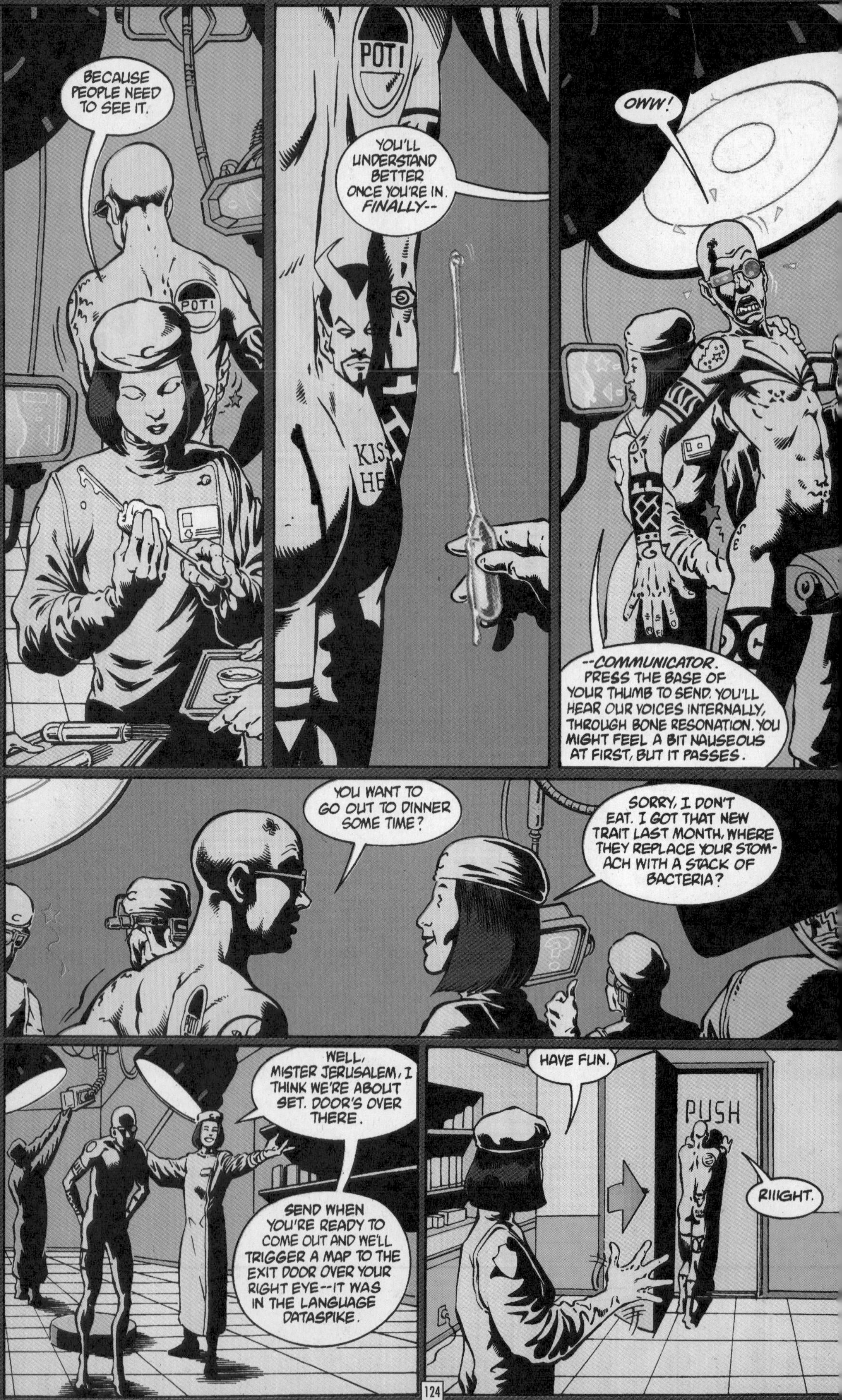

BECAUSE PEOPLE NEED TO SEE IT.
POT I
YOU'LL UNDERSTAND BETTER ONCE YOU'RE IN. *FINALLY--*
KISS HE
OWW!
--*COMMUNICATOR*. PRESS THE BASE OF YOUR THUMB TO SEND. YOU'LL HEAR OUR VOICES INTERNALLY, THROUGH BONE RESONATION. YOU MIGHT FEEL A BIT NAUSEOUS AT FIRST, BUT IT PASSES.
YOU WANT TO GO OUT TO DINNER SOME TIME?
SORRY, I DON'T EAT. I GOT THAT NEW TRAIT LAST MONTH, WHERE THEY REPLACE YOUR STOMACH WITH A STACK OF BACTERIA?
WELL, MISTER JERUSALEM, I THINK WE'RE ABOUT SET. DOOR'S OVER THERE.
SEND WHEN YOU'RE READY TO COME OUT AND WE'LL TRIGGER A MAP TO THE EXIT DOOR OVER YOUR RIGHT EYE--IT WAS IN THE LANGUAGE DATASPIKE.
HAVE FUN.
PUSH
RIIIGHT.

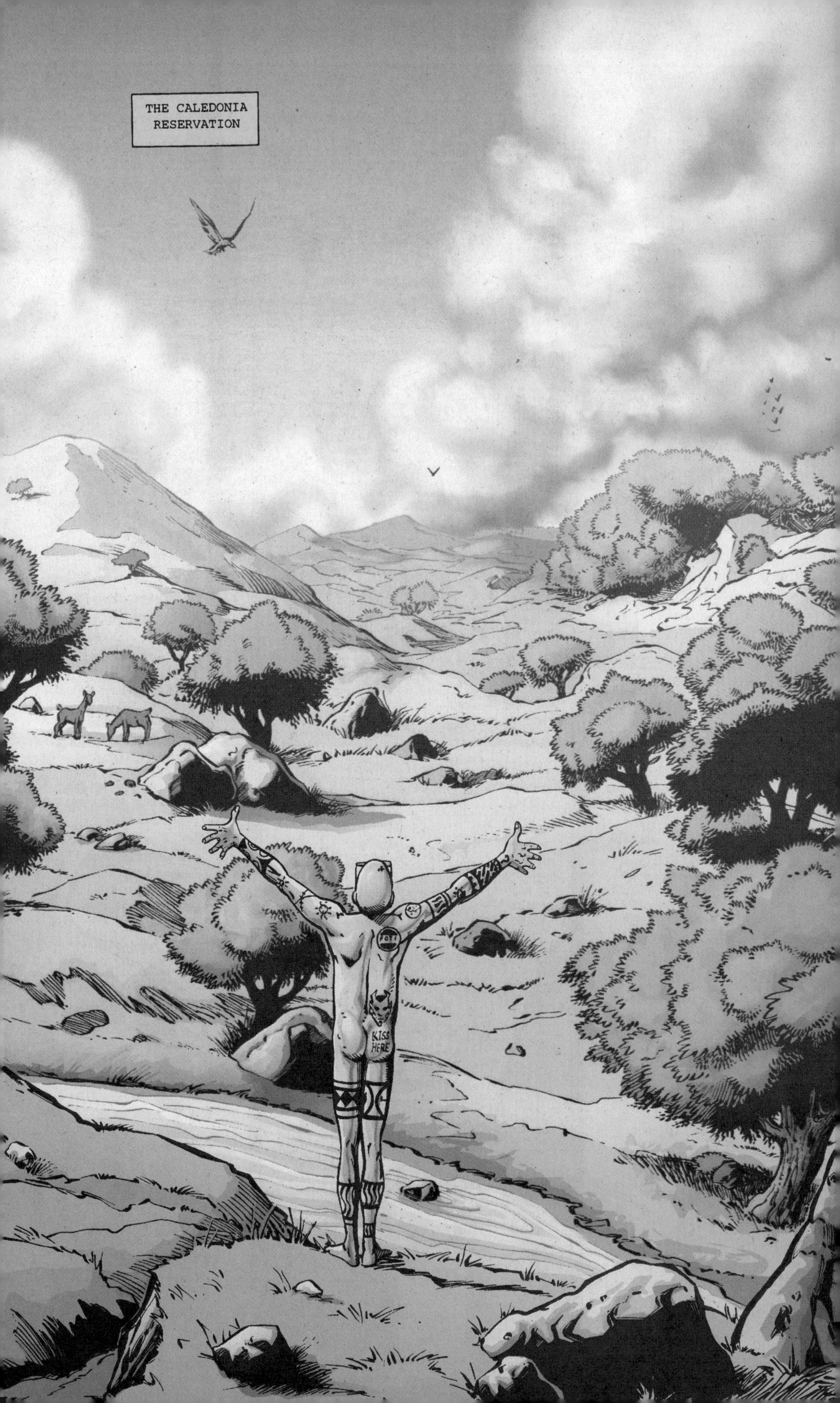
THE CALEDONIA RESERVATION
KISS HERE

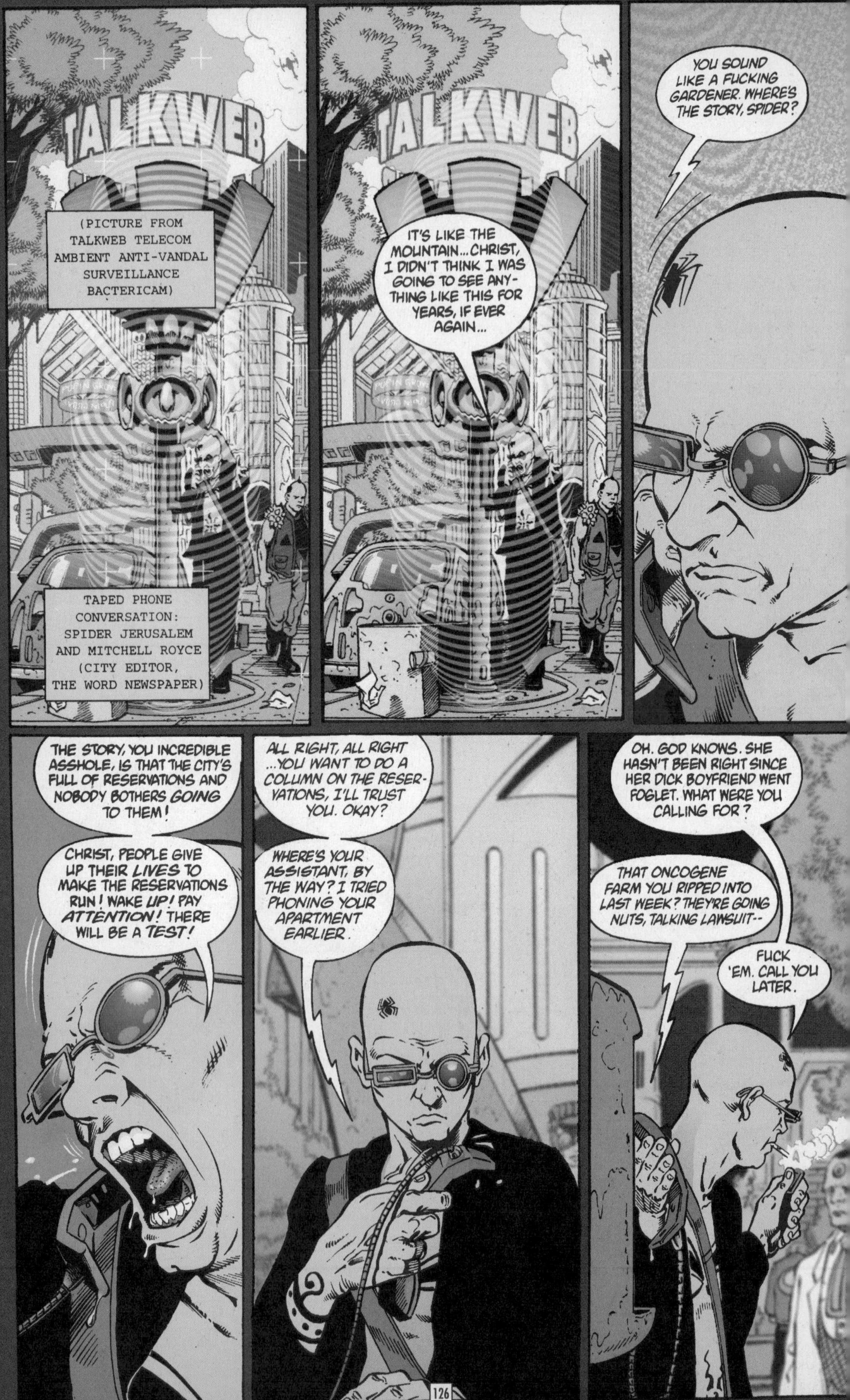
TALKWEB
(PICTURE FROM TALKWEB TELECOM AMBIENT ANTI-VANDAL SURVEILLANCE BACTERICAM)
TAPED PHONE CONVERSATION: SPIDER JERUSALEM AND MITCHELL ROYCE (CITY EDITOR, THE WORD NEWSPAPER)
TALKWEB
IT'S LIKE THE MOUNTAIN... CHRIST, I DIDN'T THINK I WAS GOING TO SEE ANYTHING LIKE THIS FOR YEARS, IF EVER AGAIN...
YOU SOUND LIKE A FUCKING GARDENER. WHERE'S THE STORY, SPIDER?
THE STORY, YOU INCREDIBLE ASSHOLE, IS THAT THE CITY'S FULL OF RESERVATIONS AND NOBODY BOTHERS GOING TO THEM!
CHRIST, PEOPLE GIVE UP THEIR LIVES TO MAKE THE RESERVATIONS RUN! WAKE UP! PAY ATTENTION! THERE WILL BE A TEST!
ALL RIGHT, ALL RIGHT ...YOU WANT TO DO A COLUMN ON THE RESERVATIONS, I'LL TRUST YOU. OKAY?
WHERE'S YOUR ASSISTANT, BY THE WAY? I TRIED PHONING YOUR APARTMENT EARLIER.
OH. GOD KNOWS. SHE HASN'T BEEN RIGHT SINCE HER DICK BOYFRIEND WENT FOGLET. WHAT WERE YOU CALLING FOR?
THAT ONCOGENE FARM YOU RIPPED INTO LAST WEEK? THEY'RE GOING NUTS, TALKING LAWSUIT--
FUCK 'EM. CALL YOU LATER.

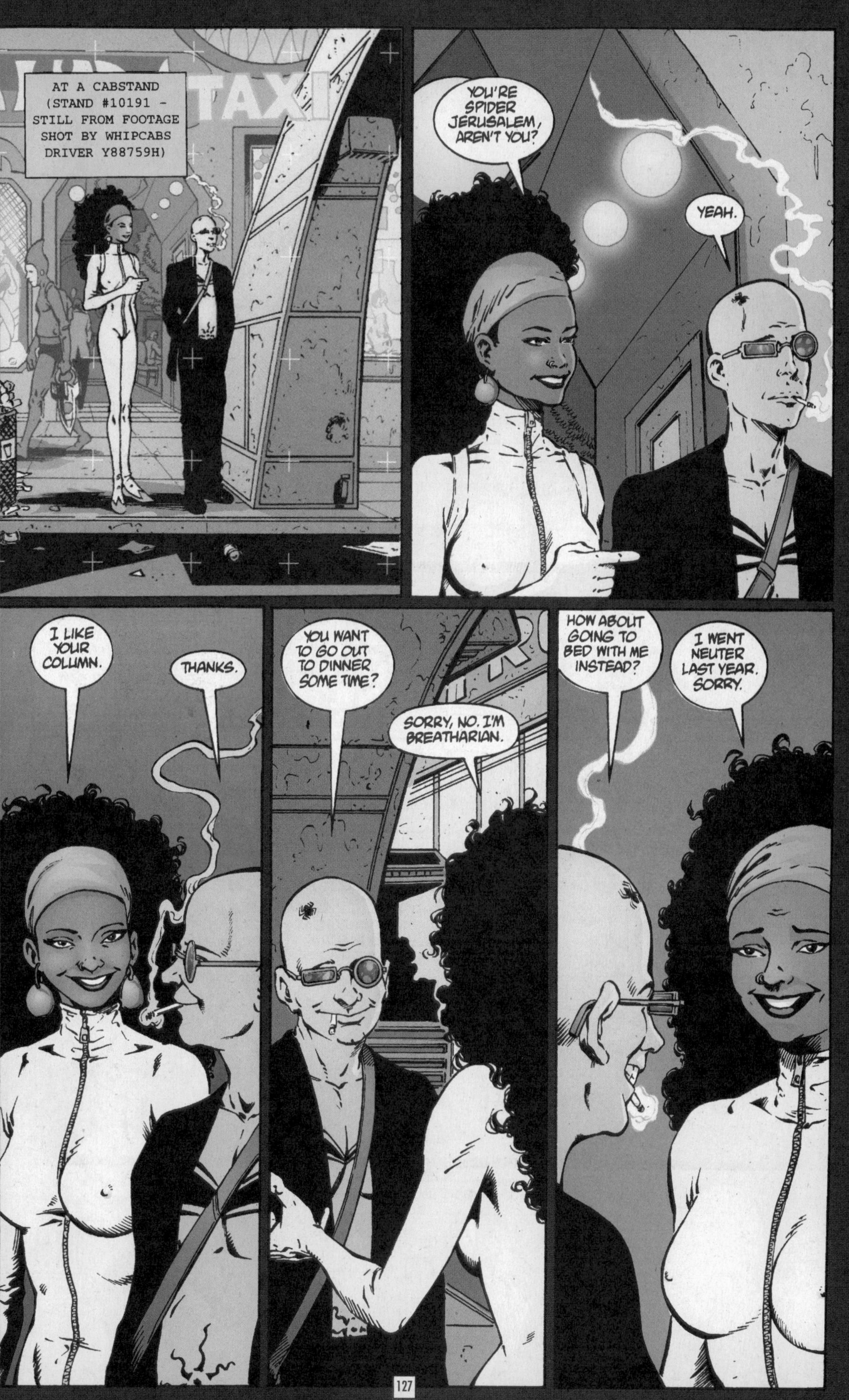

AT A CABSTAND (STAND #10191 - STILL FROM FOOTAGE SHOT BY WHIPCABS DRIVER Y88759H)
TAXI
YOU'RE SPIDER JERUSALEM, AREN'T YOU?
YEAH.
I LIKE YOUR COLUMN.
THANKS.
YOU WANT TO GO OUT TO DINNER SOME TIME?
SORRY, NO. I'M BREATHARIAN.
HOW ABOUT GOING TO BED WITH ME INSTEAD?
I WENT NEUTER LAST YEAR. SORRY.

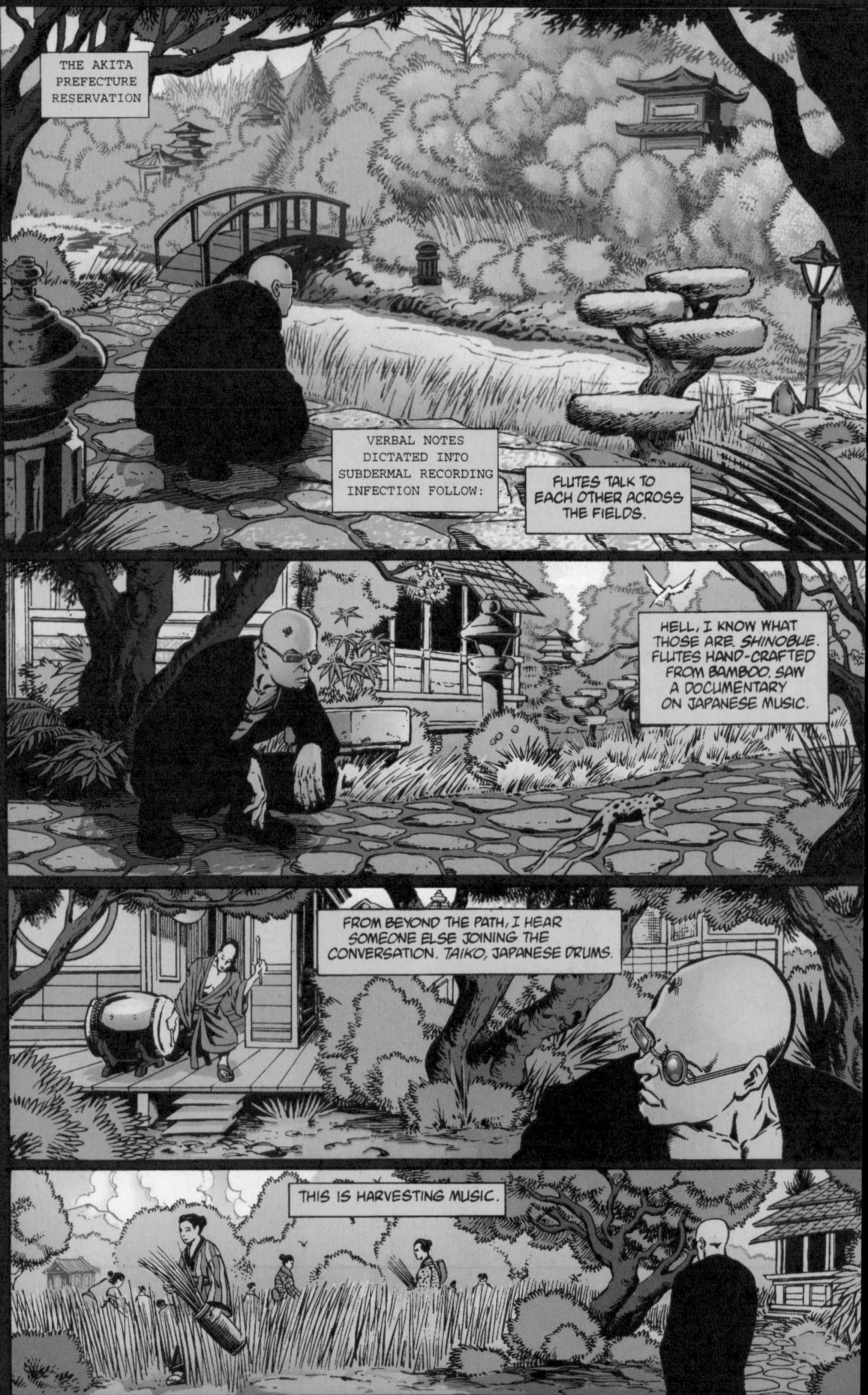
THE AKITA PREFECTURE RESERVATION
VERBAL NOTES DICTATED INTO SUBDERMAL RECORDING INFECTION FOLLOW:
FLUTES TALK TO EACH OTHER ACROSS THE FIELDS.
HELL, I KNOW WHAT THOSE ARE. *SHINOBUE*. FLUTES HAND-CRAFTED FROM BAMBOO. SAW A DOCUMENTARY ON JAPANESE MUSIC.
FROM BEYOND THE PATH, I HEAR SOMEONE ELSE JOINING THE CONVERSATION. *TAIKO*, JAPANESE DRUMS.
THIS IS HARVESTING MUSIC.

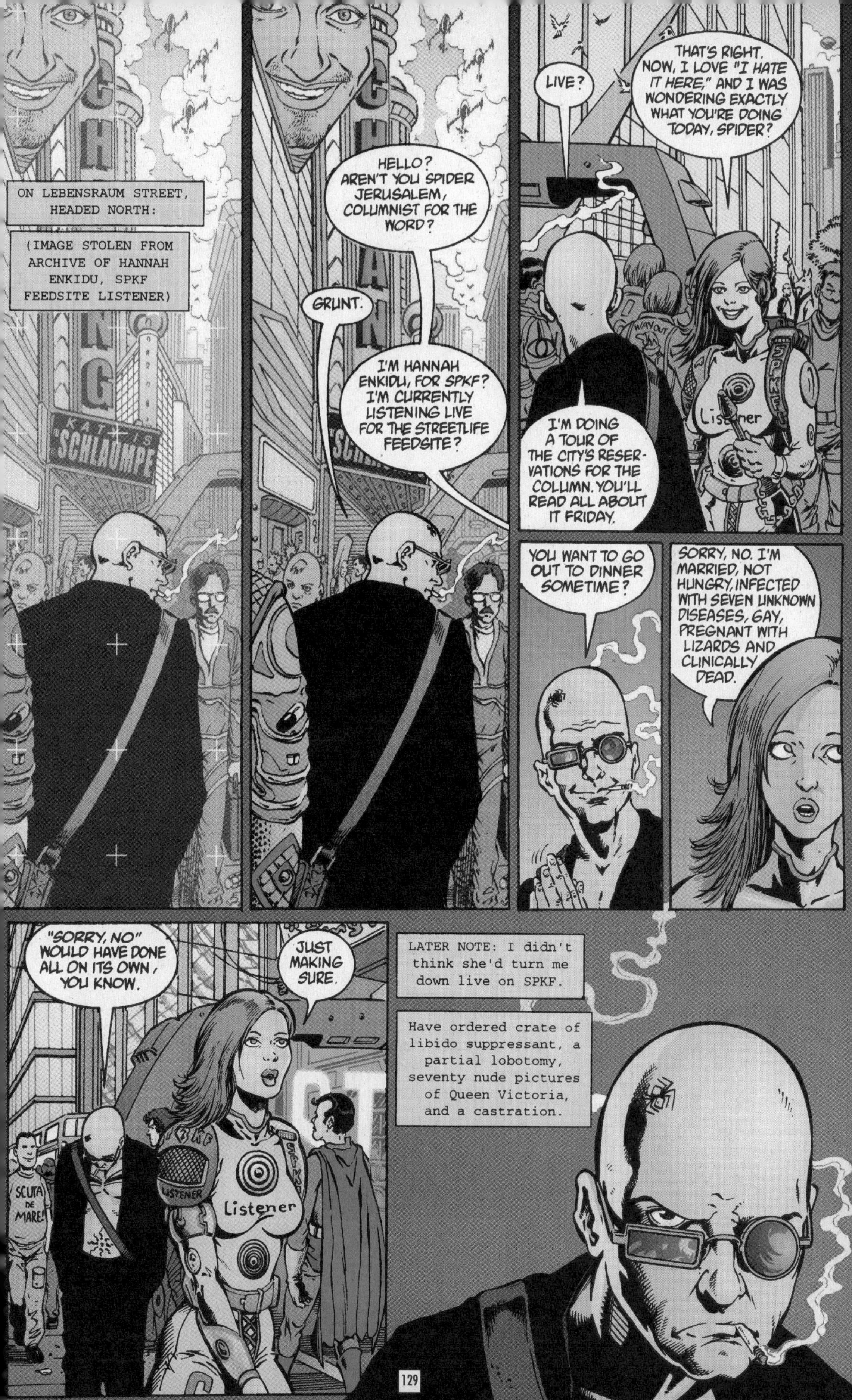
ON LEBENSRAUM STREET, HEADED NORTH:
(IMAGE STOLEN FROM ARCHIVE OF HANNAH ENKIDU, SPKF FEEDSITE LISTENER)
SCHLAUMPE
HELLO? AREN'T YOU SPIDER JERUSALEM, COLUMNIST FOR THE WORD?
GRUNT.
I'M HANNAH ENKIDU, FOR SPKF? I'M CURRENTLY LISTENING LIVE FOR THE STREETLIFE FEEDSITE?
LIVE?
THAT'S RIGHT. NOW, I LOVE "I HATE IT HERE," AND I WAS WONDERING EXACTLY WHAT YOU'RE DOING TODAY, SPIDER?
I'M DOING A TOUR OF THE CITY'S RESERVATIONS FOR THE COLUMN. YOU'LL READ ALL ABOUT IT FRIDAY.
Listener
SPKF
YOU WANT TO GO OUT TO DINNER SOMETIME?
SORRY, NO. I'M MARRIED, NOT HUNGRY, INFECTED WITH SEVEN UNKNOWN DISEASES, GAY, PREGNANT WITH LIZARDS AND CLINICALLY DEAD.
"SORRY, NO" WOULD HAVE DONE ALL ON ITS OWN, YOU KNOW.
JUST MAKING SURE.
SCUTA DE MARE!
Listener
LATER NOTE: I didn't think she'd turn me down live on SPKF.
Have ordered crate of libido suppressant, a partial lobotomy, seventy nude pictures of Queen Victoria, and a castration.

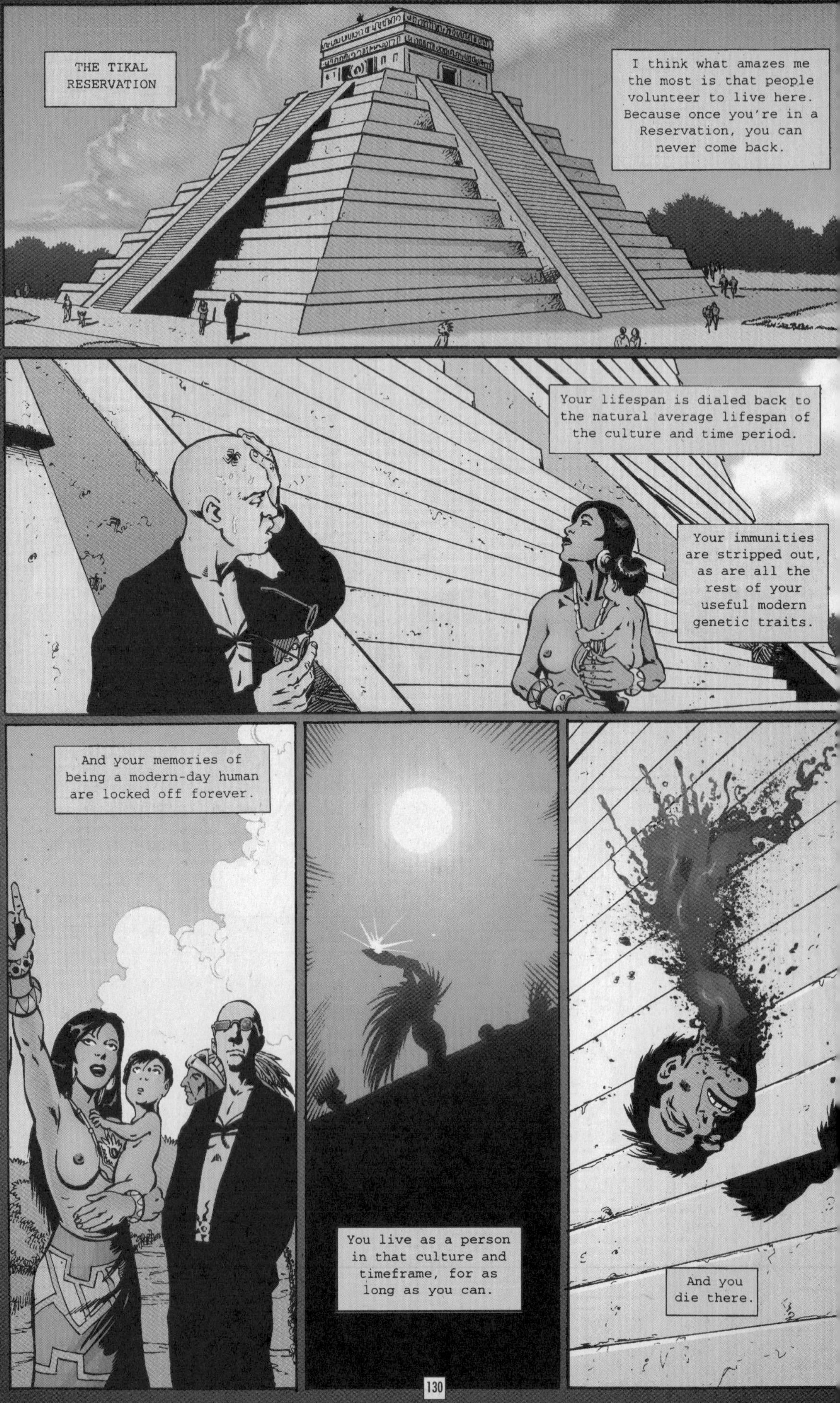
THE TIKAL RESERVATION
I think what amazes me the most is that people volunteer to live here. Because once you're in a Reservation, you can never come back.
Your lifespan is dialed back to the natural average lifespan of the culture and time period.
Your immunities are stripped out, as are all the rest of your useful modern genetic traits.
And your memories of being a modern-day human are locked off forever.
You live as a person in that culture and timeframe, for as long as you can.
And you die there.

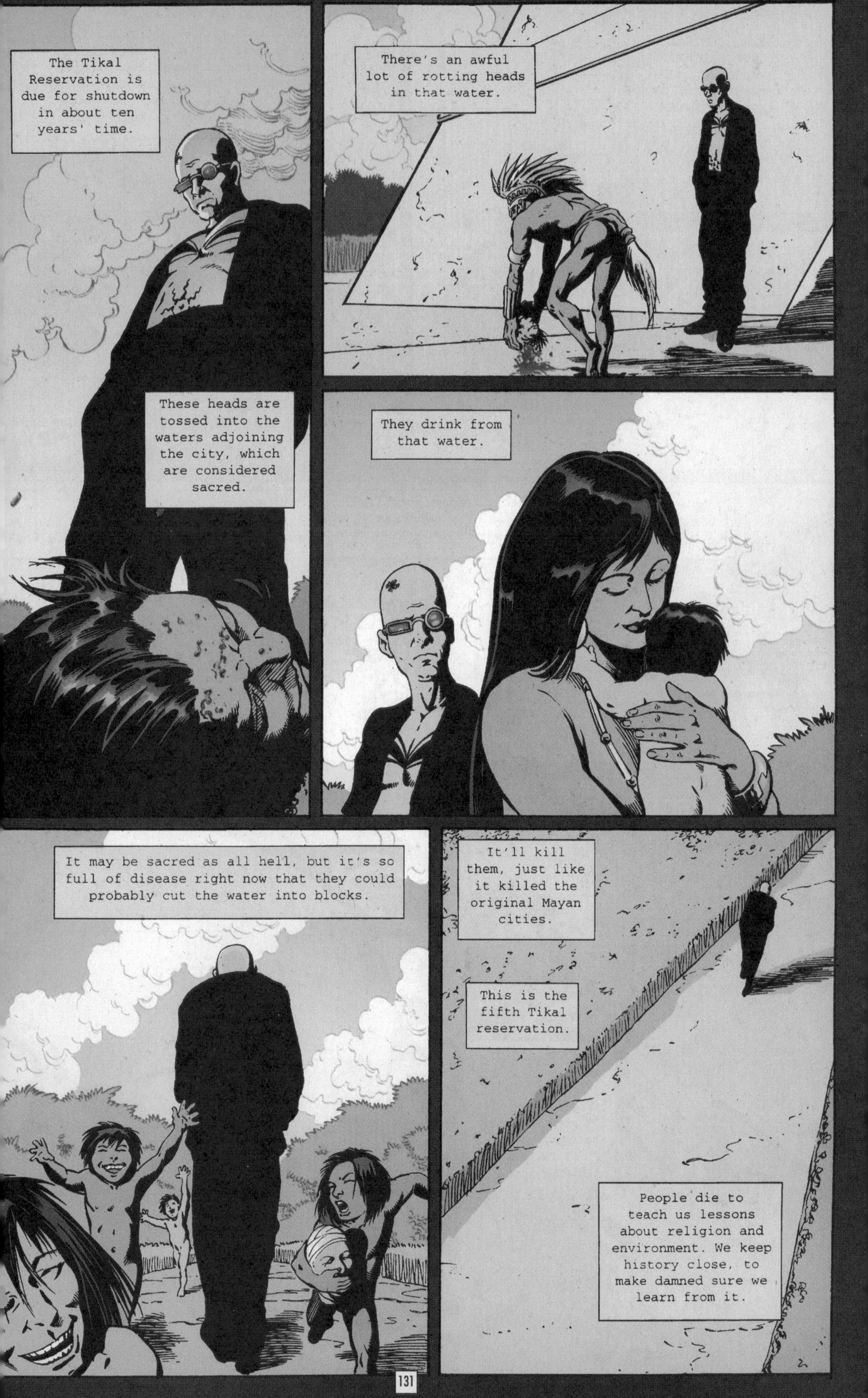

The Tikal Reservation is due for shutdown in about ten years' time.
There's an awful lot of rotting heads in that water.
These heads are tossed into the waters adjoining the city, which are considered sacred.
They drink from that water.
It may be sacred as all hell, but it's so full of disease right now that they could probably cut the water into blocks.
It'll kill them, just like it killed the original Mayan cities.
This is the fifth Tikal reservation.
People die to teach us lessons about religion and environment. We keep history close, to make damned sure we learn from it.

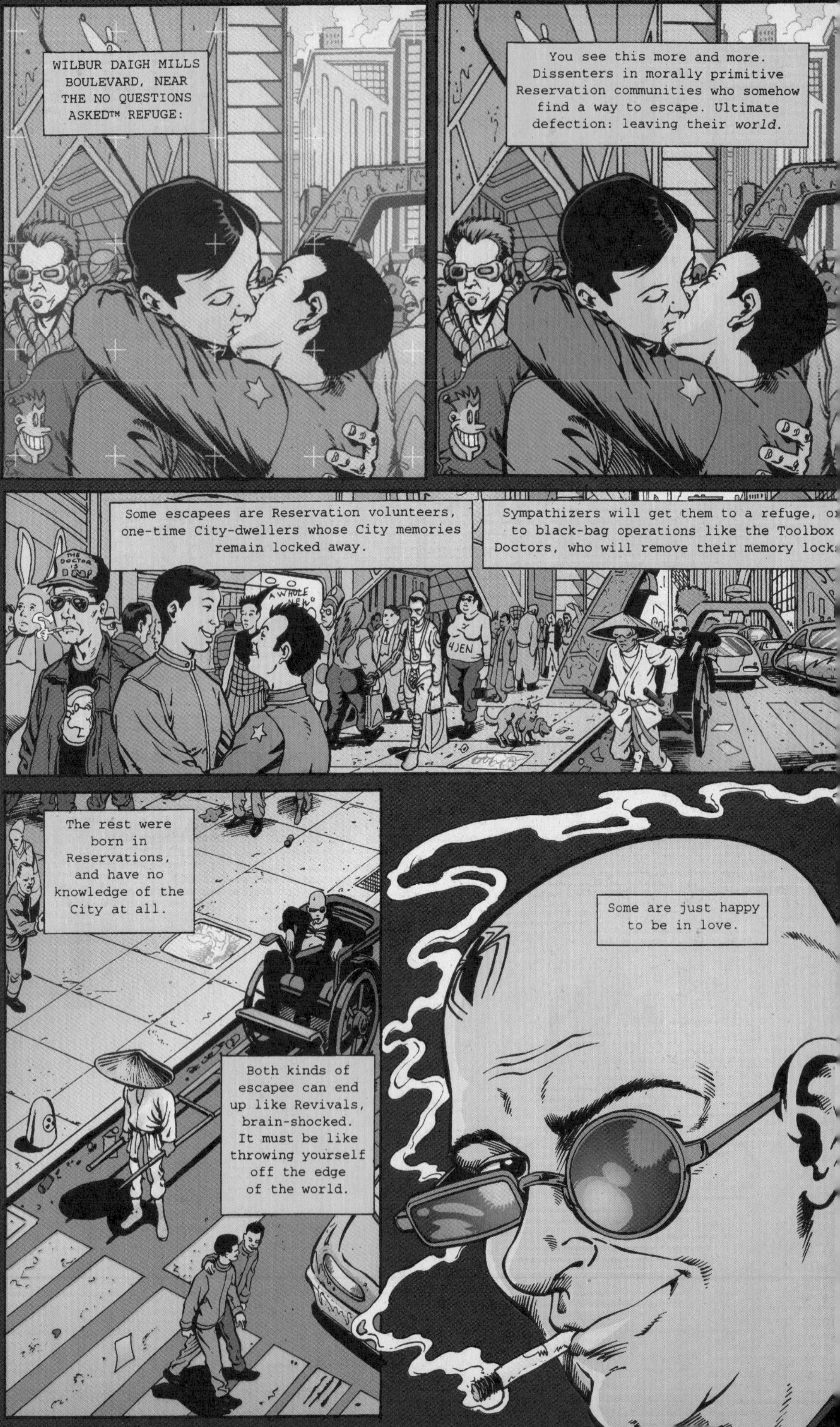
WILBUR DAIGH MILLS BOULEVARD, NEAR THE NO QUESTIONS ASKED™ REFUGE:
You see this more and more. Dissenters in morally primitive Reservation communities who somehow find a way to escape. Ultimate defection: leaving their *world*.
Some escapees are Reservation volunteers, one-time City-dwellers whose City memories remain locked away.
Sympathizers will get them to a refuge, or to black-bag operations like the Toolbox Doctors, who will remove their memory locks.
THE DOCTOR IS
4JEN
The rest were born in Reservations, and have no knowledge of the City at all.
Both kinds of escapee can end up like Revivals, brain-shocked. It must be like throwing yourself off the edge of the world.
Some are just happy to be in love.

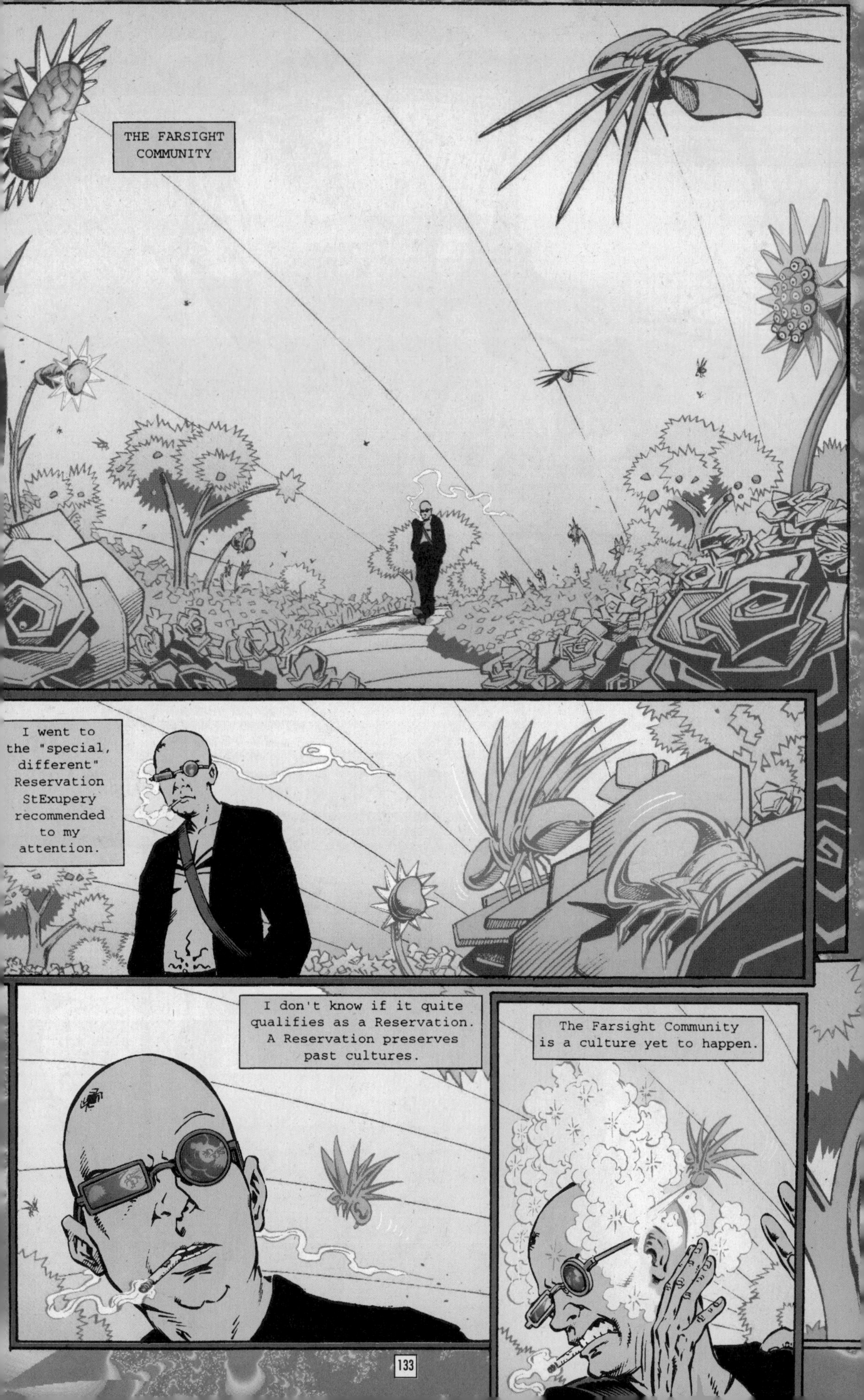
THE FARSIGHT COMMUNITY
I went to the "special, different" Reservation StExupery recommended to my attention.
I don't know if it quite qualifies as a Reservation. A Reservation preserves past cultures.
The Farsight Community is a culture yet to happen.

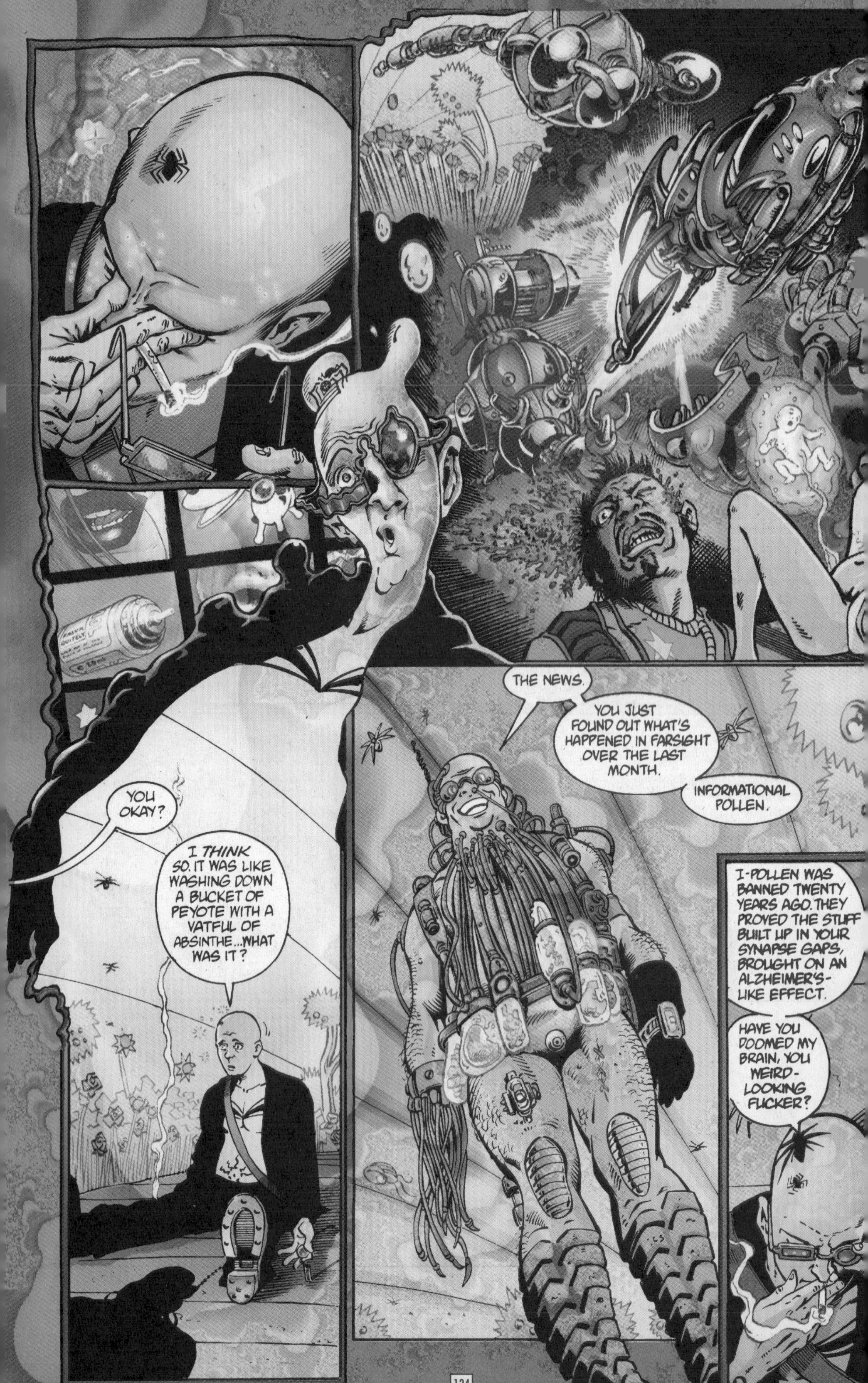
THE NEWS.
YOU JUST FOUND OUT WHAT'S HAPPENED IN FARSIGHT OVER THE LAST MONTH.
INFORMATIONAL POLLEN.
YOU OKAY?
I THINK SO. IT WAS LIKE WASHING DOWN A BUCKET OF PEYOTE WITH A VATFUL OF ABSINTHE...WHAT WAS IT?
I-POLLEN WAS BANNED TWENTY YEARS AGO. THEY PROVED THE STUFF BUILT UP IN YOUR SYNAPSE GAPS, BROUGHT ON AN ALZHEIMER'S-LIKE EFFECT.
HAVE YOU DOOMED MY BRAIN, YOU WEIRD-LOOKING FUCKER?

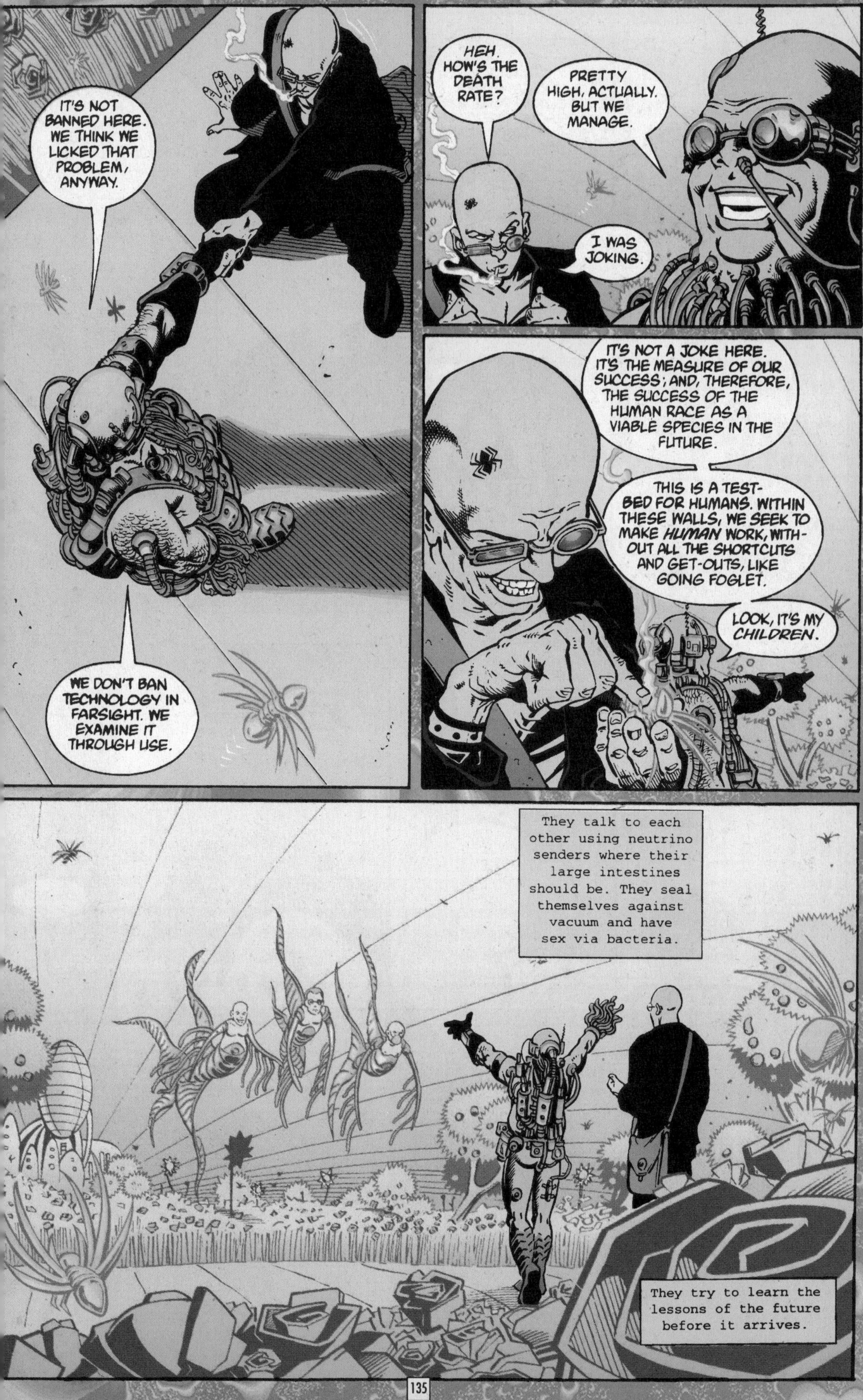

IT'S NOT BANNED HERE. WE THINK WE LICKED THAT PROBLEM, ANYWAY.
WE DON'T BAN TECHNOLOGY IN FARSIGHT. WE EXAMINE IT THROUGH USE.
HEH. HOW'S THE DEATH RATE?
PRETTY HIGH, ACTUALLY. BUT WE MANAGE.
I WAS JOKING.
IT'S NOT A JOKE HERE. IT'S THE MEASURE OF OUR SUCCESS; AND, THEREFORE, THE SUCCESS OF THE HUMAN RACE AS A VIABLE SPECIES IN THE FUTURE.
THIS IS A TEST-BED FOR HUMANS. WITHIN THESE WALLS, WE SEEK TO MAKE HUMAN WORK, WITH-OUT ALL THE SHORTCUTS AND GET-OUTS, LIKE GOING FOGLET.
LOOK, IT'S MY CHILDREN.
They talk to each other using neutrino senders where their large intestines should be. They seal themselves against vacuum and have sex via bacteria.
They try to learn the lessons of the future before it arrives.

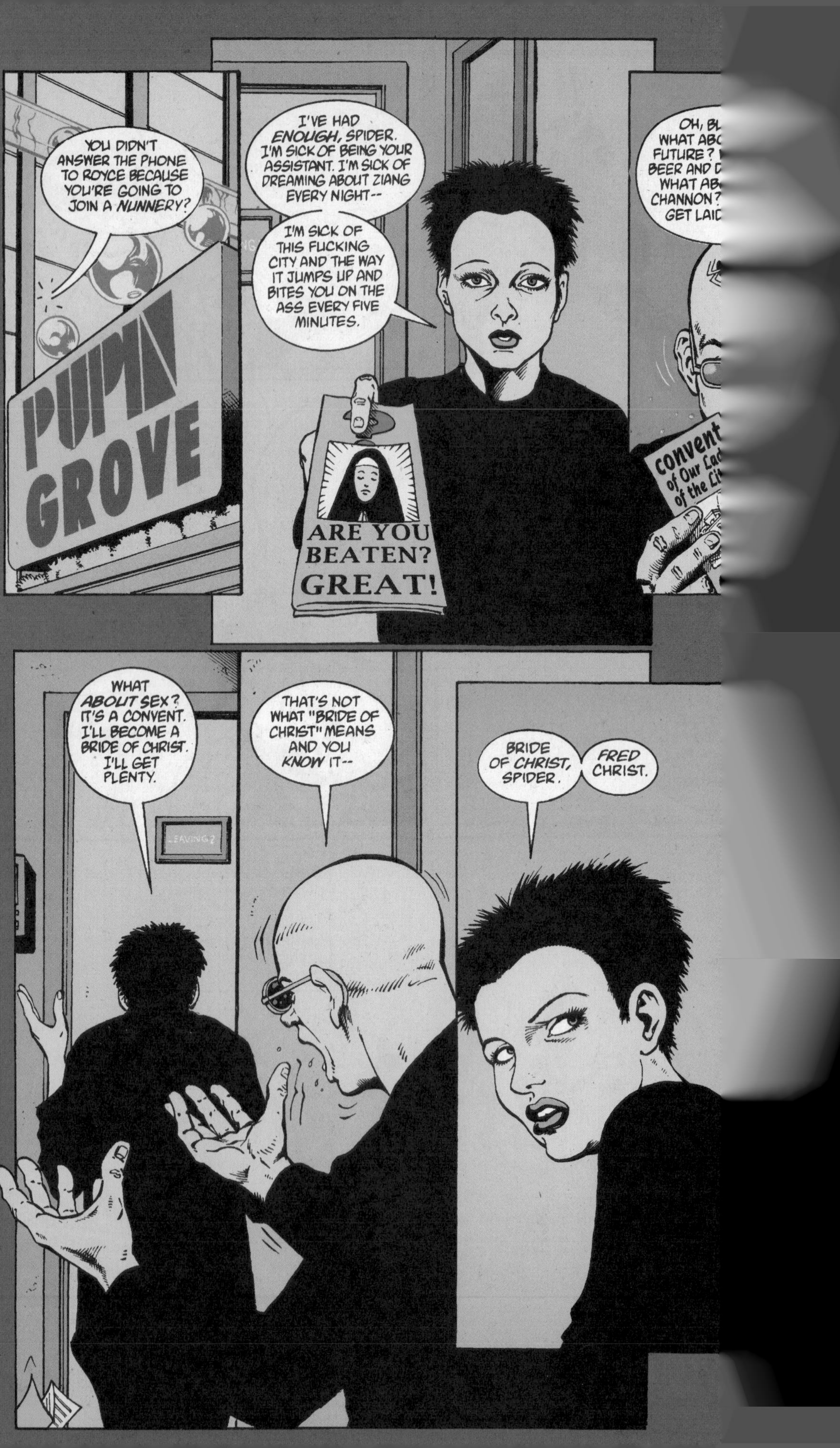
YOU DIDN'T ANSWER THE PHONE TO ROYCE BECAUSE YOU'RE GOING TO JOIN A *NUNNERY*?
PUPA GROVE
I'VE HAD *ENOUGH*, SPIDER. I'M SICK OF BEING YOUR ASSISTANT. I'M SICK OF DREAMING ABOUT ZIANG EVERY NIGHT--
I'M SICK OF THIS FUCKING CITY AND THE WAY IT JUMPS UP AND BITES YOU ON THE ASS EVERY FIVE MINUTES.
ARE YOU BEATEN? GREAT!
WHAT *ABOUT* SEX? IT'S A CONVENT. I'LL BECOME A BRIDE OF CHRIST. I'LL GET PLENTY.
LEAVING?
THAT'S NOT WHAT "BRIDE OF CHRIST" MEANS AND YOU *KNOW* IT--
BRIDE OF *CHRIST*, SPIDER.
*FRED* CHRIST.

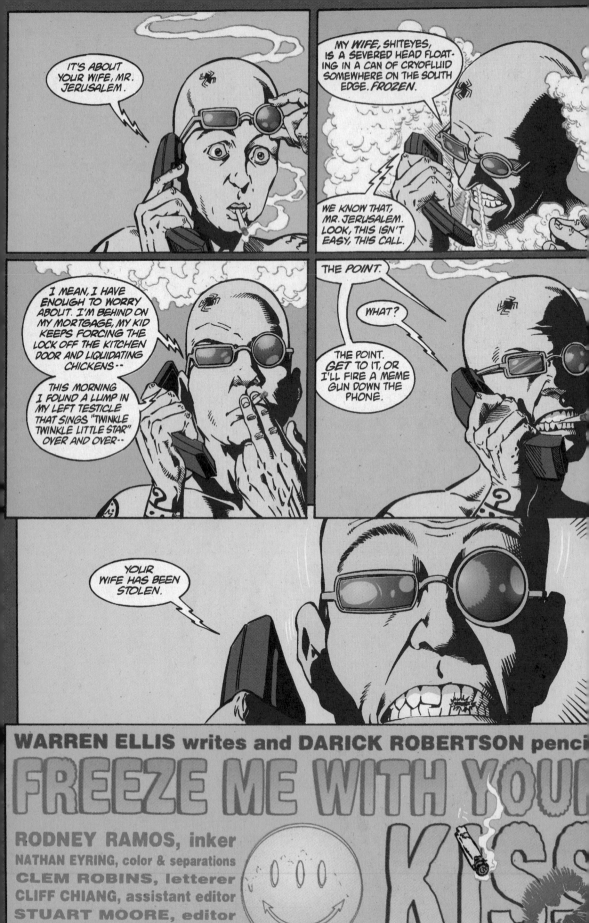

IT'S ABOUT YOUR WIFE, MR. JERUSALEM.

MY *WIFE*, SHITEYES, IS A SEVERED HEAD FLOATING IN A CAN OF CRYOFLUID SOMEWHERE ON THE SOUTH EDGE. *FROZEN.*

WE KNOW THAT, MR. JERUSALEM. LOOK, THIS ISN'T EASY, THIS CALL.

I MEAN, I HAVE ENOUGH TO WORRY ABOUT. I'M BEHIND ON MY MORTGAGE, MY KID KEEPS FORCING THE LOCK OFF THE KITCHEN DOOR AND LIQUIDATING CHICKENS--

THIS MORNING I FOUND A LUMP IN MY LEFT TESTICLE THAT SINGS "TWINKLE TWINKLE LITTLE STAR" OVER AND OVER--

THE *POINT.*

WHAT?

THE POINT. *GET* TO IT, OR I'LL FIRE A MEME GUN DOWN THE PHONE.

YOUR WIFE HAS BEEN STOLEN.

WARREN ELLIS writes and DARICK ROBERTSON penci

FREEZE ME WITH YOU

KISS

RODNEY RAMOS, inker
NATHAN EYRING, color & separations
CLEM ROBINS, letterer
CLIFF CHIANG, assistant editor
STUART MOORE, editor

TRANSMETROPOLITAN CREATED BY
WARREN ELLIS & DARICK ROBERTSON

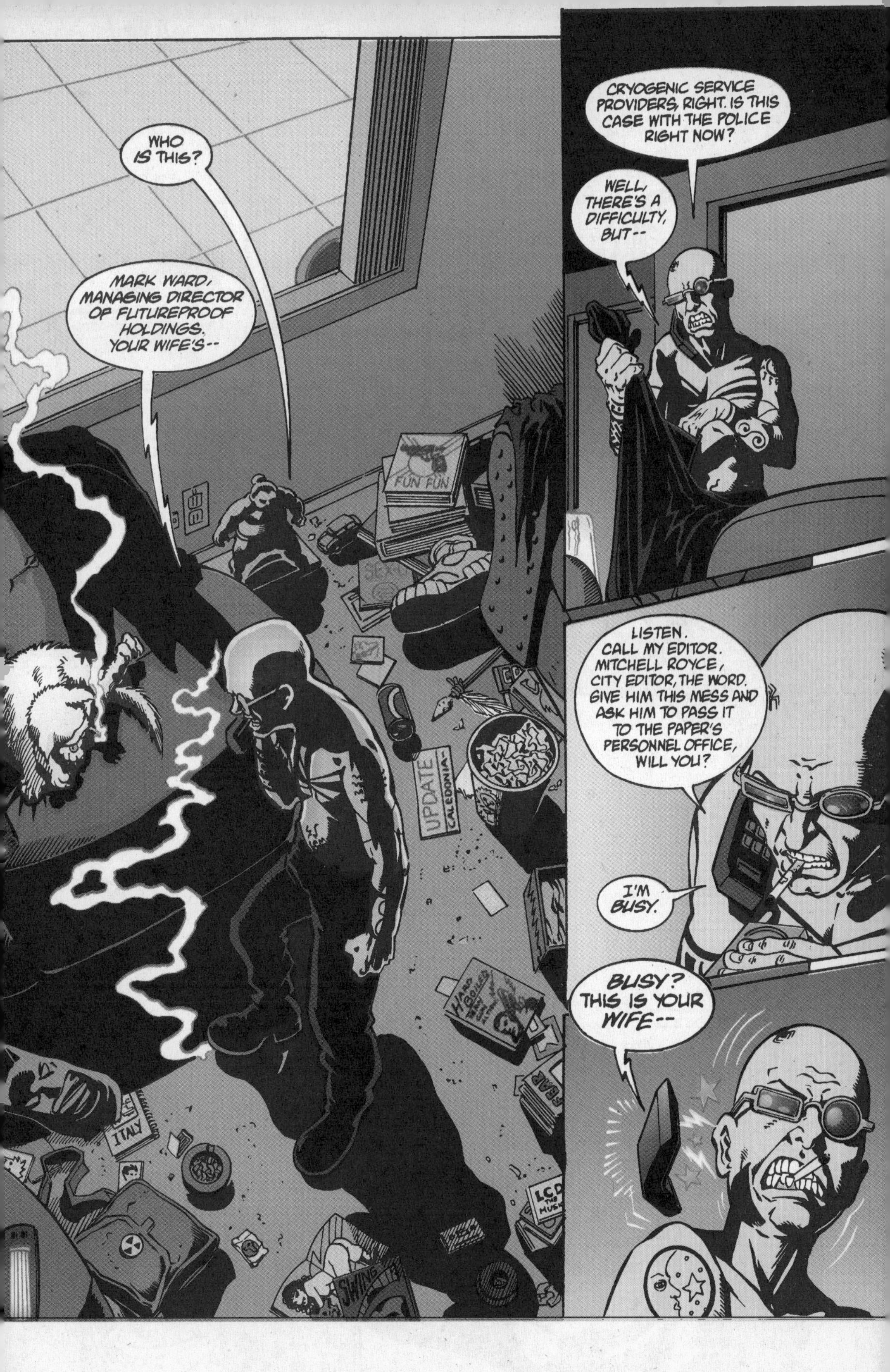
WHO IS THIS?
MARK WARD, MANAGING DIRECTOR OF FUTUREPROOF HOLDINGS. YOUR WIFE'S--
CRYOGENIC SERVICE PROVIDERS, RIGHT. IS THIS CASE WITH THE POLICE RIGHT NOW?
WELL, THERE'S A DIFFICULTY, BUT--
LISTEN. CALL MY EDITOR. MITCHELL ROYCE, CITY EDITOR, THE WORD. GIVE HIM THIS MESS AND ASK HIM TO PASS IT TO THE PAPER'S PERSONNEL OFFICE, WILL YOU?
I'M BUSY.
BUSY? THIS IS YOUR WIFE--
FUN FUN
UPDATE
CALEDONIA
ITALY
SWING

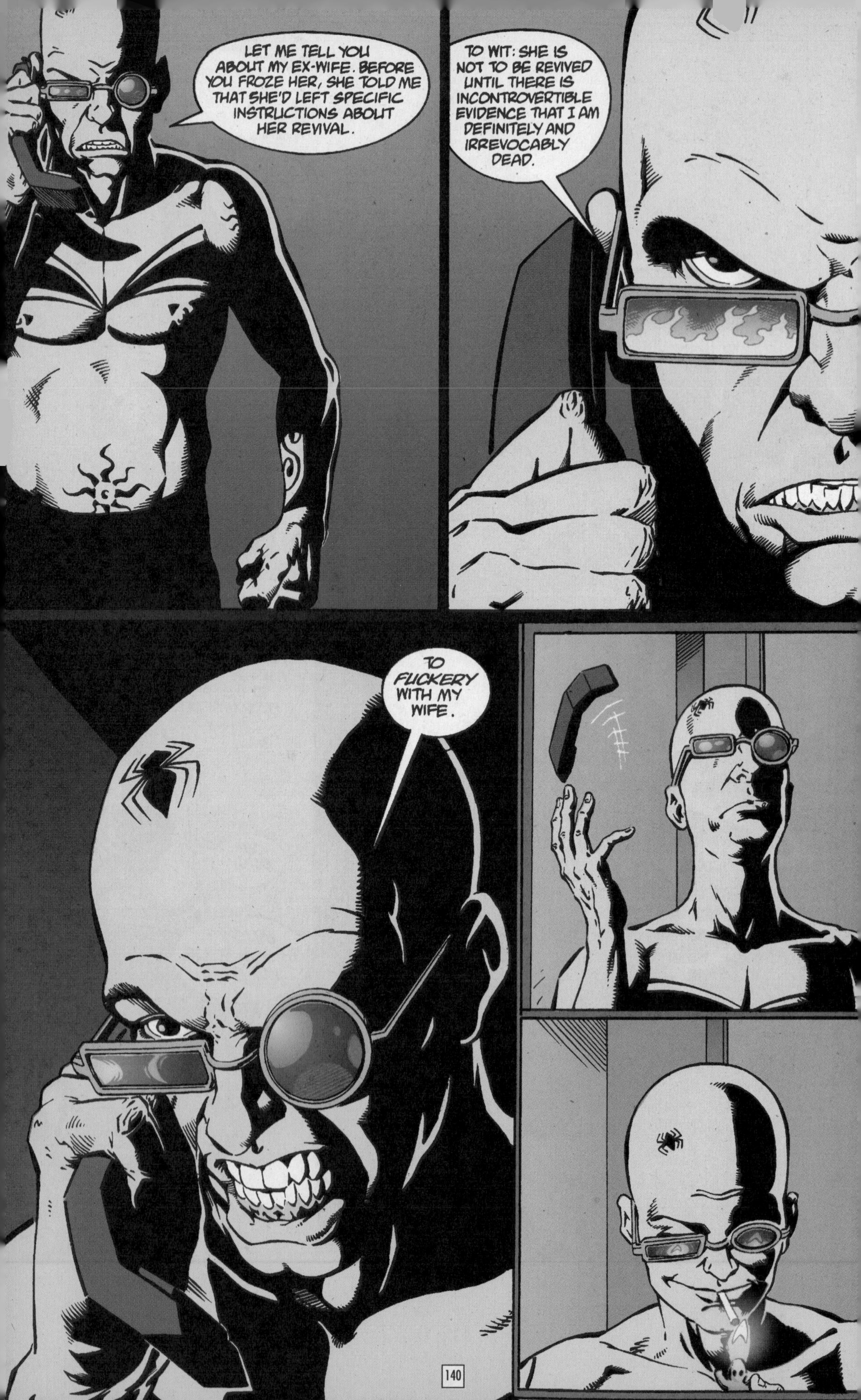
LET ME TELL YOU ABOUT MY EX-WIFE. BEFORE YOU FROZE HER, SHE TOLD ME THAT SHE'D LEFT SPECIFIC INSTRUCTIONS ABOUT HER REVIVAL.
TO WIT: SHE IS NOT TO BE REVIVED UNTIL THERE IS INCONTROVERTIBLE EVIDENCE THAT I AM DEFINITELY AND IRREVOCABLY DEAD.
TO FUCKERY WITH MY WIFE.

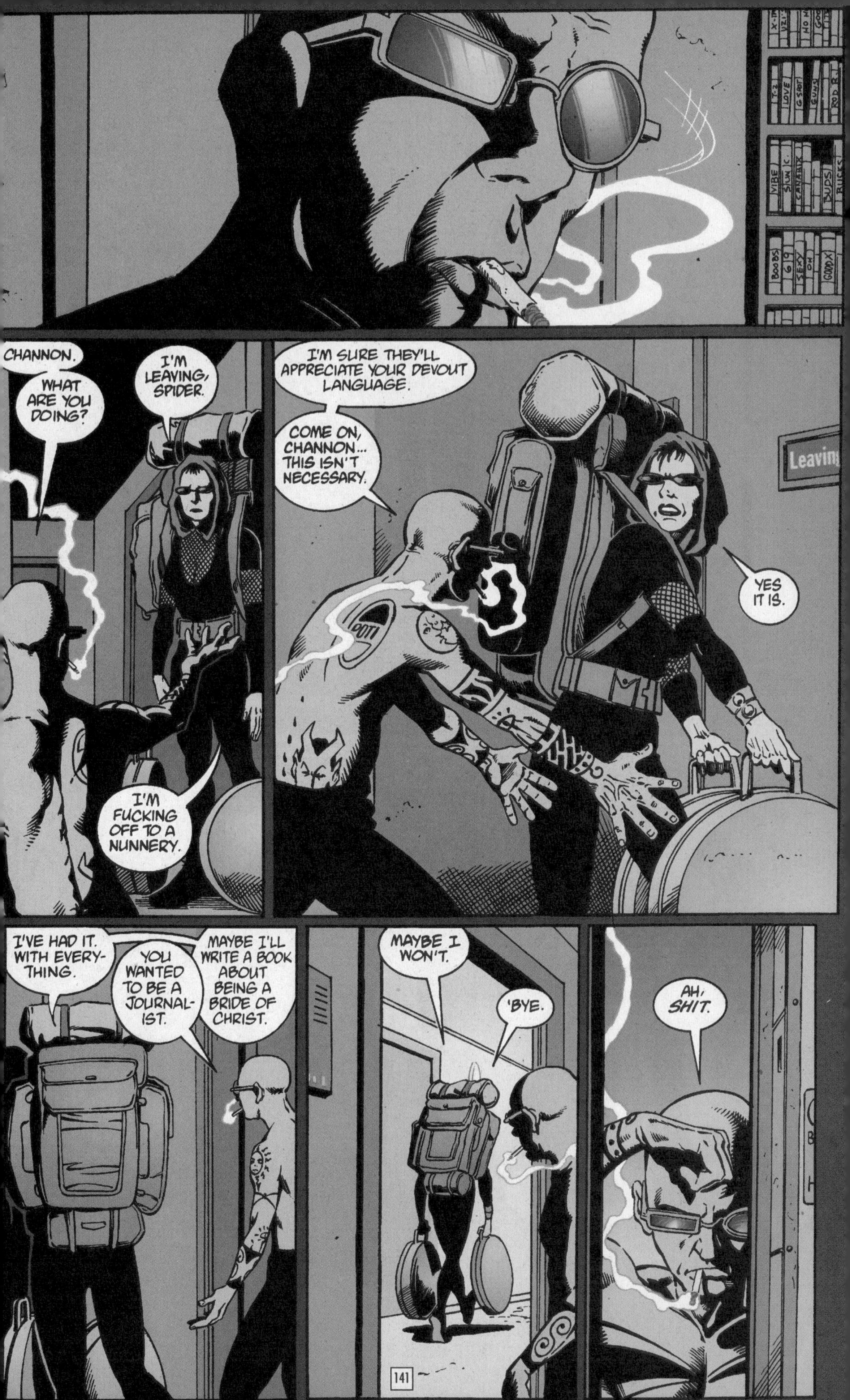
X-I
U2
HO
T-3
LOVE
GSBT
GUNS
ROD R.
VIBE
SLW C.
CANABIX
DUDS
BUCKS
BOOBS
69
SEXY
GOODX
CHANNON.
WHAT ARE YOU DOING?
I'M LEAVING, SPIDER.
I'M FUCKING OFF TO A NUNNERY.
I'M SURE THEY'LL APPRECIATE YOUR DEVOUT LANGUAGE.
COME ON, CHANNON... THIS ISN'T NECESSARY.
Leaving
YES IT IS.
I'VE HAD IT. WITH EVERY-THING.
YOU WANTED TO BE A JOURNAL-IST.
MAYBE I'LL WRITE A BOOK ABOUT BEING A BRIDE OF CHRIST.
MAYBE I WON'T.
'BYE.
AH, SHIT.

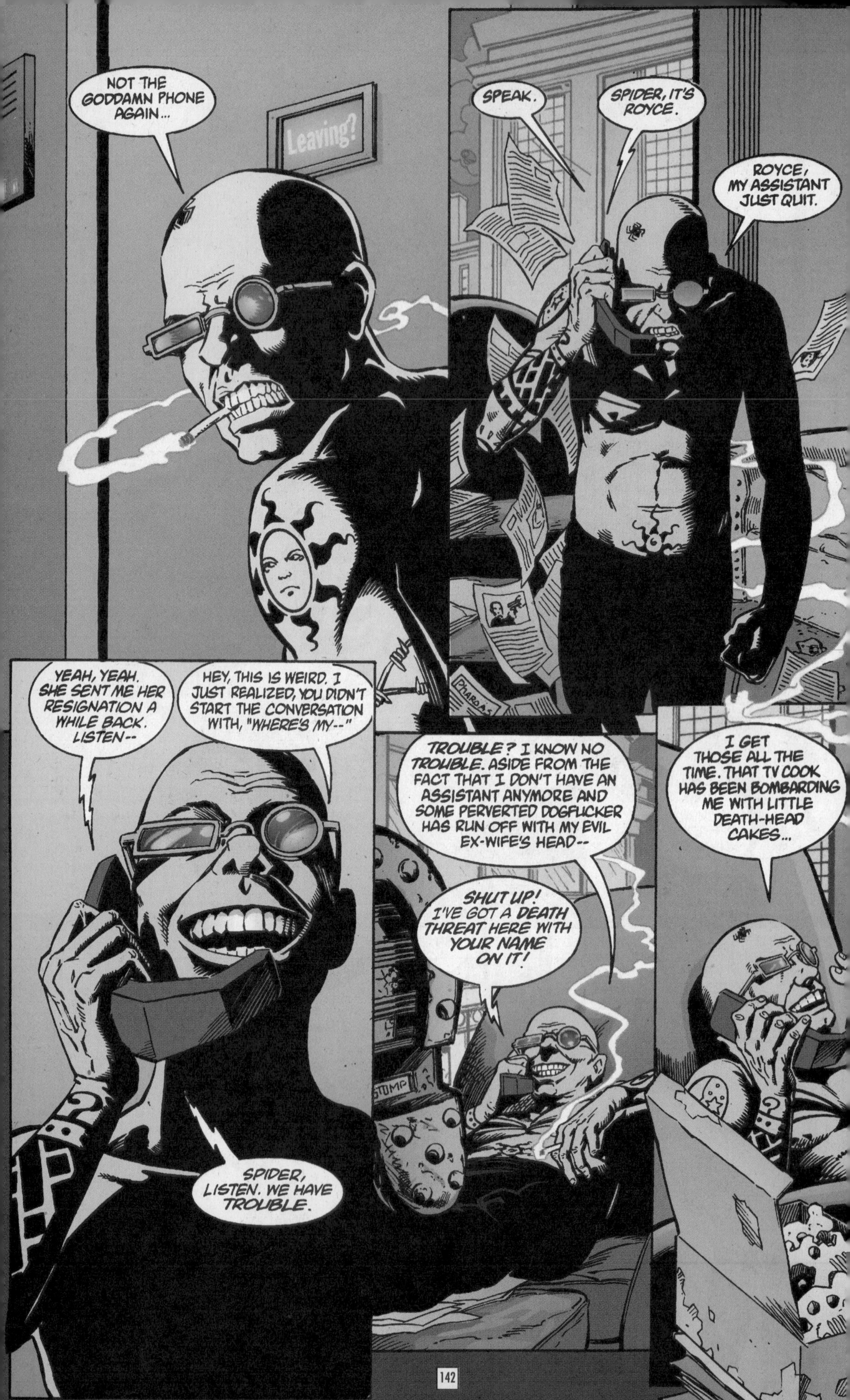
NOT THE GODDAMN PHONE AGAIN...
Leaving?
SPEAK.
SPIDER, IT'S ROYCE.
ROYCE, MY ASSISTANT JUST QUIT.
YEAH, YEAH. SHE SENT ME HER RESIGNATION A WHILE BACK. LISTEN--
HEY, THIS IS WEIRD. I JUST REALIZED, YOU DIDN'T START THE CONVERSATION WITH, "WHERE'S MY--"
SPIDER, LISTEN. WE HAVE TROUBLE.
TROUBLE? I KNOW NO TROUBLE. ASIDE FROM THE FACT THAT I DON'T HAVE AN ASSISTANT ANYMORE AND SOME PERVERTED DOGFUCKER HAS RUN OFF WITH MY EVIL EX-WIFE'S HEAD--
SHUT UP! I'VE GOT A DEATH THREAT HERE WITH YOUR NAME ON IT!
I GET THOSE ALL THE TIME. THAT TV COOK HAS BEEN BOMBARDING ME WITH LITTLE DEATH-HEAD CAKES...

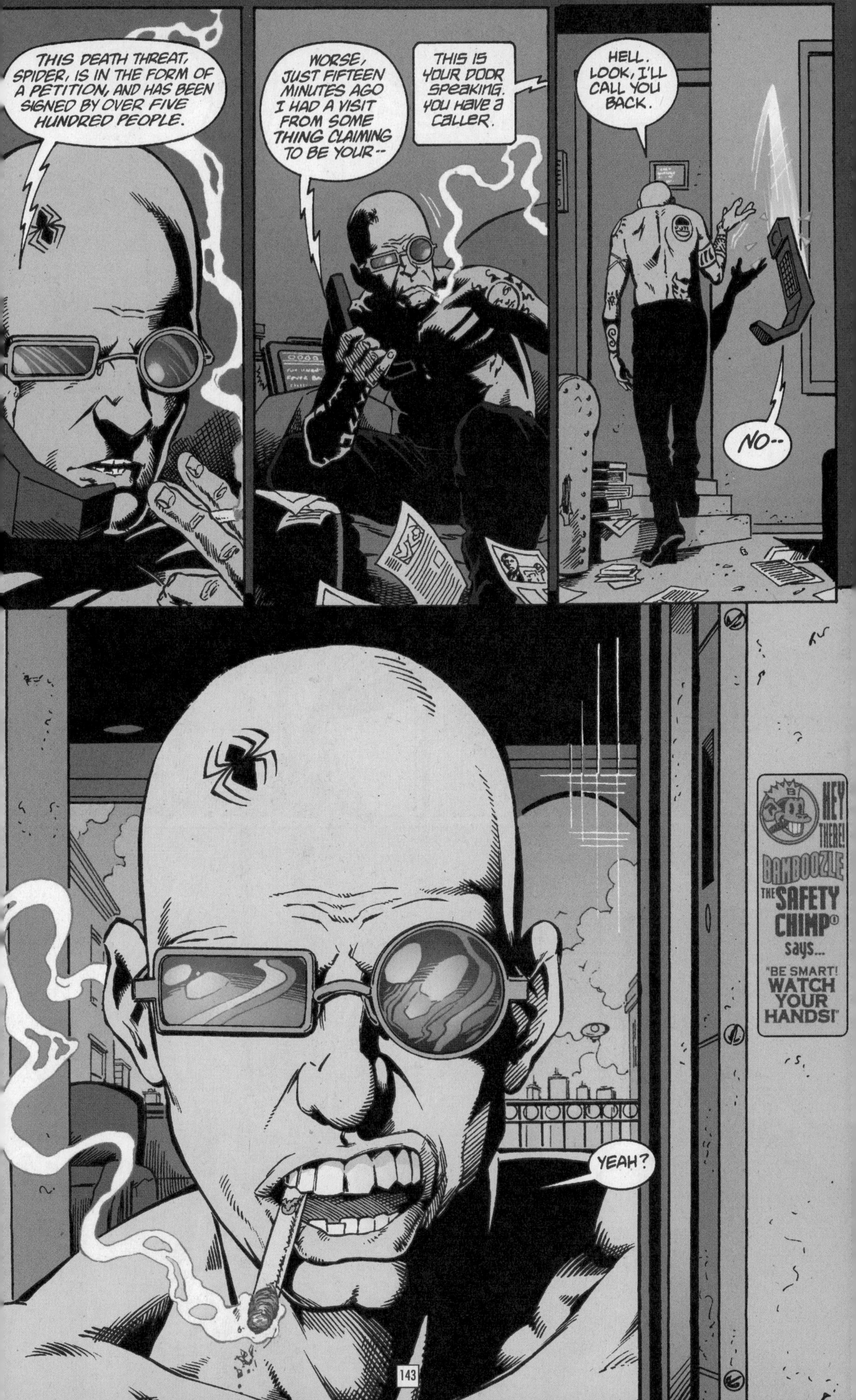
THIS DEATH THREAT, SPIDER, IS IN THE FORM OF A PETITION, AND HAS BEEN SIGNED BY OVER FIVE HUNDRED PEOPLE.
WORSE, JUST FIFTEEN MINUTES AGO I HAD A VISIT FROM SOME THING CLAIMING TO BE YOUR--
THIS IS YOUR DOOR SPEAKING. YOU HAVE A CALLER.
HELL. LOOK, I'LL CALL YOU BACK.
NO--
HEY THERE! BAMBOOZLE THE SAFETY CHIMP® says... "BE SMART! WATCH YOUR HANDS!"
YEAH?

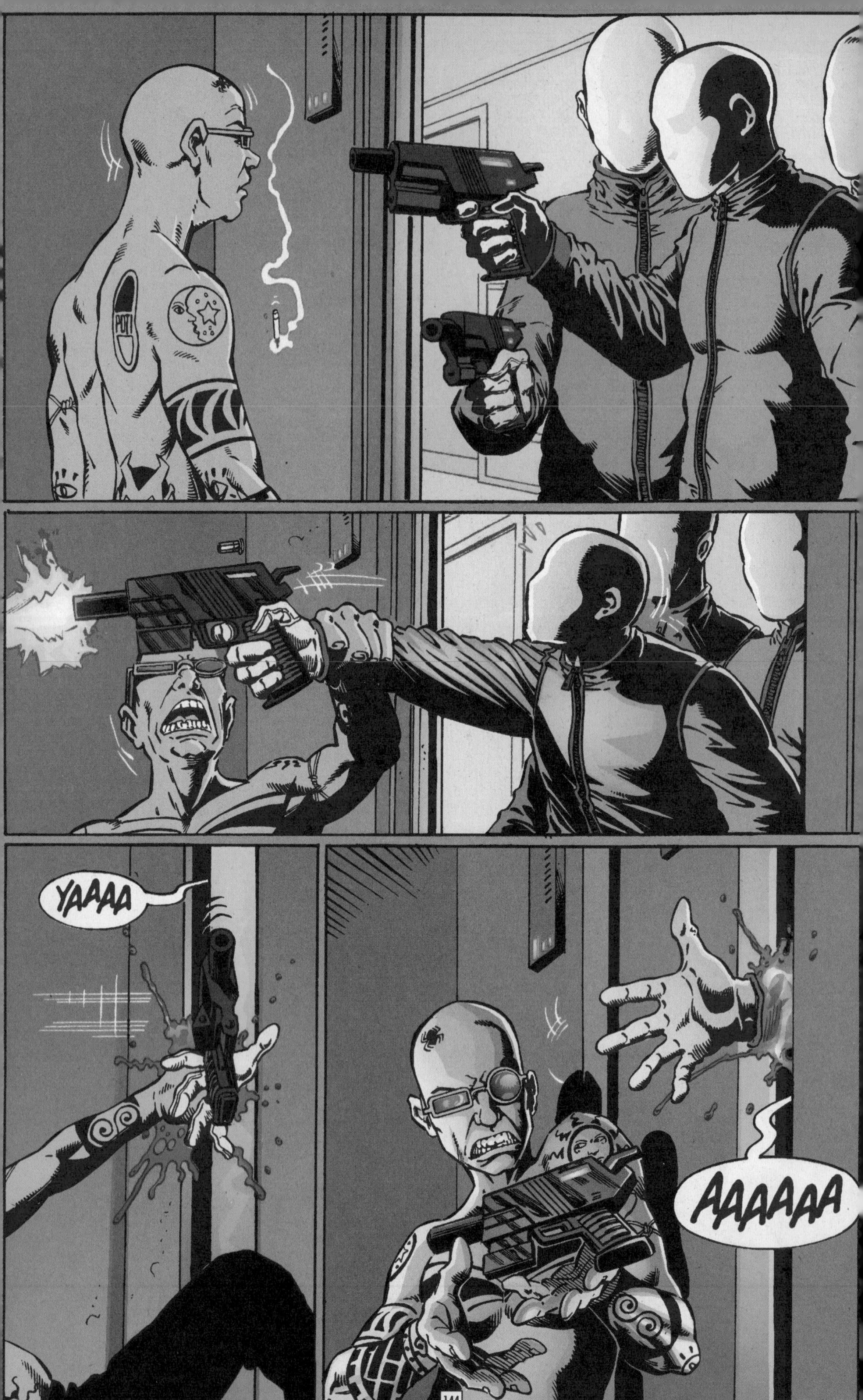
POPI
YAAAA
AAAAAA

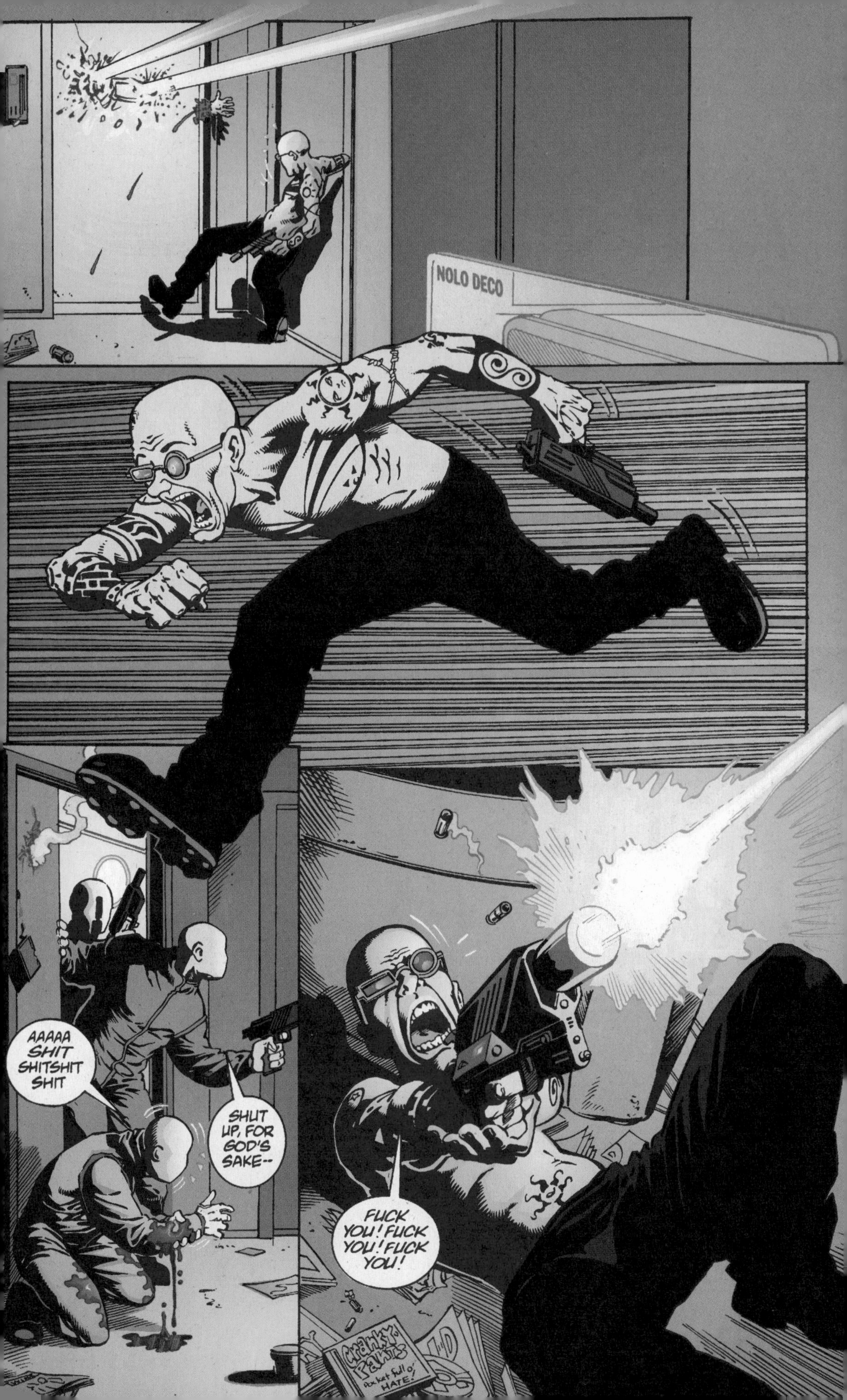
NOLO DECO
AAAAA SHIT SHITSHIT SHIT
SHUT UP, FOR GOD'S SAKE--
FUCK YOU! FUCK YOU! FUCK YOU!

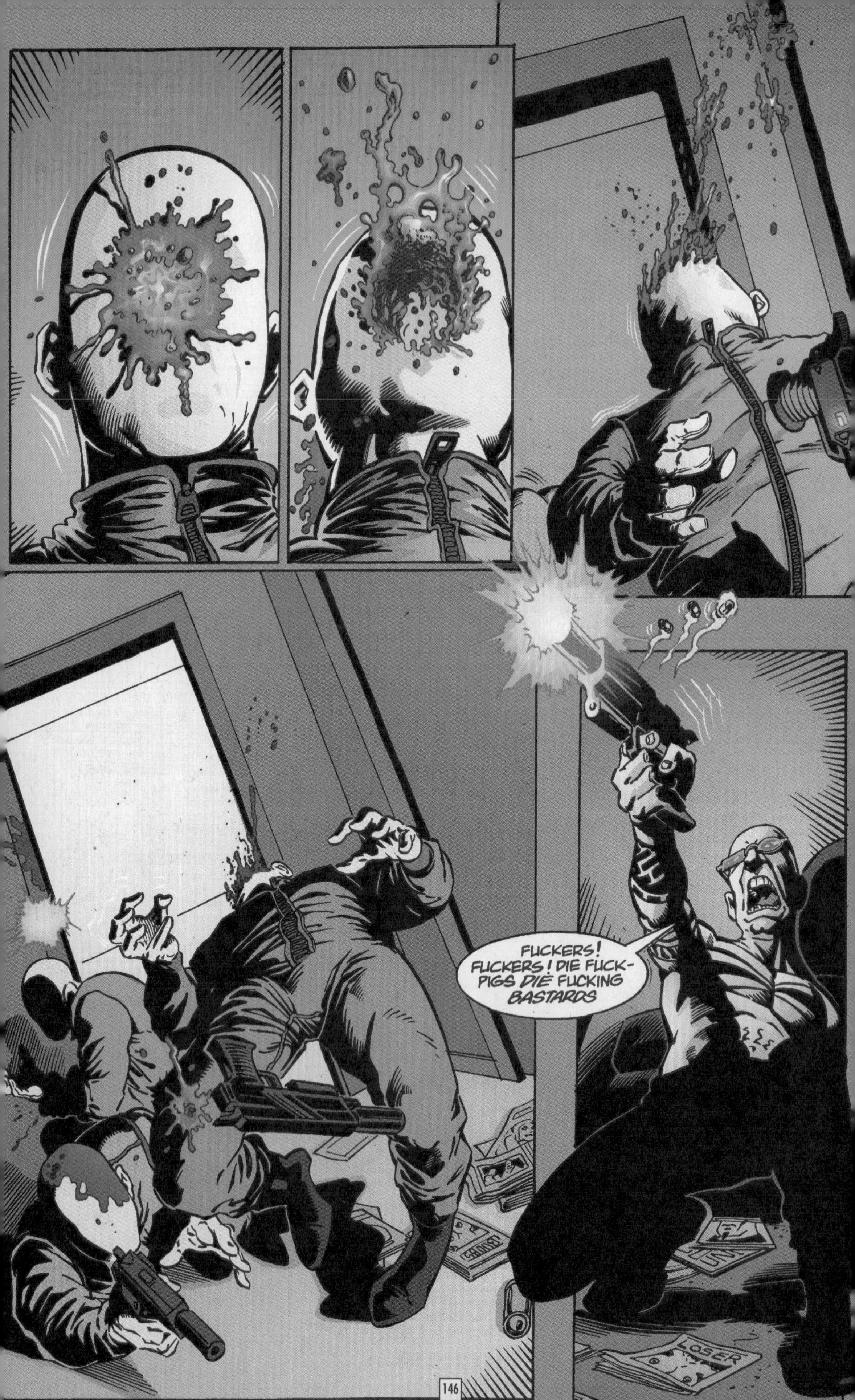
FUCKERS! FUCKERS! DIE FUCK-PIGS *DIE* FUCKING *BASTARDS*
LOSER

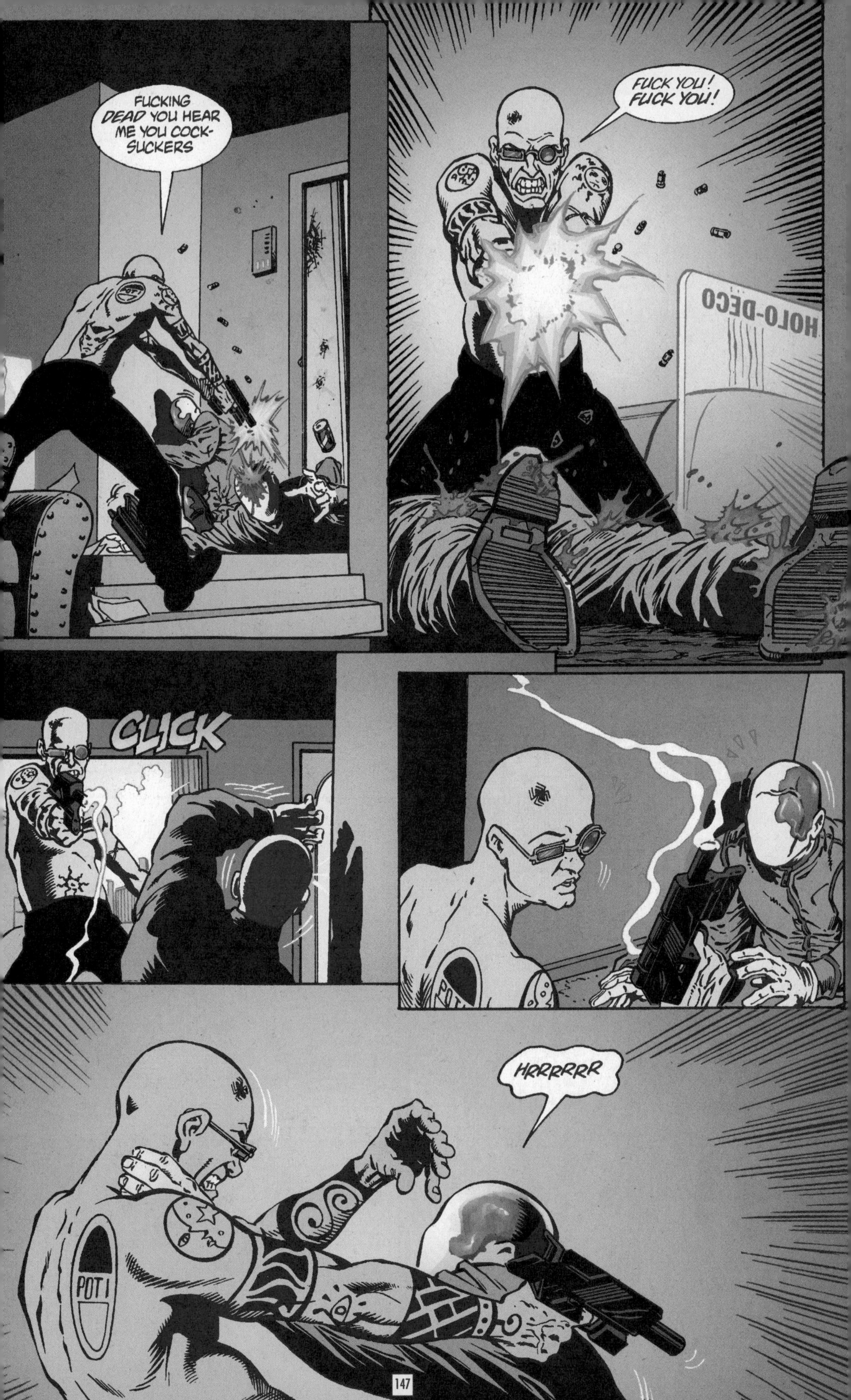
FUCKING DEAD YOU HEAR ME YOU COCK-SUCKERS
FUCK YOU! FUCK YOU!
HOLO-DECO
CLICK
POT I
HRRRRRR
POT I

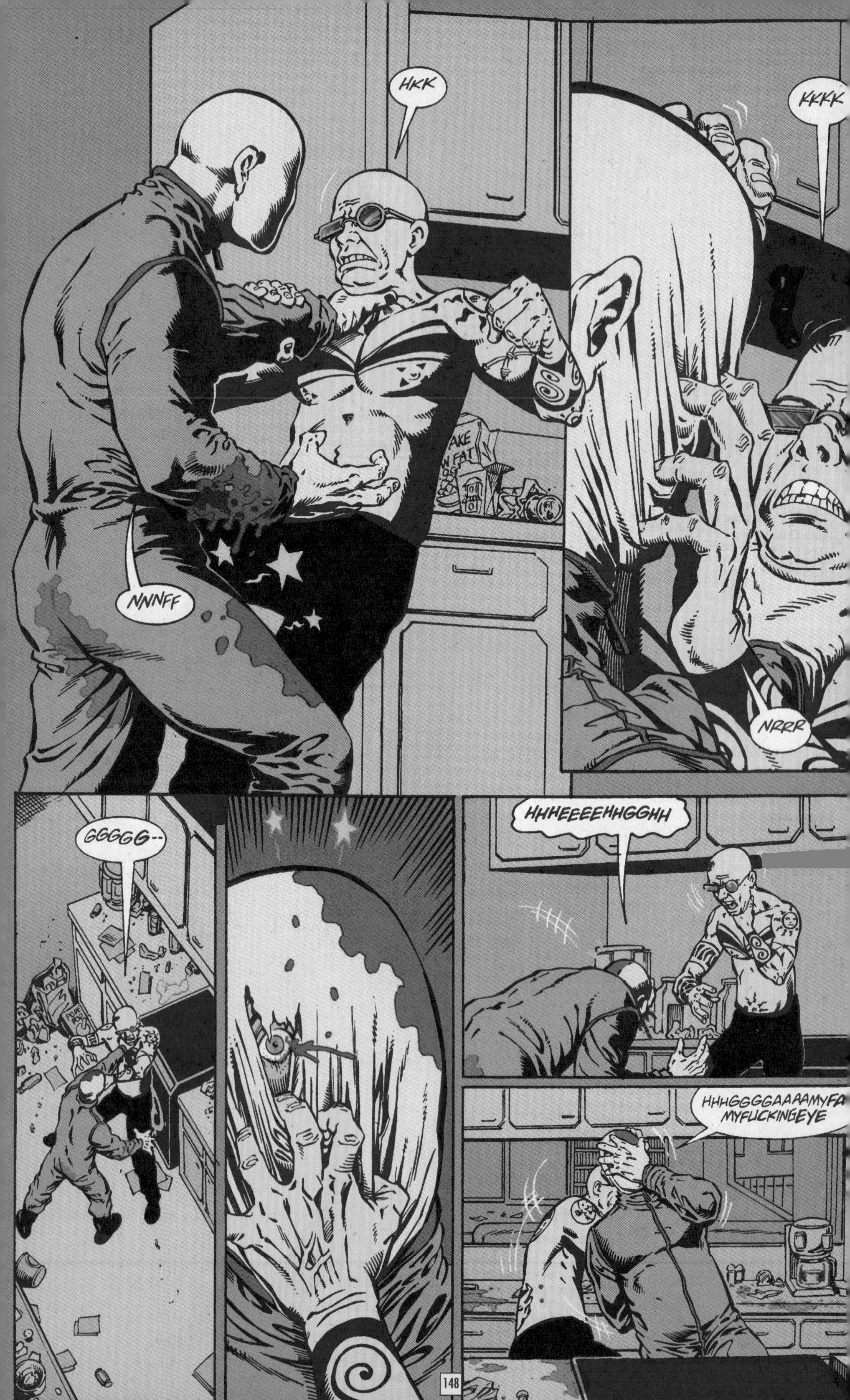

HKK
NNNFF
KKKK
NRRR
GGGGG--
HHHEEEEEHHGGHH
HHHGGGGAAAAMYFA
MYFUCKINGEYE

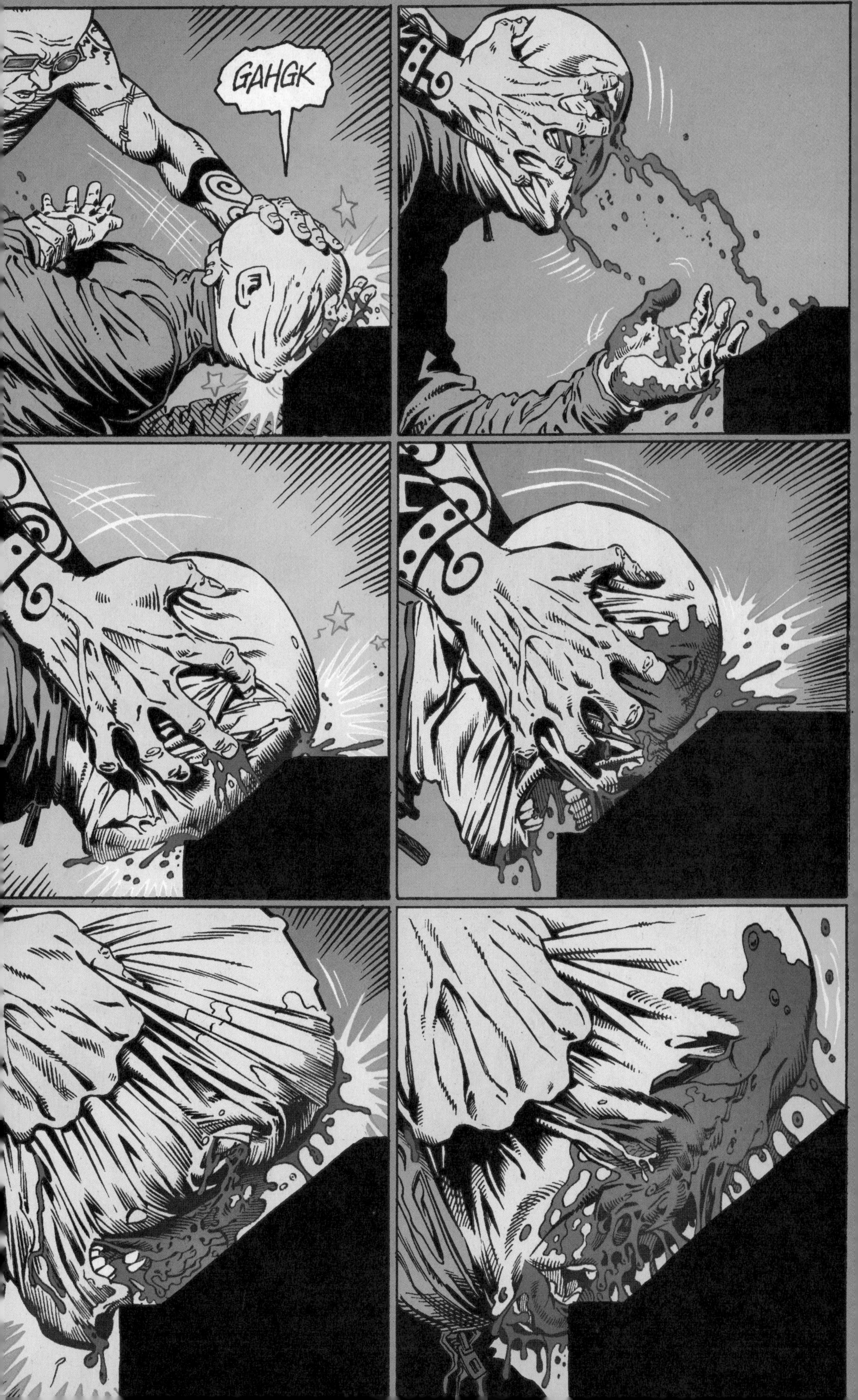
GAHGK

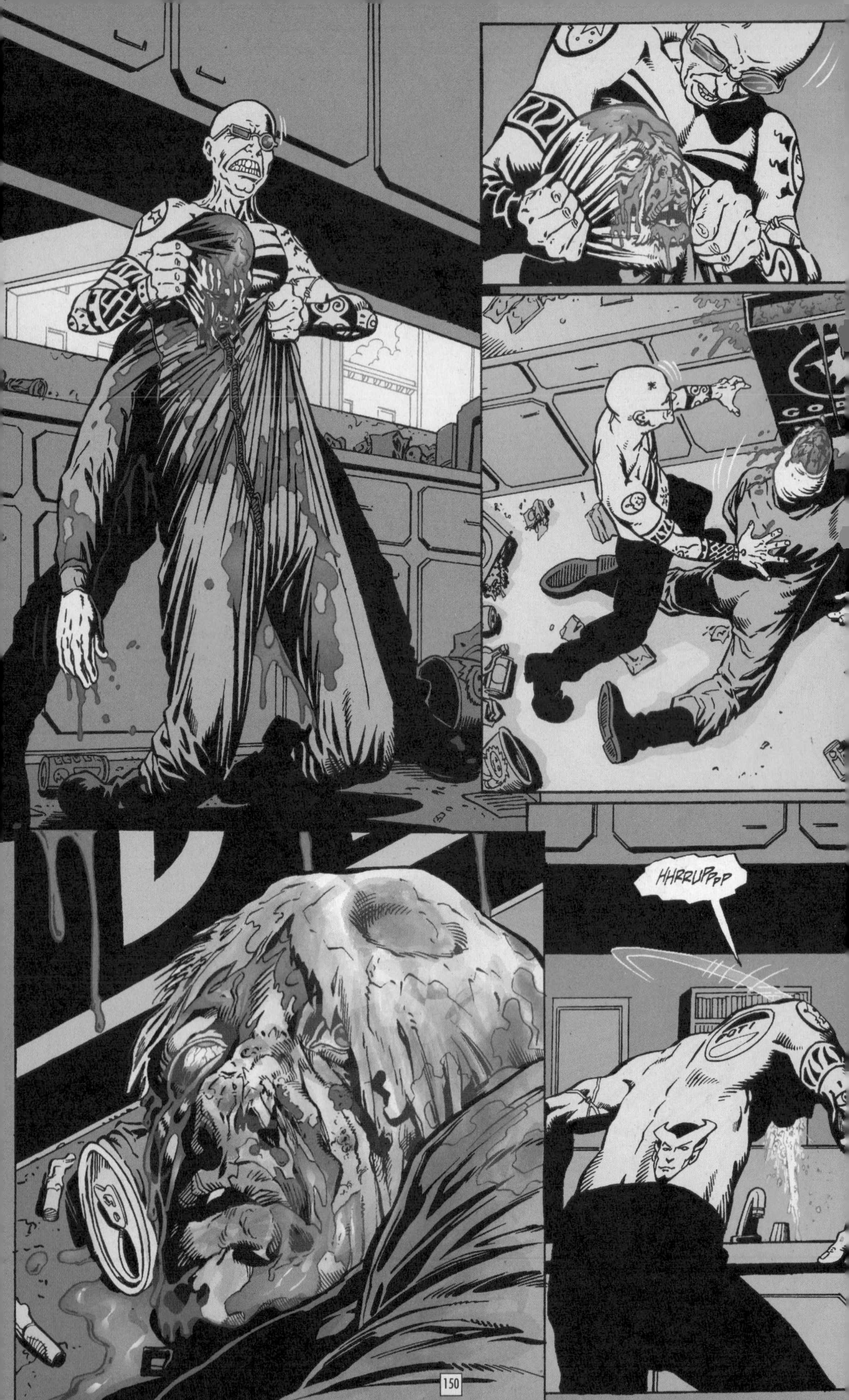
HHRRUPPPP

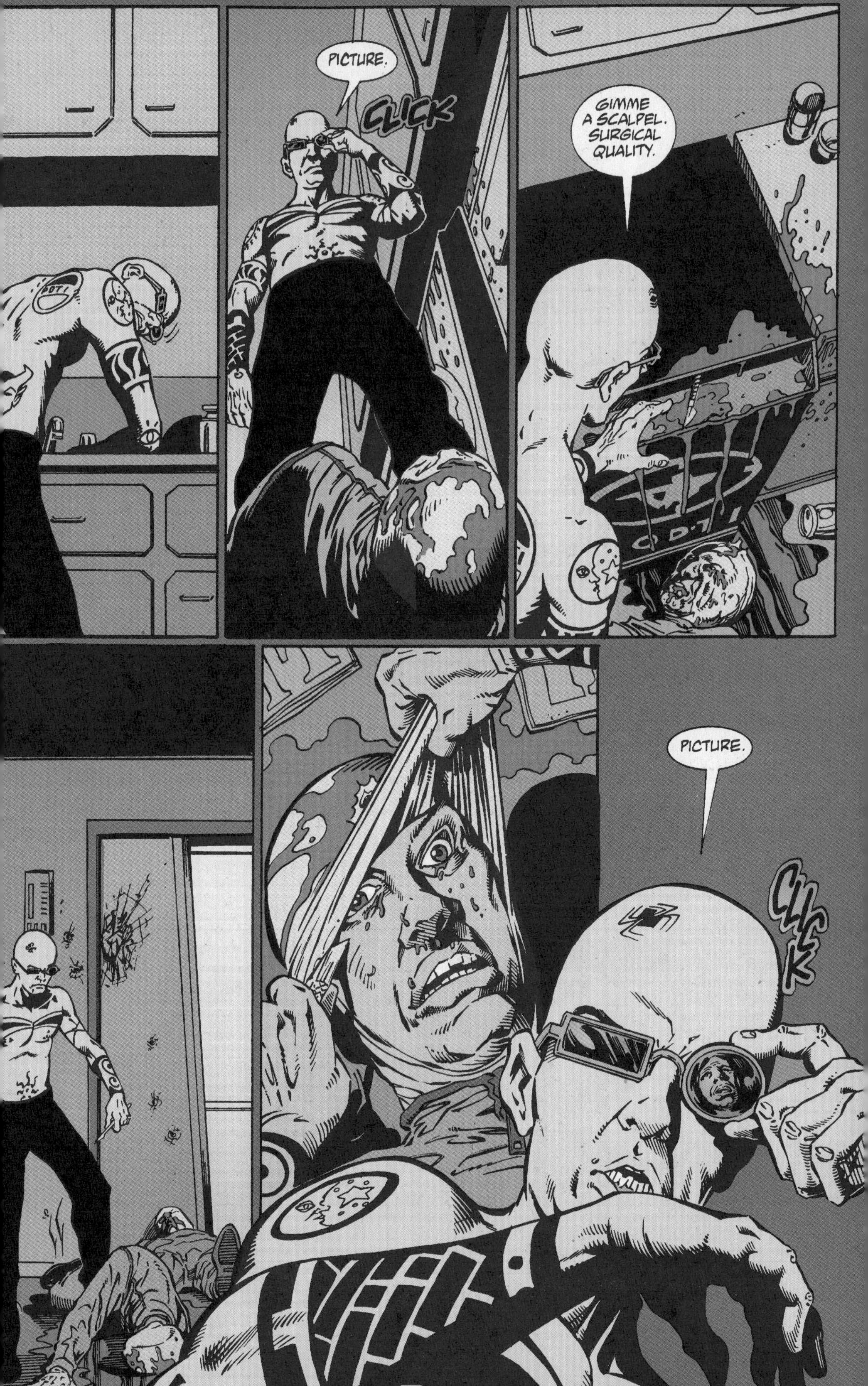
PICTURE.
CLICK
GIMME A SCALPEL. SURGICAL QUALITY.
PICTURE.
CLICK

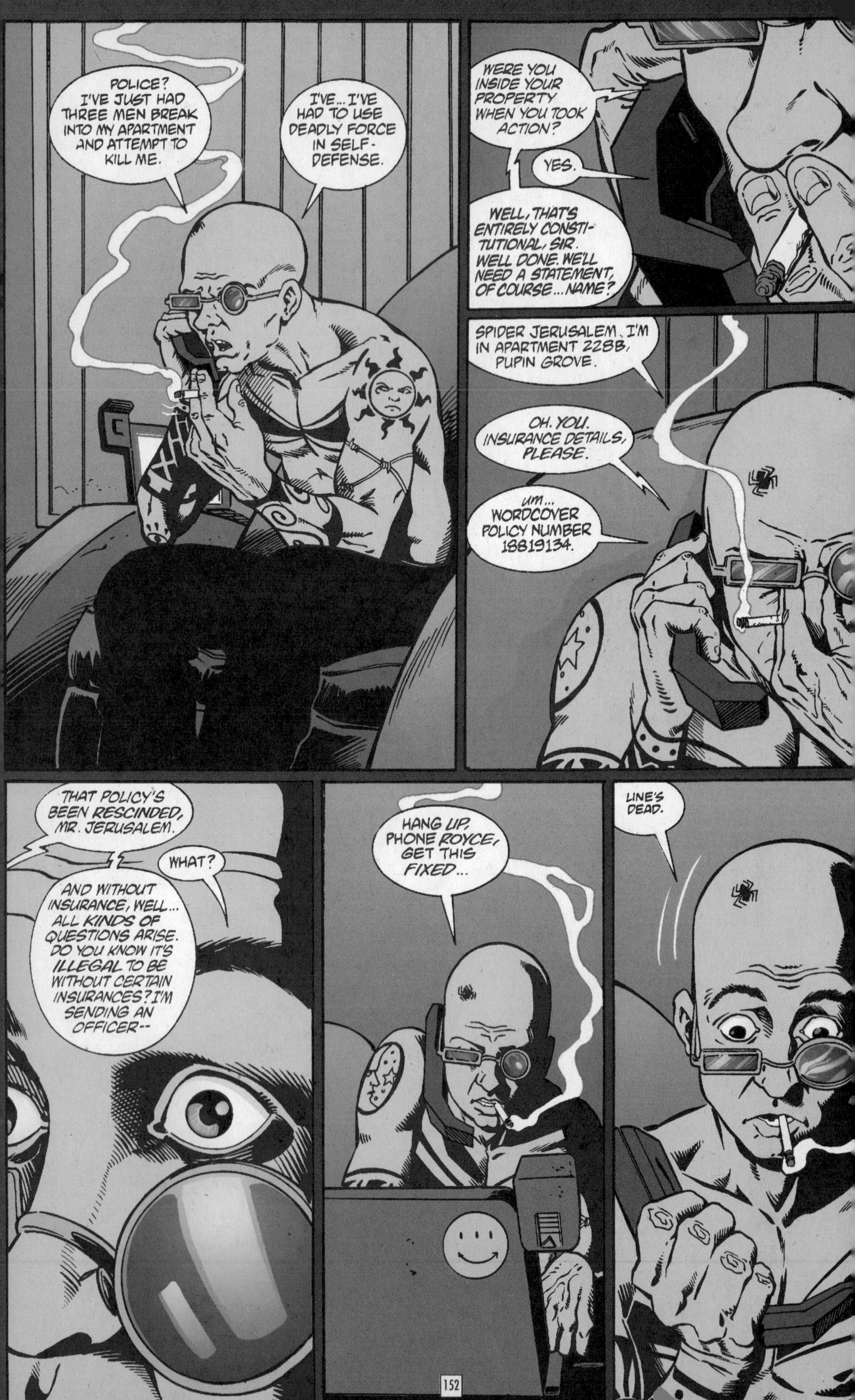
POLICE? I'VE JUST HAD THREE MEN BREAK INTO MY APARTMENT AND ATTEMPT TO KILL ME.
I'VE... I'VE HAD TO USE DEADLY FORCE IN SELF-DEFENSE.
WERE YOU INSIDE YOUR PROPERTY WHEN YOU TOOK ACTION?
YES.
WELL, THAT'S ENTIRELY CONSTITUTIONAL, SIR. WELL DONE. WE'LL NEED A STATEMENT, OF COURSE... NAME?
SPIDER JERUSALEM. I'M IN APARTMENT 228B, PUPIN GROVE.
OH. YOU. INSURANCE DETAILS, PLEASE.
UM... WORDCOVER POLICY NUMBER 18819134.
THAT POLICY'S BEEN RESCINDED, MR. JERUSALEM.
WHAT?
AND WITHOUT INSURANCE, WELL... ALL KINDS OF QUESTIONS ARISE. DO YOU KNOW IT'S ILLEGAL TO BE WITHOUT CERTAIN INSURANCES? I'M SENDING AN OFFICER--
HANG UP, PHONE ROYCE, GET THIS FIXED...
LINE'S DEAD.

# "THE POLICE DOG"

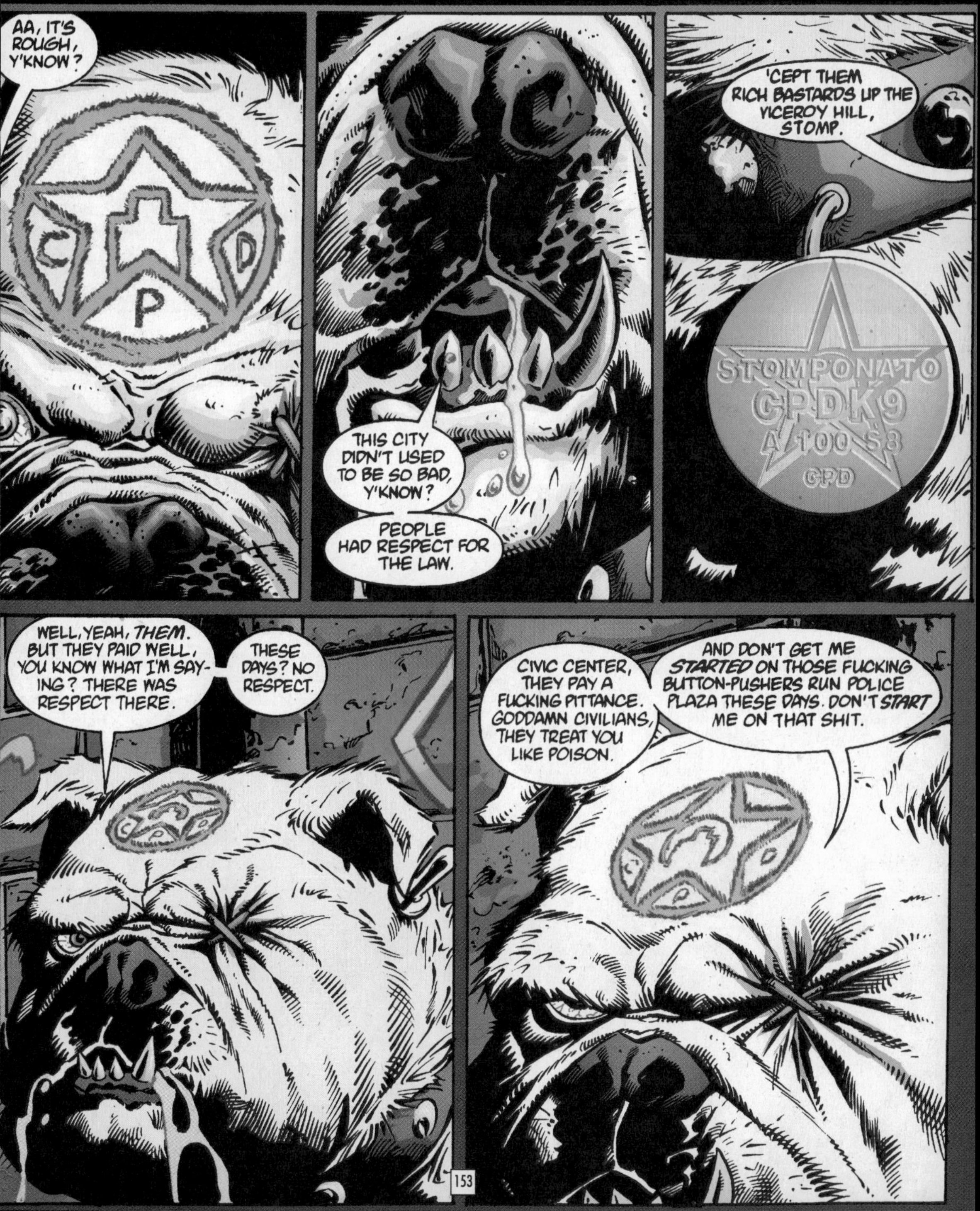
AA, IT'S ROUGH, Y'KNOW?
THIS CITY DIDN'T USED TO BE SO BAD, Y'KNOW?
PEOPLE HAD RESPECT FOR THE LAW.
'CEPT THEM RICH BASTARDS UP THE VICEROY HILL, STOMP.
STOMPONATO
CPDK9
WELL, YEAH, *THEM*. BUT THEY PAID WELL, YOU KNOW WHAT I'M SAY-ING? THERE WAS RESPECT THERE.
THESE DAYS? NO RESPECT.
CIVIC CENTER, THEY PAY A FUCKING PITTANCE. GODDAMN CIVILIANS, THEY TREAT YOU LIKE POISON.
AND DON'T GET ME *STARTED* ON THOSE FUCKING BUTTON-PUSHERS RUN POLICE PLAZA THESE DAYS. DON'T *START* ME ON THAT SHIT.

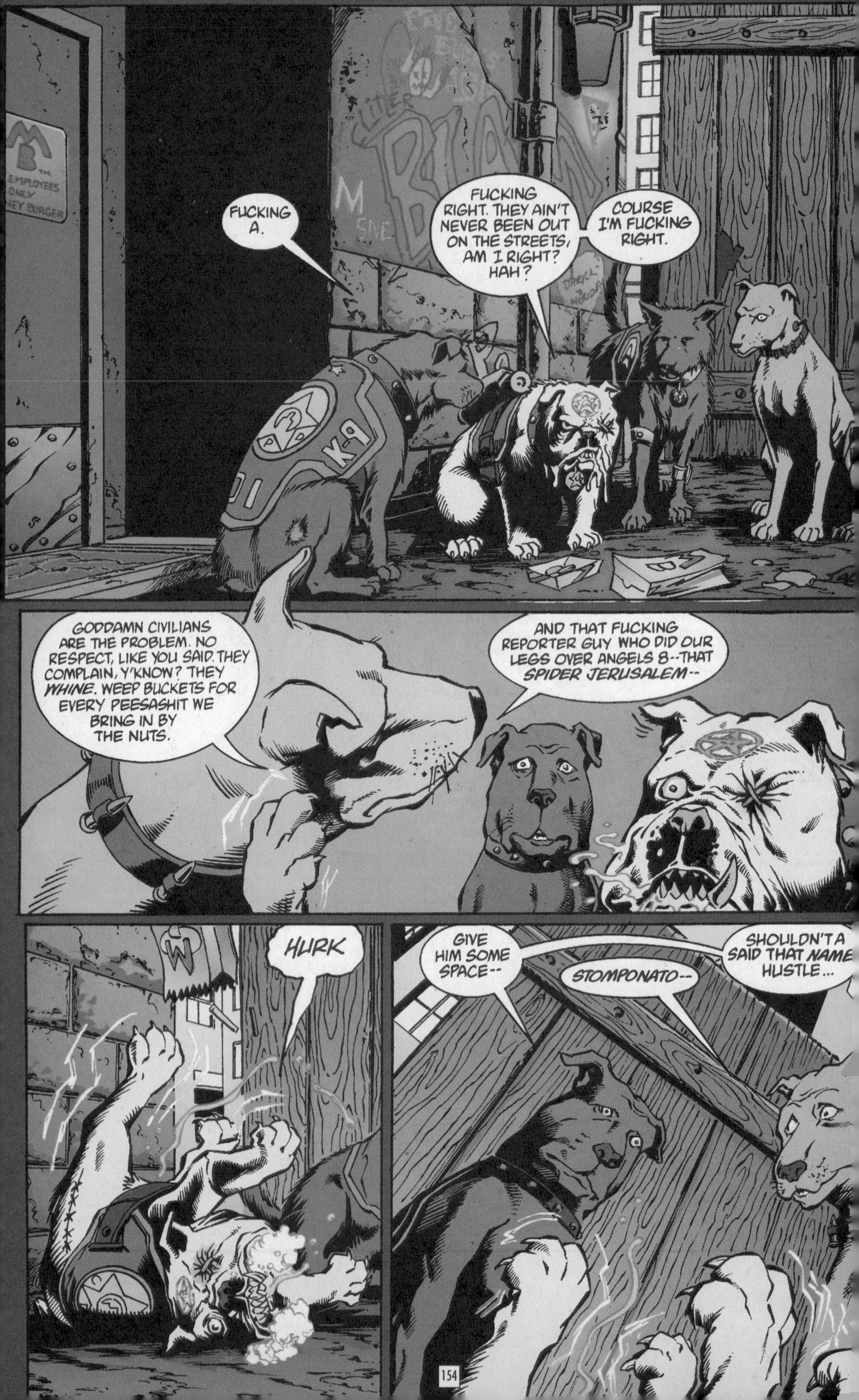
FUCKING A.
FUCKING RIGHT. THEY AIN'T NEVER BEEN OUT ON THE STREETS, AM I RIGHT? HAH?
COURSE I'M FUCKING RIGHT.
GODDAMN CIVILIANS ARE THE PROBLEM. NO RESPECT, LIKE YOU SAID. THEY COMPLAIN, Y'KNOW? THEY *WHINE*. WEEP BUCKETS FOR EVERY PEESASHIT WE BRING IN BY THE NUTS.
AND THAT FUCKING REPORTER GUY WHO DID OUR LEGS OVER ANGELS 8--THAT *SPIDER JERUSALEM*--
HURK
GIVE HIM SOME SPACE--
STOMPONATO--
SHOULDN'T A SAID THAT *NAME* HUSTLE...

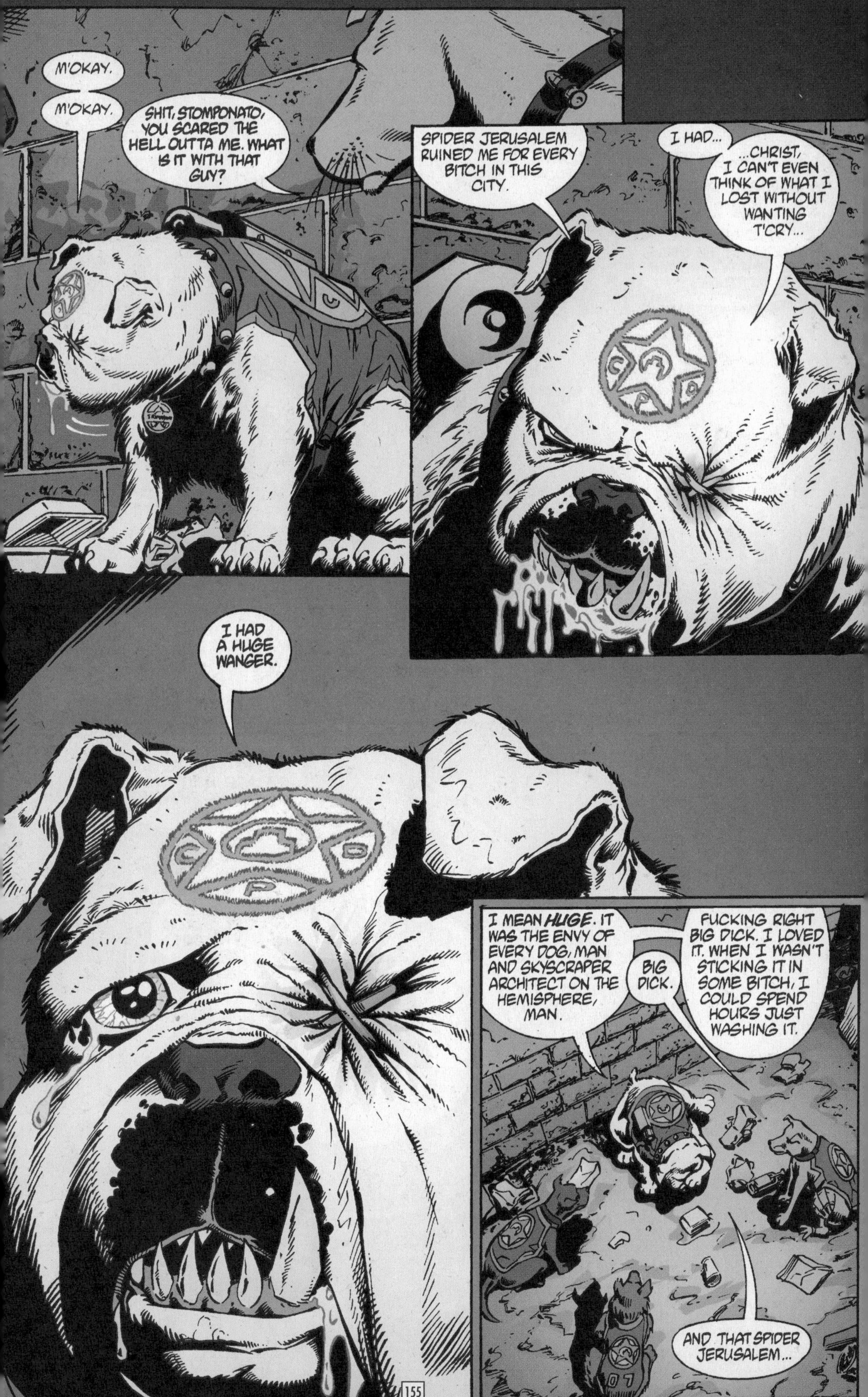

M'OKAY.
M'OKAY.
SHIT, STOMPONATO, YOU SCARED THE HELL OUTTA ME. WHAT IS IT WITH THAT GUY?
SPIDER JERUSALEM RUINED ME FOR EVERY BITCH IN THIS CITY.
I HAD...
...CHRIST, I CAN'T EVEN THINK OF WHAT I LOST WITHOUT WANTING T'CRY...
I HAD A HUGE WANGER.
I MEAN HUGE. IT WAS THE ENVY OF EVERY DOG, MAN AND SKYSCRAPER ARCHITECT ON THE HEMISPHERE, MAN.
BIG DICK.
FUCKING RIGHT BIG DICK. I LOVED IT. WHEN I WASN'T STICKING IT IN SOME BITCH, I COULD SPEND HOURS JUST WASHING IT.
AND THAT SPIDER JERUSALEM...

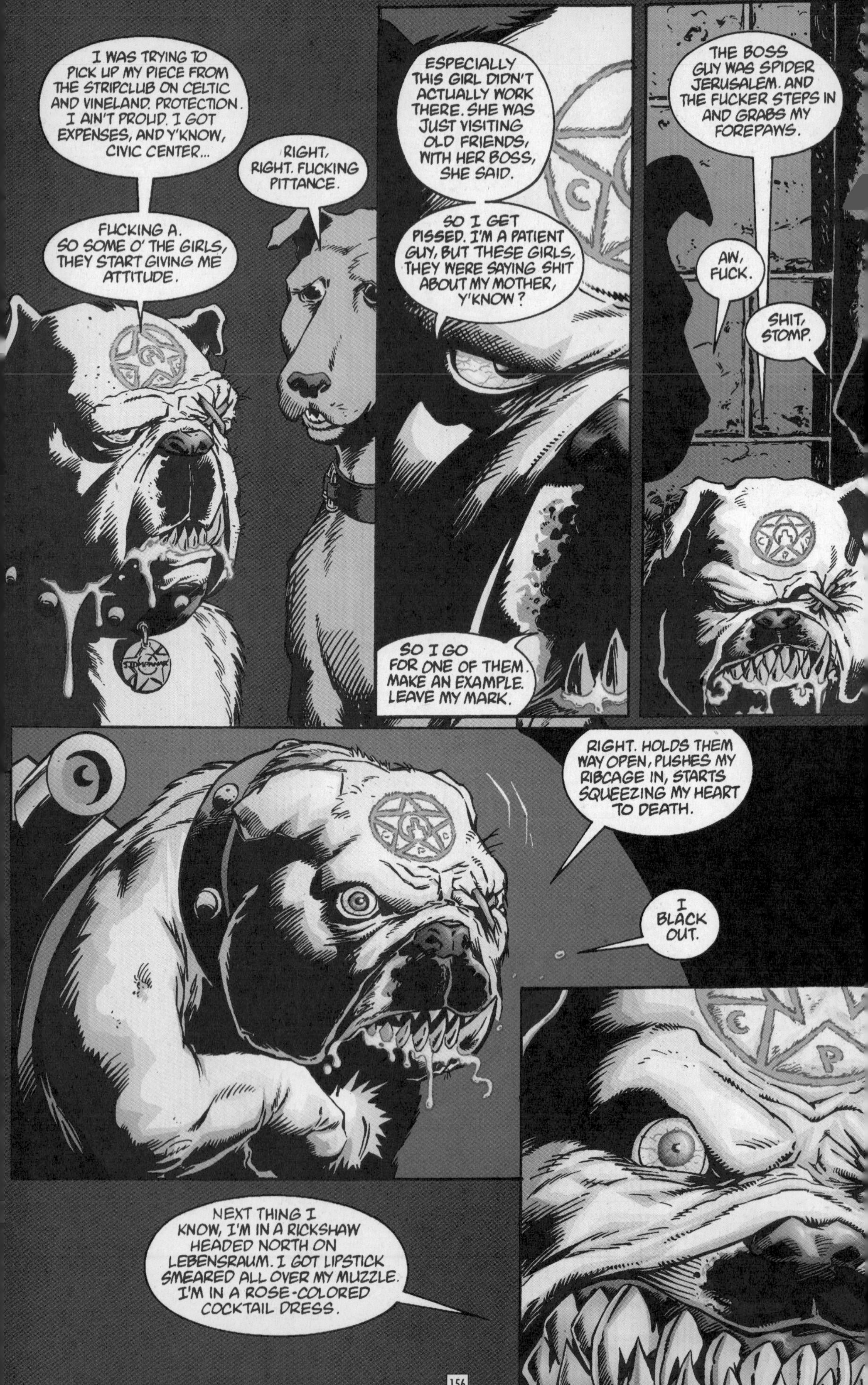
I WAS TRYING TO PICK UP MY PIECE FROM THE STRIPCLUB ON CELTIC AND VINELAND. PROTECTION. I AIN'T PROUD. I GOT EXPENSES, AND Y'KNOW, CIVIC CENTER...
RIGHT, RIGHT. FUCKING PITTANCE.
FUCKING A. SO SOME O' THE GIRLS, THEY START GIVING ME ATTITUDE.
ESPECIALLY THIS GIRL DIDN'T ACTUALLY WORK THERE. SHE WAS JUST VISITING OLD FRIENDS, WITH HER BOSS, SHE SAID.
SO I GET PISSED. I'M A PATIENT GUY, BUT THESE GIRLS, THEY WERE SAYING SHIT ABOUT MY MOTHER, Y'KNOW?
SO I GO FOR ONE OF THEM. MAKE AN EXAMPLE. LEAVE MY MARK.
THE BOSS GUY WAS SPIDER JERUSALEM. AND THE FUCKER STEPS IN AND GRABS MY FOREPAWS.
AW, FUCK.
SHIT, STOMP.
RIGHT. HOLDS THEM WAY OPEN, PUSHES MY RIBCAGE IN, STARTS SQUEEZING MY HEART TO DEATH.
I BLACK OUT.
NEXT THING I KNOW, I'M IN A RICKSHAW HEADED NORTH ON LEBENSRAUM. I GOT LIPSTICK SMEARED ALL OVER MY MUZZLE. I'M IN A ROSE-COLORED COCKTAIL DRESS.

AND MY...

...MY PRIDE AND JOY...

THAT BASTARD JERUSALEM PAID A VET TO...

OFFICER STOMPONATO, PLEASE RESPOND.

THIS IS STOMPONATO, CONTROL.

PLEASE PROCEED TO PUPIN GROVE APARTMENT COMPOUND, SUITE 22BB. OCCUPANT HAS BEEN ASSAULTED AND HAS DEFENDED HIMSELF WITH DEADLY FORCE.

HE HAS NONE OF THE USUAL LAW INSURANCES AT THIS TIME, AND SHOULD BE BROUGHT IN.

NAME.

SPIDER JERUSALEM, STOMP.

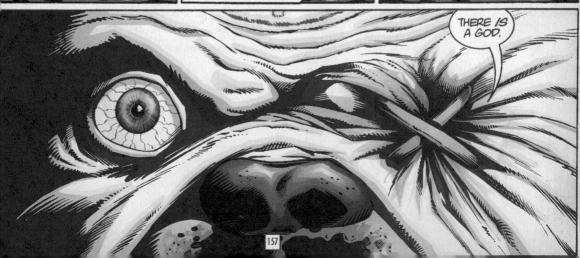

THERE IS A GOD.

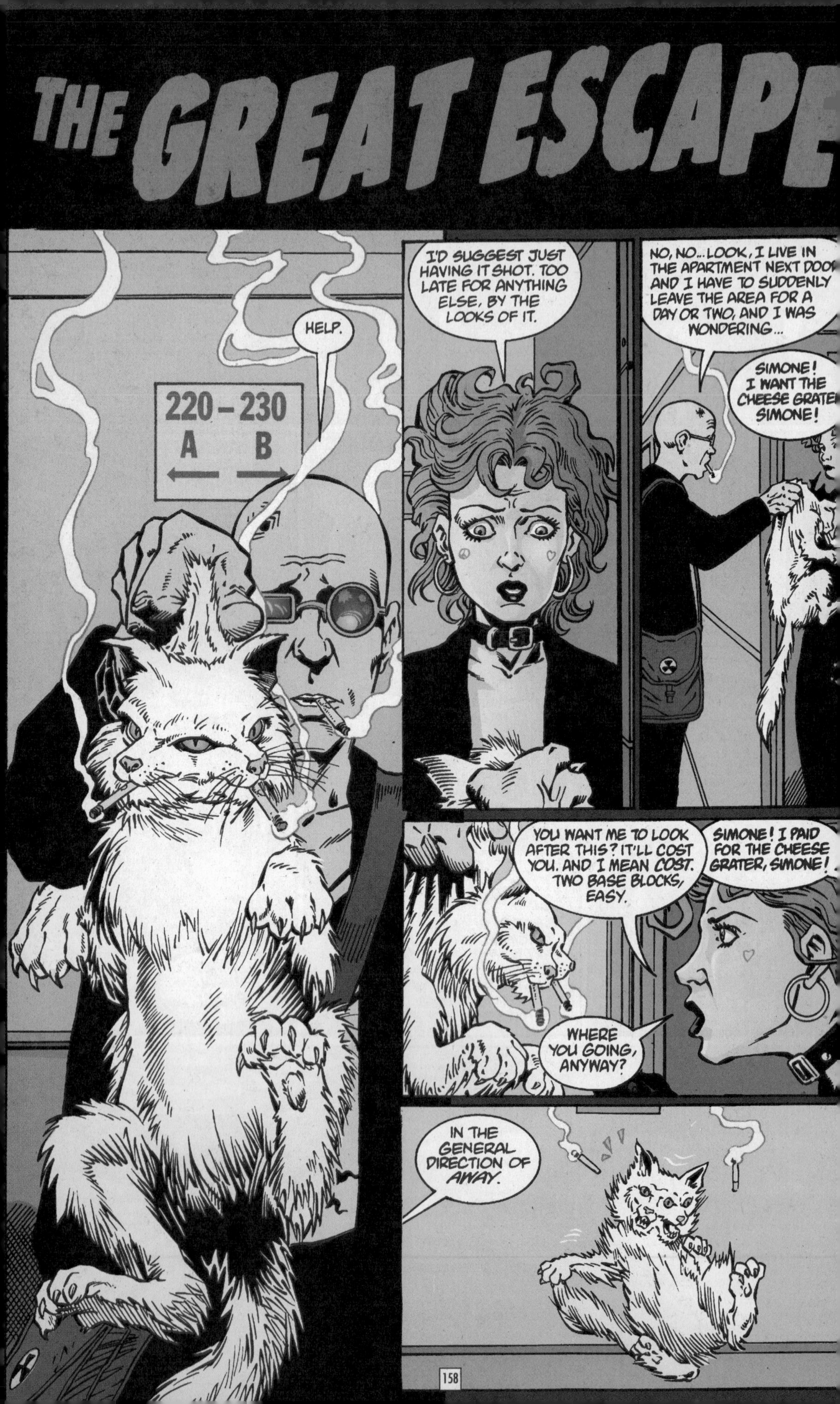
THE GREAT ESCAPE
220-230
A B
HELP.
I'D SUGGEST JUST HAVING IT SHOT. TOO LATE FOR ANYTHING ELSE, BY THE LOOKS OF IT.
NO, NO... LOOK, I LIVE IN THE APARTMENT NEXT DOOR AND I HAVE TO SUDDENLY LEAVE THE AREA FOR A DAY OR TWO, AND I WAS WONDERING...
SIMONE! I WANT THE CHEESE GRATER, SIMONE!
YOU WANT ME TO LOOK AFTER THIS? IT'LL COST YOU. AND I MEAN COST. TWO BASE BLOCKS, EASY.
SIMONE! I PAID FOR THE CHEESE GRATER, SIMONE!
WHERE YOU GOING, ANYWAY?
IN THE GENERAL DIRECTION OF AWAY.

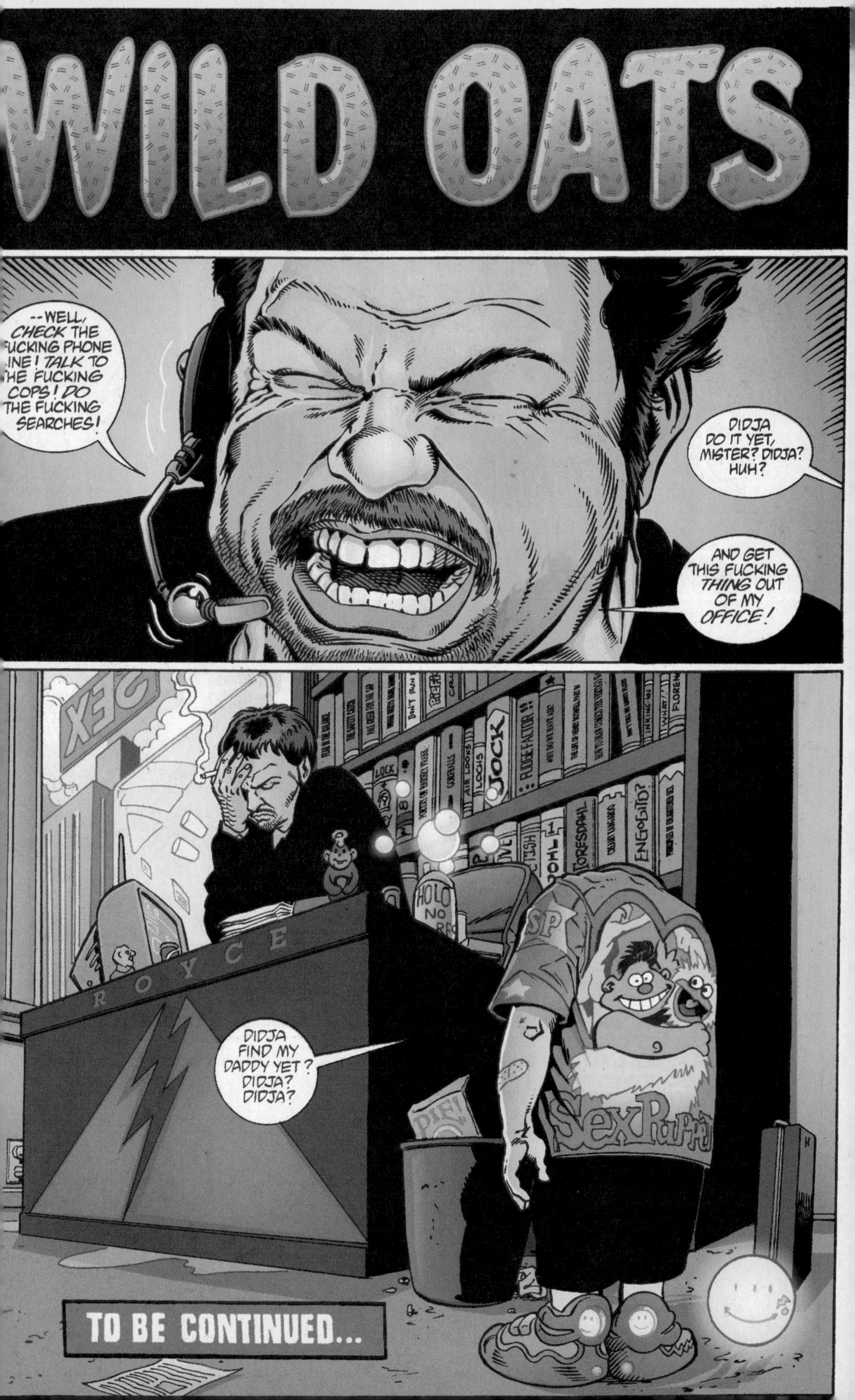
WILD OATS
--WELL, CHECK THE FUCKING PHONE LINE! TALK TO THE FUCKING COPS! DO THE FUCKING SEARCHES!
DIDJA DO IT YET, MISTER? DIDJA? HUH?
AND GET THIS FUCKING THING OUT OF MY OFFICE!
ROYCE
DIDJA FIND MY DADDY YET? DIDJA? DIDJA?
SEX PUPPET
TO BE CONTINUED...

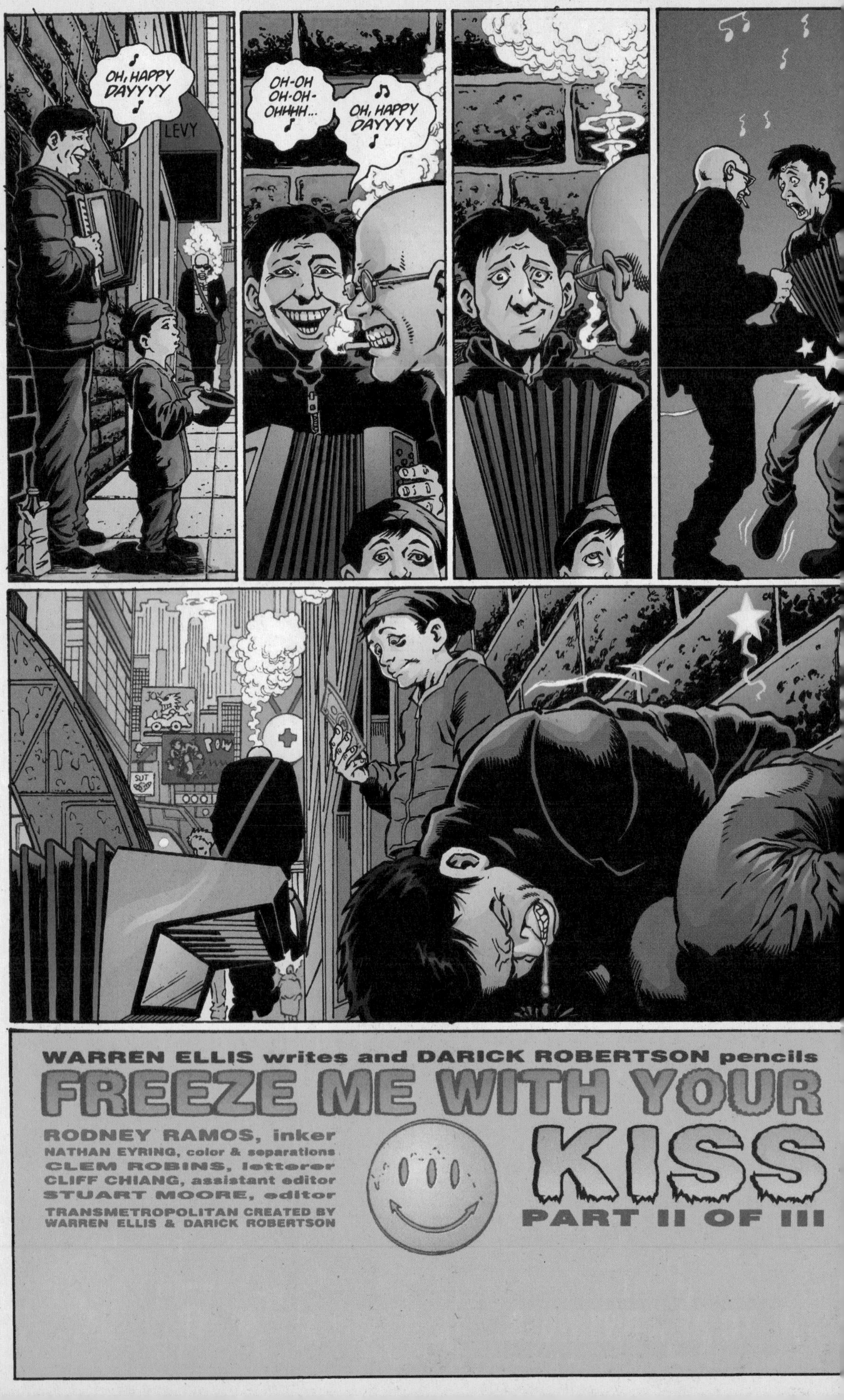
OH, HAPPY DAYYYY
LEVY
OH-OH OH-OH-OHHHH...
OH, HAPPY DAYYYY
POW

WARREN ELLIS writes and DARICK ROBERTSON pencils

# FREEZE ME WITH YOUR KISS

## PART II OF III

RODNEY RAMOS, inker
NATHAN EYRING, color & separations
CLEM ROBINS, letterer
CLIFF CHIANG, assistant editor
STUART MOORE, editor

TRANSMETROPOLITAN CREATED BY WARREN ELLIS & DARICK ROBERTSON

# the last time this happened...

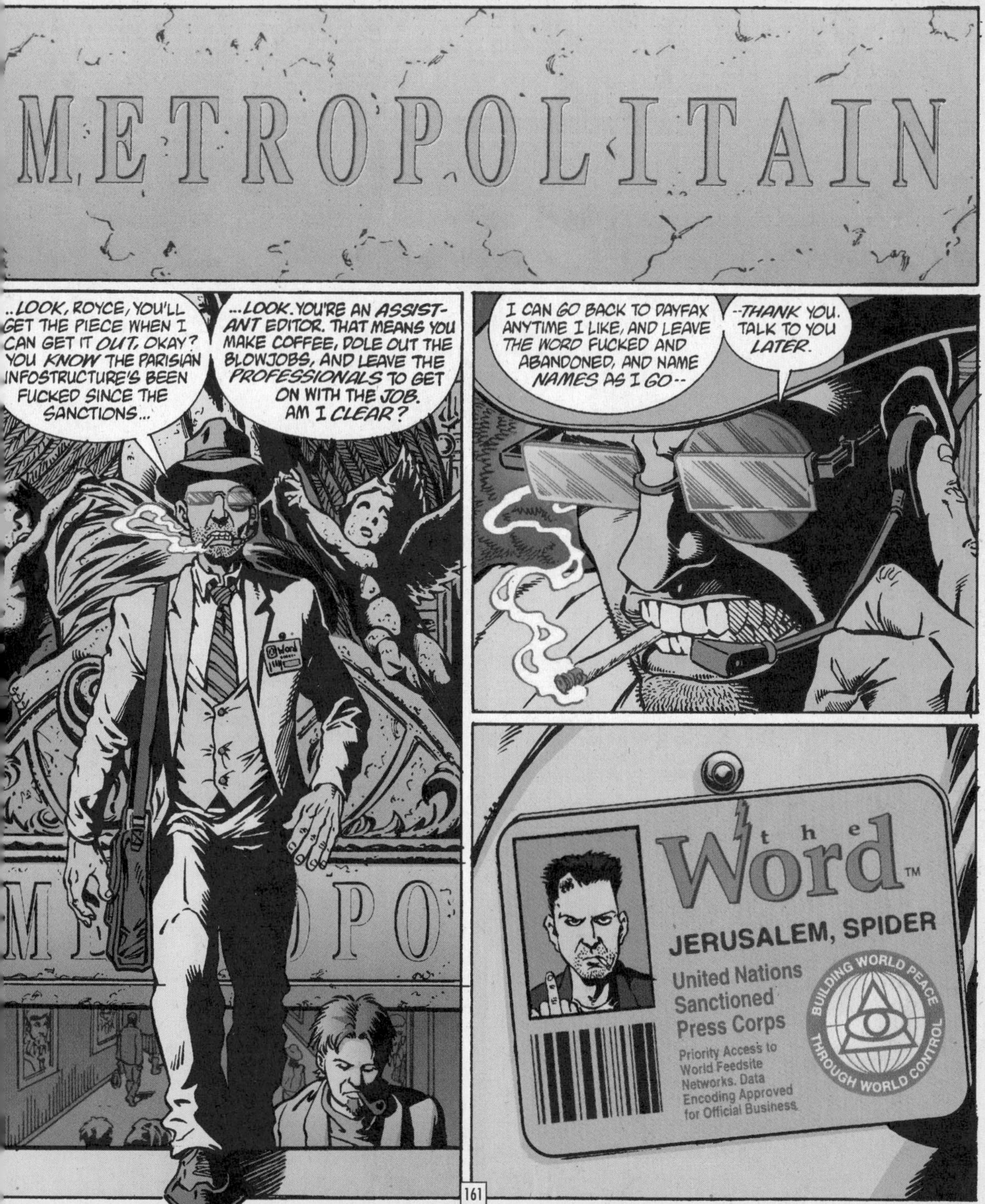
METROPOLITAIN
..LOOK, ROYCE, YOU'LL GET THE PIECE WHEN I CAN GET IT OUT, OKAY? YOU KNOW THE PARISIAN INFOSTRUCTURE'S BEEN FUCKED SINCE THE SANCTIONS...
...LOOK. YOU'RE AN ASSIST-ANT EDITOR. THAT MEANS YOU MAKE COFFEE, DOLE OUT THE BLOWJOBS, AND LEAVE THE PROFESSIONALS TO GET ON WITH THE JOB. AM I CLEAR?
I CAN GO BACK TO DAYFAX ANYTIME I LIKE, AND LEAVE THE WORD FUCKED AND ABANDONED, AND NAME NAMES AS I GO--
--THANK YOU. TALK TO YOU LATER.
the Word™
JERUSALEM, SPIDER
United Nations Sanctioned Press Corps
Priority Access to World Feedsite Networks. Data Encoding Approved for Official Business.
BUILDING WORLD PEACE THROUGH WORLD CONTROL

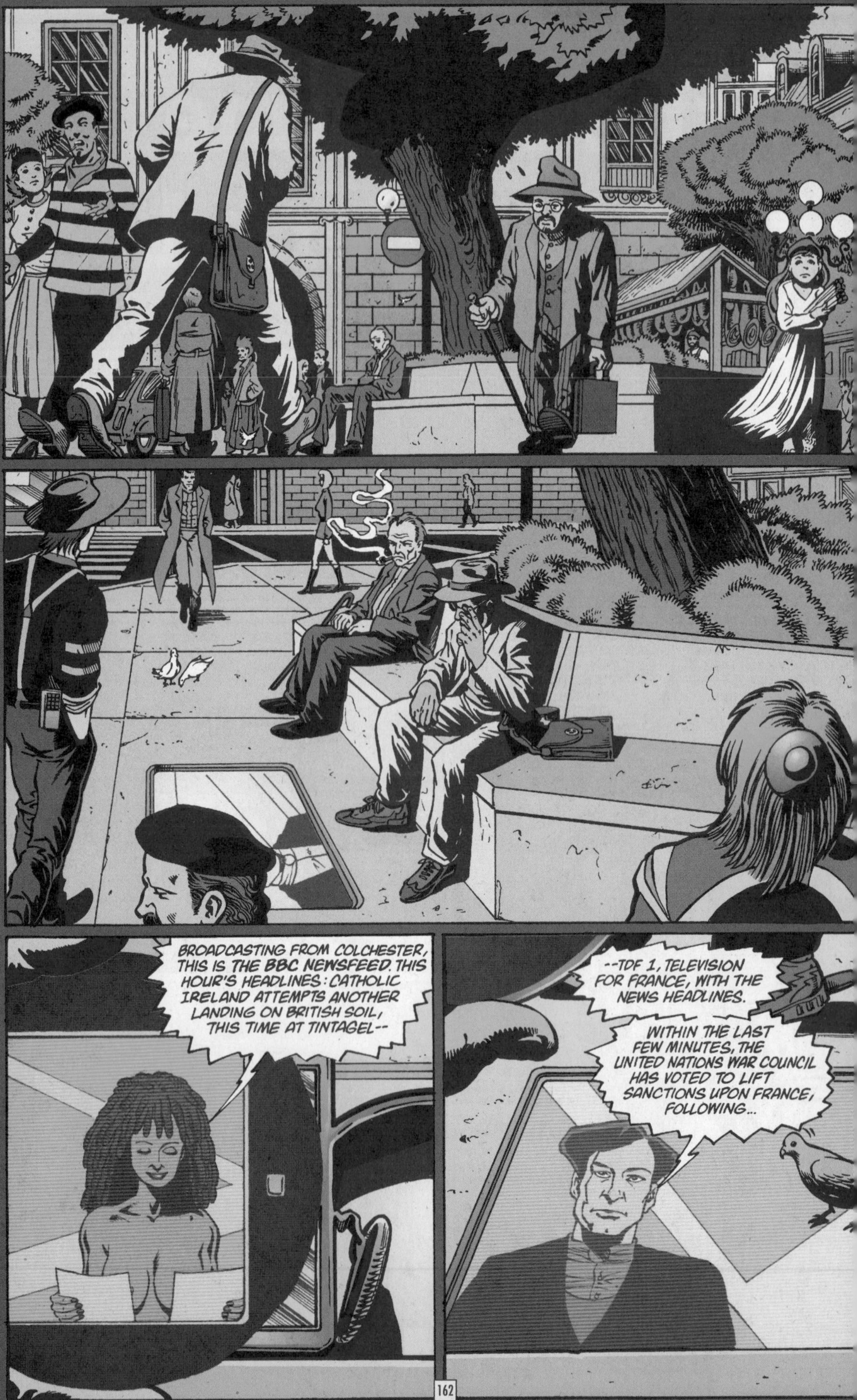
BROADCASTING FROM COLCHESTER, THIS IS THE BBC NEWSFEED. THIS HOUR'S HEADLINES: CATHOLIC IRELAND ATTEMPTS ANOTHER LANDING ON BRITISH SOIL, THIS TIME AT TINTAGEL--
--TDF 1, TELEVISION FOR FRANCE, WITH THE NEWS HEADLINES.
WITHIN THE LAST FEW MINUTES, THE UNITED NATIONS WAR COUNCIL HAS VOTED TO LIFT SANCTIONS UPON FRANCE, FOLLOWING...

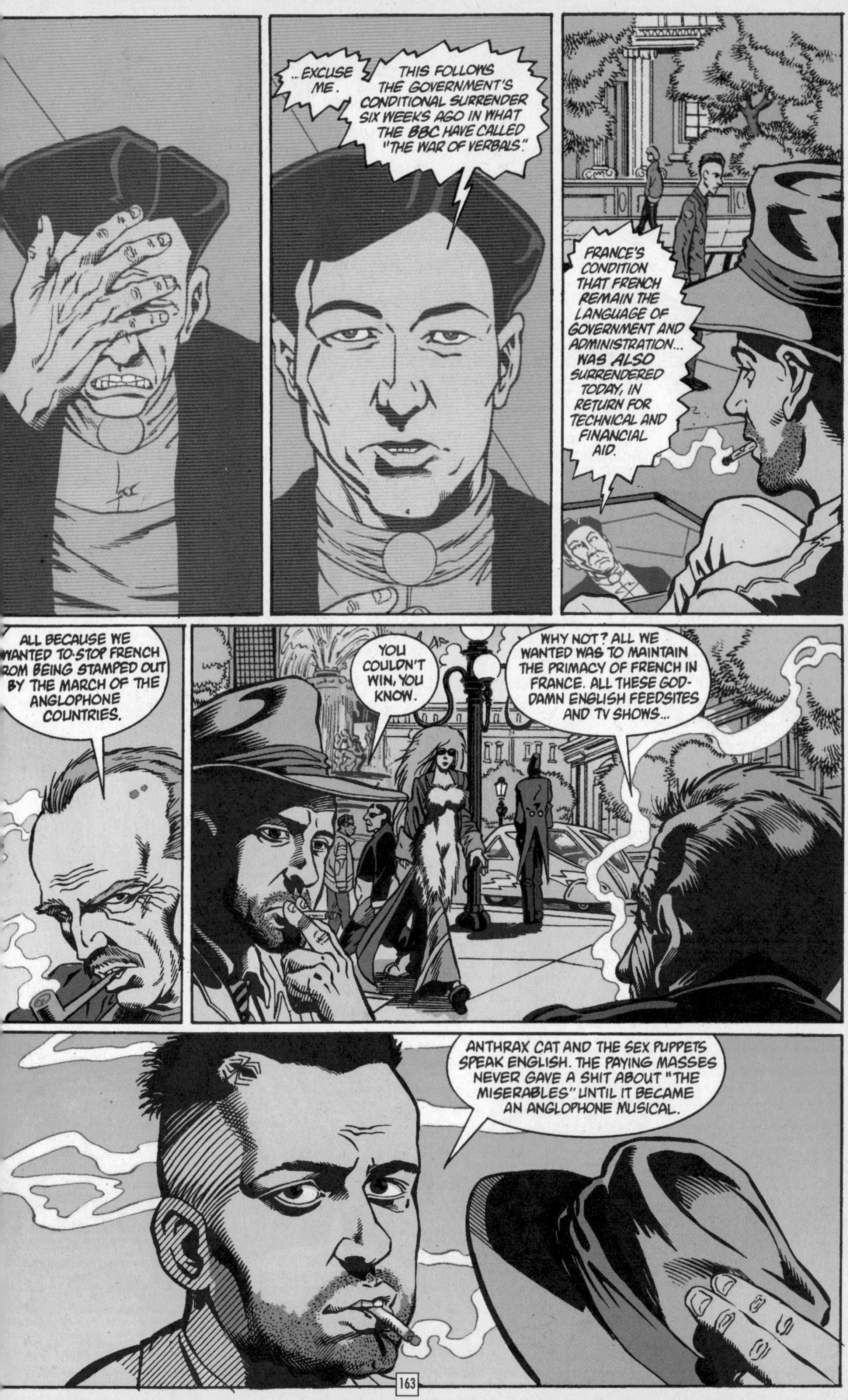
...EXCUSE ME.
THIS FOLLOWS THE GOVERNMENT'S CONDITIONAL SURRENDER SIX WEEKS AGO IN WHAT THE BBC HAVE CALLED "THE WAR OF VERBALS".
FRANCE'S CONDITION THAT FRENCH REMAIN THE LANGUAGE OF GOVERNMENT AND ADMINISTRATION... WAS ALSO SURRENDERED TODAY, IN RETURN FOR TECHNICAL AND FINANCIAL AID.
ALL BECAUSE WE WANTED TO STOP FRENCH ROM BEING STAMPED OUT BY THE MARCH OF THE ANGLOPHONE COUNTRIES.
YOU COULDN'T WIN, YOU KNOW.
WHY NOT? ALL WE WANTED WAS TO MAINTAIN THE PRIMACY OF FRENCH IN FRANCE. ALL THESE GOD-DAMN ENGLISH FEEDSITES AND TV SHOWS...
ANTHRAX CAT AND THE SEX PUPPETS SPEAK ENGLISH. THE PAYING MASSES NEVER GAVE A SHIT ABOUT "THE MISERABLES" UNTIL IT BECAME AN ANGLOPHONE MUSICAL.

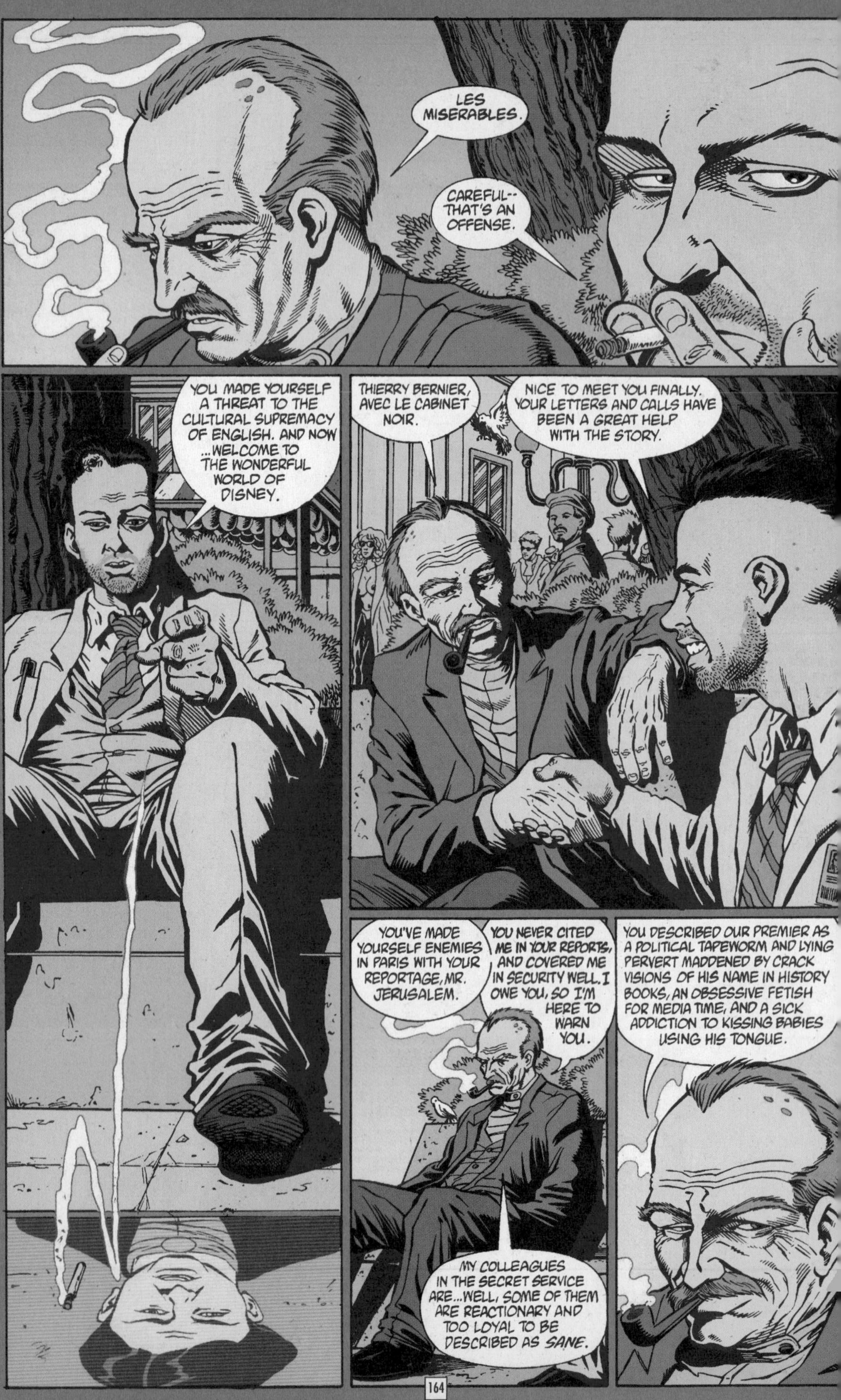
LES MISERABLES.
CAREFUL--THAT'S AN OFFENSE.
YOU MADE YOURSELF A THREAT TO THE CULTURAL SUPREMACY OF ENGLISH. AND NOW ...WELCOME TO THE WONDERFUL WORLD OF DISNEY.
THIERRY BERNIER, AVEC LE CABINET NOIR.
NICE TO MEET YOU FINALLY. YOUR LETTERS AND CALLS HAVE BEEN A GREAT HELP WITH THE STORY.
YOU'VE MADE YOURSELF ENEMIES IN PARIS WITH YOUR REPORTAGE, MR. JERUSALEM.
YOU NEVER CITED ME IN YOUR REPORTS, AND COVERED ME IN SECURITY WELL. I OWE YOU, SO I'M HERE TO WARN YOU.
MY COLLEAGUES IN THE SECRET SERVICE ARE...WELL, SOME OF THEM ARE REACTIONARY AND TOO LOYAL TO BE DESCRIBED AS *SANE*.
YOU DESCRIBED OUR PREMIER AS A POLITICAL TAPEWORM AND LYING PERVERT MADDENED BY CRACK VISIONS OF HIS NAME IN HISTORY BOOKS, AN OBSESSIVE FETISH FOR MEDIA TIME, AND A SICK ADDICTION TO KISSING BABIES USING HIS TONGUE.

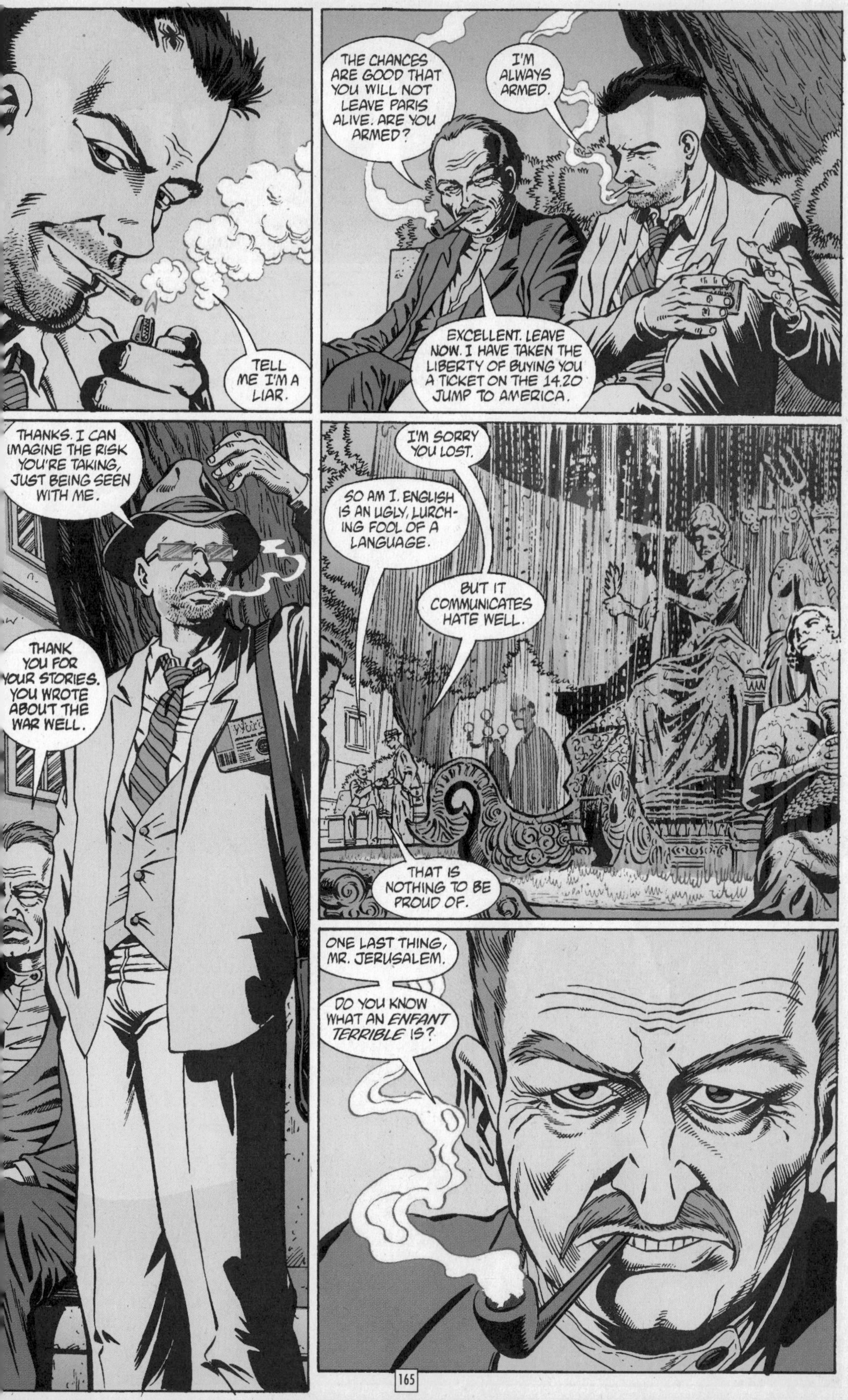
TELL ME I'M A LIAR.
THE CHANCES ARE GOOD THAT YOU WILL NOT LEAVE PARIS ALIVE. ARE YOU ARMED?
I'M ALWAYS ARMED.
EXCELLENT. LEAVE NOW. I HAVE TAKEN THE LIBERTY OF BUYING YOU A TICKET ON THE 14.20 JUMP TO AMERICA.
THANKS. I CAN IMAGINE THE RISK YOU'RE TAKING, JUST BEING SEEN WITH ME.
THANK YOU FOR YOUR STORIES. YOU WROTE ABOUT THE WAR WELL.
I'M SORRY YOU LOST.
SO AM I. ENGLISH IS AN UGLY, LURCHING FOOL OF A LANGUAGE.
BUT IT COMMUNICATES HATE WELL.
THAT IS NOTHING TO BE PROUD OF.
ONE LAST THING, MR. JERUSALEM.
DO YOU KNOW WHAT AN *ENFANT TERRIBLE* IS?

# Blood Hound

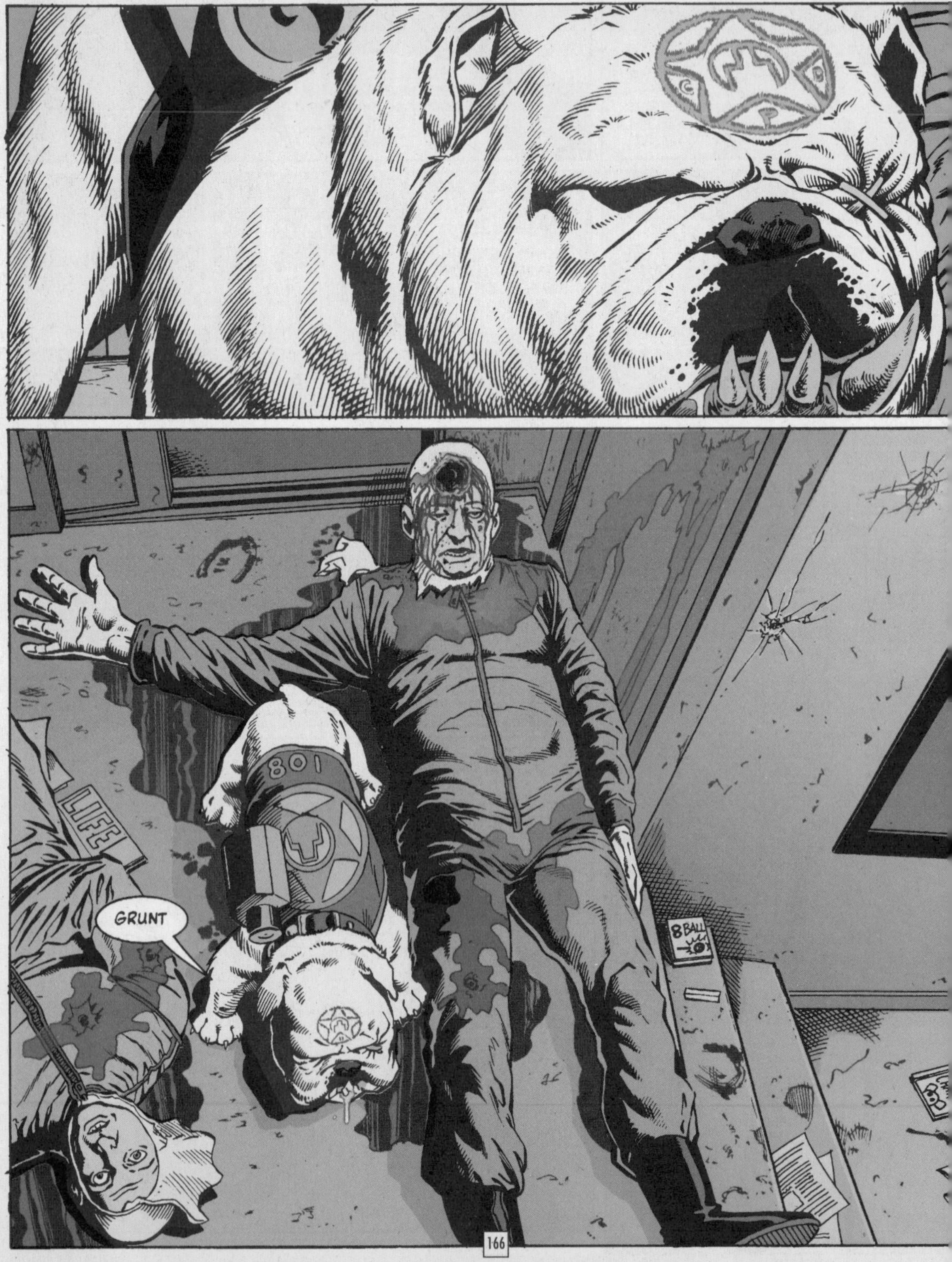

801
LIFE
GRUNT
8 BALL

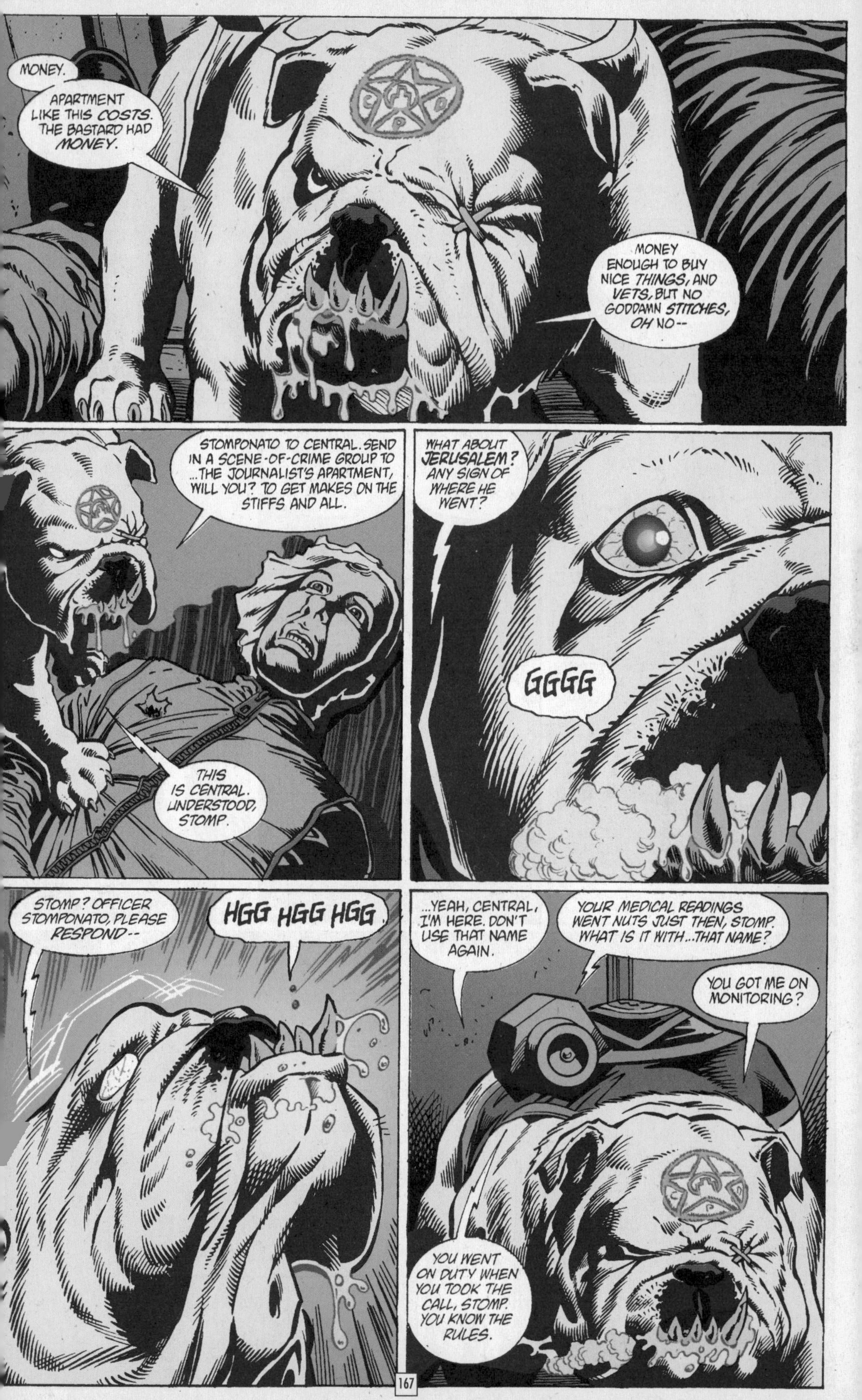

MONEY.
APARTMENT LIKE THIS COSTS. THE BASTARD HAD MONEY.
MONEY ENOUGH TO BUY NICE THINGS, AND VETS, BUT NO GODDAMN STITCHES, OH NO--
STOMPONATO TO CENTRAL. SEND IN A SCENE-OF-CRIME GROUP TO ...THE JOURNALIST'S APARTMENT, WILL YOU? TO GET MAKES ON THE STIFFS AND ALL.
THIS IS CENTRAL. UNDERSTOOD, STOMP.
WHAT ABOUT JERUSALEM? ANY SIGN OF WHERE HE WENT?
GGGG
STOMP? OFFICER STOMPONATO, PLEASE RESPOND--
HGG HGG HGG
...YEAH, CENTRAL, I'M HERE. DON'T USE THAT NAME AGAIN.
YOUR MEDICAL READINGS WENT NUTS JUST THEN, STOMP. WHAT IS IT WITH...THAT NAME?
YOU GOT ME ON MONITORING?
YOU WENT ON DUTY WHEN YOU TOOK THE CALL, STOMP. YOU KNOW THE RULES.

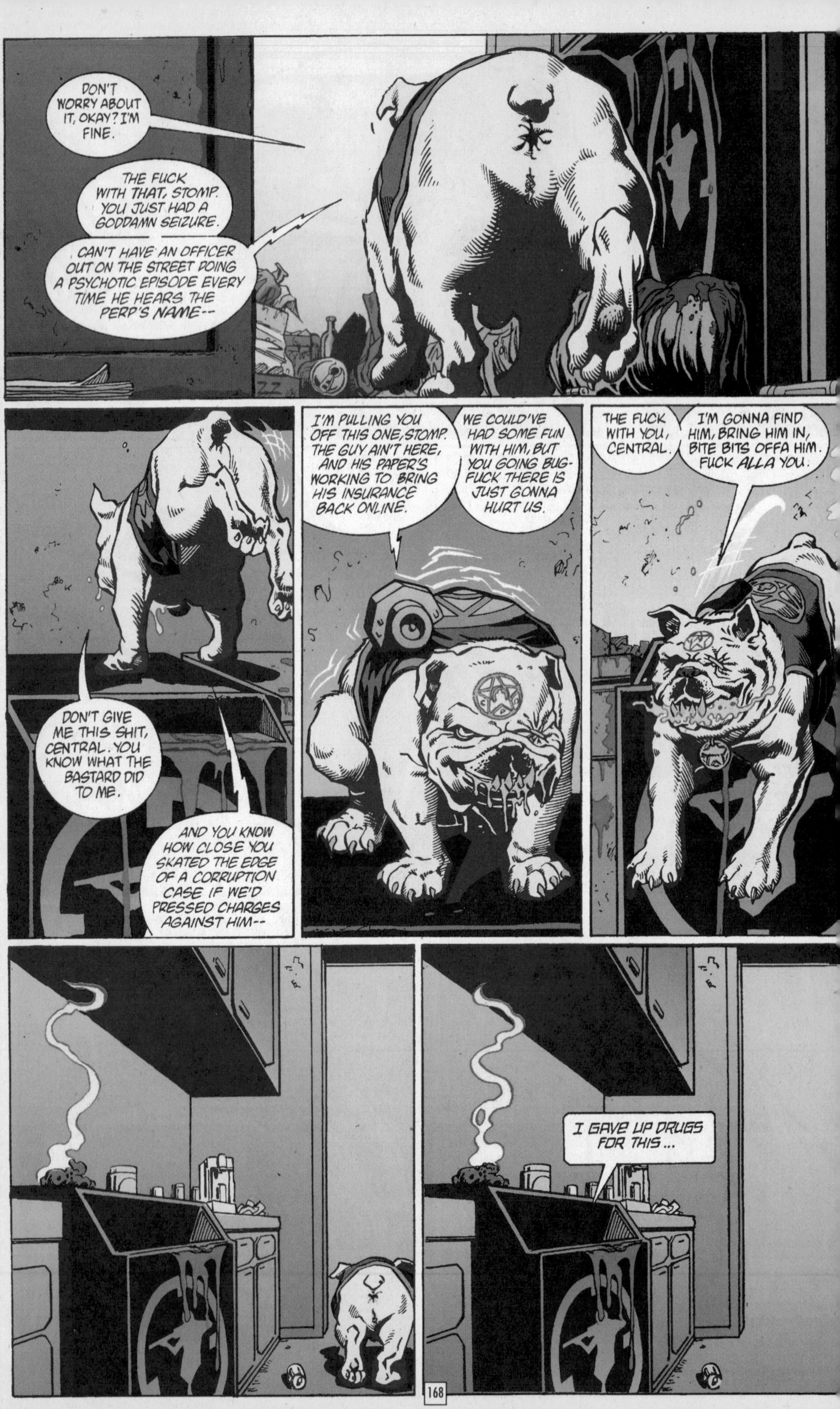
DON'T WORRY ABOUT IT, OKAY? I'M FINE.
THE FUCK WITH THAT, STOMP. YOU JUST HAD A GODDAMN SEIZURE.
CAN'T HAVE AN OFFICER OUT ON THE STREET DOING A PSYCHOTIC EPISODE EVERY TIME HE HEARS THE PERP'S NAME--
DON'T GIVE ME THIS SHIT, CENTRAL. YOU KNOW WHAT THE BASTARD DID TO ME.
AND YOU KNOW HOW CLOSE YOU SKATED THE EDGE OF A CORRUPTION CASE IF WE'D PRESSED CHARGES AGAINST HIM--
I'M PULLING YOU OFF THIS ONE, STOMP. THE GUY AIN'T HERE, AND HIS PAPER'S WORKING TO BRING HIS INSURANCE BACK ONLINE.
WE COULD'VE HAD SOME FUN WITH HIM, BUT YOU GOING BUG-FUCK THERE IS JUST GONNA HURT US.
THE FUCK WITH YOU, CENTRAL.
I'M GONNA FIND HIM, BRING HIM IN, BITE BITS OFFA HIM. FUCK ALLA YOU.
I GAVE UP DRUGS FOR THIS...

# Lost at Home

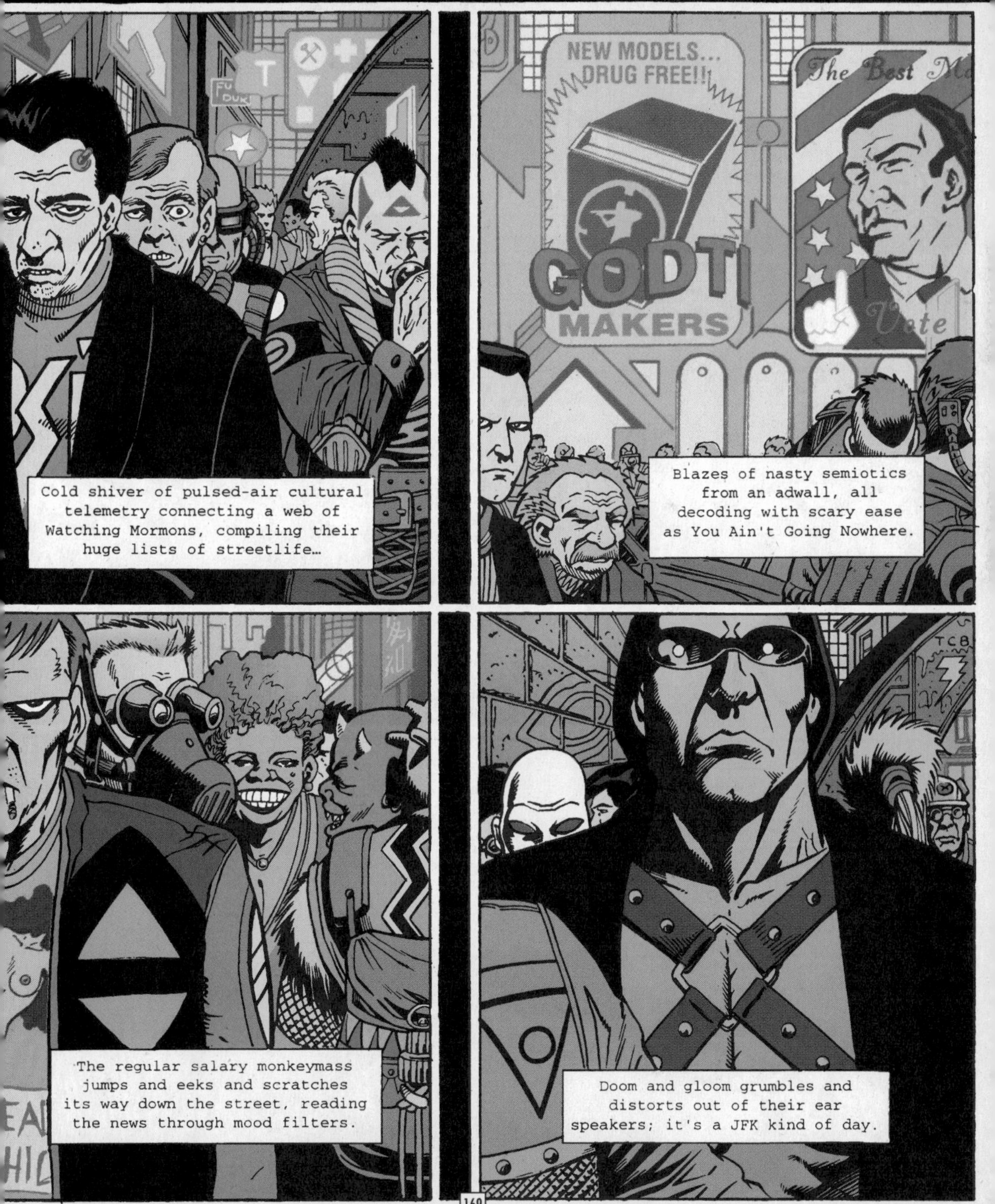

Cold shiver of pulsed-air cultural telemetry connecting a web of Watching Mormons, compiling their huge lists of streetlife…
NEW MODELS... DRUG FREE!!
GODTI MAKERS
The Best M
Vote
Blazes of nasty semiotics from an adwall, all decoding with scary ease as You Ain't Going Nowhere.
The regular salary monkeymass jumps and eeks and scratches its way down the street, reading the news through mood filters.
TCB
Doom and gloom grumbles and distorts out of their ear speakers; it's a JFK kind of day.

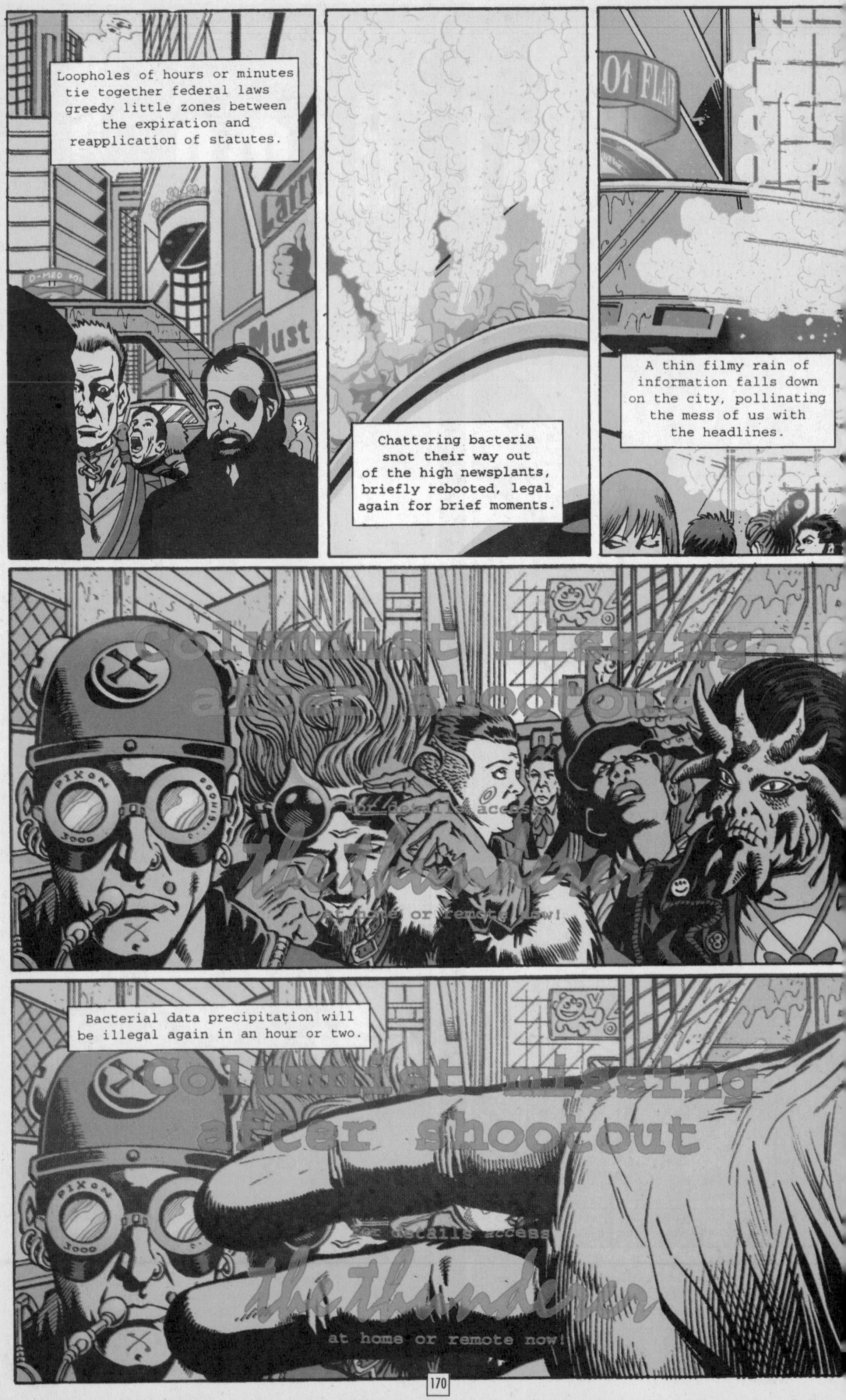
Loopholes of hours or minutes tie together federal laws greedy little zones between the expiration and reapplication of statutes.
Chattering bacteria snot their way out of the high newsplants, briefly rebooted, legal again for brief moments.
A thin filmy rain of information falls down on the city, pollinating the mess of us with the headlines.
Columnist missing after shootout
For details access
the thunderer
at home or remote now!
Bacterial data precipitation will be illegal again in an hour or two.
Columnist missing after shootout
for details access
the thunderer
at home or remote now!

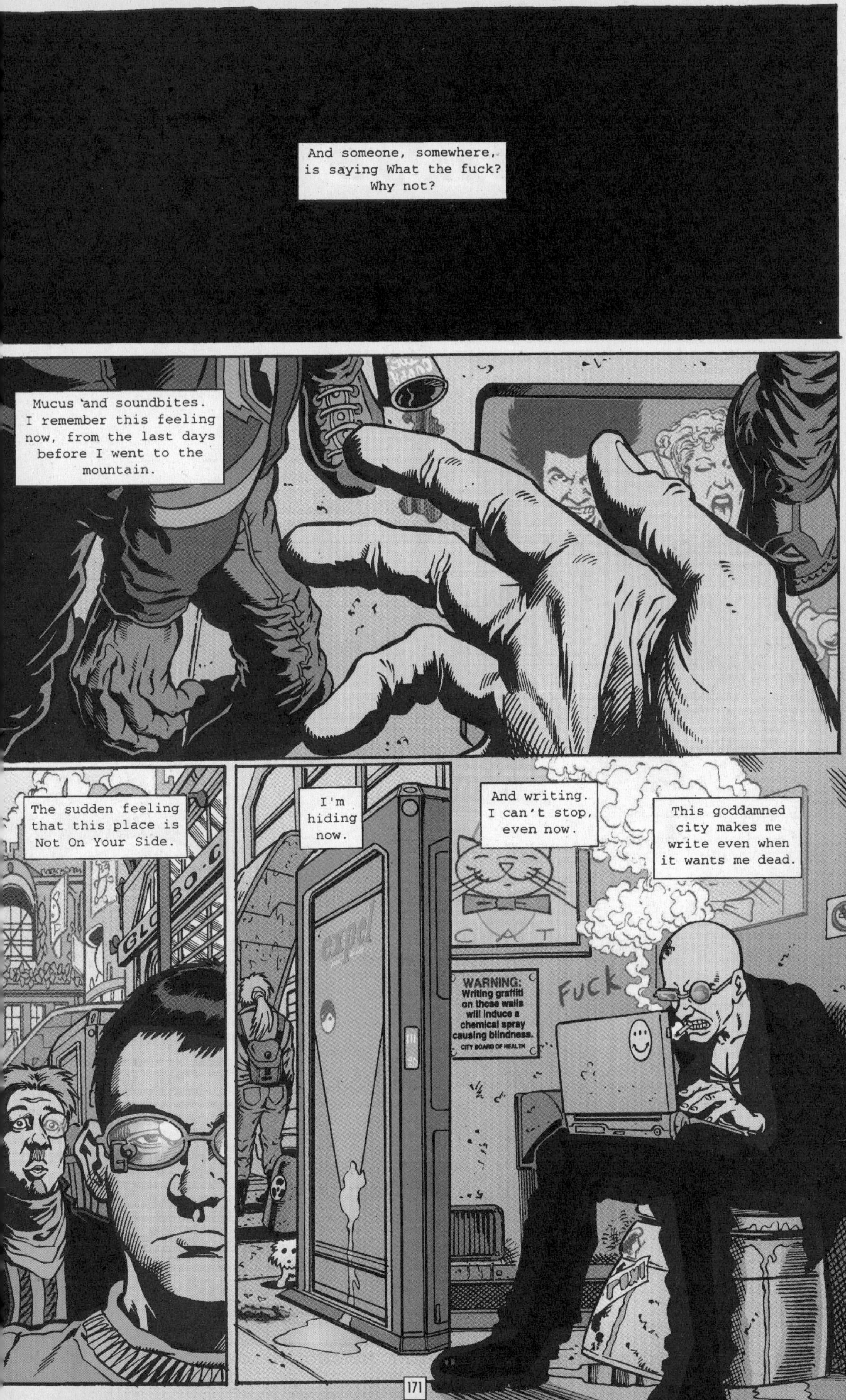
And someone, somewhere, is saying What the fuck? Why not?
Mucus and soundbites. I remember this feeling now, from the last days before I went to the mountain.
The sudden feeling that this place is Not On Your Side.
I'm hiding now.
And writing. I can't stop, even now.
This goddamned city makes me write even when it wants me dead.
CAT
WARNING: Writing graffiti on these walls will induce a chemical spray causing blindness.
CITY BOARD OF HEALTH
FUCK

# A VOYAGE ROUND MY FATHER

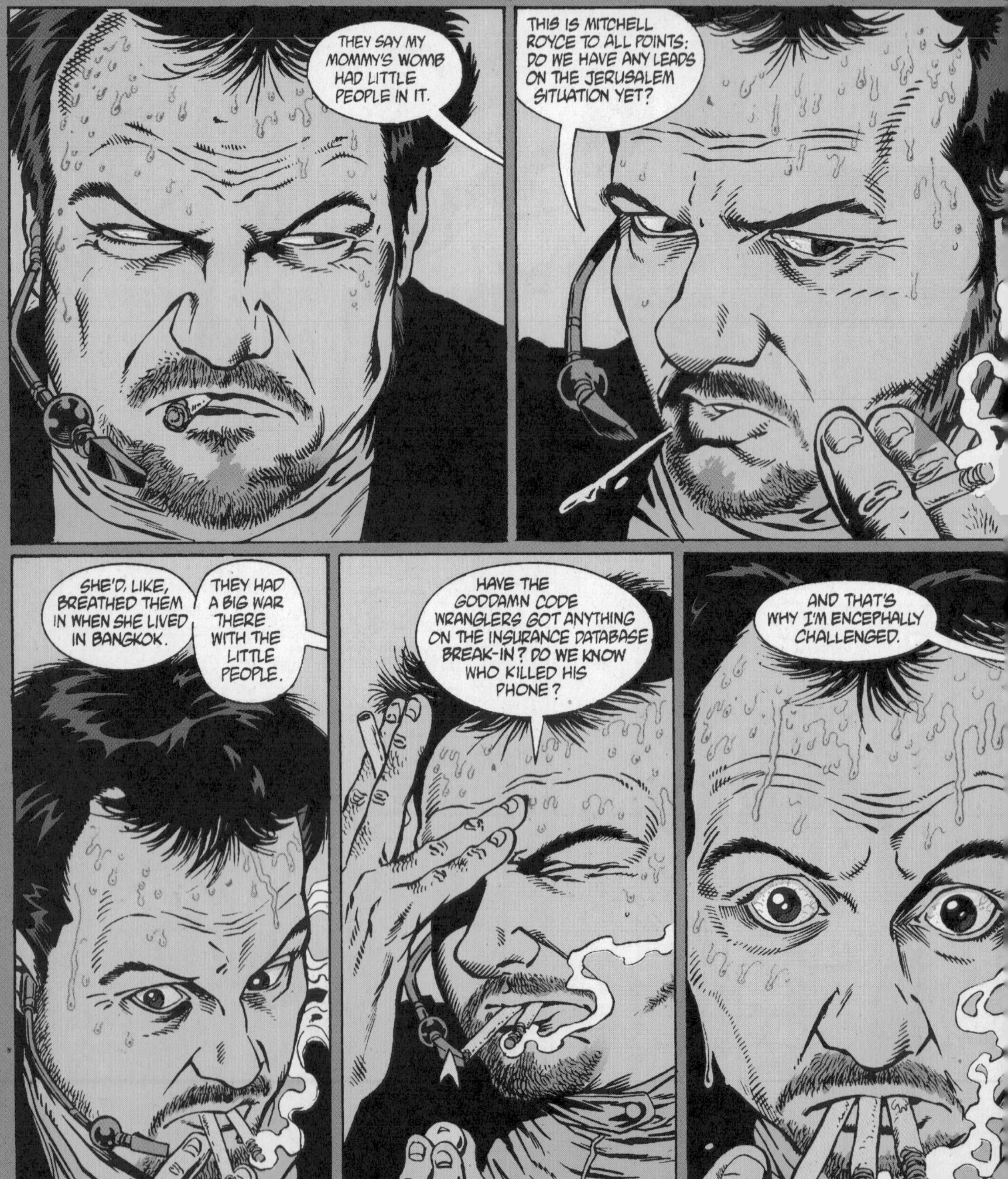
THEY SAY MY MOMMY'S WOMB HAD LITTLE PEOPLE IN IT.
THIS IS MITCHELL ROYCE TO ALL POINTS: DO WE HAVE ANY LEADS ON THE JERUSALEM SITUATION YET?
SHE'D, LIKE, BREATHED THEM IN WHEN SHE LIVED IN BANGKOK.
THEY HAD A BIG WAR THERE WITH THE LITTLE PEOPLE.
HAVE THE GODDAMN CODE WRANGLERS GOT ANYTHING ON THE INSURANCE DATABASE BREAK-IN? DO WE KNOW WHO KILLED HIS PHONE?
AND THAT'S WHY I'M ENCEPHALLY CHALLENGED.

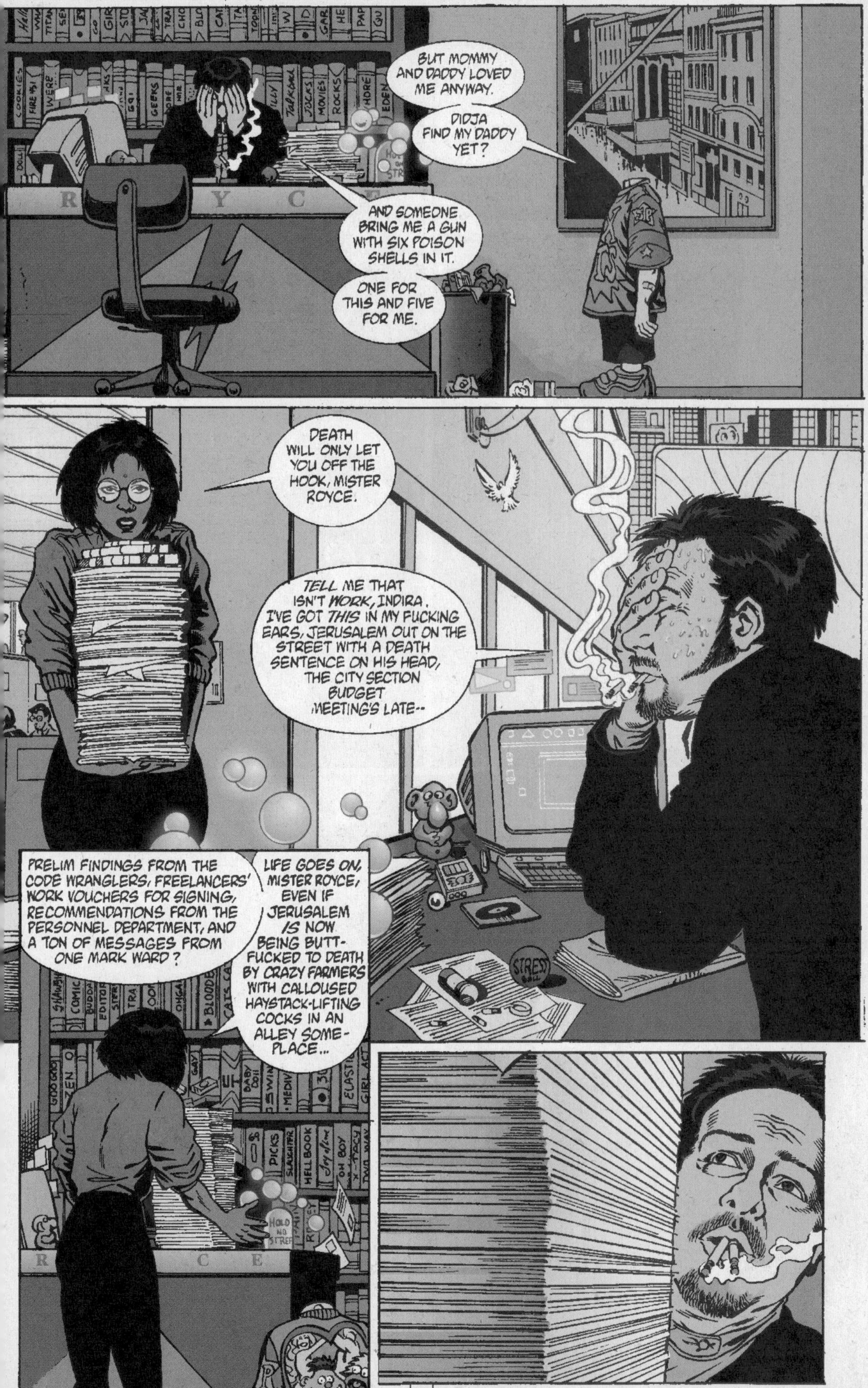

BUT MOMMY AND DADDY LOVED ME ANYWAY.
DIDJA FIND MY DADDY YET?
AND SOMEONE BRING ME A GUN WITH SIX POISON SHELLS IN IT.
ONE FOR THIS AND FIVE FOR ME.
DEATH WILL ONLY LET YOU OFF THE HOOK, MISTER ROYCE.
TELL ME THAT ISN'T WORK, INDIRA. I'VE GOT THIS IN MY FUCKING EARS, JERUSALEM OUT ON THE STREET WITH A DEATH SENTENCE ON HIS HEAD, THE CITY SECTION BUDGET MEETING'S LATE--
PRELIM FINDINGS FROM THE CODE WRANGLERS, FREELANCERS' WORK VOUCHERS FOR SIGNING, RECOMMENDATIONS FROM THE PERSONNEL DEPARTMENT, AND A TON OF MESSAGES FROM ONE MARK WARD?
LIFE GOES ON, MISTER ROYCE, EVEN IF JERUSALEM IS NOW BEING BUTT-FUCKED TO DEATH BY CRAZY FARMERS WITH CALLOUSED HAYSTACK-LIFTING COCKS IN AN ALLEY SOMEPLACE...

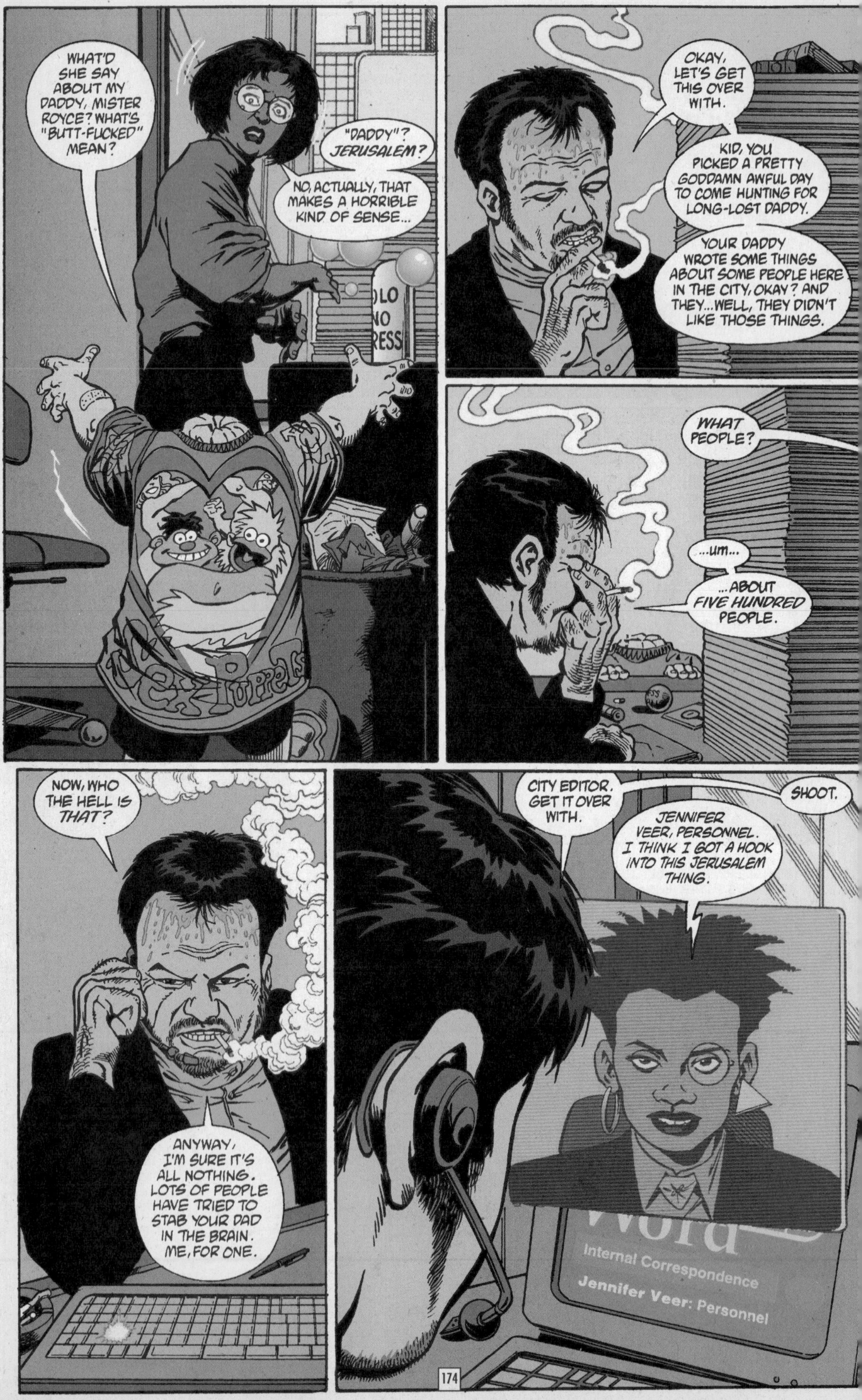
WHAT'D SHE SAY ABOUT MY DADDY, MISTER ROYCE? WHAT'S "BUTT-FUCKED" MEAN?
"DADDY"? JERUSALEM?
NO, ACTUALLY, THAT MAKES A HORRIBLE KIND OF SENSE...
OKAY, LET'S GET THIS OVER WITH.
KID, YOU PICKED A PRETTY GODDAMN AWFUL DAY TO COME HUNTING FOR LONG-LOST DADDY.
YOUR DADDY WROTE SOME THINGS ABOUT SOME PEOPLE HERE IN THE CITY, OKAY? AND THEY...WELL, THEY DIDN'T LIKE THOSE THINGS.
WHAT PEOPLE?
...um...
...ABOUT FIVE HUNDRED PEOPLE.
NOW, WHO THE HELL IS THAT?
ANYWAY, I'M SURE IT'S ALL NOTHING. LOTS OF PEOPLE HAVE TRIED TO STAB YOUR DAD IN THE BRAIN. ME, FOR ONE.
CITY EDITOR. GET IT OVER WITH.
SHOOT.
JENNIFER VEER, PERSONNEL. I THINK I GOT A HOOK INTO THIS JERUSALEM THING.
Internal Correspondence
Jennifer Veer: Personnel

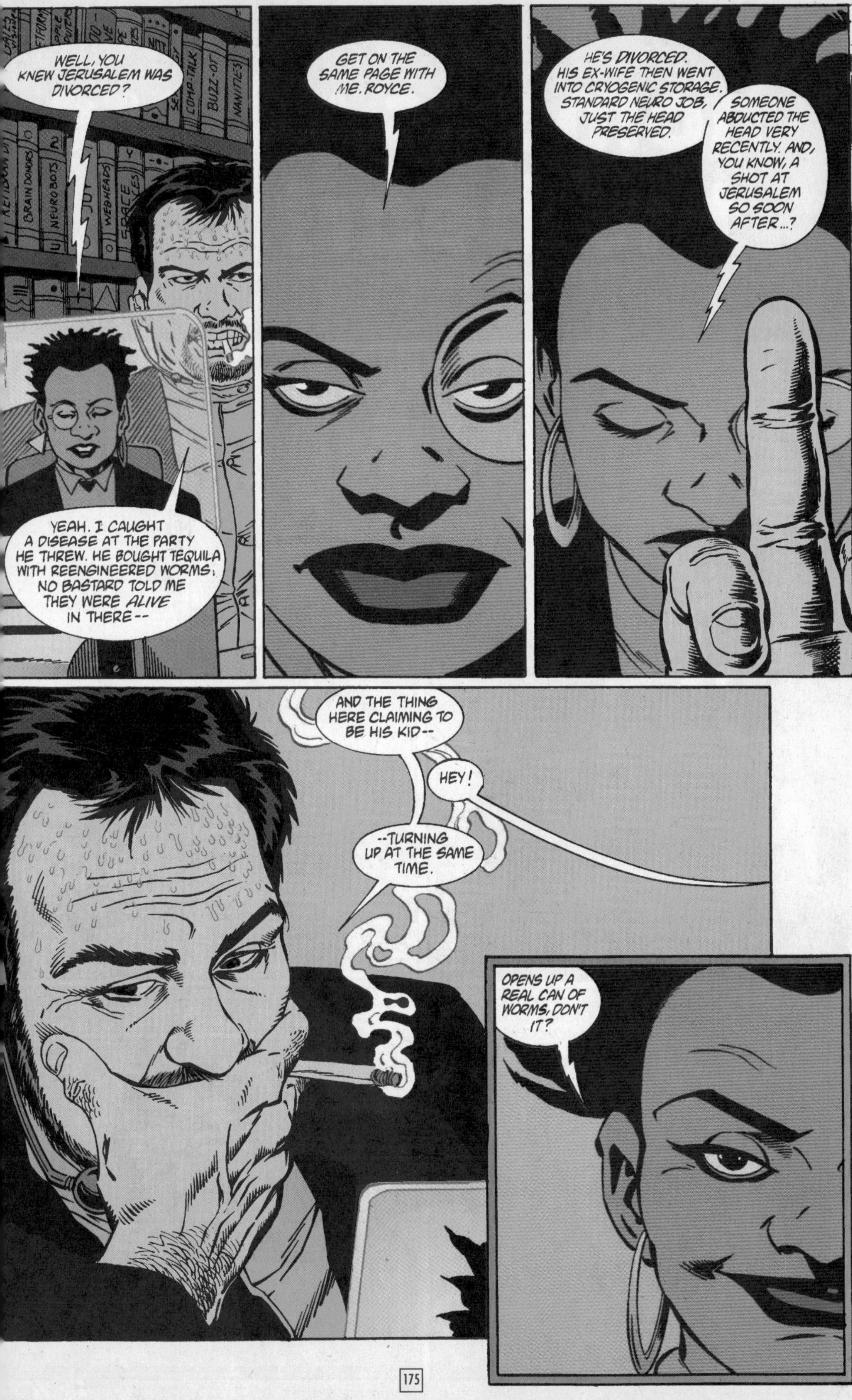
WELL, YOU KNEW JERUSALEM WAS DIVORCED?
YEAH. I CAUGHT A DISEASE AT THE PARTY HE THREW. HE BOUGHT TEQUILA WITH REENGINEERED WORMS; NO BASTARD TOLD ME THEY WERE *ALIVE* IN THERE--
GET ON THE SAME PAGE WITH ME, ROYCE.
HE'S *DIVORCED*. HIS EX-WIFE THEN WENT INTO CRYOGENIC STORAGE. STANDARD NEURO JOB, JUST THE HEAD PRESERVED.
SOMEONE ABDUCTED THE HEAD VERY RECENTLY. AND, YOU KNOW, A SHOT AT JERUSALEM SO SOON AFTER...?
AND THE THING HERE CLAIMING TO BE HIS KID--
HEY!
--TURNING UP AT THE SAME TIME.
OPENS UP A REAL CAN OF WORMS, DON'T IT?

# home is where the heart is...

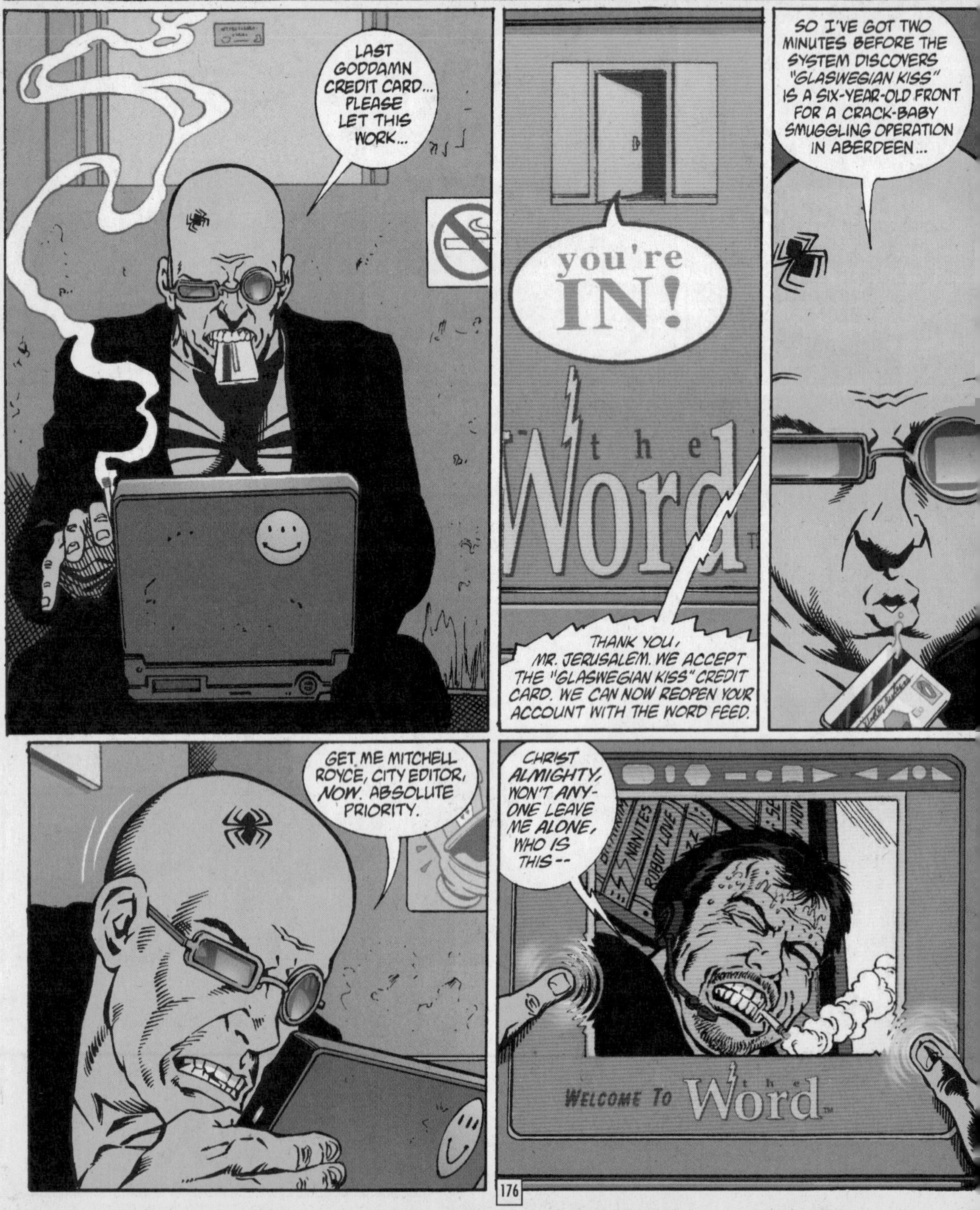
LAST GODDAMN CREDIT CARD... PLEASE LET THIS WORK...
you're IN!
the Word
THANK YOU, MR. JERUSALEM. WE ACCEPT THE "GLASWEGIAN KISS" CREDIT CARD. WE CAN NOW REOPEN YOUR ACCOUNT WITH THE WORD FEED.
SO I'VE GOT TWO MINUTES BEFORE THE SYSTEM DISCOVERS "GLASWEGIAN KISS" IS A SIX-YEAR-OLD FRONT FOR A CRACK-BABY SMUGGLING OPERATION IN ABERDEEN...
GET ME MITCHELL ROYCE, CITY EDITOR, NOW. ABSOLUTE PRIORITY.
CHRIST ALMIGHTY, WON'T ANYONE LEAVE ME ALONE, WHO IS THIS--
NANITES
ROBOT LOVE
WELCOME TO the Word

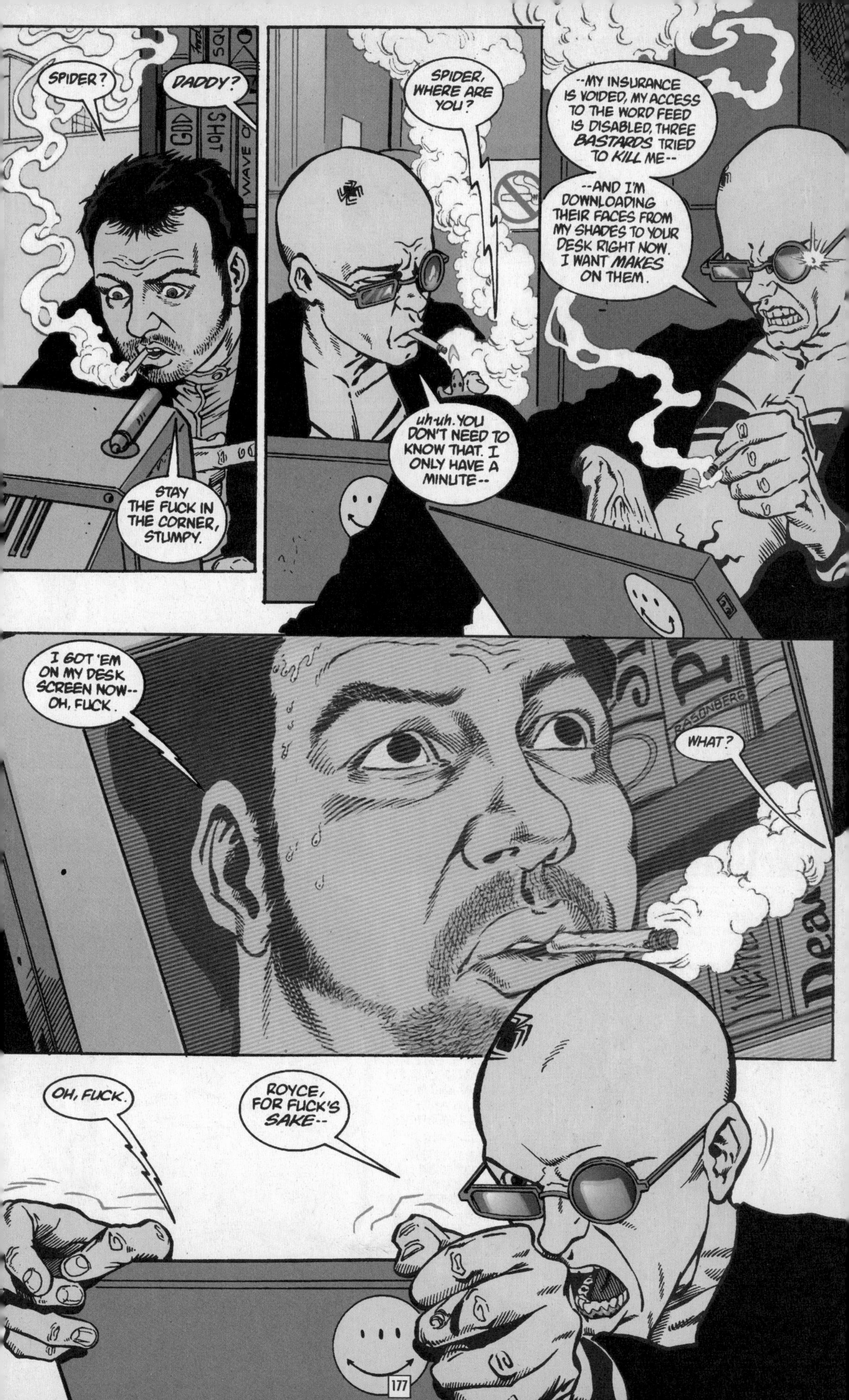
SPIDER?
DADDY?
STAY THE FUCK IN THE CORNER, STUMPY.
SPIDER, WHERE ARE YOU?
uh-uh. YOU DON'T NEED TO KNOW THAT. I ONLY HAVE A MINUTE--
--MY INSURANCE IS VOIDED, MY ACCESS TO THE WORD FEED IS DISABLED, THREE BASTARDS TRIED TO KILL ME--
--AND I'M DOWNLOADING THEIR FACES FROM MY SHADES TO YOUR DESK RIGHT NOW. I WANT MAKES ON THEM.
I GOT 'EM ON MY DESK SCREEN NOW-- OH, FUCK.
WHAT?
OH, FUCK.
ROYCE, FOR FUCK'S SAKE--

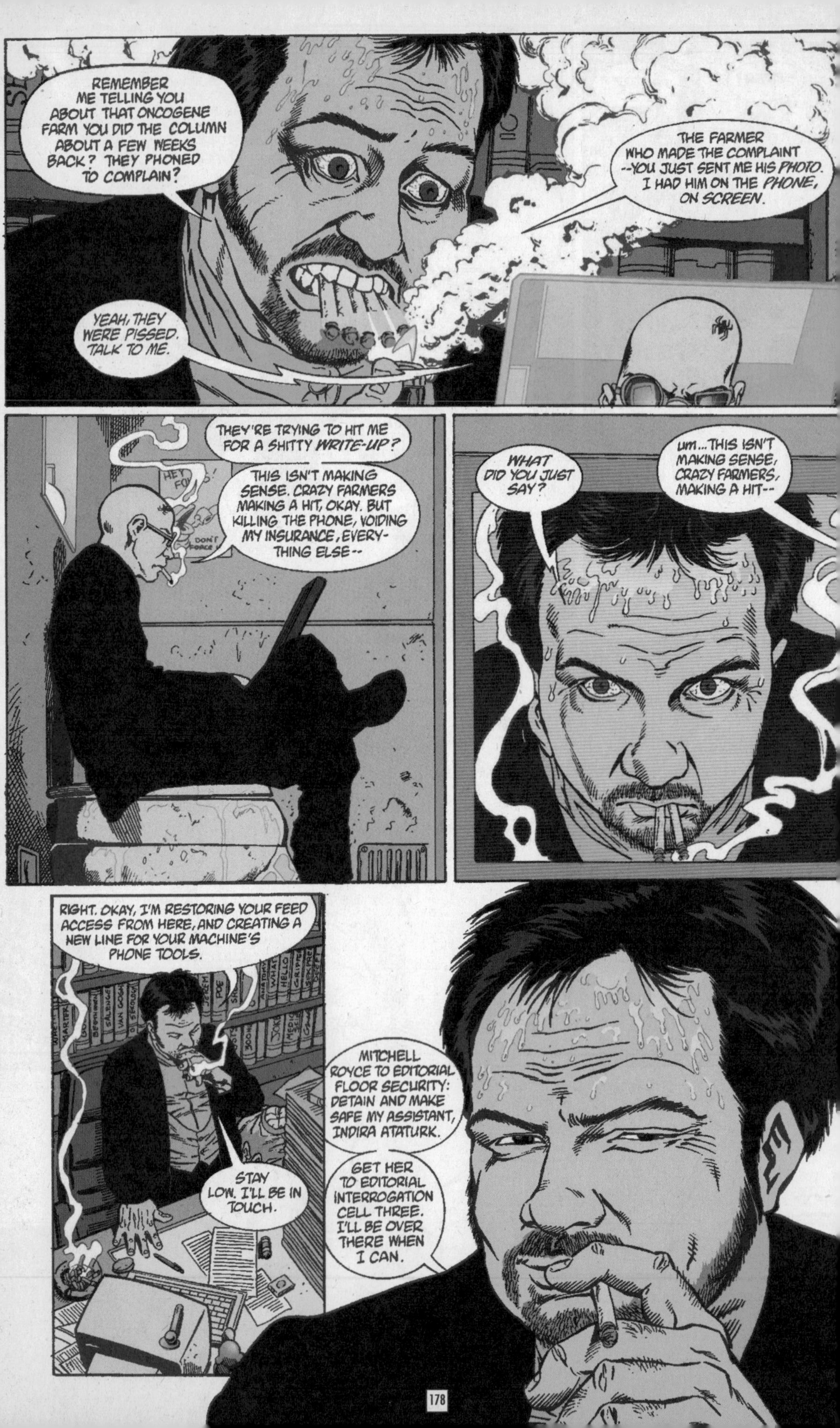
REMEMBER ME TELLING YOU ABOUT THAT ONCOGENE FARM YOU DID THE COLUMN ABOUT A FEW WEEKS BACK? THEY PHONED TO COMPLAIN?
THE FARMER WHO MADE THE COMPLAINT --YOU JUST SENT ME HIS PHOTO. I HAD HIM ON THE PHONE, ON SCREEN.
YEAH, THEY WERE PISSED. TALK TO ME.
THEY'RE TRYING TO HIT ME FOR A SHITTY WRITE-UP?
THIS ISN'T MAKING SENSE. CRAZY FARMERS MAKING A HIT, OKAY. BUT KILLING THE PHONE, VOIDING MY INSURANCE, EVERYTHING ELSE--
WHAT DID YOU JUST SAY?
um... THIS ISN'T MAKING SENSE, CRAZY FARMERS, MAKING A HIT--
RIGHT. OKAY, I'M RESTORING YOUR FEED ACCESS FROM HERE, AND CREATING A NEW LINE FOR YOUR MACHINE'S PHONE TOOLS.
STAY LOW. I'LL BE IN TOUCH.
MITCHELL ROYCE TO EDITORIAL FLOOR SECURITY: DETAIN AND MAKE SAFE MY ASSISTANT, INDIRA ATATURK.
GET HER TO EDITORIAL INTERROGATION CELL THREE. I'LL BE OVER THERE WHEN I CAN.

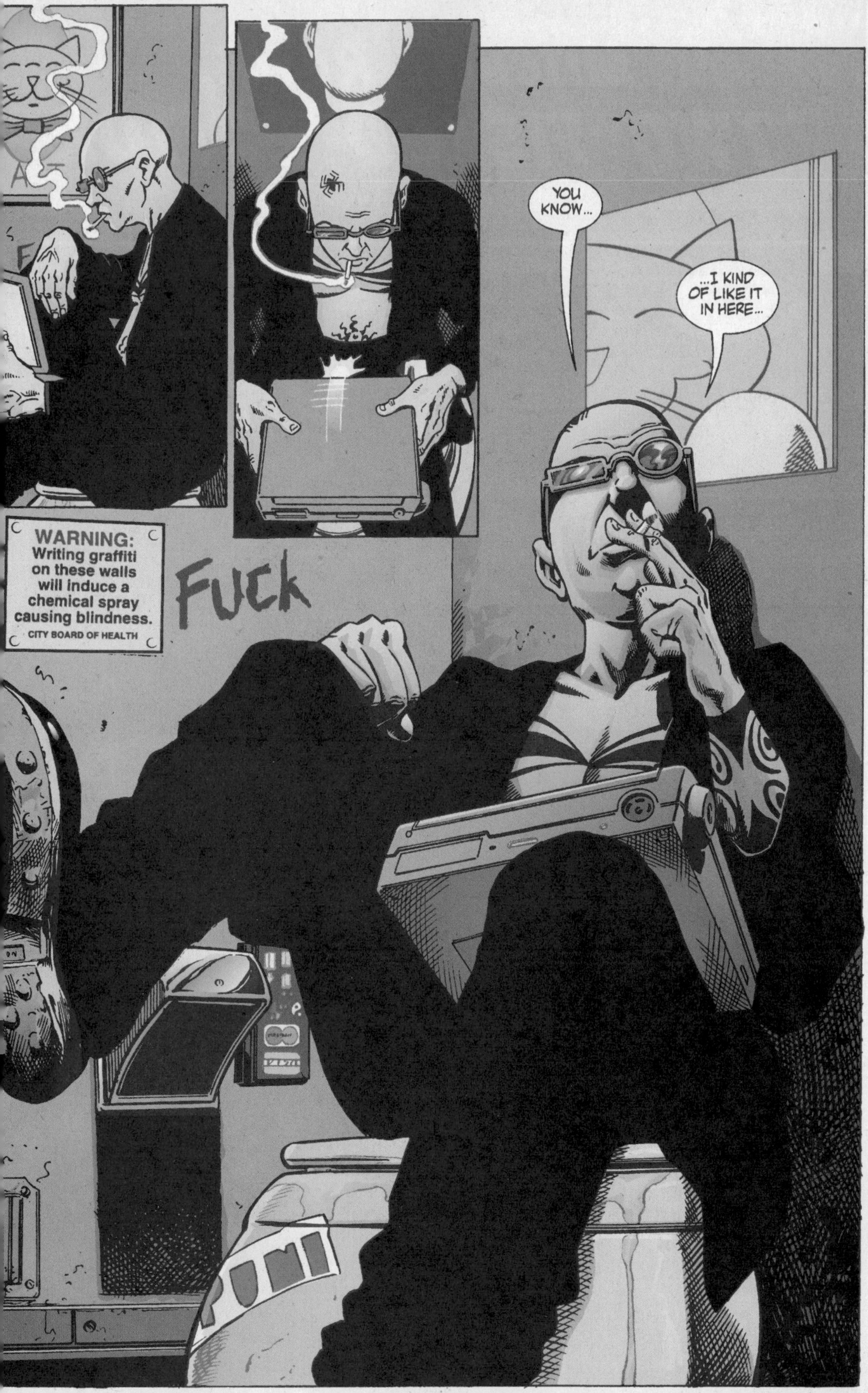
WARNING:
Writing graffiti on these walls will induce a chemical spray causing blindness.
CITY BOARD OF HEALTH
FUCK
YOU KNOW...
...I KIND OF LIKE IT IN HERE...

# MITCHELL ROYCE, TWO-FISTED EDITOR

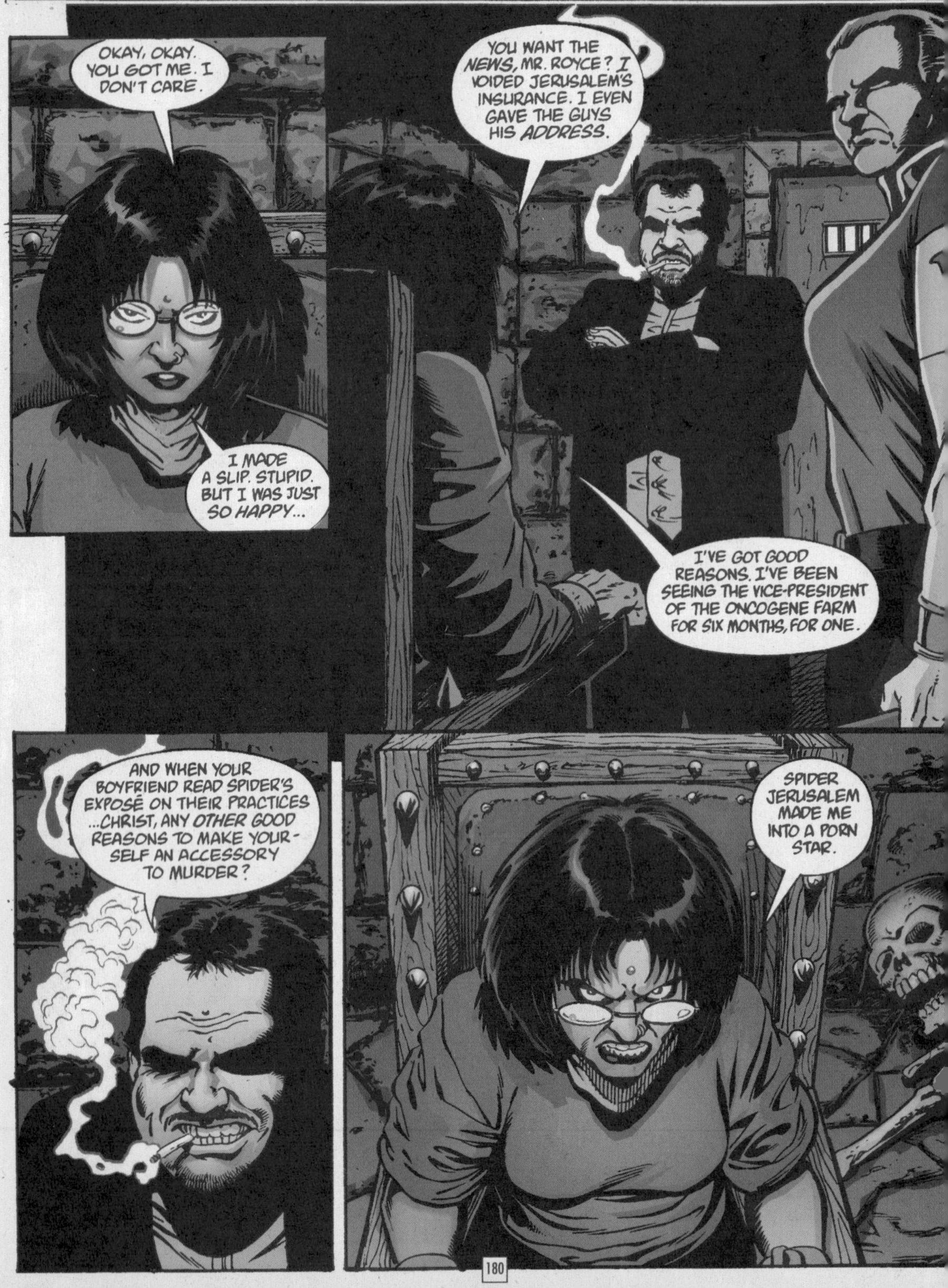

OKAY, OKAY. YOU GOT ME. I DON'T CARE.
I MADE A SLIP. STUPID. BUT I WAS JUST SO *HAPPY*...
YOU WANT THE *NEWS*, MR. ROYCE? *I* VOIDED JERUSALEM'S INSURANCE. I EVEN GAVE THE GUYS HIS *ADDRESS*.
I'VE GOT GOOD REASONS. I'VE BEEN SEEING THE VICE-PRESIDENT OF THE ONCOGENE FARM FOR SIX MONTHS, FOR ONE.
AND WHEN YOUR BOYFRIEND READ SPIDER'S EXPOSÉ ON THEIR PRACTICES ...CHRIST, ANY *OTHER GOOD* REASONS TO MAKE YOURSELF AN ACCESSORY TO MURDER?
SPIDER JERUSALEM MADE ME INTO A PORN STAR.

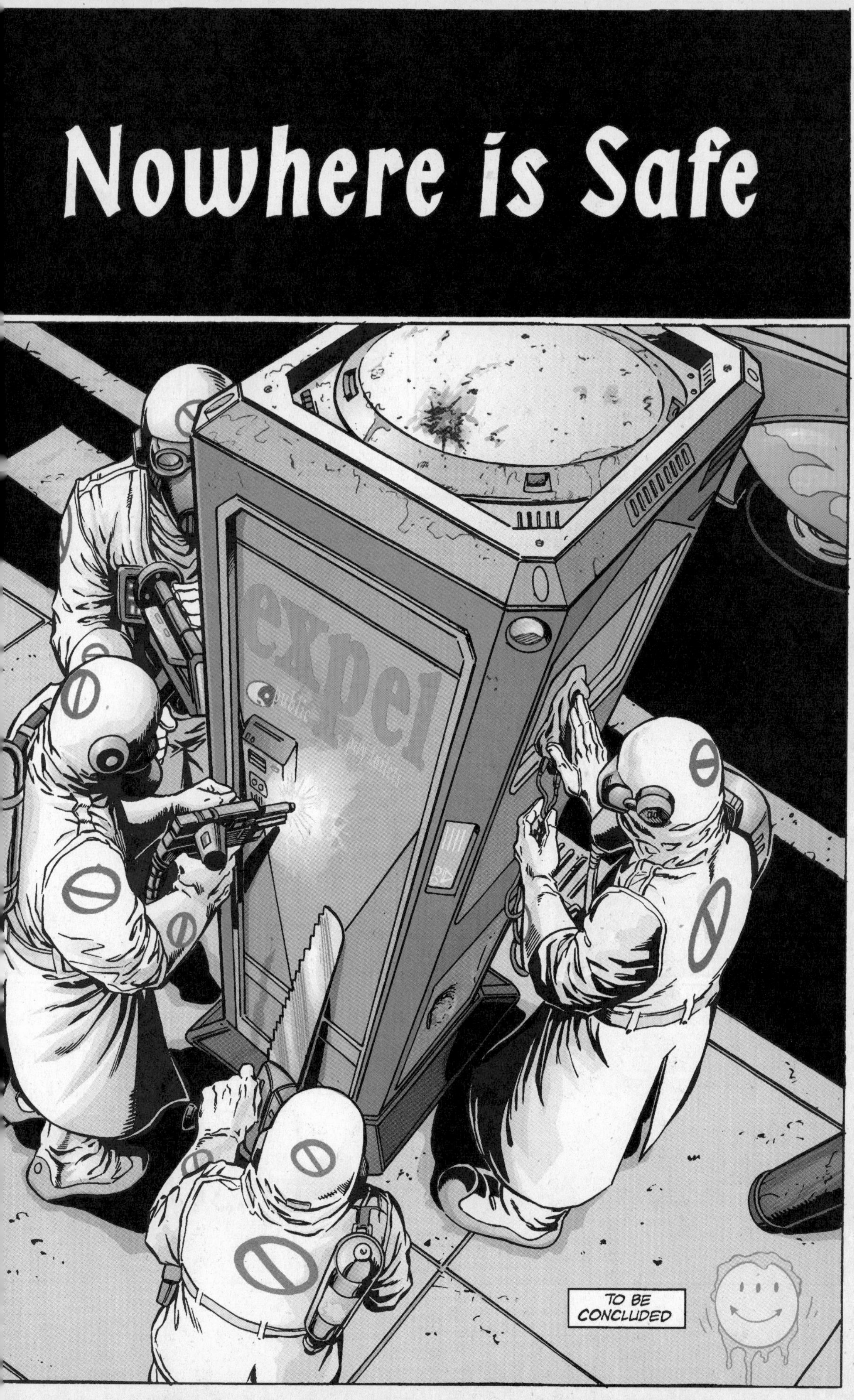
Nowhere is Safe
expel
public
pay toilets
TO BE CONCLUDED

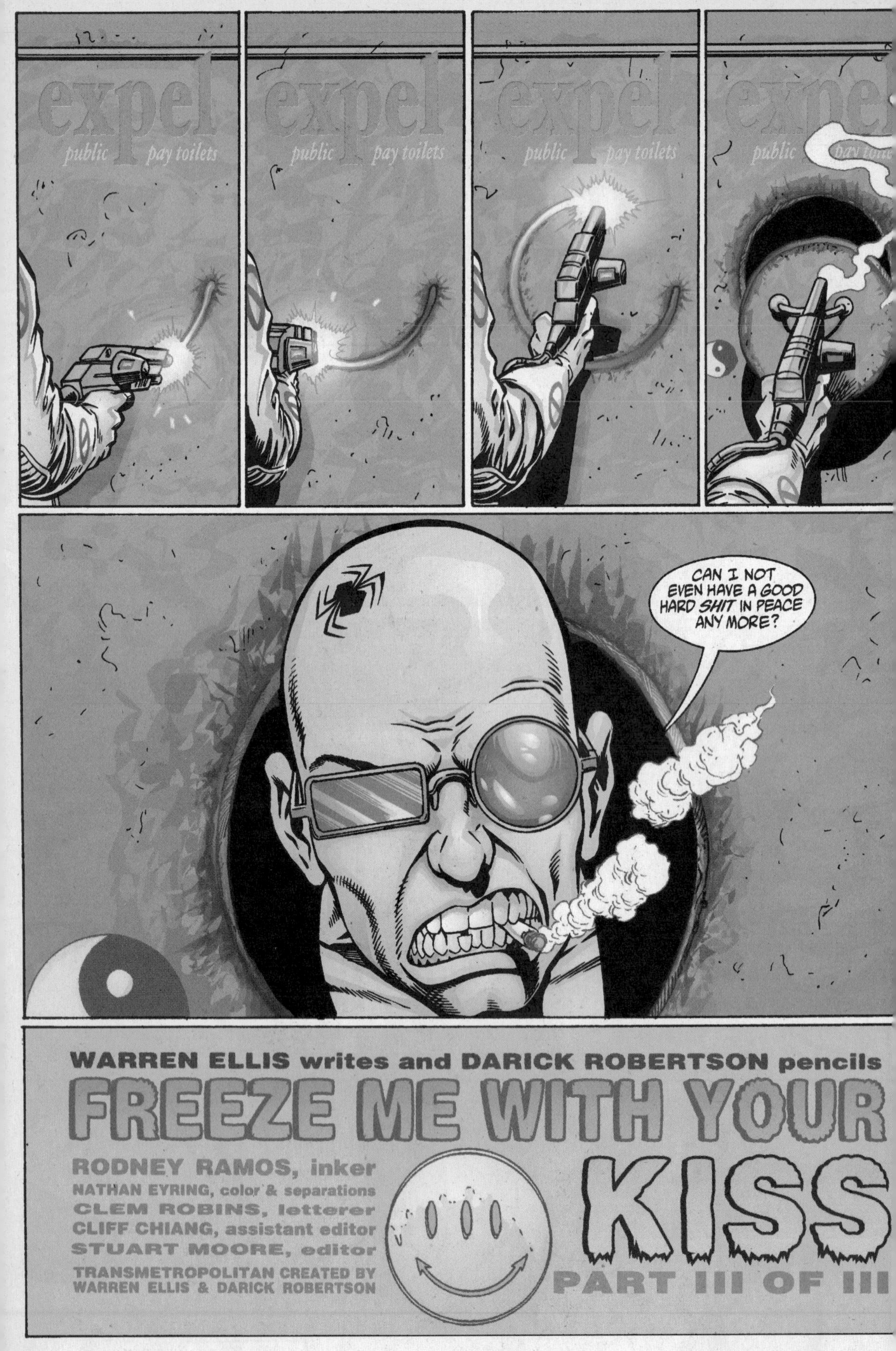
expel
public pay toilets
CAN I NOT EVEN HAVE A GOOD HARD *SHIT* IN PEACE ANY MORE?

**WARREN ELLIS writes and DARICK ROBERTSON pencils**

# FREEZE ME WITH YOUR KISS

## PART III OF III

**RODNEY RAMOS, inker**
**NATHAN EYRING, color & separations**
**CLEM ROBINS, letterer**
**CLIFF CHIANG, assistant editor**
**STUART MOORE, editor**
**TRANSMETROPOLITAN CREATED BY WARREN ELLIS & DARICK ROBERTSON**

# True Confessions

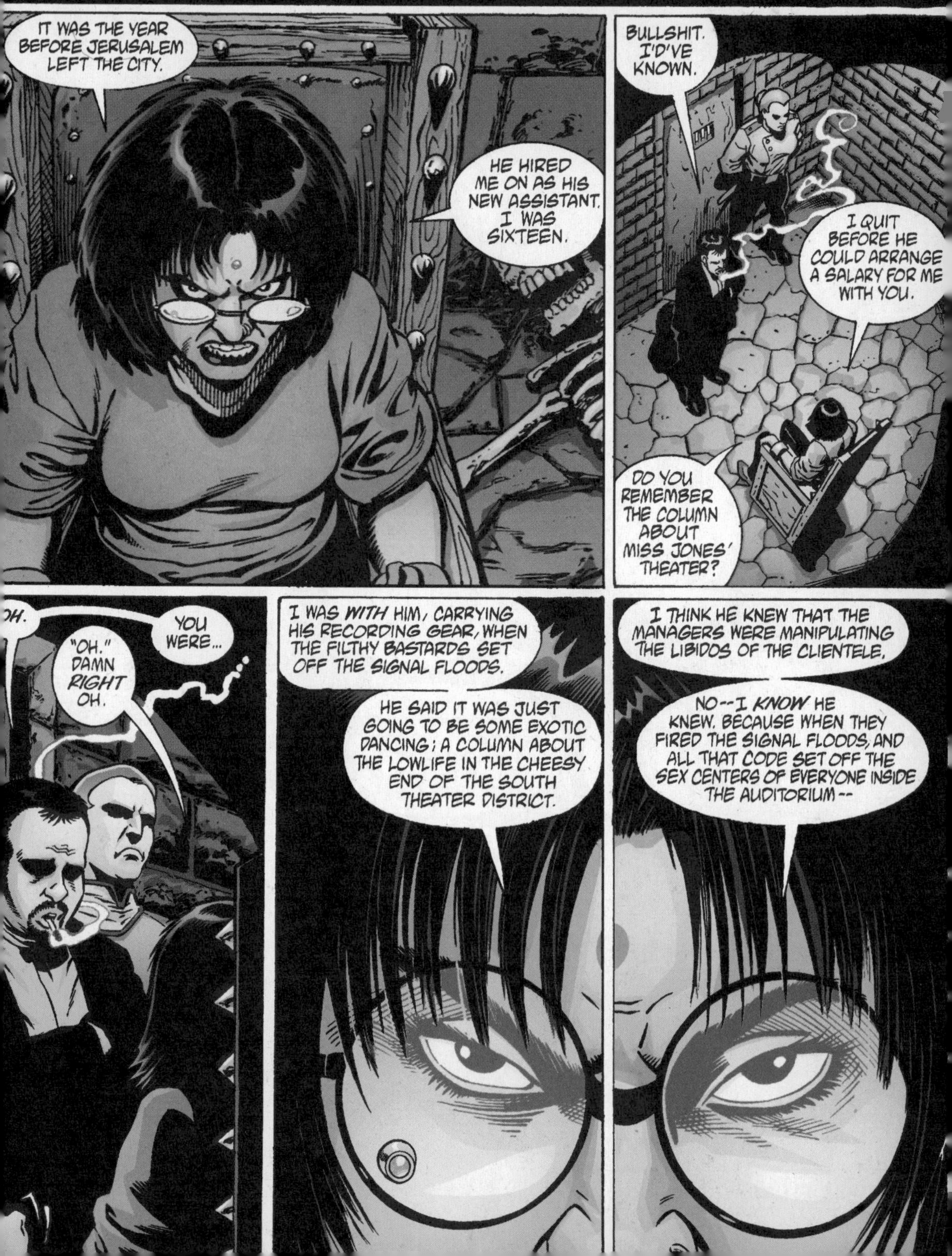

IT WAS THE YEAR BEFORE JERUSALEM LEFT THE CITY.
HE HIRED ME ON AS HIS NEW ASSISTANT. I WAS SIXTEEN.
BULLSHIT. I'D'VE KNOWN.
I QUIT BEFORE HE COULD ARRANGE A SALARY FOR ME WITH YOU.
DO YOU REMEMBER THE COLUMN ABOUT MISS JONES' THEATER?
OH.
YOU WERE...
"OH." DAMN *RIGHT* OH.
I WAS *WITH* HIM, CARRYING HIS RECORDING GEAR, WHEN THE FILTHY BASTARDS SET OFF THE SIGNAL FLOODS.
HE SAID IT WAS JUST GOING TO BE SOME EXOTIC DANCING; A COLUMN ABOUT THE LOWLIFE IN THE CHEESY END OF THE SOUTH THEATER DISTRICT.
I THINK HE KNEW THAT THE MANAGERS WERE MANIPULATING THE LIBIDOS OF THE CLIENTELE.
NO--I *KNOW* HE KNEW. BECAUSE WHEN THEY FIRED THE SIGNAL FLOODS, AND ALL THAT CODE SET OFF THE SEX CENTERS OF EVERYONE INSIDE THE AUDITORIUM--

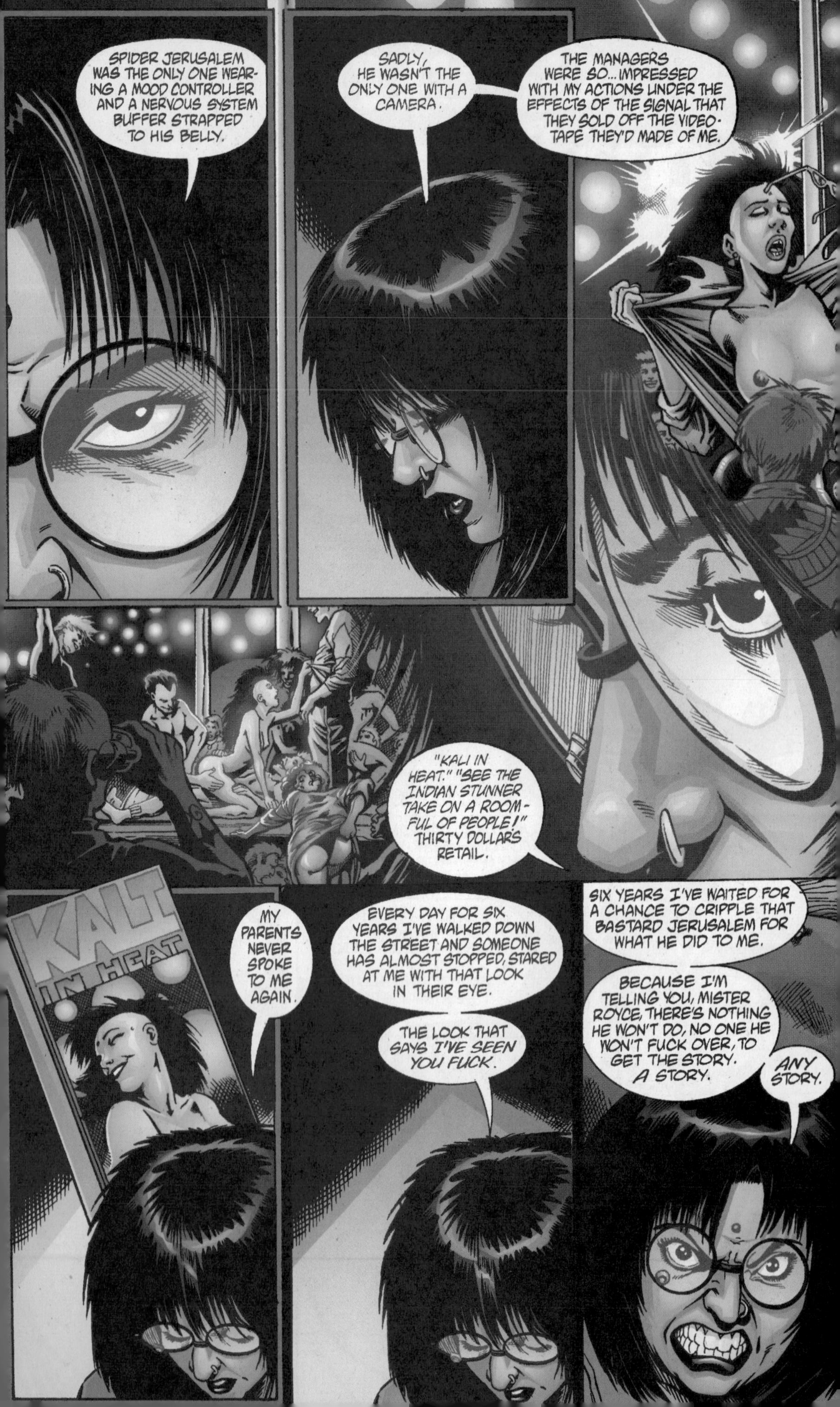
SPIDER JERUSALEM WAS THE ONLY ONE WEARING A MOOD CONTROLLER AND A NERVOUS SYSTEM BUFFER STRAPPED TO HIS BELLY.
SADLY, HE WASN'T THE ONLY ONE WITH A CAMERA.
THE MANAGERS WERE SO... IMPRESSED WITH MY ACTIONS UNDER THE EFFECTS OF THE SIGNAL THAT THEY SOLD OFF THE VIDEOTAPE THEY'D MADE OF ME.
"KALI IN HEAT." "SEE THE INDIAN STUNNER TAKE ON A ROOMFUL OF PEOPLE!" THIRTY DOLLARS RETAIL.
KALI IN HEAT
MY PARENTS NEVER SPOKE TO ME AGAIN.
EVERY DAY FOR SIX YEARS I'VE WALKED DOWN THE STREET AND SOMEONE HAS ALMOST STOPPED, STARED AT ME WITH THAT LOOK IN THEIR EYE.
THE LOOK THAT SAYS *I'VE SEEN YOU FUCK*.
SIX YEARS I'VE WAITED FOR A CHANCE TO CRIPPLE THAT BASTARD JERUSALEM FOR WHAT HE DID TO ME.
BECAUSE I'M TELLING YOU, MISTER ROYCE, THERE'S NOTHING HE WON'T DO, NO ONE HE WON'T FUCK OVER, TO GET THE STORY. *A STORY.*
*ANY STORY.*

# BAD DOGGIE

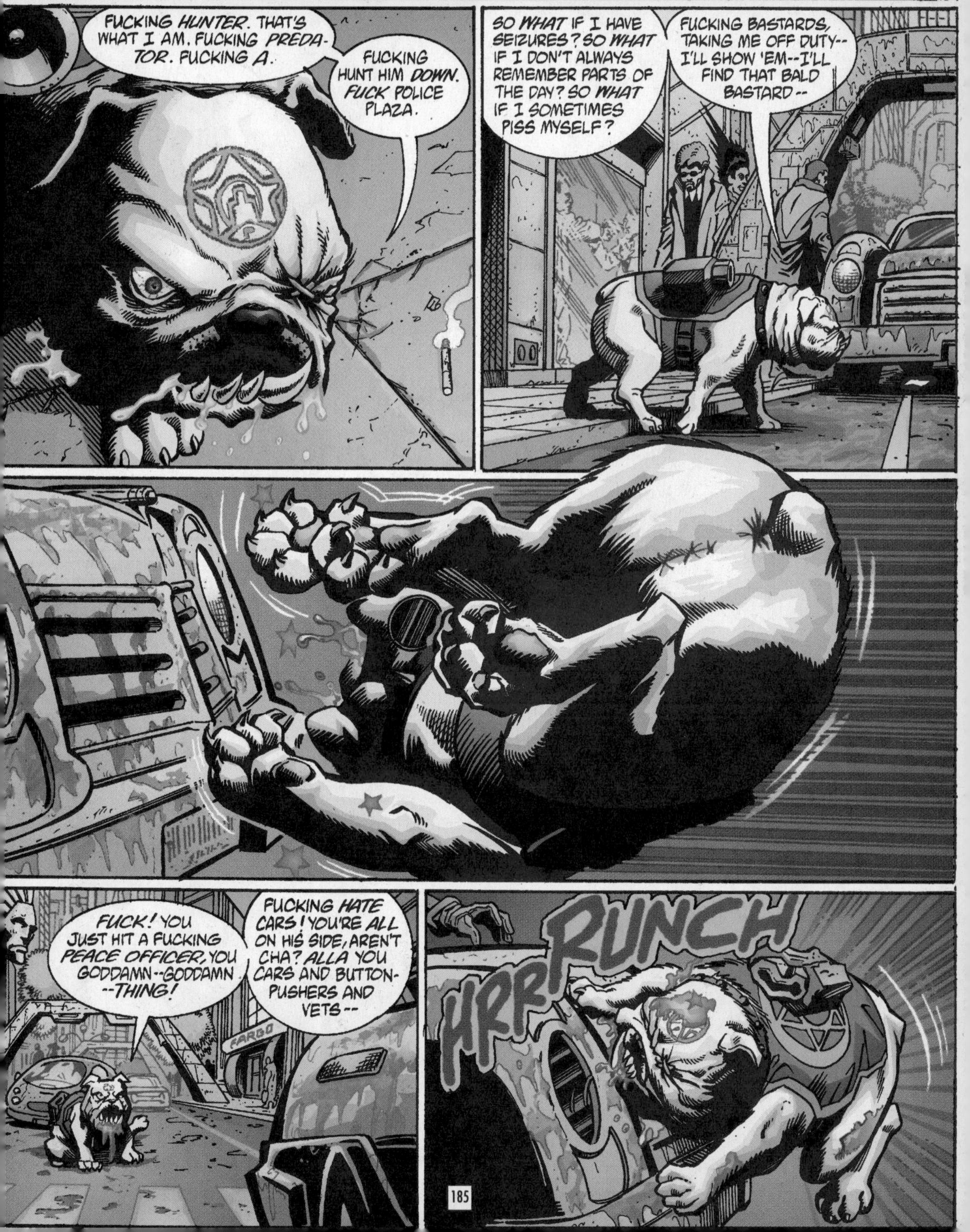
FUCKING HUNTER. THAT'S WHAT I AM. FUCKING PREDATOR. FUCKING A.
FUCKING HUNT HIM DOWN. FUCK POLICE PLAZA.
SO WHAT IF I HAVE SEIZURES? SO WHAT IF I DON'T ALWAYS REMEMBER PARTS OF THE DAY? SO WHAT IF I SOMETIMES PISS MYSELF?
FUCKING BASTARDS, TAKING ME OFF DUTY-- I'LL SHOW 'EM--I'LL FIND THAT BALD BASTARD--
FUCK! YOU JUST HIT A FUCKING PEACE OFFICER, YOU GODDAMN--GODDAMN --THING!
FUCKING HATE CARS! YOU'RE ALL ON HIS SIDE, AREN'T CHA? ALLA YOU CARS AND BUTTON-PUSHERS AND VETS--
FARBO
HRRRUNCH

# To Live and Die on a Toilet

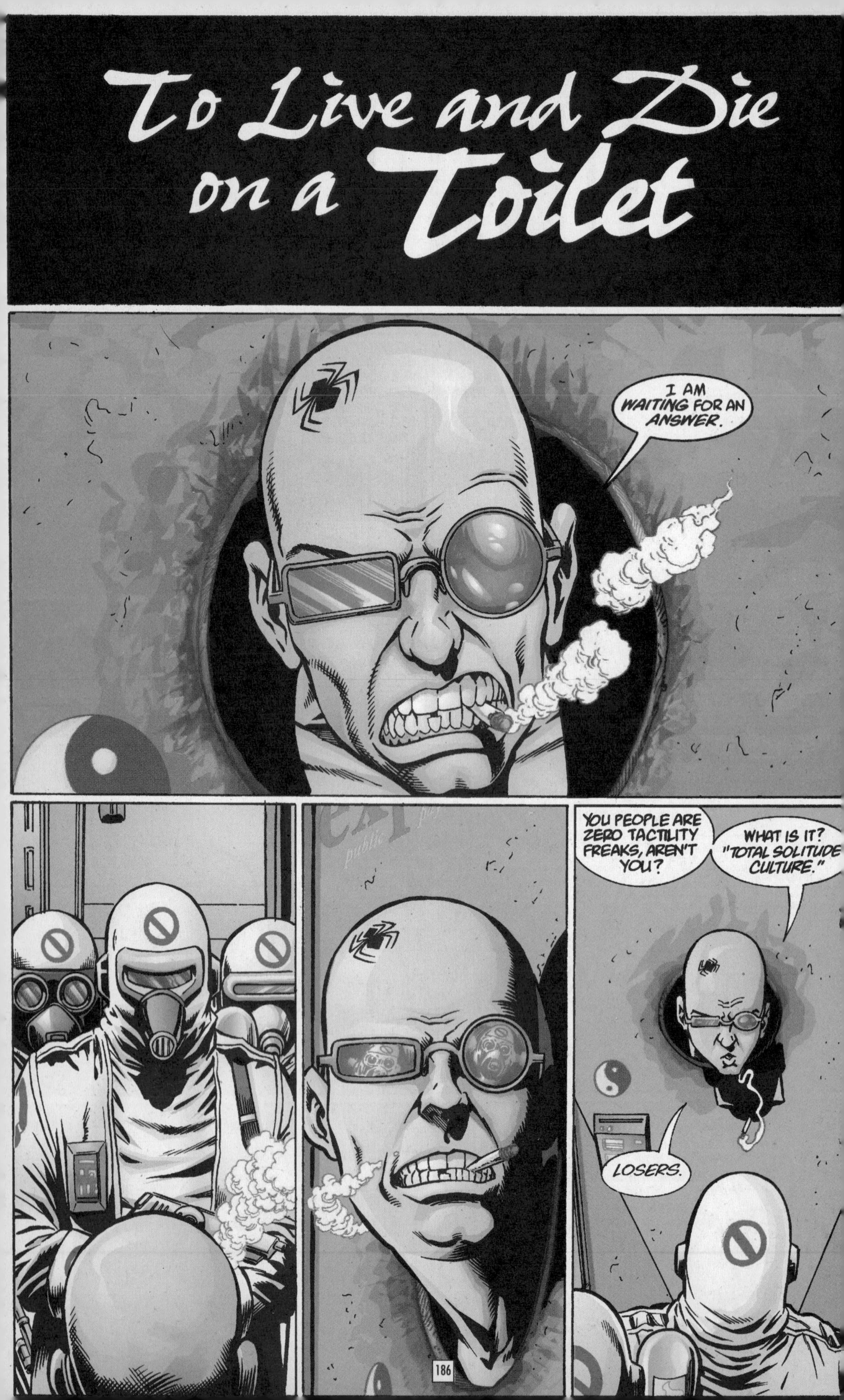

I AM WAITING FOR AN ANSWER.
YOU PEOPLE ARE ZERO TACTILITY FREAKS, AREN'T YOU?
WHAT IS IT? "TOTAL SOLITUDE CULTURE."
LOSERS.

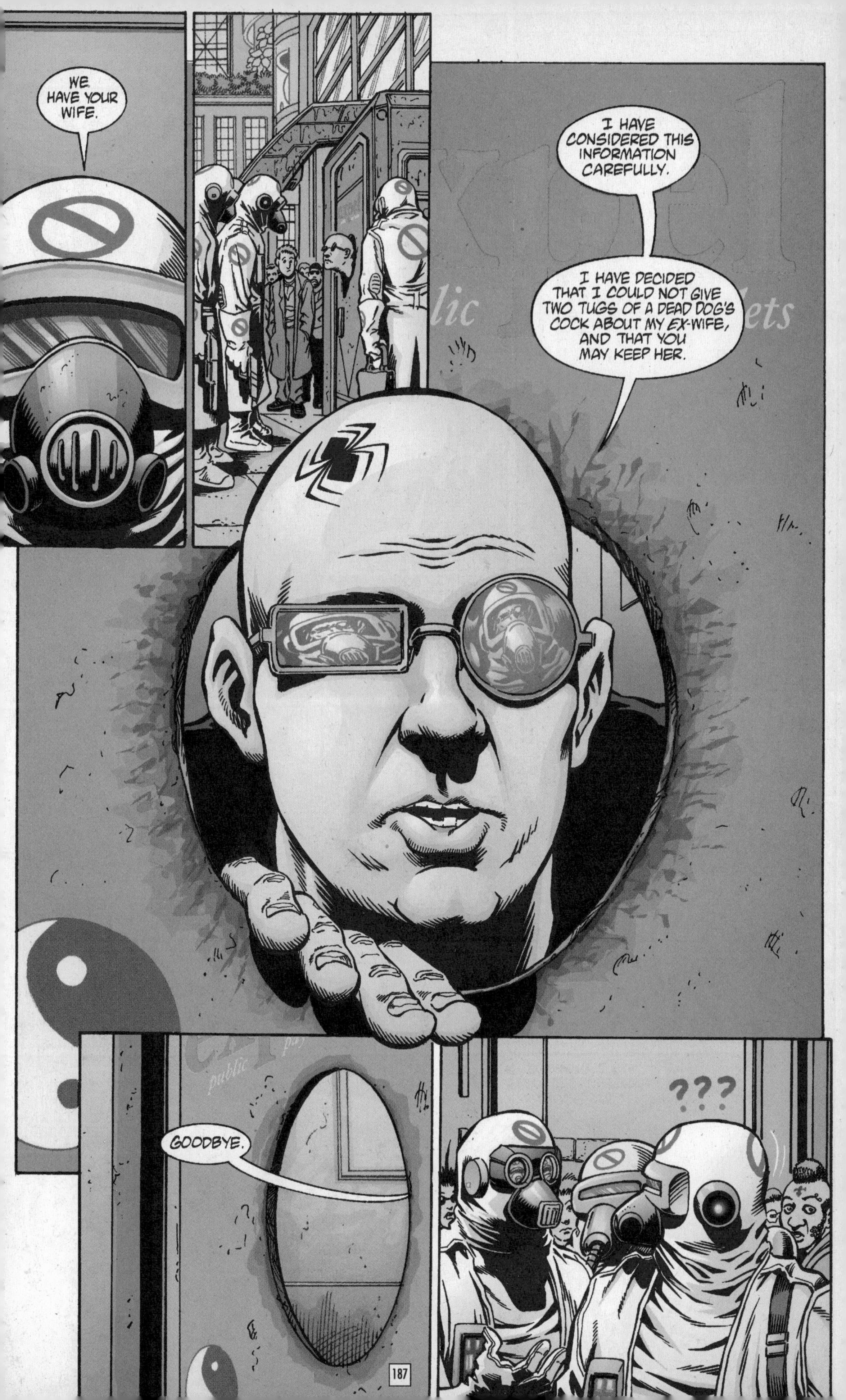
WE HAVE YOUR WIFE.
I HAVE CONSIDERED THIS INFORMATION CAREFULLY.
I HAVE DECIDED THAT I COULD NOT GIVE TWO TUGS OF A DEAD DOG'S COCK ABOUT MY *EX*-WIFE, AND THAT YOU MAY KEEP HER.
GOODBYE.
???

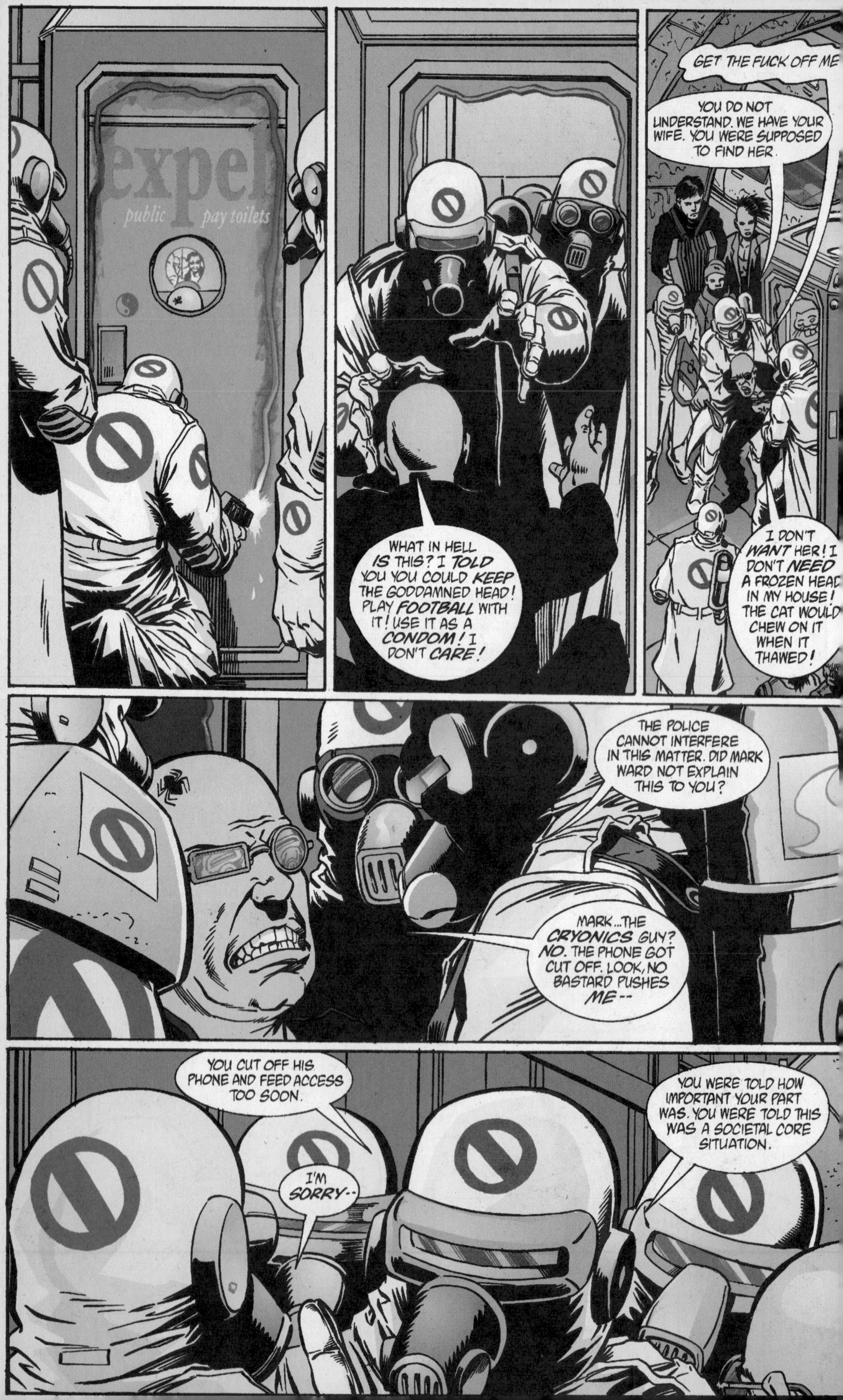
expel
public pay toilets
WHAT IN HELL IS THIS? I TOLD YOU YOU COULD KEEP THE GODDAMNED HEAD! PLAY FOOTBALL WITH IT! USE IT AS A CONDOM! I DON'T CARE!
GET THE FUCK OFF ME
YOU DO NOT UNDERSTAND. WE HAVE YOUR WIFE. YOU WERE SUPPOSED TO FIND HER.
I DON'T WANT HER! I DON'T NEED A FROZEN HEAD IN MY HOUSE! THE CAT WOULD CHEW ON IT WHEN IT THAWED!
THE POLICE CANNOT INTERFERE IN THIS MATTER. DID MARK WARD NOT EXPLAIN THIS TO YOU?
MARK...THE CRYONICS GUY? NO. THE PHONE GOT CUT OFF. LOOK, NO BASTARD PUSHES ME--
YOU CUT OFF HIS PHONE AND FEED ACCESS TOO SOON.
I'M SORRY--
YOU WERE TOLD HOW IMPORTANT YOUR PART WAS. YOU WERE TOLD THIS WAS A SOCIETAL CORE SITUATION.

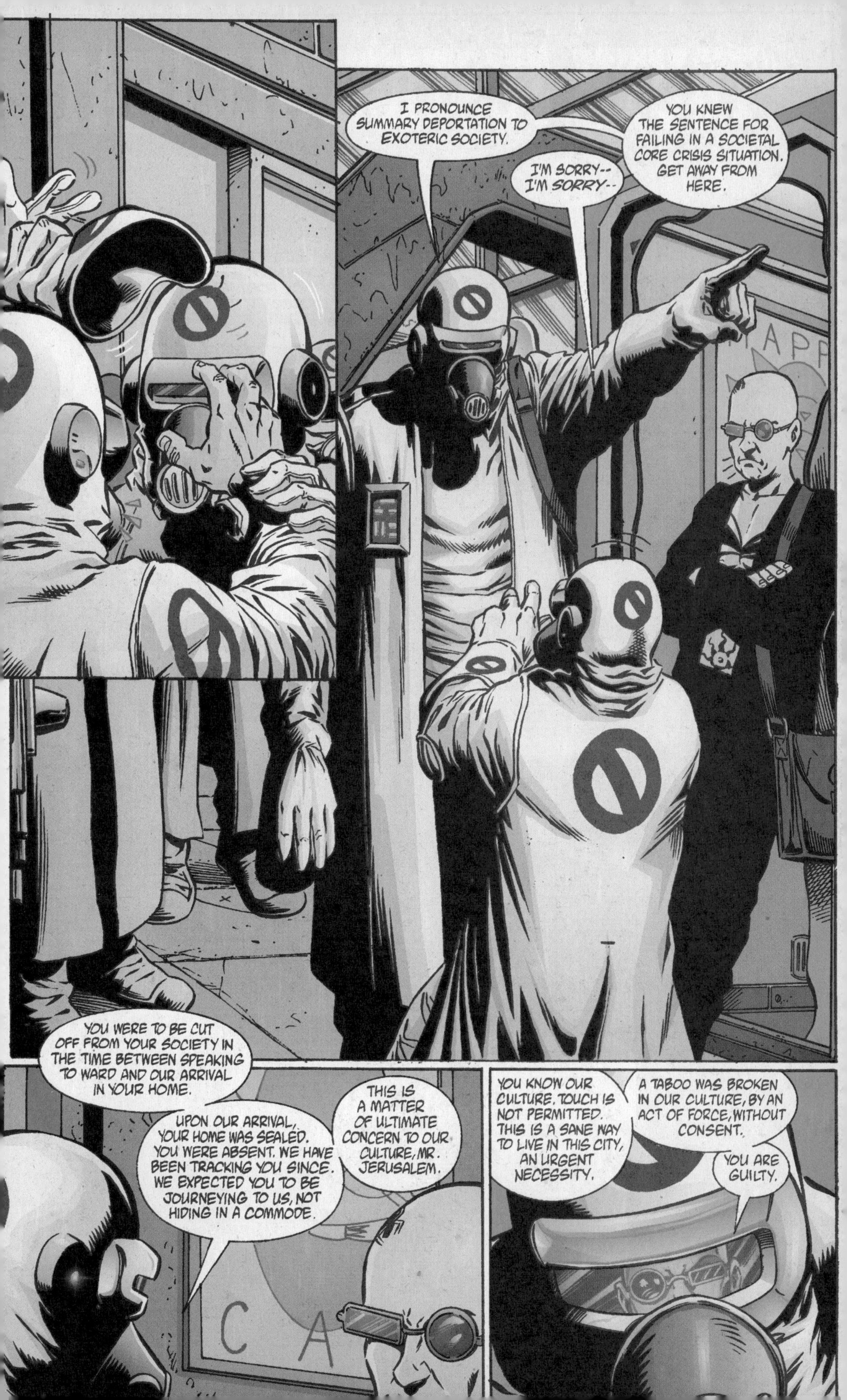
I PRONOUNCE SUMMARY DEPORTATION TO EXOTERIC SOCIETY.
YOU KNEW THE SENTENCE FOR FAILING IN A SOCIETAL CORE CRISIS SITUATION. GET AWAY FROM HERE.
I'M SORRY-- I'M SORRY--
YOU WERE TO BE CUT OFF FROM YOUR SOCIETY IN THE TIME BETWEEN SPEAKING TO WARD AND OUR ARRIVAL IN YOUR HOME.
UPON OUR ARRIVAL, YOUR HOME WAS SEALED. YOU WERE ABSENT. WE HAVE BEEN TRACKING YOU SINCE. WE EXPECTED YOU TO BE JOURNEYING TO US, NOT HIDING IN A COMMODE.
THIS IS A MATTER OF ULTIMATE CONCERN TO OUR CULTURE, MR. JERUSALEM.
YOU KNOW OUR CULTURE. TOUCH IS NOT PERMITTED. THIS IS A SANE WAY TO LIVE IN THIS CITY, AN URGENT NECESSITY.
A TABOO WAS BROKEN IN OUR CULTURE, BY AN ACT OF FORCE, WITHOUT CONSENT.
YOU ARE GUILTY.

# "TRUTH, JUSTICE, ALL THAT"

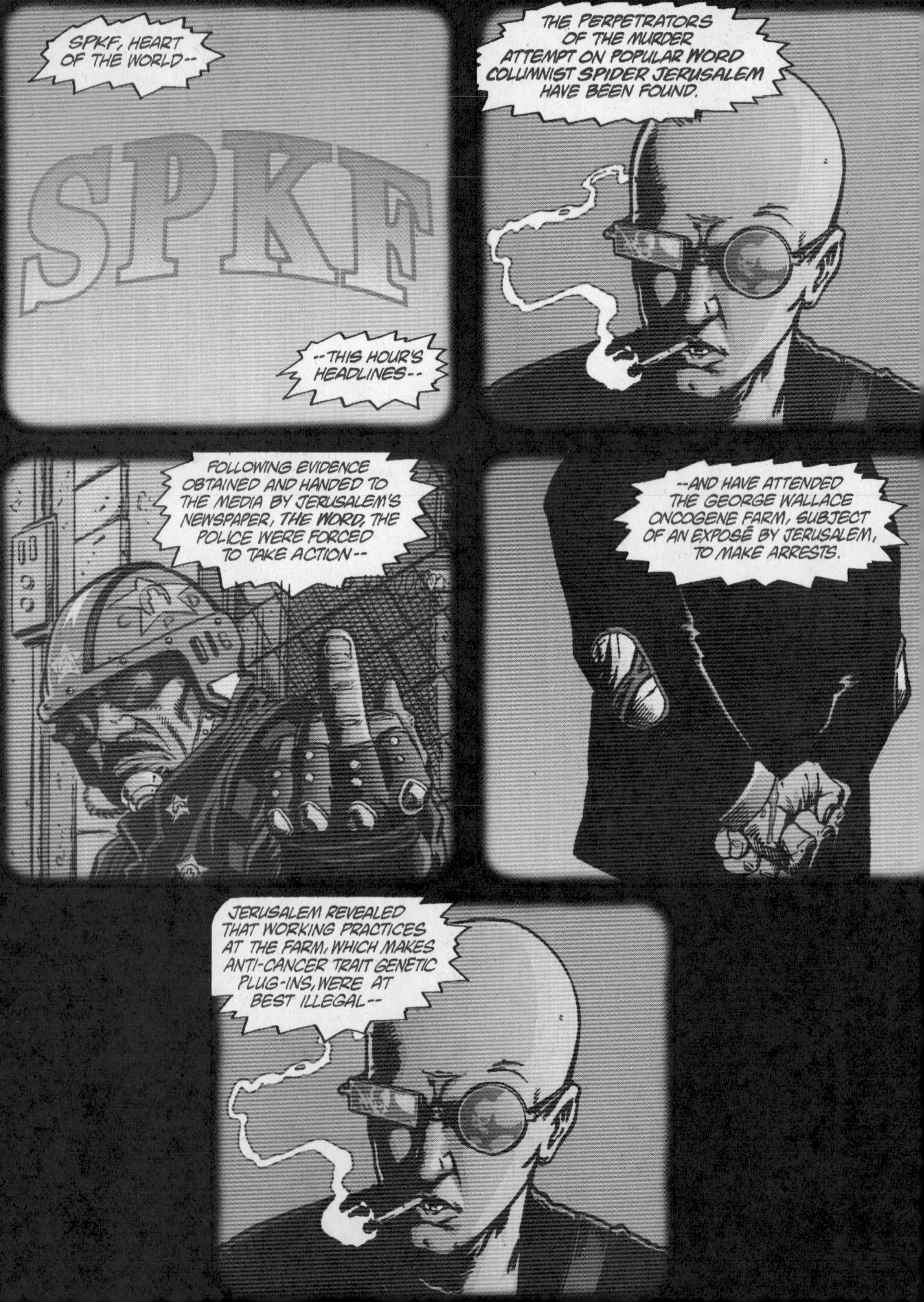
SPKF, HEART OF THE WORLD--
SPKF
--THIS HOUR'S HEADLINES--
THE PERPETRATORS OF THE MURDER ATTEMPT ON POPULAR WORD COLUMNIST SPIDER JERUSALEM HAVE BEEN FOUND.
FOLLOWING EVIDENCE OBTAINED AND HANDED TO THE MEDIA BY JERUSALEM'S NEWSPAPER, THE WORD, THE POLICE WERE FORCED TO TAKE ACTION--
--AND HAVE ATTENDED THE GEORGE WALLACE ONCOGENE FARM, SUBJECT OF AN EXPOSÉ BY JERUSALEM, TO MAKE ARRESTS.
JERUSALEM REVEALED THAT WORKING PRACTICES AT THE FARM, WHICH MAKES ANTI-CANCER TRAIT GENETIC PLUG-INS, WERE AT BEST ILLEGAL--

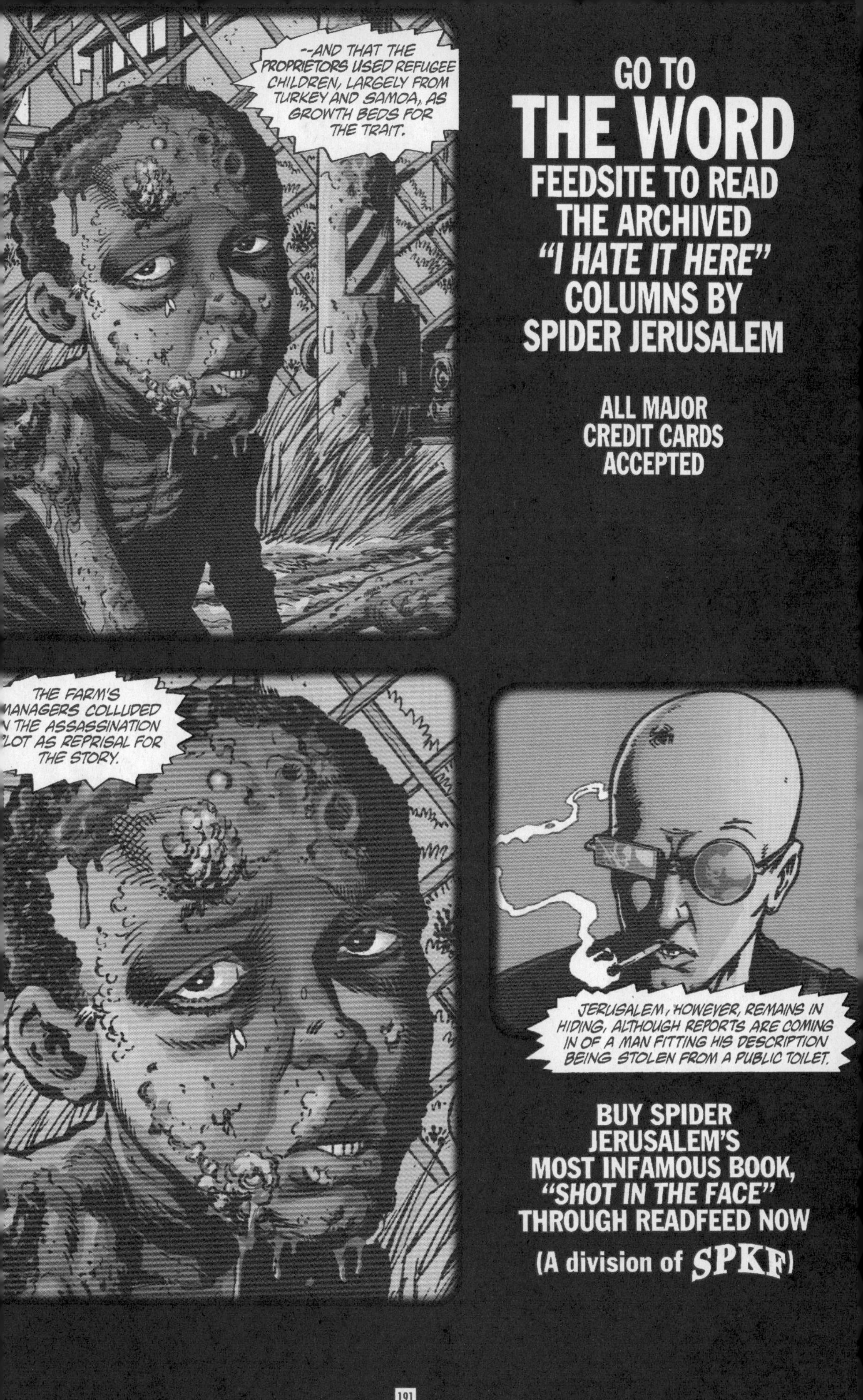
--AND THAT THE PROPRIETORS USED REFUGEE CHILDREN, LARGELY FROM TURKEY AND SAMOA, AS GROWTH BEDS FOR THE TRAIT.
GO TO THE WORD FEEDSITE TO READ THE ARCHIVED "I HATE IT HERE" COLUMNS BY SPIDER JERUSALEM
ALL MAJOR CREDIT CARDS ACCEPTED
THE FARM'S MANAGERS COLLUDED N THE ASSASSINATION LOT AS REPRISAL FOR THE STORY.
JERUSALEM, HOWEVER, REMAINS IN HIDING, ALTHOUGH REPORTS ARE COMING IN OF A MAN FITTING HIS DESCRIPTION BEING STOLEN FROM A PUBLIC TOILET.
BUY SPIDER JERUSALEM'S MOST INFAMOUS BOOK, "SHOT IN THE FACE" THROUGH READFEED NOW
(A division of SPKF)

# THE TRUTH ABOUT CATS AND DOGS

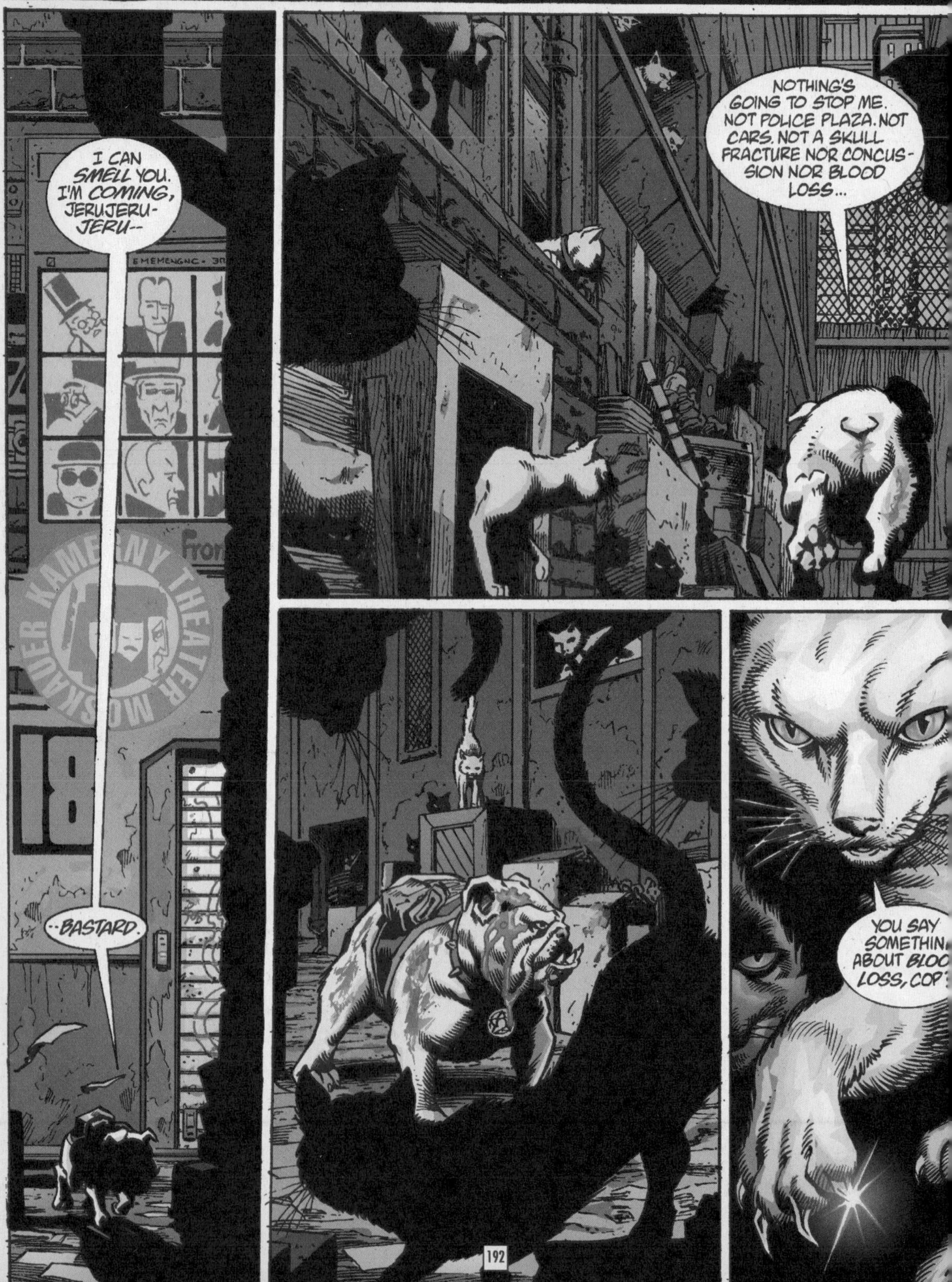

I CAN SMELL YOU. I'M COMING, JERUJERU-JERU--
NOTHING'S GOING TO STOP ME. NOT POLICE PLAZA. NOT CARS. NOT A SKULL FRACTURE NOR CONCUSSION NOR BLOOD LOSS...
KAMERNY THEATER MOSKAUER
18
--BASTARD.
YOU SAY SOMETHIN ABOUT BLOO LOSS, COP

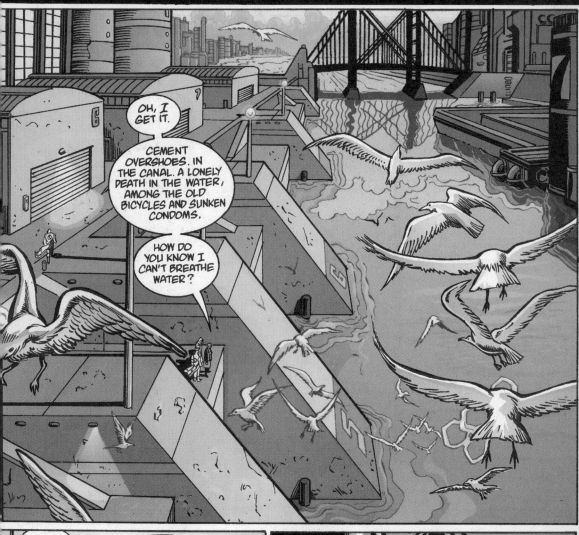

OH, I GET IT.

CEMENT OVERSHOES. IN THE CANAL. A LONELY DEATH IN THE WATER, AMONG THE OLD BICYCLES AND SUNKEN CONDOMS.

HOW DO YOU KNOW I CAN'T BREATHE WATER?

WHAT?

COME ON. YOU STAY CUT OFF FROM THE CITY. YOU DON'T KNOW WHAT WE DO, WHAT WE HAVE.

WE'VE CURED CANCER. MOST WOMEN CAN ABORT UNWANTED PREGNANCIES JUST BY THINKING ABOUT IT. WE LIVE TO ONE HUNDRED WITHOUT TRYING.

HOW DO YOU KNOW I CAN'T KILL YOU BY STARING HARD?

YOU KNOW NOTHING ABOUT ME.

IF I WERE YOU I'D START EXPLAINING YOURSELVES IN A VAIN EFFORT TO DELAY YOUR IMMINENT HORRIFIC EXECUTION.

BEGIN WITH THE LOCATION OF MY EX-WIFE'S HEAD.

IT BEGINS WITH A VERY DRUNK WOMAN WHO DROVE THROUGH OUR PLACE ONE NIGHT.

SHE FOLDED HER CAR NEATLY INTO A TELE-GRAPH POLE, AND THEN STAG-GERED INTO OUR COMMUNITY HALL.

FIRST SHE DEMANDED ALCOHOL. THEN SHE REQUESTED CERTAIN EXOTIC NARCOTICS.

FINALLY, SHE HARASSED OUR YOUNG MEN FOR SEXUAL FAVORS OF AN UNUSUAL AND EXPLICITLY DETAILED NATURE.

WHEN SHE MET WITH NO ANSWER, SHE GRABBED ONE YOUTH, RIPPED OFF HIS MASK--

--AND PUT HER TONGUE IN HIS MOUTH.

"SHE THEN SHOUTED HER NAME SEVERAL TIMES AND LEFT QUICKLY.

"POLICE WERE WAITING FOR HER. WE SOUGHT TO LODGE A COMPLAINT. BUT THE WOMAN GAVE THE POLICE SOMETHING IN EXCESS OF TEN THOUSAND DOLLARS AND ASKED FOR A RIDE HOME."

DARROW'S SIN GIN

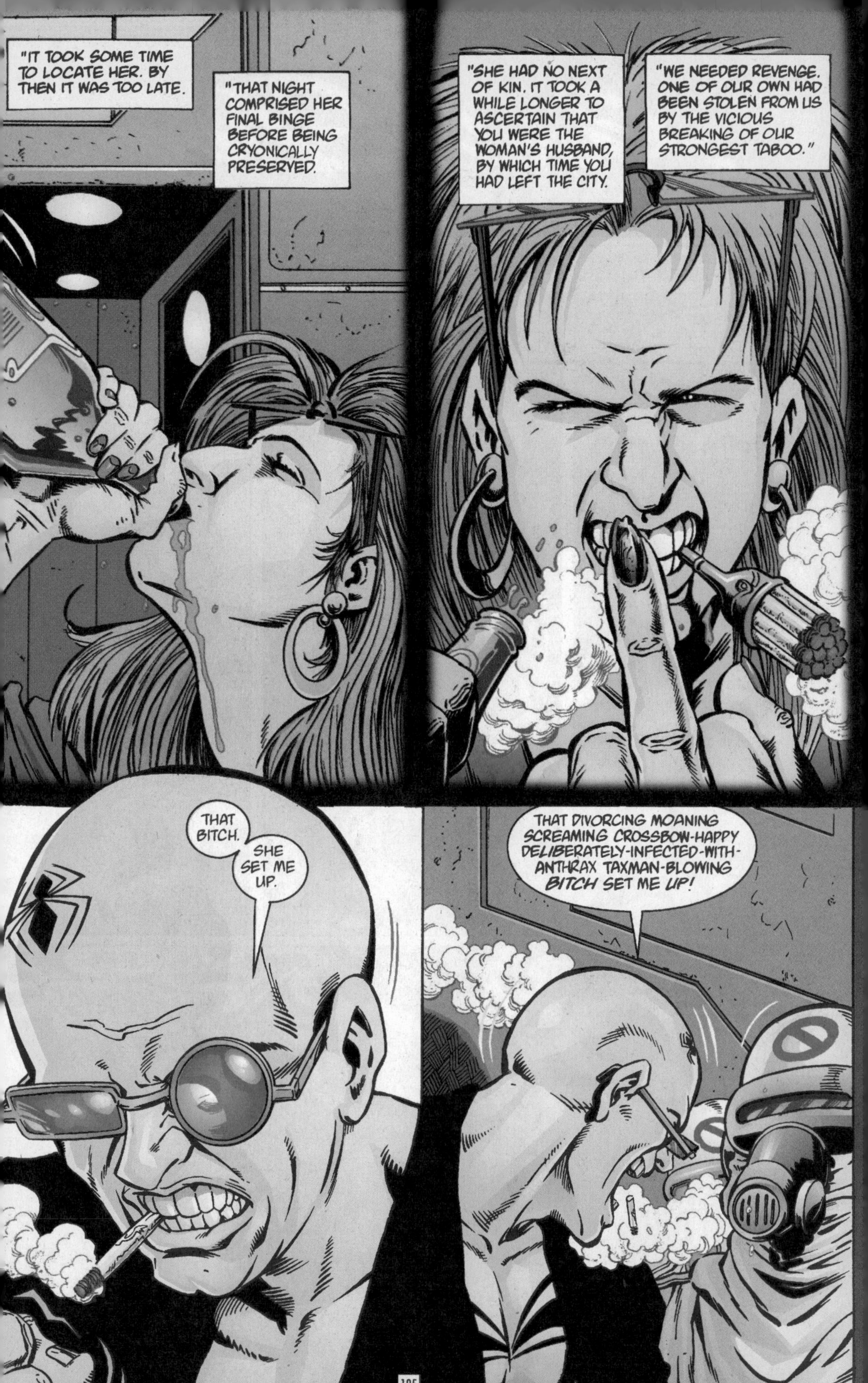
"IT TOOK SOME TIME TO LOCATE HER. BY THEN IT WAS TOO LATE.
"THAT NIGHT COMPRISED HER FINAL BINGE BEFORE BEING CRYONICALLY PRESERVED.
"SHE HAD NO NEXT OF KIN. IT TOOK A WHILE LONGER TO ASCERTAIN THAT YOU WERE THE WOMAN'S HUSBAND, BY WHICH TIME YOU HAD LEFT THE CITY.
"WE NEEDED REVENGE. ONE OF OUR OWN HAD BEEN STOLEN FROM US BY THE VICIOUS BREAKING OF OUR STRONGEST TABOO."
THAT BITCH.
SHE SET ME UP.
THAT DIVORCING MOANING SCREAMING CROSSBOW-HAPPY DELIBERATELY-INFECTED-WITH-ANTHRAX TAXMAN-BLOWING *BITCH* SET ME *UP*!

# God / Dog

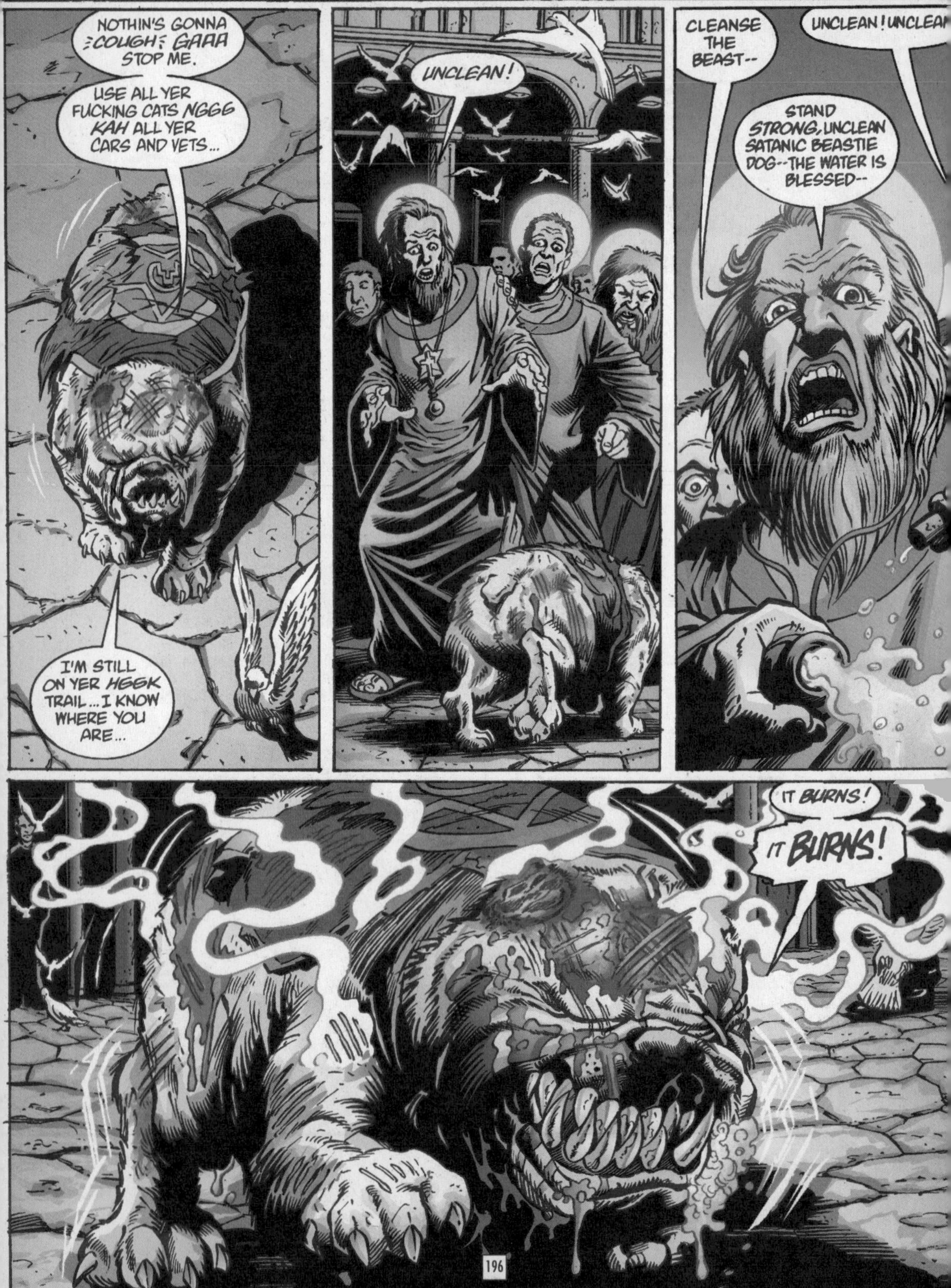
NOTHIN'S GONNA
:COUGH: GAAA
STOP ME.
USE ALL YER FUCKING CATS NGGG KAH ALL YER CARS AND VETS...
I'M STILL ON YER HGGK TRAIL... I KNOW WHERE YOU ARE...
UNCLEAN!
CLEANSE THE BEAST--
UNCLEAN! UNCLEAN
STAND STRONG, UNCLEAN SATANIC BEASTIE DOG--THE WATER IS BLESSED--
IT BURNS!
IT BURNS!

# spider explains it all

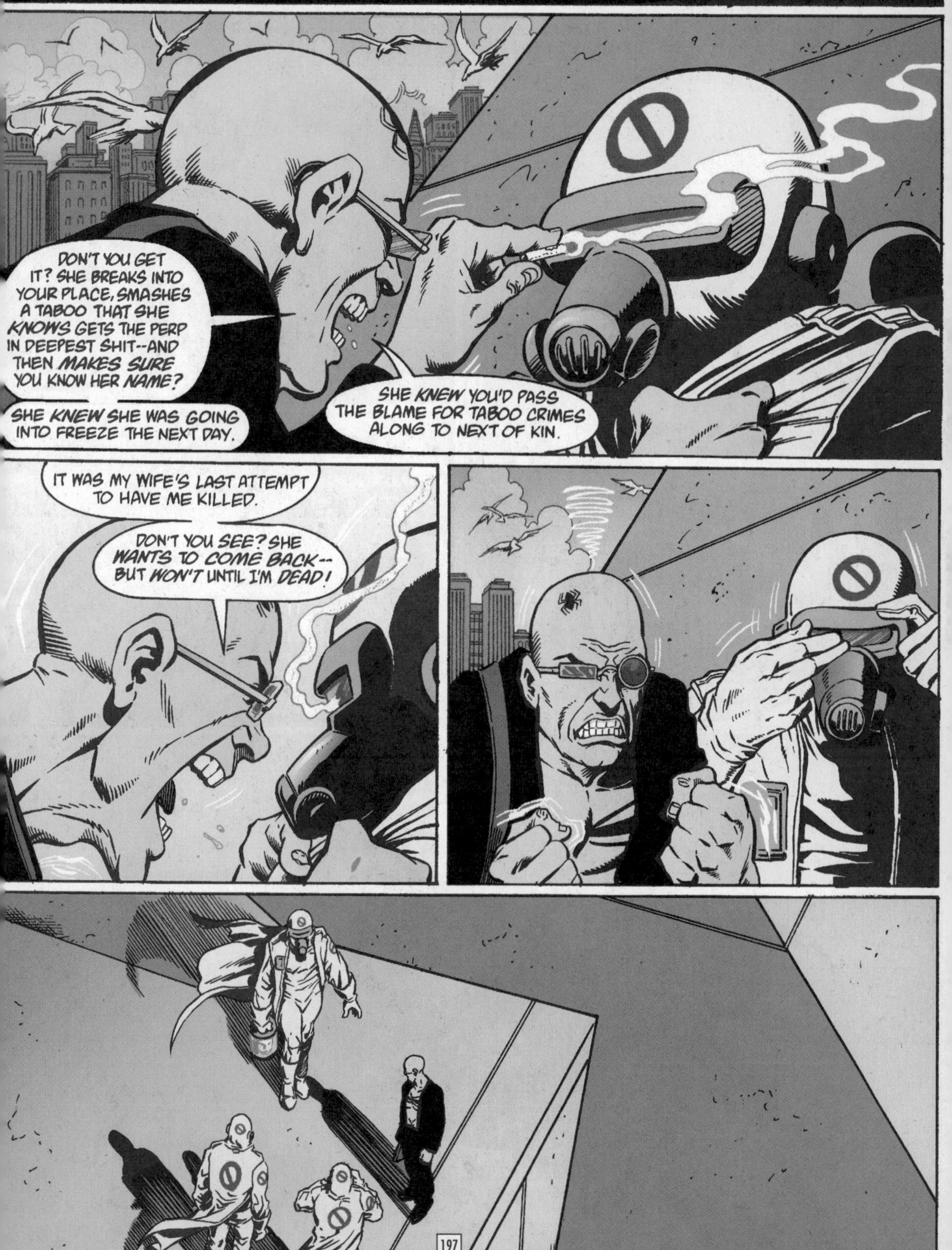
DON'T YOU GET IT? SHE BREAKS INTO YOUR PLACE, SMASHES A TABOO THAT SHE KNOWS GETS THE PERP IN DEEPEST SHIT--AND THEN MAKES SURE YOU KNOW HER NAME?
SHE KNEW SHE WAS GOING INTO FREEZE THE NEXT DAY.
SHE KNEW YOU'D PASS THE BLAME FOR TABOO CRIMES ALONG TO NEXT OF KIN.
IT WAS MY WIFE'S LAST ATTEMPT TO HAVE ME KILLED.
DON'T YOU SEE? SHE WANTS TO COME BACK--BUT WON'T UNTIL I'M DEAD!

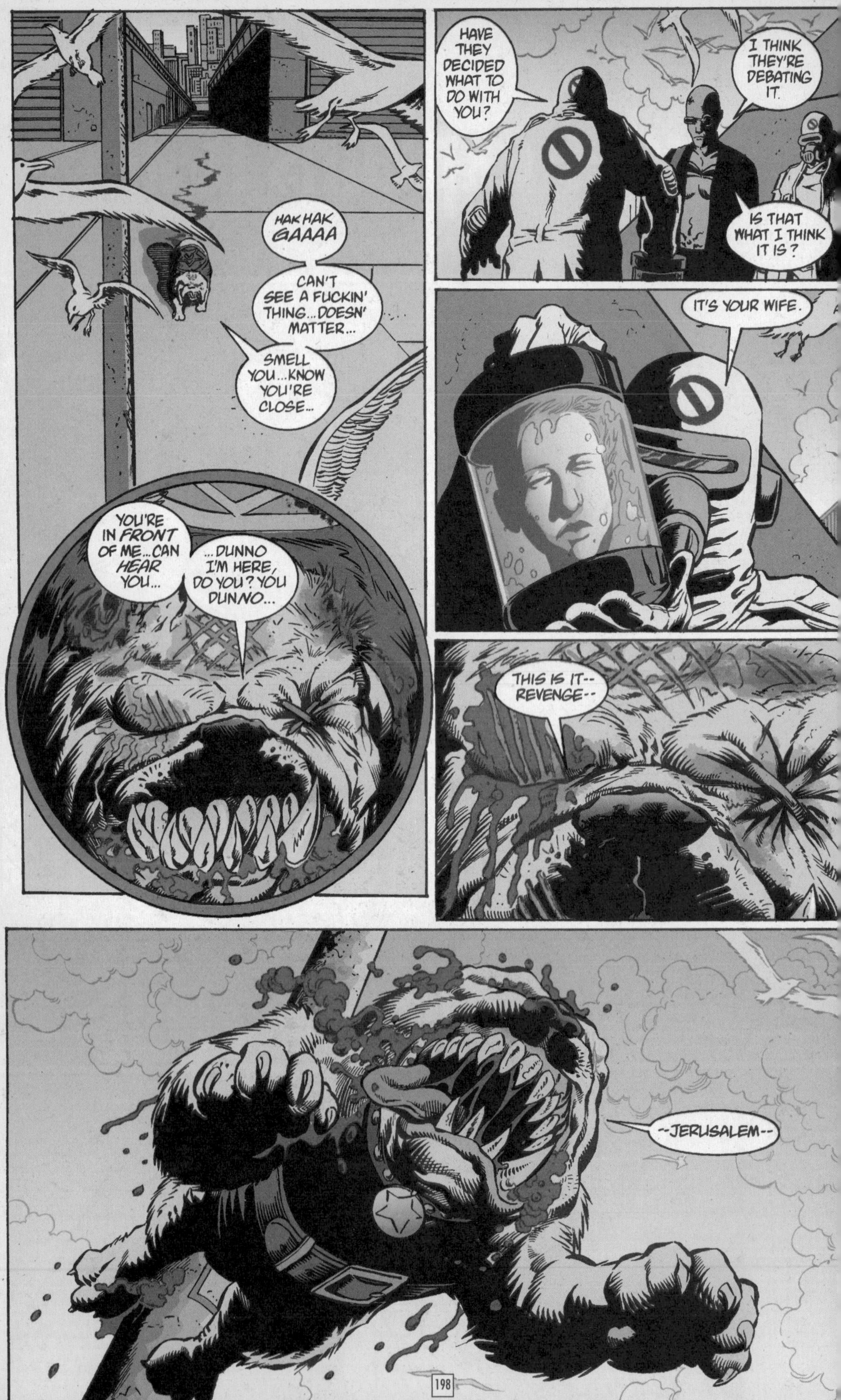
HAK HAK GAAAA
CAN'T SEE A FUCKIN' THING...DOESN' MATTER...
SMELL YOU...KNOW YOU'RE CLOSE...
HAVE THEY DECIDED WHAT TO DO WITH YOU?
I THINK THEY'RE DEBATING IT.
IS THAT WHAT I THINK IT IS?
IT'S YOUR WIFE.
YOU'RE IN FRONT OF ME...CAN HEAR YOU...
...DUNNO I'M HERE, DO YOU? YOU DUNNO...
THIS IS IT-- REVENGE--
--JERUSALEM--

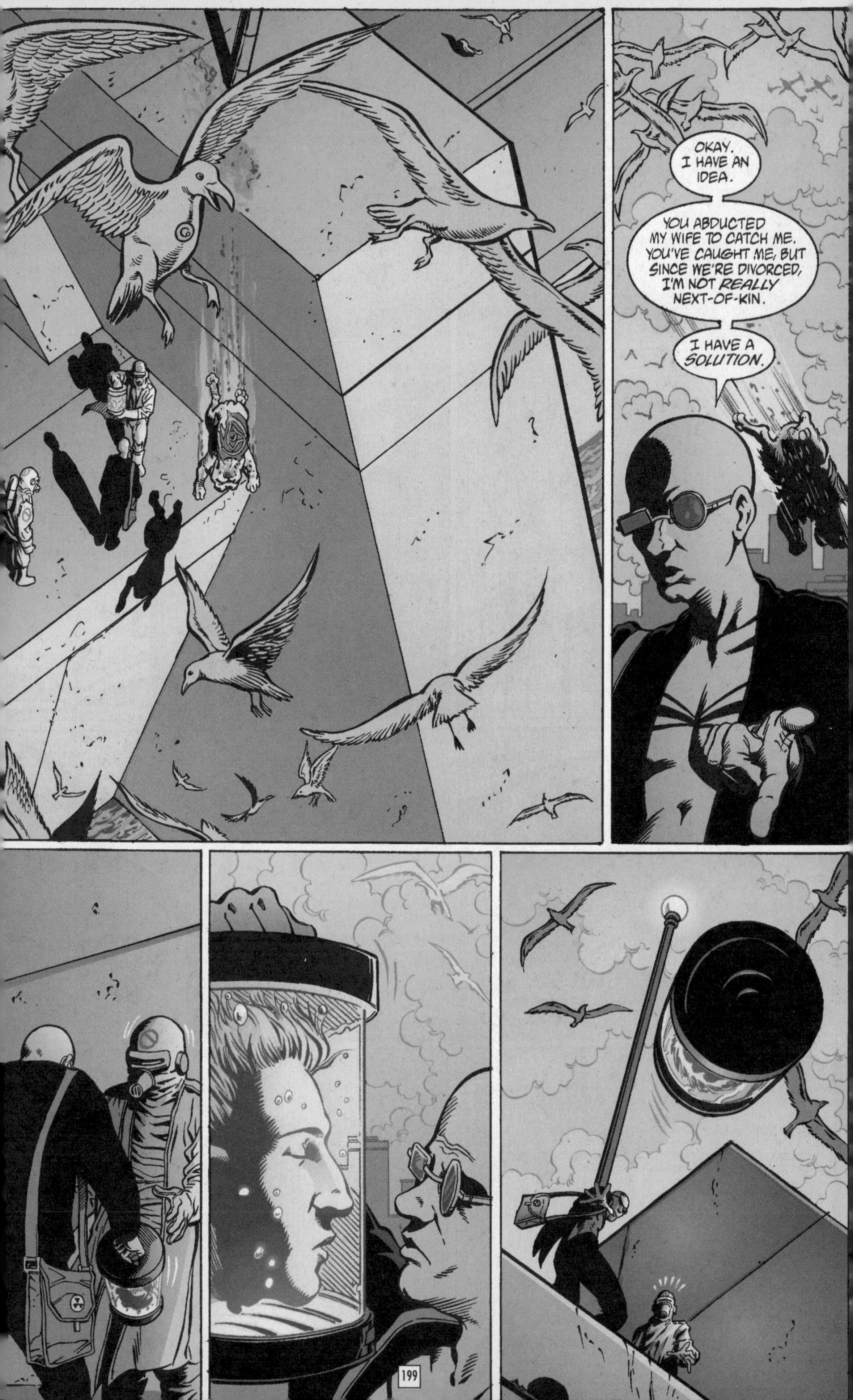

OKAY. I HAVE AN IDEA.
YOU ABDUCTED MY WIFE TO CATCH ME. YOU'VE CAUGHT ME, BUT SINCE WE'RE DIVORCED, I'M NOT REALLY NEXT-OF-KIN.
I HAVE A SOLUTION.

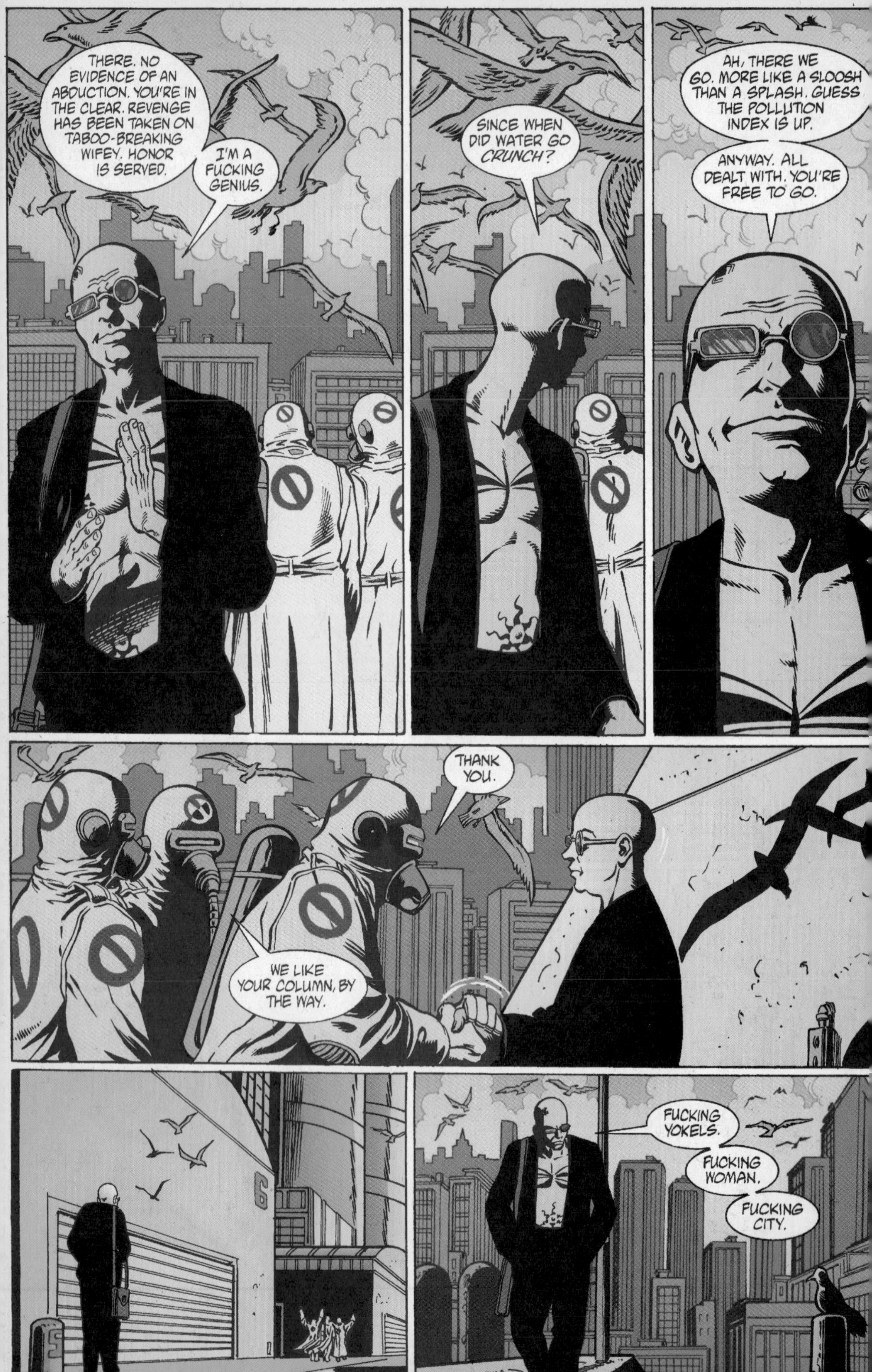
THERE. NO EVIDENCE OF AN ABDUCTION. YOU'RE IN THE CLEAR. REVENGE HAS BEEN TAKEN ON TABOO-BREAKING WIFEY. HONOR IS SERVED.
I'M A FUCKING GENIUS.
SINCE WHEN DID WATER GO *CRUNCH?*
AH, THERE WE GO. MORE LIKE A SLOOSH THAN A SPLASH. GUESS THE POLLUTION INDEX IS UP.
ANYWAY. ALL DEALT WITH. YOU'RE FREE TO GO.
THANK YOU.
WE LIKE YOUR COLUMN, BY THE WAY.
FUCKING YOKELS.
FUCKING WOMAN.
FUCKING CITY.

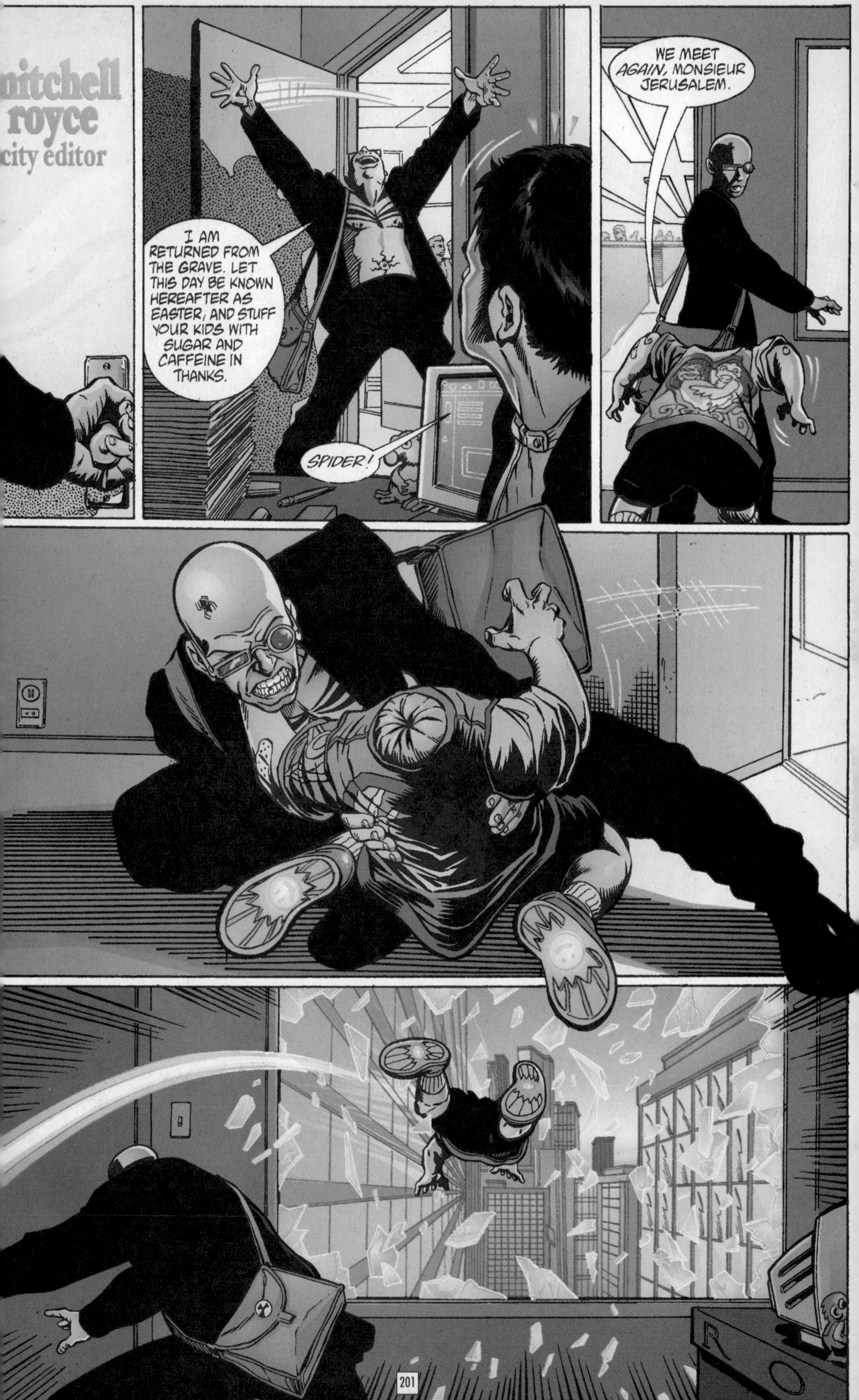
mitchell royce city editor
I AM RETURNED FROM THE GRAVE. LET THIS DAY BE KNOWN HEREAFTER AS EASTER, AND STUFF YOUR KIDS WITH SUGAR AND CAFFEINE IN THANKS.
SPIDER!
WE MEET AGAIN, MONSIEUR JERUSALEM.

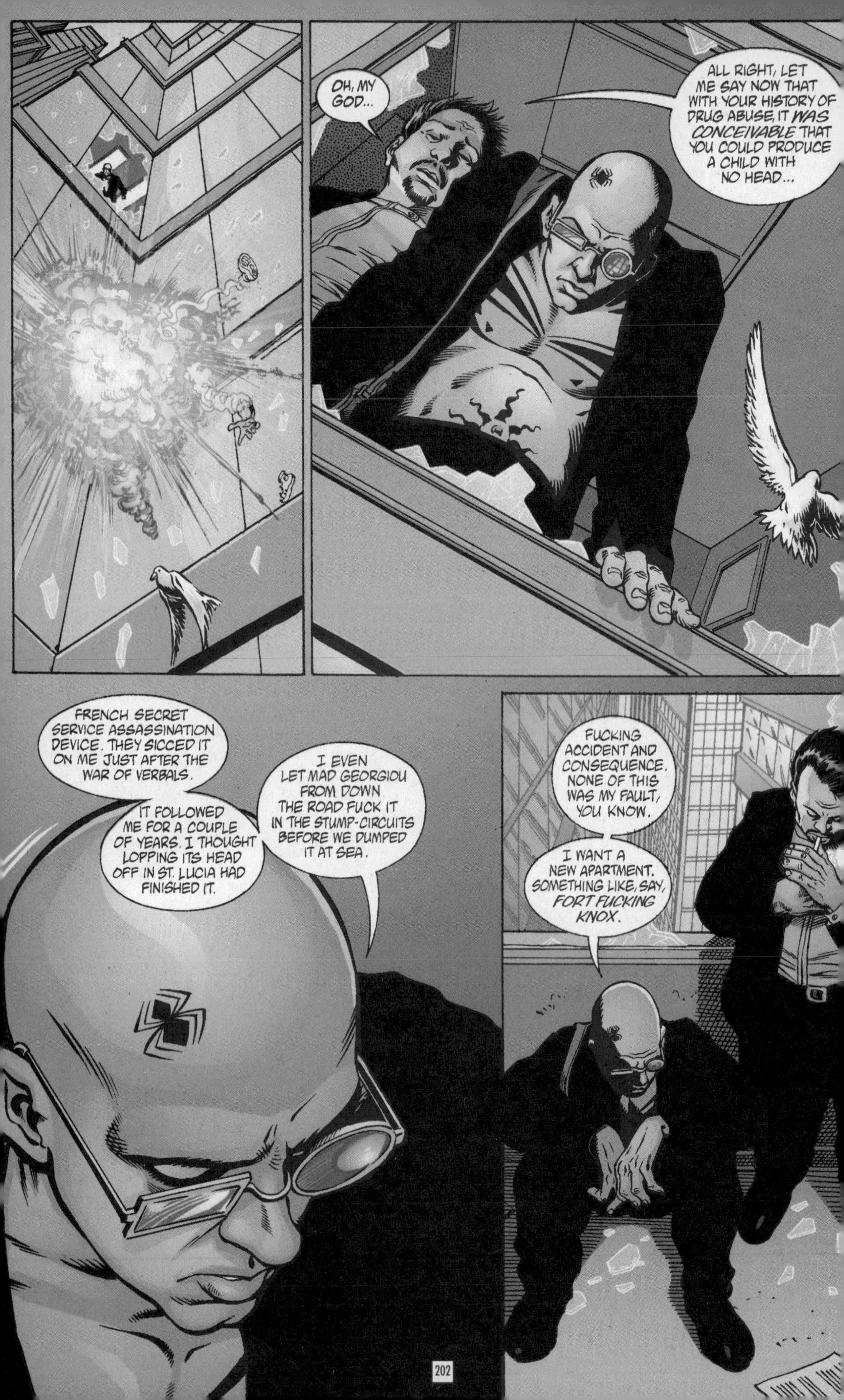
OH, MY GOD...
ALL RIGHT, LET ME SAY NOW THAT WITH YOUR HISTORY OF DRUG ABUSE, IT *WAS* *CONCEIVABLE* THAT YOU COULD PRODUCE A CHILD WITH NO HEAD...
FRENCH SECRET SERVICE ASSASSINATION DEVICE. THEY SICCED IT ON ME JUST AFTER THE WAR OF VERBALS.
IT FOLLOWED ME FOR A COUPLE OF YEARS. I THOUGHT LOPPING ITS HEAD OFF IN ST. LUCIA HAD FINISHED IT.
I EVEN LET MAD GEORGIOU FROM DOWN THE ROAD FUCK IT IN THE STUMP-CIRCUITS BEFORE WE DUMPED IT AT SEA.
FUCKING ACCIDENT AND CONSEQUENCE. NONE OF THIS WAS MY FAULT, YOU KNOW.
I WANT A NEW APARTMENT. SOMETHING LIKE, SAY, *FORT FUCKING KNOX*.

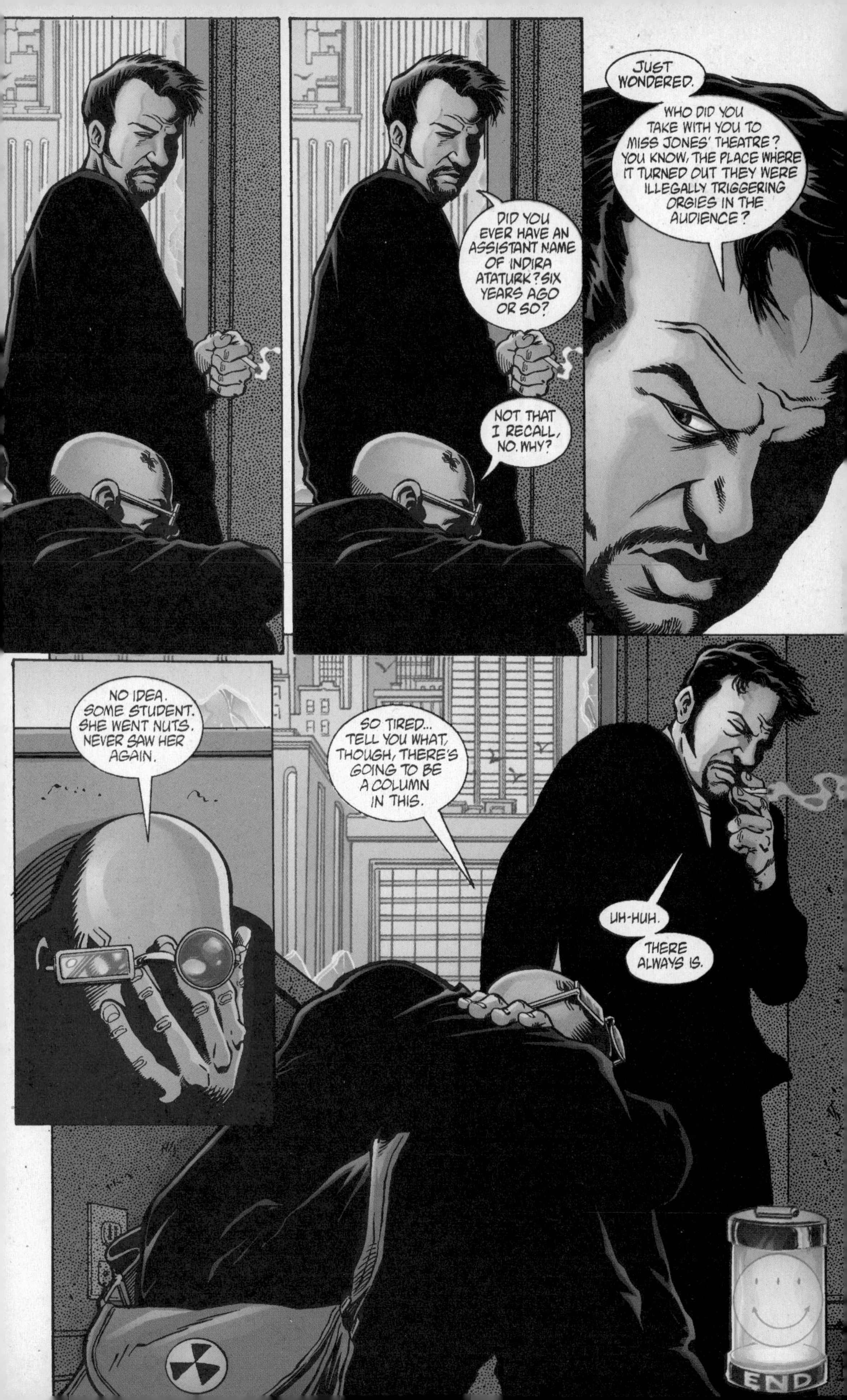
DID YOU EVER HAVE AN ASSISTANT NAME OF INDIRA ATATURK? SIX YEARS AGO OR SO?
NOT THAT I RECALL, NO. WHY?
JUST WONDERED.
WHO DID YOU TAKE WITH YOU TO MISS JONES' THEATRE? YOU KNOW, THE PLACE WHERE IT TURNED OUT THEY WERE ILLEGALLY TRIGGERING ORGIES IN THE AUDIENCE?
NO IDEA. SOME STUDENT. SHE WENT NUTS. NEVER SAW HER AGAIN.
SO TIRED... TELL YOU WHAT, THOUGH, THERE'S GOING TO BE A COLUMN IN THIS.
UH-HUH.
THERE ALWAYS IS.
END

# COVER GALLERY

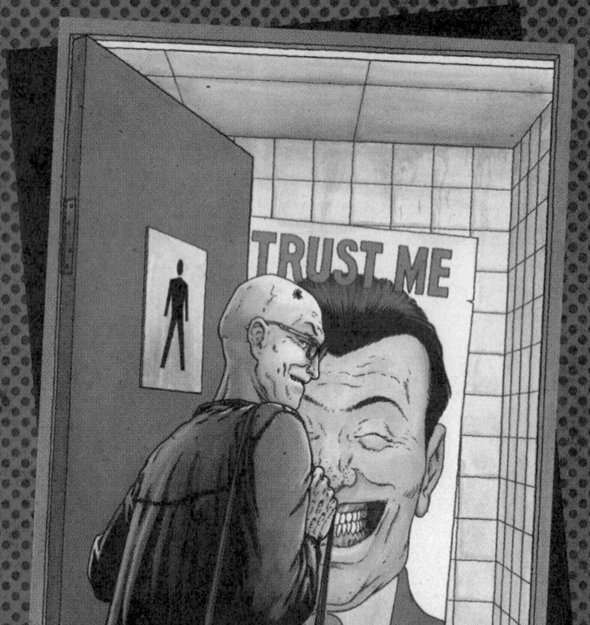
TRUST ME

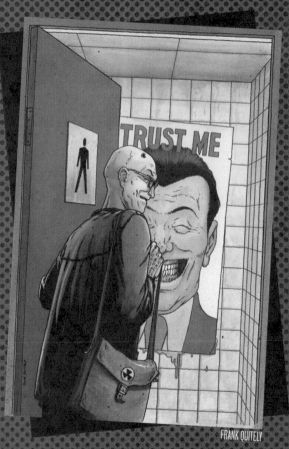

FRANK QUITELY

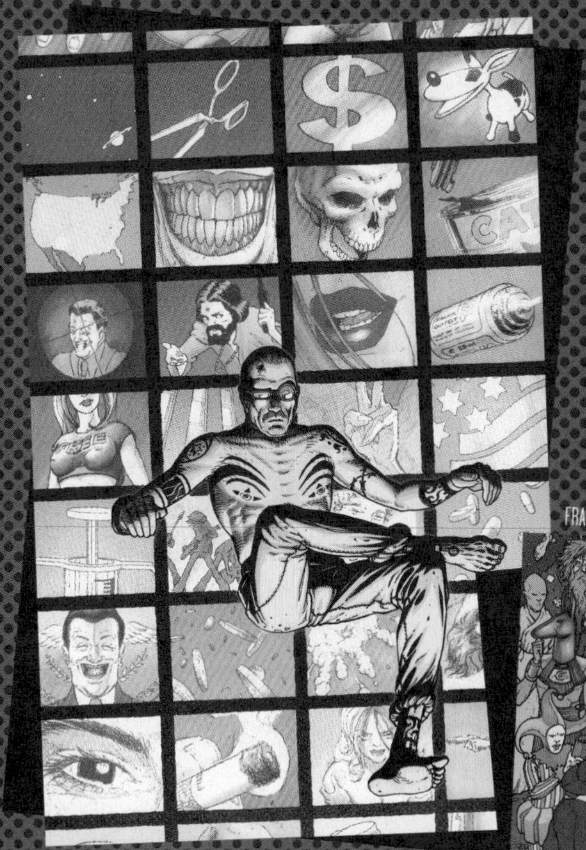
$
CAT

FRANK QUITELY

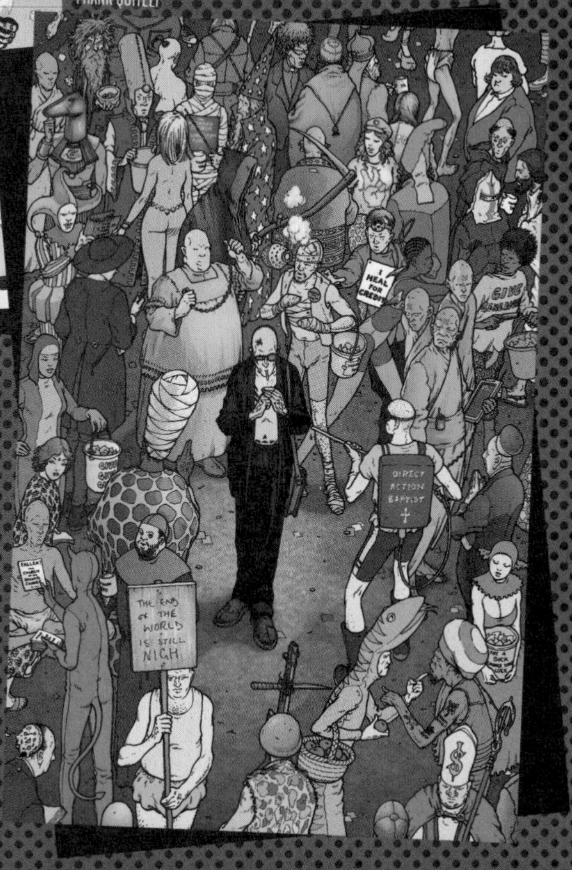
I HEAL FOR CREDIT
DIRECT ACTION BAPTIST
THE END OF THE WORLD IS STILL NIGH

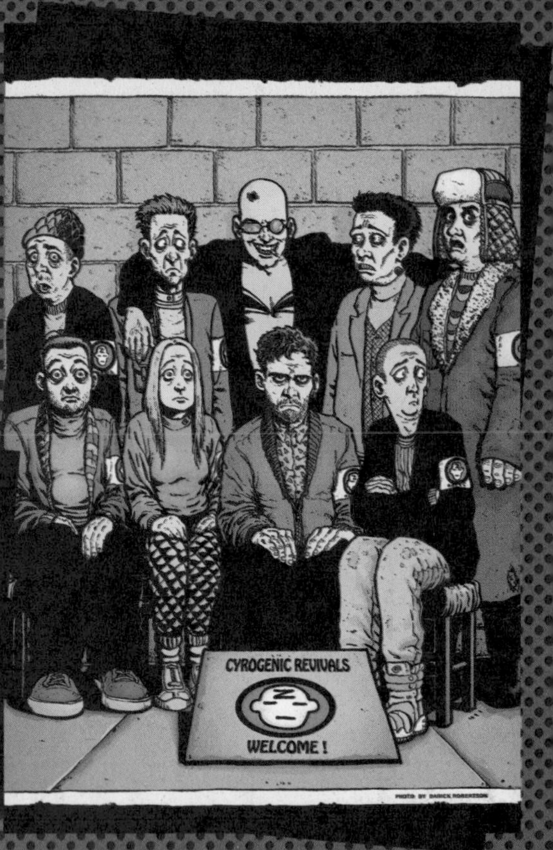
CYROGENIC REVIVALS
WELCOME !
PHOTO BY DARICK ROBERTSON

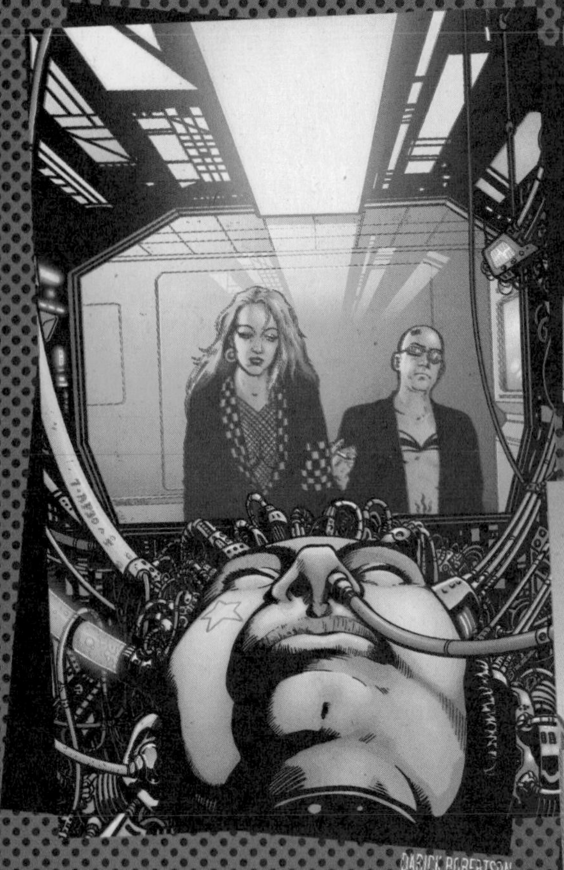

DARICK ROBERTSON

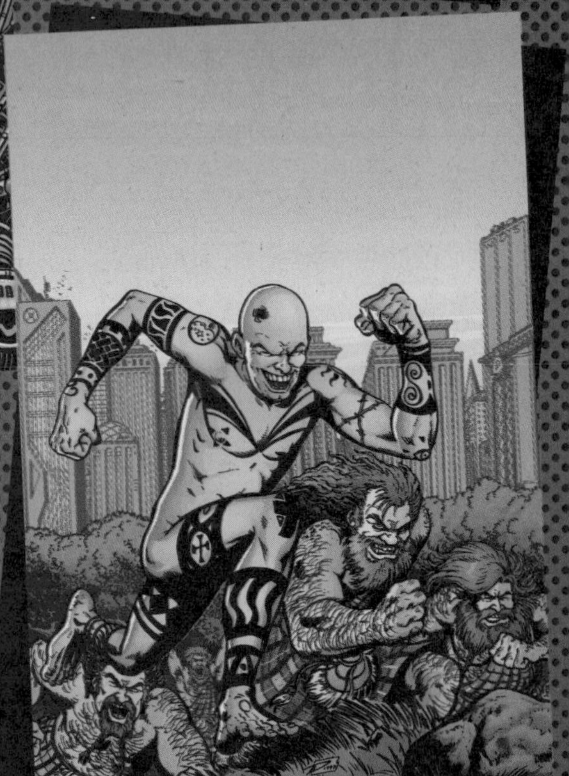

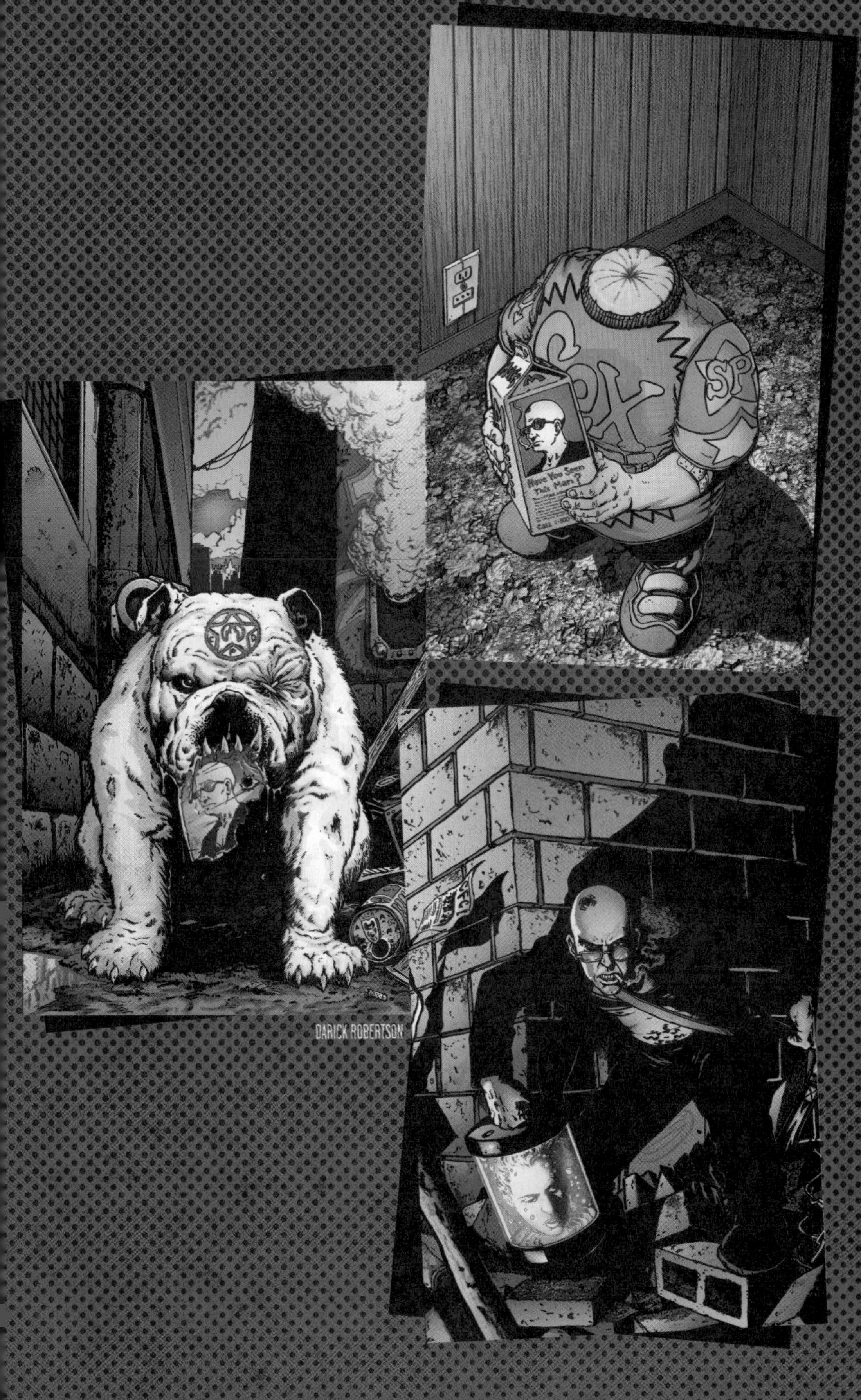
Have You Seen This Man?
SP
DARICK ROBERTSON

# THE TRANSMETROPOLITAN LIBRARY

**BY WARREN ELLIS, DARICK ROBERTSON, RODNEY RAMOS AND VARIOUS**

An exuberant trip into a frenetic future, where outlaw journalist Spider Jerusalem battles hypocrisy, corruption, and sobriety.

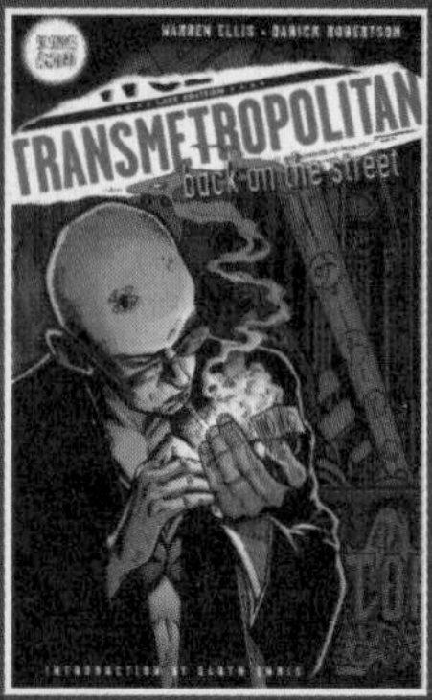
WARREN ELLIS • DARICK ROBERTSON
TRANSMETROPOLITAN
back on the street

Volume One:
BACK ON THE STREET

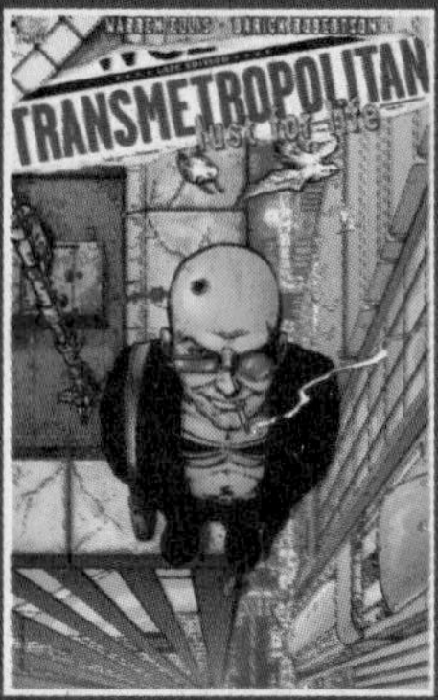
TRANSMETROPOLITAN
lust for life

Volume Two:
LUST FOR LIFE

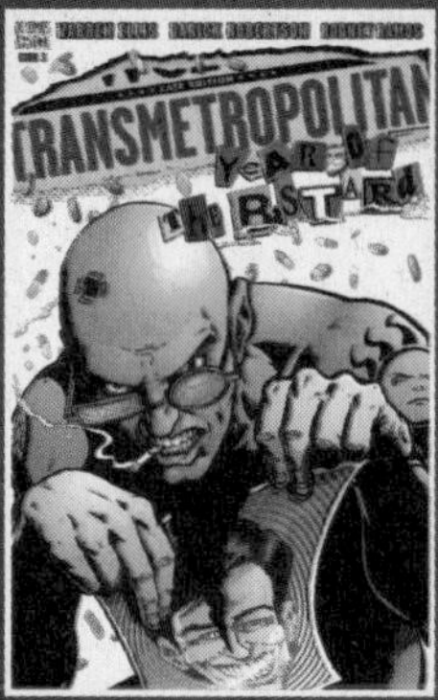
TRANSMETROPOLITAN
YEAR OF THE BASTARD

Volume Three:
YEAR OF THE BASTARD

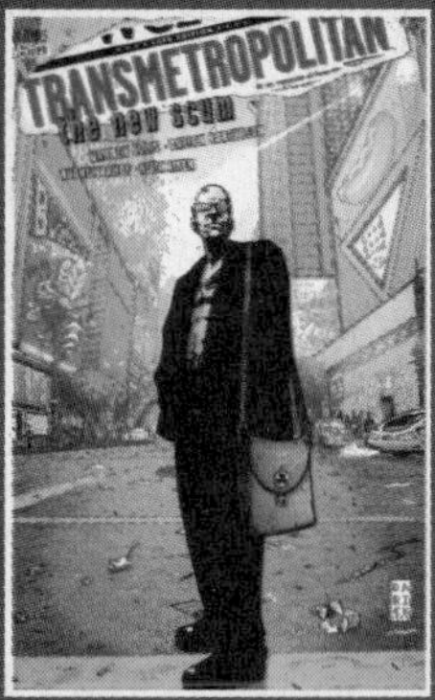
TRANSMETROPOLITAN
the new scum

Volume Four:
THE NEW SCUM

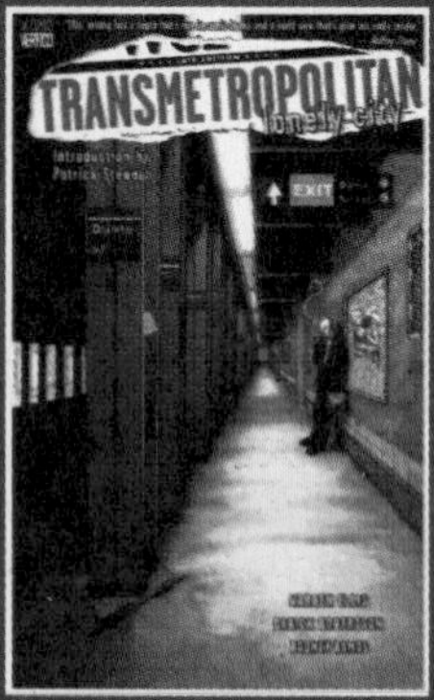
TRANSMETROPOLITAN
lonely city
EXIT

Volume Five:
LONELY CITY

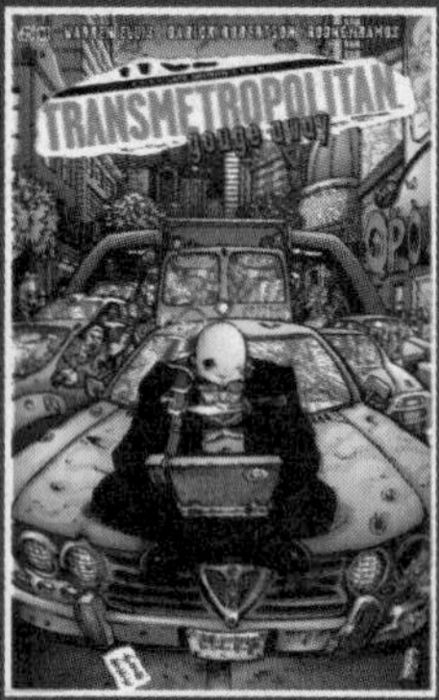
TRANSMETROPOLITAN
gouge away

Volume Six:
GOUGE AWAY

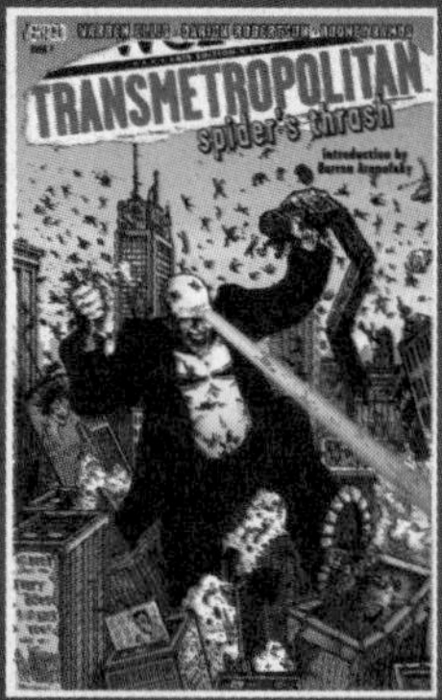
TRANSMETROPOLITAN
spider's thrash

Volume Seven:
SPIDER'S THRASH

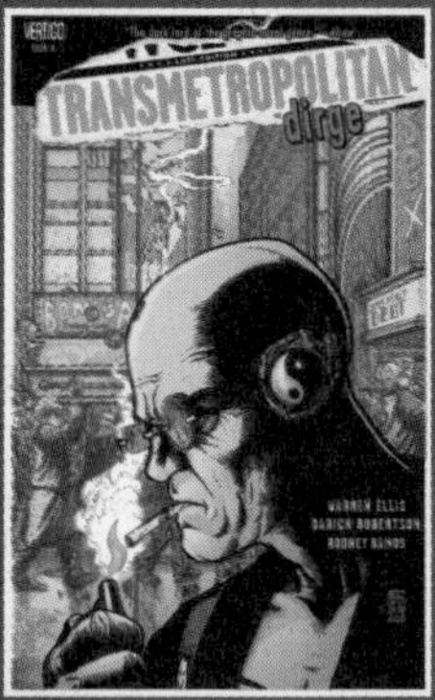
TRANSMETROPOLITAN
dirge
WARREN ELLIS
DARICK ROBERTSON
RODNEY RAMOS

Volume Eight:
DIRGE

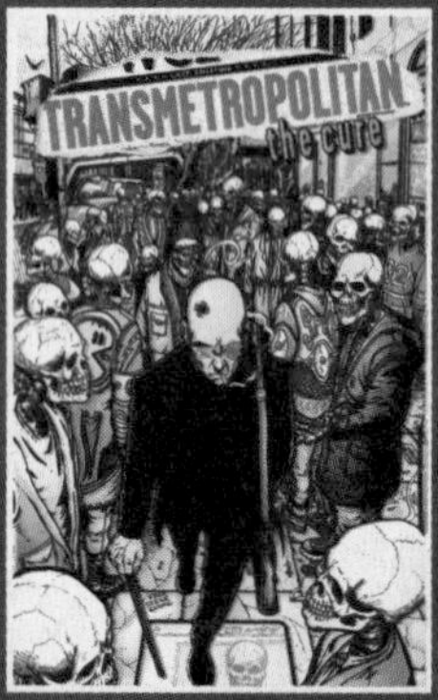
TRANSMETROPOLITAN
the cure

Volume Nine:
THE CURE

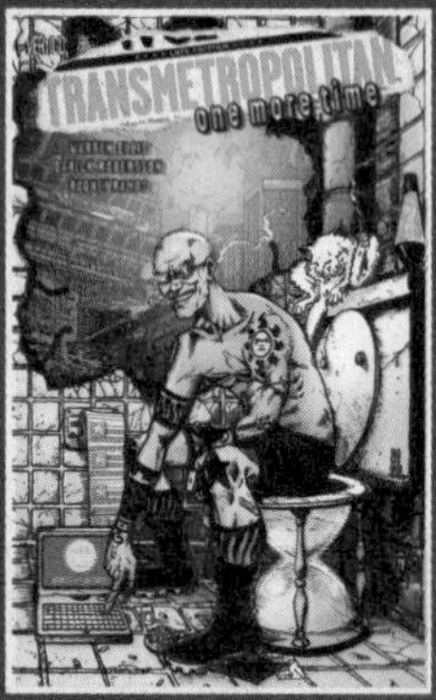
TRANSMETROPOLITAN
one more time

Volume Ten:
ONE MORE TIME

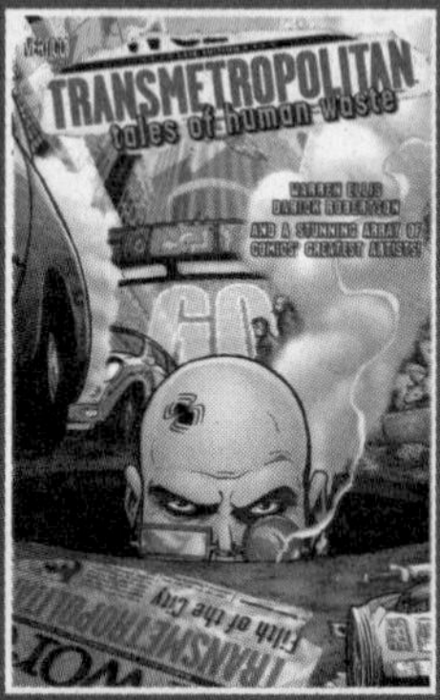
TRANSMETROPOLITAN
tales of human waste
WARREN ELLIS
DARICK ROBERTSON
AND A STUNNING ARRAY OF COMICS' GREATEST ARTISTS

Volume Zero:
TALES OF HUMAN WASTE

## ALSO FROM WRITER WARREN ELLIS

**HELLBLAZER: HAUNTED**
with John Higgins

**ORBITER**
with Colleen Doran

**GLOBAL FREQUENCY: PLANET ABLAZE**
with various

**RELOAD/MEK**
with various

**RED/TOKYO STORM WARNING**
with various

**THE AUTHORITY: RELENTLESS**
with Bryan Hitch and Paul Neary

**THE AUTHORITY: UNDER NEW MANAGEMENT**
with Mark Millar and various

**PLANETARY: ALL OVER THE WORLD**
with John Cassaday

**PLANETARY: THE FOURTH MAN**
with John Cassaday

**PLANETARY: CROSSING WORLDS**
with John Cassaday, Phil Jimenez and Jerry Ordway

**STORMWATCH: FORCE OF NATURE**
with Tom Raney and Randy Elliott

**STORMWATCH: LIGHTNING STRIKES**
with Tom Raney, Randy Elliott and Jim Lee

**STORMWATCH: CHANGE OR DIE**
with Tom Raney and Oscar Jimenez

**STORMWATCH: A FINER WORLD**
with Bryan Hitch and Paul Neary

**STORMWATCH: FINAL ORBIT**
with various

Search the Graphic Novels section of vertigocomics.com for art and info on every one of our hundreds of books, or call 1-888-COMIC BOOK for the comics shop nearest you, or go to your local book store.